The Politics of Food in Modern Morocco

UNIVERSITY PRESS OF FLORIDA

Florida A&M University, Tallahassee
Florida Atlantic University, Boca Raton
Florida Gulf Coast University, Ft. Myers
Florida International University, Miami
Florida State University, Tallahassee
New College of Florida, Sarasota
University of Central Florida, Orlando
University of Florida, Gainesville
University of North Florida, Jacksonville
University of South Florida, Tampa
University of West Florida, Pensacola

# The Politics of Food in Modern Morocco

STACY E. HOLDEN

University Press of Florida
Gainesville/Tallahassee/Tampa/Boca Raton
Pensacola/Orlando/Miami/Jacksonville/Ft. Myers/Sarasota

Copyright 2009 by Stacy E. Holden
All rights reserved
Printed in the United States of America on acid-free paper

First cloth printing, 2009
First paperback printing, 2015

Library of Congress Cataloging-in-Publication Data
Holden, Stacy E.
The politics of food in modern Morocco / Stacy E. Holden
p. cm.
Includes bibliographical references and index.
ISBN 978-0-8130-3373-0 (cloth: alk. paper)
ISBN 978-0-8130-6090-3 (pbk.)
1. Food supply—Political aspects—Morocco—History—20th century.
2. Morocco—Politics and government—20th century. 3. Morocco—Economic conditions—20th century. 4. Morocco—Social conditions—20th century.
5. Hunger—Political aspects—Morocco—History—20th century. 6. Nutrition policy—Morocco—History—20th century. 7. Islam and politics—Morocco—History—20th century. 8. Social classes—Morocco—History—20th century. 9. Power (Social sciences)—Morocco—History—20th century.
10. Nationalism—Morocco—History—20th century. I. Title.
HD9017.M82H65 2009
338.1'964—dc22    2009006566

The University Press of Florida is the scholarly publishing agency for the State University System of Florida, comprising Florida A&M University, Florida Atlantic University, Florida Gulf Coast University, Florida International University, Florida State University, New College of Florida, University of Central Florida, University of Florida, University of North Florida, University of South Florida, and University of West Florida.

University Press of Florida
15 Northwest 15th Street
Gainesville, FL 32611-2079
http://www.upf.com

# Contents

Acknowledgments  vii
Note on Transliteration  ix

Introduction: Food and Politics in the Arab-Islamic World  1

**Part I. The More Things Change . . .**

1. The Political Economy of Moroccan Hunger  17
2. Industrialism and Participatory Politics at the Water Mill  41
3. Commerce and Class Tensions at the Butcher Shop  65

**Part II. . . . the More They Stay the Same**

4. The Economic and Political Order of Colonial Morocco  93
5. The Colonial Preservation of the Miller's Trade  119
6. Fiscal Politics at the Municipal Slaughterhouse  143

**Part III. Continuity and Change**

7. Struggles for Scarce Resources in the 1930s  173
8. Famine and the Emergence of Popular Nationalism  197

Conclusion  213

Glossary  219
Notes  225
Bibliography  263
Index  277

# Acknowledgments

I am deeply indebted to many people for their support and assistance since I began this project. In particular, I thank Diana Wylie for her sharp criticism of my work and for her constant moral support. I also thank Jim McCann, an invaluable resource in regard to the environmental aspects of this study. Nasser Rabbat has inspired me with his strong opinions and challenging questions, always pushing me to rethink the broader implications of the events that I document. For reading all or part of the manuscript and commenting on it, I also owe an intellectual debt to Susan Miller, Thomas Glick, Sarah Phillips, Susan Slyomovics, Jonathan Katz, Mark Bernstein, and John Larson.

In Morocco, I developed a wonderful network of colleagues and friends. For hospitality and assistance with all aspects of the research, I thank Khalid ben Srhir, Abderrahman Benhada, Jamaa Baida, and Mina Elmghari. Among fellow researchers who let me blather on about my "soucis," both professional and personal, I must mention Mahfoud Asmahri, Kashia Pieprzak, Madia Thomson, Lisa Bernasek, Ghislaine Lydon, Kathy Roberts, Geoff Porter, Bonnie Kaplan, Ann Hawley, Irene Siegel, Malika Khandagui, and Mohamed Bourras. Aicha Hariri and Myriam Bousta offered wellsprings of friendship that I greatly appreciated. I undoubtedly owe the largest debt of gratitude to Abdellah Larhmaid, a gifted historian and a very dear friend.

Family connections are an important part of all of our lives, and this truism is particularly relevant in my case. Given that I am a granddaughter of a janitor and an auto mechanic, it is no surprise that I focused my historical interest in African cities on urban workers. My late father provided a model of strength and tenacity. My mother's curiosity about the world has always been an inspiration. And my brothers have patiently listened to me droning on about the book and other sundry topics for years and years. Since every good historian of Africa and the Middle East knows that family is a constructed entity, I would also like to acknowledge the support of my long-time girlfriends Amy Clark, Cindy Smith, Maryclaire Paullis, and Susan Akram.

I am grateful for the encouragement of my colleagues in the history department at Purdue University. I would like to thank in particular Randy Roberts, Frank Lambert, Dawn Marsh, Mike Ryan, Darren Dochuk, and Juan Wang.

Finally, I want to express my gratitude to the institutions that funded the research for this book, and these include the Graham Foundation, the American Institute of Maghrib Studies, and the Fulbright Association.

# Note on Transliteration

Transliteration is a persistent problem for scholars of Moroccan history. We want to do justice to the Arabic language when transliterating a term, but we also want to keep such words in a form that is recognizable to Moroccans. This is not easy. Moroccans speak Modern Standard Arabic as well as a regional dialect of Arabic. Complicating this linguistic dualism is a Latin overlay that stems from Morocco's long relationship with France. For most terms, I have used a simplified version of the system of transliteration detailed by the *International Journal of Middle East Studies*. The transliterated terms have no diacritical markers except for the ayn and hamza. If a word is found in Webster's Dictionary—such as the names of the months in the Islamic calendar or a common noun like mellah—then I have left it in the form in which it was adopted into English. Personal and place names are particularly challenging for the scholar. When in doubt about rendering a proper or common noun, I have erred on the side of a more familiar French form of transliteration that would be more recognizable to Moroccans than the academically transliterated version. In this way, I believe that this book about ordinary Moroccans also provides the auditory and visual flavor, so to speak, of everyday life in Fez. I ask for the reader's indulgence regarding any inconsistencies.

# Introduction

Food and Politics in the Arab-Islamic World

The exercise of power in the Arab-Islamic world puzzles politicians and pundits alike and leads scholars to engage in intensive debates on the nature of authority in the Middle East and North Africa. This region includes countries that regularly headline the news, such as Libya, Algeria, Israel, Palestine, Egypt, Syria, and Iraq. In this region, it seems that despots dominate authoritarian political systems, establishing the state as their personal fiefdom. They use oppressive measures to crush the masses and to enforce their authority. And yet, more often than not, the revolutions organized to oust such tyrants replace their rule with another of the same ilk, and not with a democracy.

This political pattern raises a number of seemingly intractable questions: Why do authoritarian regimes thrive in the Middle East and North Africa? Why do ordinary people acquiesce to such exploitive political systems? Why do they seem instinctively to shy away from Western modernity, defined here as both a liberal political system and an industrialized capitalist economy? Does this situation stem from Arab backwardness? From irrational religious fanaticism? What accounts for the excessive violence and political turmoil that plague all too many places in the Arab-Islamic world? These questions were most provocatively summed up in Bernard Lewis's best seller *What Went Wrong? The Clash between Islam and Modernity in the Middle East*.[1] Lewis proposes that the political and economic stagnation in the Middle East is an outgrowth of a narrow worldview by Muslims, one that rejects innovation.

It is difficult to redefine the questions raised in a field of study that often promotes Islam as the engine of historical process. Islamic principles are presented as definitive of the relationships between state and society, and religion is viewed as the determining factor in the political life of Arab-Islamic states.[2] Scholars often limit themselves to persuading readers that Islam does not provide a blueprint for understanding political behavior in the Middle East. This self-imposed limitation results not in an explanation of the actual forces shaping the region but instead in an assertion that there are "conflicts which primarily pit Muslims against Muslims, and . . . a growing gulf between Shia and Sunnis."[3] Even when authors challenge the concept of a monolithic Islam, they still suggest that local interpretations of Islamic beliefs and adaptations of Islamic practices, albeit in all their myriad forms, define relations between state and society.[4]

This book does not deny the importance of Islam in the Middle East and North Africa. It suggests, though, that a religiously based system of moral obligations is shaped by the mundane concerns of everyday life in a semi-arid land. All countries of the Middle East and North Africa fall between 40 and 20 degrees latitude, where insufficient rainfall often fails to sustain the harvesting of a plentiful food supply. The challenge of food provisioning promotes highly centralized governments. This statement should not be read as a blind endorsement of Karl Wittfogel's teleology of "Oriental despotism," whereby the control of water in drought-prone lands leads inevitably to a repressive state.[5] And yet, it is undeniable that the challenge of feeding people shapes state institutions and political ideology. The study of food provisioning and the distribution of natural resources in a society—whether equitable or exploitive—merits attention for the insights it provides into the nature of political authority.

Ensuring access to affordable food is a basic task of all governments across time and space, but it is particularly difficult in lands where drought is a constant threat. Even in the United States, drought and concomitant concerns for food security advance the authoritarian tendencies of the state. David Worster refers to the Wittfogel thesis when he deems the American West a "modern hydraulic society," showing that the need to control water led to an antidemocratic centralization of power. In analyzing the control of irrigation systems, Worster shows that the American West's governance over the course of the nineteenth and twentieth centuries was "increasingly a coercive, monolithic, and hierarchical system, ruled by a power elite based on the ownership of capital and expertise."[6] This centralizing tendency increased during the Depression, when a need to distribute natural resources promoted the expansion of the federal government's powers.[7]

An approach highlighting the importance of agricultural production and food distribution as a means of understanding social and political relationships has already emerged in Ottoman studies. The Ottomans forged a military state, with successive caliphs constantly seeking to expand the empire's borders. The Ottoman Empire got its start in the Anatolian peninsula in the thirteenth century and encompassed eight million square kilometers on three continents by the sixteenth century. At that time, Ottoman caliphs were the rulers of twenty-five million people. Turks were but a fraction of this population, and Muslims only slightly more numerous than Christians. The caliphs legitimized their rule by claiming Islamic authority, but their subjects freely practiced their different religions, evidence that spiritual practices were not a pressing Ottoman concern.[8]

Instead, Ottoman caliphs spent much time and energy addressing their subjects' quotidian needs. The highest echelons of administrators ensured that wheat was equitably distributed throughout the empire, from the arable Balkans to the semiarid Levant.[9] Focusing on "food matrices," Amy Singer elucidates how "giving and taking food symbolized and actualized the dense networks of patronage woven with implications of rights and obligations."[10] Amnon Cohen argues that the workings of this empire are best understood at the level of the local economy, and not in the detailing of imperial intentions or international imbroglios, thereby revealing the influence butchers and millers exercised in sixteenth-century Jerusalem.[11] Rhoads Murphey attributes the empire's staying power to "the feeding and providing for the basic needs of the population, adjusting imbalances between the 'haves' and 'have nots.'"[12]

Western powers did not fully disband the Ottoman Empire until after World War I, when the imperial system was replaced with a set of modern states. A modern state is a political entity in which the government, whether it takes the form of a democratic republic or an authoritarian monarchy, exercises direct control over a distinct territory and population, and not through the intermediaries of communal organizations, as often occurred under the Ottomans' millet system. It is premised on a centralized bureaucracy and standardization. With its monopoly on the legitimate use of force, a modern state's government has the power to impose policy on its citizens.

Thus, there is by definition an element of authoritarianism underpinning all modern states, even democracies. As analyzed by James C. Scott, the purveyors of power forcibly impose agricultural and industrial policies that—despite the government's enunciated intention to improve the lives of its citizens and the productivity of the nation as a whole—often wreak havoc. That such interventions often produce unhappy results stems from the fact that governments tend to be run from the center by technocrats who set aside the practical knowledge of the people to be affected by policy. Such technocratic centralization is found not only in Tanzania or China but also in the United States, where the regional planning agency of the Tennessee Valley Authority reflects the ideals of a top-down scheme of economic development imposed on Americans.[13]

But if there is an element of authoritarianism even in democracies, there is conversely an element of popular participation in authoritarian regimes. British administrators of colonial Kenya forged one of the most authoritarian regimes of the past century. Nevertheless, they recognized a need to accede on some issues in order to gain the acquiescence of subject peoples and so avoid a military occupation that would be costly in terms of money and manpower.[14]

Scholars in Middle Eastern studies illuminate how Egypt's authoritarian regime addresses the aspirations of the majority in modern Cairo. Much as in colonial Kenya, the government wants to avoid using its monopoly on force against its own citizens. Egyptian elections, however, do no more than rubber-stamp the rule of President Mubarak and his cohorts, resulting in few formal means for people to assert their interests. Despite this institutional vacuum, even the poor participate vigorously in political life, albeit in an informal sphere outside of government institutions, which makes such political mechanisms difficult to detect.

In Cairo, "food issues are highly politicized," and a rise in the price of staples threatens violent riots.[15] The government has set up subsidies to keep prices low, although such a policy does not always ensure the provisioning of the markets. As a consequence, some residents shop for food in the black market. It is this sort of everyday choice by regular Egyptians, when repeated over and over, that allows the government to perceive and to address the concerns of the Egyptian majority in order to prevent unrest. In this case, Islam does not explain political behavior; at most, it validates the rational choices of Egyptian people.[16]

Provisioning policies remain a pressing concern of rulers in the Middle East and North Africa, just as in past centuries. In too many Arab-Islamic countries, excessive violence continues to shape the environment of power. This book ultimately suggests a need to consider geoclimatic conditions as a factor in regional instability. Is it coincidence that Afghanistan's Taliban rose to power during a drought? Or that Algeria's civil war began after bread riots in 1988?[17] Or that President Mouayya Ould Sid'Ahmed Taya of Mauritania was overthrown in 2005, the second year of a famine threatening one million people in North and West Africa?[18] Or that insurgents in Baghdad target bakeries in poor quarters during the present Iraq War? Given the conclusions of this study, it is reasonable to expect that our understanding of other places in the Middle East and North Africa would be deepened if scholars—and U.S. policymakers—focused on how governments deal with the unique shortcomings of geography and climate instead of on the ethnicity and religion of the peoples living there.

A Moroccan Case Study

Morocco is the only country in the Arab-Islamic world that has exhibited consistent political stability, and it has done so not just over the course of the last one hundred years but over the course of the past four centuries. Situated on the westernmost limits of this cultural region, Morocco does not share the Ottoman past of other states in that part of the world, a historical circumstance that contributes to its identification as "exceptional." Nevertheless, this North African kingdom experiences the same geoclimatic challenges as other states in the region. Just like these other countries, Morocco is a centralized state under an unquestioned leader perceived as authoritarian. But, and here is the critical difference between Morocco and other states of the region, the same dynasty has ruled over this monarchy for 350 years, a notable case of political continuity that merits attention.

In terms of being a focus of scholarly analysis, however, Morocco is a victim of its political success. Morocco rarely headlines U.S. newspapers, and relatively few books are published about it. Instead, journalists and authors prefer to address the history and politics of countries wracked with problems. While voyeuristically satisfying, such analytical preferences for so-called failed states only generate ever more unanswered questions in regard to the effective wielding of power. This study focuses on the distribution of scarce resources in the kingdom of Morocco and the supply of food in its urban markets in order to demonstrate how Moroccan rulers have, if you will excuse the pun, found a "recipe for success."

The Alaouite dynasty has ruled Morocco since 1664, overseeing and shaping this country's transformation as a modern monarchal state that exudes stability. The modern history of state formation began in the early nineteenth century, when Sultan Moulay Abderrahman (1822–1859) and his successor, Sidi Mohamed ben Abderrahman (1859–1873), expanded Morocco's trading networks with Europe. Sultan Moulay Hassan (1873–1894) centralized the royal administration, making sure that his officials ruled in both fact and theory in the furthest reaches of his kingdom. His son Moulay Abdelaziz (1894–1908) continued his policies, as did Moulay Abdelhafid (1908–1912), who forcibly, though without a war, replaced his brother fourteen years after his initial ascent to the throne.

It was in 1912, under Moulay Abdelhafid, that the French established the protectorate of Morocco, ruling on behalf of the Alaouite sultans for the next forty-four years. Louis-Hubert Lyautey was the first resident-general appointed by the colonizing foreigners, and he oversaw Moulay Abdelhafid's abdication in favor of his brother Moulay Youssef (1912–1927). Lyautey constructed and implemented a policy of indirect rule that ensured the continuance of the Alaouites as putative rulers of Morocco even during the colonial era.[19] It would be Sultan Sidi Mohamed (1927–1961), the son of Moulay Youssef, who would partner with the sons of elite notables and forge a nationalist movement that would lead in 1956 to an independent Morocco ruled by Alaouites.

These sultans perpetuated a conservative ideology that shaped state institutions and the wielding of power. As a general term, conservatism signifies a social and political outlook premised on the preservation of benefits associated with prior institutions and patterns of social life. In Morocco, this term has taken shape as a social system based on the perpetuation of patriarchal relations of subordination organized as patron-client networks. As an economic philosophy, it signifies the communal organization of manual labor as well as the blocking of full-scale industrialization. As a political system, it connotes divine kingship and dynastic rule. Toward this last, the Alaouites legitimize their authority by virtue of their descent from the Prophet Mohamed. The sultan—now having the title of king—claims the title of *imam*, which, designating the head of an Islamic community, gives the Moroccan ruler not only secular authority over his subjects but also a moral obligation to serve them.

This study focuses on Fez, an interior city of northern Morocco and the center of sultanic power wielded by the makhzan. In Morocco, the term *makhzan* connotes the sultan and all personnel associated with his monarchal administration. Fez—along with Marrakesh, Rabat, and Meknes—was one of four imperial capitals where the Alaouites maintained a palace. The sultan, however, at least in the late nineteenth century, spent more of his reign in Fez than in other imperial cities. Moulay Hassan, for example, spent nearly half of his reign there, dividing the rest of his time between the other three imperial capitals as well as on military excursions in the south.[20]

Given climatic patterns in the late nineteenth and early twentieth centuries, food supply was the issue of most concern to a preponderant majority in Fez and throughout the kingdom. Lasting from 1878 to 1884, the Great Famine was one episode, albeit the worst, in a devastating cycle of environmental catastrophes in the thirty-five years that preceded French colonization. When the Great Famine began, Moroccans had hardly recovered from a drought that destroyed harvests between 1867 and 1869. In the mid-1890s and again between 1903 and 1907, Morocco's parched land produced few crops. Between 1867 and 1912, drought and locusts destroyed at least seventeen wheat harvests in the region of Fez.[21] After the French established the protectorate of Morocco in 1912, colonial administrators would also need to address environmental crises. Famine loomed again as drought and locusts struck in 1915 and 1927, and throughout most of the 1930s.

Flour and meat were basic foods sold in urban markets, so mills and slaughterhouses offer an ideal prism through which to view relations between state and society. Millers served the poor, but they were influential members of urban society; butchers served the rich, but they were at the bottom rung of Fez's social hierarchy. The sultan implemented fiscal policies, market regulations, and industrial plans to increase or decrease access to the flour and meat sold by millers and butchers. In other words, Alaouite sultans doggedly defined access to the commodities sold by these artisans. Such policies show that Islamic rulers in this kingdom secured absolute power by supplying flour (a staple) to workers and the poor, who constituted the majority of the king's subjects, rather than access to meat (a consumable luxury) to influential notables.

In considering the political history of Morocco from the perspective of ordinary workers, this case study of urban food supply breaks new historiographical ground. First, this book moves away from postcolonial questions linked to foreign conquest and subsequent nationalist movements aimed at independence. All too often, foreign intervention dictates the organization of books on Moroccan history, with either the first or the last chapter focused on French colonization in 1912.[22] This chronology unwittingly leads scholars to frame the questions to which they respond in terms of either the nineteenth-century origins of the colonial encounter or the twentieth-century struggle for independence. Arid weather patterns were a constant in both the precolonial and colonial eras, and this book shows that popular responses to the threat of famine shaped Morocco's political system.

In reconfiguring the chronology of Moroccan history, this book reevaluates the colonial policy of "association." Scholars have defined this policy as a partnership between colonial administrators and Moroccan merchants and scholars. The French, however, also adopted the sultan's precolonial defense of workers and the poor, protecting them from the avarice of their social superiors. Although workers and the poor were generally of a lower status, having neither the economic power of merchants nor the political authority of religious leaders, they made up the preponderant majority of urban residents. The French ensured employment and affordable food to these ordinary Moroccans in order to forestall sociopolitical unrest.

By addressing the plight of workers, this book shows that a nationalist movement aiming at independence did not develop in Morocco until drought and global recession in the 1930s led the French to eliminate colonial programs of social welfare. Members of the nationalist party stepped into this economic vacuum. Consisting primarily of young men from notable families, they adopted the paternalistic activities of their forefathers to forge sociopolitical networks. In this sense, it was the weakness of the colonial state—and not its oppressive strength—that fostered a conservative form of nationalism intent on independence and the perpetuation of Alaouite rule.

Finally, this book shows that the economic system engendered by environmental conditions explains social and political conservatism in Morocco. Studies of Morocco invariably emphasize the Islamic underpinnings of the region's social and political life. Abdellah Hammoudi argues that Moroccan Islam fosters a hierarchical system between an all-powerful master and submissive disciples.[23] This book extends explanations of social and political development beyond Islamic beliefs by examining the environmental and economic conditions in which Moroccan events transpired. In doing so, it shows that mundane concerns, and not just religious beliefs, fostered a conservative political system premised on a highly centralized state under an autocratic monarch.

This study gives empirical form to theoretical discussions of state development and challenges a general belief that Muslims instinctively retreat from modernity. I base my findings on the correspondence of Moroccan officials in the precolonial era (1878–1912) and French officials of the protectorate (1912–1956). I examine the interpretation and enactment of Islamic law as it affected market controls, property rights, and charitable endowments. Twenty-five octogenarians—millers and butchers trained by their fathers and grandfathers—contributed family histories that shed new light on official documents. By enunciating the concerns of urban residents from diverse socioeconomic statuses, these sources reveal that Morocco's political leaders and private residents consciously debated the efficacy of models of modernity emerging in the late nineteenth and early twentieth centuries. The sultan and his subjects ultimately chose a conservative form of modernity that adapted institutions of the past and continued to rely on an autocratic monarch to ensure urban food supply.

## Chapter Descriptions

This book is organized into three distinct chronological periods that trace the construction of the modern state via urban food provisioning. Part I is subtitled "The More Things Change . . . " In this section, I discuss Morocco in the context of the Arab-Islamic world, thereafter focusing on how royal policies affected urban food supply between 1878 and 1912. Part II is subtitled ". . . the More They Stay the Same." Here, I set out colonial intentions to preserve stability by maintaining precolonial provisioning policies between 1912 and 1929, the first seventeen years of French rule. "Continuity within Change" is the final section, and it evaluates the effects of the global depression and local drought that plagued Morocco between 1930 and 1937. Ultimately, it traces the fashion by which the nationalist movement carried over the tenets of personalized rule developed by precolonial Alaouite rulers.

"The Political Economy of Moroccan Hunger" (chapter 1): The socioeconomic connotations conveyed by the term "famine" changed dramatically in the late nineteenth and early twentieth centuries. The epicenter of starvation shifted from the city (its location in previous centuries) to the countryside, and rural migrants flocked to Fez when famine loomed. Such food crises, however, revealed a growing gap between the rich and the poor. The sultan ensured equitable distribution of wheat through tax collection, and his royal officials oversaw the price and quality of foodstuffs in the marketplace. Further, the sultan counted on the elite to sustain informal networks of patronage supplying food to the poor. Religious affiliation often defined the membership of these groupings, but food provisioning was their primary mission. This chapter demonstrates that the Alaouites forestalled unrest by providing the urban poor with wheat, even if it meant redistributing the wealth of influential Moroccans.

"Industrialism and Participatory Politics at the Water Mill" (chapter 2): Contrary to Western stereotypes, neither ignorance nor lack of capital prevented industrialism in the Arab-Islamic world. Flour was a staple food, so an economic decline, even if caused by a poor harvest, led to a paradoxical increase in demand for this filling starch. To satisfy increased demand for flour, royal officials and private entrepreneurs set up some steam mills. And yet, the sultan and his subjects deliberately blocked full-scale mechanization due to fears of foreign incursion, of the misuse of natural resources, and of the high cost of flour produced by steam mills. This collective check on industrialism highlights the importance of political consensus, even under authoritarian rule. This chapter argues that drought provoked some mechanization of flour production, but the sultan, millers, and struggling consumers together perpetuated a reliance on traditional technology.

"Commerce and Class Tensions at the Butcher Shop" (chapter 3): Meat was a consumable luxury that provided tangible evidence of wealth and status among both the Muslim majority and the Jewish minority. To increase profits, butchers serving each of these communities tried to lower the price of their commodity, which, by enlarging their base clientele, would then increase their volume of sales. They slaughtered cheaper female animals, but the sultan prohibited such action so as to preserve livestock during periods of drought. The sultan also increased the cost of meat by imposing a tax on slaughter in order to fund social welfare programs for those impoverished by drought. Slaughter is regulated by both Islamic and Jewish law, so butchers practicing the two different faiths should have embodied religious division in this kingdom. Instead, this chapter shows that their joint effort to render meat a staple reflected a struggle to change economic policy, with class interests, not religion, shaping the political action of Muslim and Jewish workers.

"The Economic and Political Order of Colonial Morocco" (chapter 4): After the protectorate's establishment in 1912, the French ruled on behalf of the Alaouites, incorporating Fez's elite in local and national government. To prevent social unrest among common peoples, the French also created employment programs in order to ensure workers' access to affordable food. By providing colonized workers with opportunities to earn money, however, colonial policies unintentionally fostered social mobility. Some workers assumed the outward trappings of notables, like home ownership. Ultimately, building projects in the medina revealed emerging class tensions in Morocco. Fez's elite advocated a modern city, with wide roads for cars and houses designed by French architects, while workers supported a colonial vision of Fez as a medieval relic relying on the work of independent artisans. This chapter reevaluates the policy of association, showing how the French defended the economic interests of workers against initiatives by the elite with whom they forged a formal political partnership.

"Colonial Preservation of the Miller's Trade" (chapter 5): Like Moroccan sultans, French administrators tried to ensure the provisioning of affordable flour to urban workers and the poor. Requiring massive amounts of start-up capital, industrial mills proved a costly and inefficient means of achieving this objective. The French therefore implemented policies that privileged the continued operation of water mills by Moroccan millers. Entrepreneurial investments highlighted the profits of the water mill's small-scale flour production. A continued reliance on the water mill also served colonial policies aimed at full employment of Moroccan workers. Factories required less manpower than water mills, and to forestall social and political unrest, French officials wanted to protect Moroccans from the dislocation of rapid modernization. This chapter argues that water mills, in terms of both cost and productive capacity, outperformed the industrial facilities operated by Europeans during the first seventeen years of the protectorate.

"Fiscal Politics at the Municipal Slaughterhouse" (chapter 6): Meat played a central role not only in legitimizing the protectorate but also in funding its operation. To advertise respect for Islam, colonial officers amplified the celebrations for 'Id al-Adha, or 'Id al-Kabir, as it was called by Moroccans, when the sultan sacrificed a ram on behalf of his subjects. For ordinary meals, however, the French expected urban residents to buy meat from local butchers at a municipal slaughterhouse. To increase demand for commercially butchered meat, the French banned private slaughter, curtailing a time-honored elite prerogative. By collecting a tax on each slaughtered animal, the French forced two hundred butchers, or only .002 percent of the population, to provide 10 percent of Fez's municipal income. Butchers increased their clientele among workers by exploiting colonial tax laws and slaughtering female animals, thereby providing customers with cheaper meat. This chapter argues that the colonial regulation of the meat industry transformed the way that social classes conducted daily life, with workers and the poor increasing their access to meat, an influential luxury.

"Struggles for Scarce Resources in the 1930s" (chapter 7): In the 1930s, drought and global recession caused a severe food shortage in Moroccan cities. Given the extent of the crisis, French officers could no longer guarantee urban workers a minimum standard of living in exchange for their political quiescence. The weakness of the colonial state—and not its oppressive strength—led some members of Fez's mercantile elite to court discontented workers by securing their access to meat and flour. These nationalists organized a movement that advocated some commercial and technological modernization, but they rejected outright industrialization.

This nationalist movement maintained conservative concepts of sociopolitical organization by which the elite cared for their social inferiors through patron-client networks.

"Famine and the Emergence of Popular Nationalism" (chapter 8): Nationalist initiatives included soup kitchens for the poor and public sacrifices conducted before the masses, time-honored methods of forging sociopolitical networks of patronage. The success of these nationalist programs culminated in massive demonstrations protesting colonial rule in October 1937. To quell unrest, the French ordered troops to occupy the medina, thereby revealing, for the first time since the conquest in 1912, the coercive force underpinning colonial rule. This chapter demonstrates that grievances over the distribution of local resources, and not over legal rights, sparked the movement that eventually led to Moroccan independence.

Conclusion

This is the story of ordinary workers and their strategies to engage the state and to assert their interests. The Alaouite sultans who ruled these subject peoples claimed the right to undisputed authority in their kingdom. Political participation, however, comes in many forms, and a system of divine kingship does not necessarily signal that workers are unwitting pawns. Through their social networks, commercial innovations, and technological choices, Moroccans ensured that their government recognized and acknowledged the interests of the working majority. The Morocco of today is much like the Morocco of yesterday, but this is not a sign of stagnation. Instead, it is the result of a dynamic process and rigorous debate.

Moroccans from a variety of socioeconomic groups with varying status have deliberately adapted and changed Western models of modernity in order to perpetuate a conservative regime headed by a ruler often perceived and analyzed as authoritarian. In these semiarid lands, food security was—and still is—a core concern of ordinary people, and popular interests shaped the dictatorial policies of Alaouites intent on prolonging their regime. Sociopolitical conservatism in this theocratic state has offered a rational response to economic and environmental conditions. This study concludes that sultans gave priority to the provisioning of the city with food in the nineteenth and twentieth centuries in order to secure the loyalty of workers and the poor, the lynchpins of their authority.

Although not a royal apologist by nature, I do recognize that this effort to show the logic underpinning sociopolitical and economic conservatism in Morocco invites criticism from those averse to political systems based on paternalism and divine kingship. Environmental conditions, however, exercise their own logic on the wielding of political authority, one that may force first-world academics beyond their comfort range. This study of political legitimacy and state construction in Morocco strongly suggests that the poor environmental conditions of the semiarid lands of the Arab-Islamic world create a paradoxically fertile field for authoritarianism, albeit, in this instance, as a form of participatory paternalism whereby the state heeds the specific needs of its people and bases its policy on their system of moral values as well as their practical knowledge about the local economy.

# PART I

# The More Things Change . . .

# 1

# The Political Economy of Moroccan Hunger

In 1878, swarms of locusts destroyed Morocco's crops of hard wheat, and a drought followed in their wake. For the next six years, little rain fell in the kingdom, ushering in an environmental crisis that caused a dire food shortage. Foreign observers estimated that a third of the rural population died during the Great Famine.[1]

Witnessing the death of family and friends, starving peasants fled the parched countryside. Rural settlements began to disappear. In the south, a French explorer stopped in a hamlet with half its normal population.[2] In the north, a frustrated English diplomat could not find most villages previously charted between Tangier and Fez.[3] Emaciated corpses at the sides of Moroccan byways testified to desperate efforts to flee the villages and to reach the closest city.[4]

Those who reached Fez did not necessarily find instant relief. The stench emanating from shallow graves outside the city walls offered indigent newcomers a telling reminder of the mortal stakes of a bad harvest and the resulting food penury.[5] Inside the city, women and children took to the streets, emitting wails of distress in order to draw attention to their hunger.[6] Status, wealth, religion, and, given the rural influx, even provincial origins highlighted potential fault lines running through a society threatened with a seismic upheaval.

For royal officials, crop failure in the hinterland generated an urgent need to procure a filling starch in order to soothe hungry multitudes in the city with little left to lose. Fez had a population of nearly one hundred thousand people at the turn of the twentieth century, and this city was among the economic and political centers of the sultan's power.[7] Residents of the densely populated urban centers were restive and prone to protest, especially when they went hungry. The sultans who ruled Morocco between

1873 and 1912 could not run the political risk of allowing the masses to go hungry. To provide for their neediest subjects, Alaouite rulers equalized the distribution of scarce resources in the city; they also sought to foster paternalistic links between residents of differing socioeconomic status.

## The Medina of Fez

Starving peasants flocked to the medina of Fez in search of food. This northeastern city was located in the foothills of the Middle Atlas Mountains on the fertile Sais Plain. There, the Oued Sebou flows south from the Middle Atlas Mountains. This river flowed year-round and not, like the Oued Draa of the pre-Saharan south, just seasonally, after winter rains replenished it. Seasonal rains would normally render Fez's hinterland a fertile place for harvesting hard wheat, a crop dependent on rainfall, not on canals from the river. For this reason, drought rendered bare most fields surrounding Fez.

These inhospitable fields reached the very edge of the medina, for there was—and still is—a very abrupt line demarcating city and countryside in Fez. The term *medina* refers to the walled quarters of the premodern urban center of Moroccan cities. From afar, migrants would have noticed that Fez's walled medina consisted of two distinct zones. They would have seen a large circle and a smaller one to its east, with a narrow and barely visible passage between the two. Describing the city to modern readers, one writer refers to it as "an uneven dumbbell."[8]

Together, Fez al-Bali and Fez al-Jadid formed an urban conglomeration of five square miles. The cityscape consisted in each zone of a dense urban center. The tightly packed houses at the medina's midpoint, however, thinned toward the outskirts, which had yet to be built up to their present form. The open spaces of orchards near the walls made a pleasant place to relax and picnic for the wealthy families owning the walled gardens.

Fez al-Bali was the larger zone, and, as an outgrowth of a town settled by Arabs in the ninth century, it represented the medina's core. It straddled the Oued Fas, a tributary of the Oued Sebou. From the surrounding foothills, the eye would inevitably be drawn to the green roof and square minaret at the center of the medina. This complex marked the Qarawiyyin Mosque and Madrasa. It produced the kingdom's most important scholars, so the mosque's presence made Fez the unquestioned cultural capital of Morocco. Given the jurisprudence of scholars, it was arguably also the kingdom's legal center.

A taller and more slender minaret in this same quarter marked the mausoleum of Moulay Idriss. Idriss II was the founder of Fez and therefore was honored as the city's patron saint. Long thought to have been buried in the nearby town of Volubulis, his putative remains were found and reburied in this mausoleum in the early fourteenth century. The ordinary Fassi, or resident of Fez, came here to pray for the intercession of this saint with any of life's problems. For criminals, the mausoleum was a place of political asylum. Many of the impoverished rural migrants looking down at Fez from the surrounding hills would soon become familiar with this area of the city. Given the devotion of visitors to the shrine, it offered an ideal site for hungry migrants to beg for charity.

Fez al-Bali's principal axis was the Talaa Saghira, which began at the main entry to the Qarawiyyin Mosque. Heading west, this street immediately passed through the Qissariyya, a market where residents could buy luxury items like silk, perfume, ribbons, candles, and jewelry. By the late nineteenth century, the wares sold in this market, or *suq*, as a Moroccan would call it, included imported goods, like brightly colored bolts of cloth from England. Arranged on a set of parallel roads, the shops were small, with most measuring no more than a few square meters. The shopkeeper stood inside with his merchandise, while his clients perused these items from the street. A wooden roof covered the suq, protecting clients from the heat of direct sunlight. The doors to this commercial center closed at night, so the area physically resembled the European market hall.[9]

Continuing along the Talaa Saghira, pedestrians kept to the left, for Fassis had not yet adopted the French practice of walking on the right side of the road.[10] It was here that they began to encounter porters and their mules, which were not allowed in the area surrounding the Qarawiyyin Mosque or the Qissariyya market. A porter's cry of "baalek!" signified that pedestrians should move to the side of the narrow road so that he and his mule could pass. The Talaa Saghira was not paved at that time, for macadamized pavement was a novelty even in Europe, where it was invented. The road turned to mud during the rainy winter months. Residents may have hated walking along such muddy byways, but the sultan and his officials appreciated that the rains washed them at no cost to the royal treasury.

Once having passed through the Qissariyya market and the nearby spice market of the Suq al-Attarin, this concourse veered uphill, past the Cherabliyyin Mosque. The walls of the surrounding houses loomed high over pedestrians, with each structure contiguous to the next one. Constructed in the fourteenth century, however, the minaret of the Cherabliyyin Mosque juts into the street, thereby ensuring visibility from afar. In this way, it exemplifies architectural embellishments designed specifically for the narrow streets of the medina.

Heading uphill, the sounds of this vibrant city must have overwhelmed rural migrants. As a tributary of the Oued Sebou, the Oued Fas had a strong current, flowing even in dry seasons. For this reason, a migrant heard the burbling of water as underground canals parceled out the waters of the Oued Fas throughout the medina. Some canals supplied fresh water to private houses, mosques, and public baths; others carried sewage downstream, beyond the Oued Fas's southeastern walls. The scraping of millstones accompanied this babble, for water mills were set up all along the canals, operating twenty-four hours a day. A cannon blast punctuated these sounds five times a day, with each announcing the time of one of five daily prayers.

Tight passages off Talaa Saghira provided entry to some of this zone's eighteen residential neighborhoods. At the turn of the twentieth century, a French consular agent counted 5,300 houses in Fez al-Bali, thereby extrapolating a population of 78,000.[11] A miniscule number of these residents could be identified as notables whose family status or personal wealth gave them influence. They were usually scholars—often *shurafa'* who claimed descent from the Prophet—or merchants. Fez's workers had numeric superiority over their social betters. Based on statistics collected in the early twentieth century, two-thirds of the active male population in Fez earned a living by producing a good, as tailors or carpenters, for example, or by rendering a service, as, for example, porters or barbers.[12]

Fez's wealthiest residents did not live in this central corridor, for most had commissioned the construction of grandiose courtyard houses in the orchards on the margins of Fez. Royal officials from mercantile families sparked a building boom during the last quarter of the nineteenth century. In the central areas off Talaa Saghira, the courtyard house was a modest endeavor, with no more than a small fountain in the paved open patio. These new houses, however, had a central patio large enough not only for a fountain but also for an expansive rectangular garden. Usually two or three stories tall, the top floor was adorned with grilled windows looking onto the surrounding mountains or the orchard below. A French official later denigrated them for the "European elements" of the construction and the decorative embellishments.[13]

The clothing of pedestrians in the medina reflected the socioeconomic diversity of Fez's residents. Millers wore a white skullcap, while beggars often adorned a red one that they humbly pulled down to their eyes. Royal officials wrapped a conical fez in a band of muslin. Members of different tribes had different ways of dressing. Some covered their head with a black turban, while others used the hood of their jellaba, a cylindrical robe reaching from the shoulders to the ankles.[14] Rural migrants might pass hundreds of people if they walked along Talaa Saghira in the late afternoon, when the streets and markets in the medina were most crowded. Approximately one and a half miles from the Qarawiyyin Mosque, a food market on Talaa Saghira preceded the end of Fez al-Bali's Talaa Saghira.

To leave Fez al-Bali, one passed through the Boujeloud Gate, originally designed as a narrow zigzag to prevent invasion. This gate offered entry into the Boujeloud esplanade, where some exiled peasants sought shelter. During a drought, many migrants would beg there, and the rags they wore offered tangible evidence of their dire straits. The wide space of this esplanade offered the rural migrant a place to set up a tent or to construct a temporary shelter of straw or reeds. The esplanade, as explained by one French visitor, became a village within the city during a drought, for the shelters he saw there in 1905 were like those he had just seen as he traveled the countryside on his way to this imperial capital.[15]

This esplanade separates Fez al-Bali from Fez al-Jadid, to which the entry is found on the western side. This second zone was founded by the Merenids (1258–1420). After emerging victorious from a hard-fought war with the Almohads, this dynasty constructed a fortified camp to protect the royal court from tribal marauders. Over the course of five centuries, it would in itself become an urban conglomeration replete with houses, public baths, water mills, mosques, and marketplaces.

In the late nineteenth century, Fez al-Jadid sheltered fifteen thousand residents. This second zone was home to the royal court and Moroccan Jews, both distinct minorities in this precolonial capital. The elite members of the royal court included three thousand retainers permanently residing at Fez's royal palace.[16] Such retainers included members of the Alaouite family as well as the workers who served them, with distinct groups formed to cook for the royal family or to serve them tea. Ordinary Muslims not associated in any way with the palace also lived in Fez al-Jadid, with one French sociologist counting six thousand Muslims at the turn of the twentieth century.[17]

Fez's Jewish minority lived next to the palace in a quarter called the mellah. There, Moroccan Jews engaged in activities forbidden to practicing Muslims, like producing and drinking a fruity wine called *mahiya*. They also set up their own institutions, such as a religious court where rabbis judged civil suits. In this sense, the mellah was "a town within itself, separate from the rest of Fez, yet attached to it through filaments of economic, social and political dependency."[18] In 1879, a rabbi counted 5,844 Jews in the mellah.[19]

Some rural refugees settled on the margins of the western quarters of Fez al-Jadid.[20] Much as in the Boujeloud esplanade, they constructed makeshift shelters of impermanent building materials. Such temporary housing offered a stark contrast to the new homes being built toward the margins of Fez al-Bali. Today, the neighborhood on the southeastern outskirts of the mellah, where these migrants first settled, preserves a memory of environmental crisis, for residents call it *Nawa'il*, for the huts usually found in the countryside.

Tempers could run high among this diverse population, especially during a severe drought that wrought food shortages and threatened famine. Two Muslim peasants learned this on 17 January 1880 as did one Jewish resident of Fez's mellah. Abdelkader and his wife Fatima were from the neighboring region of Aslad al-Hadj. They had come to Fez's biweekly *extra muro* market to purchase, among other things, dried fruit. Their purchases nearly complete, Abdelkader told his wife to meet him at the Sidi Bou Nafa Gate. According to Fatima, a Tetouani Jew named Mordecai ben Yashua then "assaulted her, and placed his hands within her clothes and commenced to pull her and to drag her from the road."[21] When her husband interceded, Yashua shot him in the head. Claiming a protected status from France for military service, Yashua resisted arrest by royal officials.

The incident acted as a catalyst for rising frustrations during the Great Famine, and a riot soon broke out in both Fez al-Jadid and Fez al-Bali. Many Jewish merchants dealt in grain, so it is not surprising that hungry Muslims targeted the mellah. Although rioters threatened the lives and property of all Jewish residents, the incident led to only one casualty. A small group of men—one witness described them as young boys—beat a Jewish resident. Afterward, they covered his body with wood and petrol and set him on fire. The sultan's officials came down hard on the rioters. Eight Muslim shopkeepers in the food market were jailed for instigating the masses and provoking the riot. The locus of the riot as well as the arrests of these purveyors of foodstuffs strongly suggests that popular anxieties about food insecurity acted as the catalyst for the violence.

## A Socioeconomic Definition of Famine

Moroccan survival strategies of the late nineteenth century differed from those of previous centuries, transforming the socioeconomic connotations conveyed by the term *famine*. Famine had once signified an absolute absence of food in the city, a situation that threatened all residents, irrespective of wealth or social status. By the nineteenth century, however, new commercial networks with Europe allowed for the importation of wheat when local crops failed. Some urban residents, a wealthy mercantile minority, began to reap profits from drought, while others, the working majority, needed to submit to high prices for basic foodstuffs. Thus, environmental crises highlighted an increasing gap between the rich and the poor.

Although Moroccans flocked to the cities during the Great Famine, their forebears had fled from them when drought or locusts destroyed crops. In the seventeenth and eighteenth centuries, a failed harvest led to an absolute absence of food in the marketplace. During the famine of 1662, most residents of Fez tried to outrun starvation, abandoning their houses and belongings. In the countryside, they could forage for edible roots.[22] A chronicle from that time reports that some urban residents resorted to cannibalism.[23] When Fez experienced yet another famine in 1724, there was again an urban exodus.

In this premodern era, starvation threatened all urban residents, regardless of their religion, wealth, or political influence. One Jewish survivor of the famine in 1724 recorded that "the heads of the household and the rabbis leave to beg in the countryside."[24] In late 1825, drought and crop failure augured extreme suffering in the city.[25] That winter, as many as two hundred residents of Fez starved to death every day, and victims included members of Fez's most influential Muslim families.[26]

By 1825, however, commercial exchanges with Europe began allowing for the importation of wheat to urban markets during a drought, thereby transforming the socioeconomic consequences of crop failure. Morocco's integration into European networks of exchange began when Moulay Abderrahman signed commercial treaties with Great Britain and Portugal in 1822.[27] The drought that struck three years later acted as the catalyst for engaging in the trade foreseen in these agreements.

Within the first three months of 1826, the sultan purchased—with cash, not credit—25,000,000 kilograms of European wheat in order to supply Morocco's urban markets. The order required transport on twenty-five French boats, more than had docked in Moroccan ports during the previous five years.[28] As the century progressed, Alaouite sultans continued to rely on European suppliers when crops in the kingdom failed. Thus, in 1878, the first year of the Great Famine, 11,118,000 kilograms of cereals entered the southern port of Essaouira.[29] That year, boats loaded with grain also docked in Rabat, Casablanca, and Safi. These European purchases filled the stalls of Moroccan grain markets, assuaging fears of urban shortage. But the price of foreign foodstuffs was high because they required transport by boat and then overland.[30] As a result of European commerce, peasants began to starve to death more often than residents of cities, and, within urban centers, the poor suffered more than the rich.

An elite group of Moroccan merchants quickly took advantage of the opening of commercial exchanges with Europe. As early as 1860, merchants from Fez had settled in Manchester and Lancashire, where they purchased English goods, especially tea and cotton, for export to Morocco. They established headquarters in Europe, but associates, usually members of their family, often set up "branch offices" in the Middle East, particularly Cairo, or West Africa, particularly Senegal's St. Louis. Azouz Benkirane was one of these merchants, transacting business in his native Fez as well as in Lyon, Marseilles, Tangier, Casablanca, and St. Louis.[31] In a like manner, Bireim Soussi moved merchandise between England and St. Louis, where he would eventually retire.[32] Fez's merchants served one of Morocco's most populated cities, and they excelled in exploiting this new commercial opportunity. By 1892, forty Moroccans lived in Manchester, and most were from Fez.[33]

As the fortunes of these merchants grew in the second half of the nineteenth century, the sultan began incorporating the merchants into the makhzan, the term signifying Morocco's royal administration. Until that time, families traditionally serving the sultan, often of sub-Saharan African descent, filled the ranks of the government. In these families, positions usually passed from father to son. Thus, Moulay Hassan's chamberlain Ahmed ben Moussa, later called Ba Ahmed, inherited his post from his father, who had, in his turn, inherited it from another member of his family who had served Moulay Abderrahman. In a like manner, Moulay Hassan's chief of protocol, Mohamed ben Aich, legated his post to his son Driss, who then served Moulay Abdelaziz.[34] The sultan appointed members of the mercantile elite alongside these traditional families of royal servants for two reasons. First, the merchants used political service as a means of furthering their economic interests, so they had a vested interest in remaining loyal to the sultan. Second, they had experience dealing with Europeans, who were beginning to exercise a significant influence in the kingdom.[35]

These long-distance merchants often profited from the failure of the kingdom's crops. When drought struck Morocco in 1850, for example, it killed off the kingdom's herds, rendering local wool very expensive. Fez's merchants then increased the volume of English cotton imported for sale in Morocco.[36] Many Moroccans, however, given the extent of the crisis, stopped purchasing nonessential food items. To foster sales, cotton merchants flooded the market with an inferior imported cloth, which decreased prices by 40 percent. Thus, cotton accounted for 31 percent of Moroccan imports during the Great Famine.[37]

Tea was another foreign commodity that became prevalent during the Great Famine, and increased consumption of tea among workers and the poor created fortunes for some merchants. Tea was a luxury when first imported in the 1840s, but the opening of the Suez Canal in 1869 decreased its cost. Poor Moroccans then started drinking it to stave off hunger. In 1878, the first year of the Great Famine, merchants imported only 168,701 kilograms of tea. Five years later, that figure would increase to 191,001 kilograms. When rains ended the drought in 1884, 275,000 kilograms of tea entered Moroccan ports, confirming its place as the domestic beverage of choice.[38]

These elite merchants participated in the grain trade with Europe when local crops failed. When the sultan purchased wheat in Europe in 1826, he sold it at the ports to Moroccan merchants. Once purchased, they took responsibility for its transport to urban markets, selling it for a profit. Moulay Abderrahman initially intended to monopolize grain purchases in Europe, but as the century progressed, his royal successors allowed private merchants, both European and Moroccan, to import wheat from Europe. The kingdom's local grain merchants, those transporting wheat from the countryside to a given city, did not have the money for large purchases overseas. Thus, long-distance merchants were the only Moroccans able to take advantage of this profitable business venture.[39]

Trade was not the only means by which Fez's elite merchants managed to reap the rewards of crop failure. When drought struck, merchants often acquired the land of starving peasants. Within a sixty-kilometer radius of Fez, peasants worked the land that supplied the city with wheat and livestock. Private property has always been a cherished right protected by Islamic law, but the elite merchants' experiences in their European host countries led them to consider real estate investments in Morocco.[40] In some cases, a merchant acquired a farm if a struggling peasant could not pay back a debt.[41] In other cases, a merchant would buy the farm outright—and often at a cut-rate price. The children of some peasants later reported that families accepted a sack of wheat as payment for one hectare of land during the Great Famine.[42] During that crisis, Fez's merchants acquired most of the land of the northern Lemta tribe. By 1912, absentee landlords controlled, depending on the area, 50 to 95 percent of the hinterland.[43]

The palatial houses constructed by merchants in the late nineteenth and early twentieth centuries reflect the profits of business ventures made during periods of looming famine. When André Chevrillon visited Fez during a drought in 1905, Mohamed al-Moqri was constructing a palatial house even as the price of food skyrocketed. Born into a family of merchants, Si Mohamed was a royal official, though still six years away from his appointment as grand vizier. His grandfather had moved from Tlemcen to Fez in 1805. His uncle Hadj Mekki traded in Egypt, where he would live for most of his life. Si Mohamed's father, Hadj Abdeselam, served Moulay Hassan by overseeing royal expenses in Fez. Si Mohamed, who studied English as a young boy and lived in England for two years, started his career in the makhzan as assistant to his father.[44]

The opulent residence of al-Moqri reflected the family's newfound wealth and political privilege. The house had two courtyards, each the center of a building commissioned by patriarchs of prior generations. It would eventually have fifty rooms and a sculpted garden with a marble fountain.[45] As Chevrillon toured the house in 1905, he saw no signs of food insecurity. The French visitor watched as artisans meticulously decorated the interior walls of the house with blue and gold paint.[46] In paying these workers, al-Moqri underscored that he was immune to the economic downturn caused by crop failure. Many of Si Mohamed's socioeconomic peers constructed similar ostentatious displays of wealth at that time, contributing to a building boom among merchants. Thus, the French consul reported that builders were one of the few groups of workers in Fez who did not fear starvation during the drought of 1905.[47]

The lot of rural migrants offered a stark contrast to this mercantile wealth. As destitute peasants flocked to the city in search of food, the number of urban poor increased. The peasants fleeing environmental crises caused the population of cities to explode, and Morocco, like most semiarid regions of the Arab world, experienced a "high degree of urbanization during a period of economic decline."[48] In many instances, rural refugees went to coastal cities, where they hoped to gain access either to jobs or to the relief supplies delivered on foreign boats. When the Great Famine began, the population of Essaouira doubled in less than a month.[49] Inland cities also experienced significant growth. In the south, so many beggars crowded the narrow streets of Marrakesh that one foreign adviser to the sultan claimed that he could not walk from one neighborhood to another.[50] These rural migrants created a mass of "conjunctural poor," meaning their plight was temporary.[51] Destitute peasants flocked to the city during hard times, but they usually returned to rural areas when they could resume cultivation.

It would not have been easy for rural migrants to integrate into urban society since workers often organized their trades as closed groups. The number of people working in a single industry, such as weaving, indicates the large number of working families in Fez. In 1905, Charles René-LeClerc counted five hundred looms in Fez, each run by a master craftsman who employed at least one worker and one young apprentice. If each worker and his employer headed a household, which averaged six people, then as much as 6 percent of the city's population depended on this industry alone. Even these numbers, however, do not fully account for the people depending on this trade, for weavers used wool spun by women who worked at home.[52] These urban workers subsisted on the precipice of poverty, so they resented rural outsiders who threatened their livelihood.

High food prices invariably caused urban workers to protest. When Moulay Hassan ascended the throne in 1873, for example, Fez's tanners led other workers in a vigorous protest against the infamous *maks*, a gate tax that caused the cost of food to rise. At that time, four tanneries employed about 1,700 men.[53] The workers demanded the abrogation of the maks imposed by Sultan Sidi Mohamed, by which the government collected revenue on goods entering the city. Such products included not only the skins worked by tanners but also cereals and oil, staples in their diet.[54] In this way, tanners lost revenue just as the price of staple foods increased.

Moulay Hassan refused to lift this tax. Angry workers attacked the home of Fez's tax collector, who then sought asylum in the mausoleum of Moulay Idriss.[55] To quell the revolt, the sultan would eventually order his army to lay siege to the city.[56] Since Moulay Hassan had to pay indemnities to Spain after losing the Battle of Tetouan and the Spanish Moroccan War (1859–60), he did not eliminate this tax for another twelve years.[57] Not until the Great Famine did the sultan try to lighten the fiscal burden on his subjects by extending the tax to Europeans.[58]

Thirty-one years after the Tanners' Revolt, shoemakers in Marrakesh led other urban workers in a protest against the high cost of food fostered by the monetary policy of Moulay Abdelaziz. In 1902, the sultan issued a new bronze coin and then minted an excess of the coin.[59] Two years later, workers expressed their dislike of this money and did so just before the January celebration of the holiday 'Id al-Kabir. As recounted by one official, merchants and peasants, or those supplying the city's food, refused to accept this new money. As a result, wheat and barley sold for astronomical prices, while other basic foods, like cooking fat, disappeared altogether from the market.

Shoemakers protested by taking refuge in the mausoleum of a local saint, where they escaped the sultan's jurisdiction. Other residents took to the streets, hurling insults at royal administrators. Some workers pillaged the house of the *muhtasib*, the royal official overseeing urban markets. To prevent further unrest, the sultan's representative in the southern capital, his brother Moulay Abdelhafid, met with the shoemaker Allal ben Ahsan. Afterward, the sultan repealed the new copper money, causing the price of wheat to fall by half.[60] With the royal resolution favoring workers and the poor, calm once again reigned in the city.

The food shortages of this period undoubtedly contributed to political uprisings in the countryside, and rural unrest aggravated food shortages in nearby cities. The most important revolt at this time was the revolt of Abu Himara, especially since it coincided with a drought lasting from 1902 to 1907. This pretender to the throne began his challenge in 1902, and within a year he headed an army of 15,000 horsemen.[61]

Abu Himara's revolt cut off transport routes in Fez's hinterland, thus imperiling the medina's precarious food supply. At that time, Fez received no wheat from the fields surrounding Taza, which, only 120 kilometers away, was Abu Himara's headquarters. Further, any wheat harvested near Meknes, only 60 (very flat) kilometers away, reached its final destination via a circuitous route requiring maritime transport from Rabat to Larache. The wheat avoided capture by hostile tribes, but these security measures had a distinct downside for local consumers.[62] Merchants factored surcharges for transport into wheat's final cost. Drought increased such surcharges since porters, unable to graze mules or camels, had to purchase feed.[63]

In response to Abu Himara's challenge, the sultan stationed troops in Fez, which exercised a negative influence on the lives of urban workers. At first, saddle makers, weavers, potters, and tanners must have welcomed the troops. In 1902, the French vice-consul reported that the military presence had increased demand for their goods, doubling the earnings of some workers.[64] Over the next four years, however, the sultan struggled against both Abu Himara and the effects of a major drought. By 1906, the sultan was no longer able to ensure regular payment of his troops, which decreased the demand for local crafts. And yet, the continued presence of thousands of royal soldiers increased the demand for staple goods, causing the price of food to rise.[65] In this way, the earnings of workers decreased as the price of food increased. A French diplomat reported that "numerous families are reduced to begging." Tanners and shoemakers exhibited an ominous restlessness as they criticized officials for their plight.[66]

Royal Distributions of Wheat and Flour

Drought brought to light a growing gap between rich and poor, offering a provocative contradiction of local wisdom. "When misfortune is widespread," North Africans say, "it is easy to bear."[67] To offset this socioeconomic disequilibrium, the sultan implemented policies designed to provide his poorest subjects with affordable wheat. The sultan was the designated imam of his Moroccan subjects, so he needed to serve the struggling majority. This was especially true since the suffering of urban workers and the poor augured social unrest in Moroccan cities, the kingdom's administrative and commercial centers. By preserving life, this monarch ensured the political stability of his kingdom and also perpetuated his own power.

Hungry Moroccans have always held the sultan responsible for their plight. Consequently, extensive drought in the seventeenth century contributed to the fall of the Saadian dynasty.[68] After a civil war of fifty years, Moulay Rachid (1664–1672) assumed power, with his reign marking the start of the Alaouite dynasty. His successor, Moulay Ismail (1672–1727), consolidated his family's control over Morocco. As recorded by one scholar in the late nineteenth century, an abundant wheat supply secured his success as a ruler, especially since its price increased only once during his reign of fifty-five years.[69] This insight is important because it was recorded one and a half centuries later, when, with the Alaouites still in power, the kingdom again suffered an extended period of environmental crises.

Wheat was an important product in urban markets because flour was a staple in the Moroccan diet both for rich merchants and poor migrants. In Fez, the wealthy purchased their own wheat, ordering it ground from custom millers (*tahaniyyin*) as needed for their household's meals. Working families and the destitute relied on commercial millers (*tarrahiyyin*), who purchased wheat and then retailed flour at shops. The weights used by shopkeepers in Fez permitted the sale of very small amounts of flour, as little as twenty-two grams.[70]

Even a small bit of flour could be used to prepare a simple dish. For breakfast, residents of Fez ate soup of finely ground flour steeped in milk. Poor families substituted a roughly ground flour that they boiled in water. For lunch, the principal meal, wealthy households served couscous, rolled semolina covered by a sauce of meat and vegetables. Most families, however, dipped flat bread in stew, with the ratio of stew to bread reflecting a household's income. In this way, poor Moroccans consumed more flour than the wealthy. There were more urban poor than rich, and a greater percentage of their diet depended on this starch.

Even during the Great Famine, people in Fez did not seek alternatives to wheat, thereby highlighting their expectation of a stable wheat supply in urban markets. In the hinterland, peasants cultivated maize in response to the drought, for it was a quickly maturing crop that compensated for a failed wheat harvest. Fez's officials and millers complained that this agricultural strategy led many peasants to divert water of the Oued Fas away from their city. These complaints highlight the fact that Fez's residents were not dependent on maize, which was intended for rural, not urban, sustenance.[71]

Fez's residents also rejected an innovation proposed by a British adviser who wanted residents to grow potatoes during the Great Famine. Given this tuber's role in alleviating famine in the British Isles, it is not surprising that the adviser tried to encourage Moroccan consumption of potatoes. Guests at his home expressed polite appreciation for this culinary novelty when served as part of their meal, but they refused his offer of seed.[72] The notables who dined with him might not have deigned to substitute wheat in their diet, but, given their shrewd ability to reap profits during famine, some would have cultivated potatoes if they perceived a market for new starches.

These examples of dietary conservatism underscore the extent to which the sultan implemented policies that stabilized the wheat supply. During the Great Famine, the sultan began to collect taxes in kind, not money. Moroccan peasants had been linked to a money economy since the eighteenth century, when Alaouite sultans began collecting taxes at rural markets.[73] For this reason, rural tribes paid annual tithes in money or in agricultural goods such as livestock or wheat. In the early 1880s, Moulay Hassan required all rural tribes to pay their taxes in kind, increasing the collection of wheat and barley. In this way, he replenished the royal silos that allowed him to increase urban distributions of wheat when crops failed. During the drought that plagued Morocco between 1867 and 1868, officials in Fez had distributed no more than 43 metric tons of wheat and barley. Twenty-six years later, when drought once again destroyed Moroccan crops, the sultan's government could distribute 340 metric tons of wheat in this same city.[74]

The royal distribution of wheat reinforced the sultan's political legitimacy. For this reason, the sultan used wheat stocked in the silos of Fez to feed not only indigent locals but also the poor in other cities. When drought destroyed the north's wheat crops in 1897, for example, Moulay Abdelaziz sent some of Fez's wheat to Tlemcen, a city beyond Morocco's official borders. The French had ruled this city since 1830, but many people there remained loyal to the Moroccan monarch.[75] Some of Fez's most influential families originated there. Most of this city's five thousand Algerians, such as the wealthy merchant Si Mohamed Moqri, were originally from Tlemcen.[76] They would undoubtedly have supported the sultan's benevolent gesture. The sultan sent Tlemcen enough wheat to feed 1,800 poor families, hoping, it seems, to retain the allegiance of his own subjects.[77]

Financial obligations to foreign creditors led Moulay Abdelaziz to suppress taxes in kind in 1901 in order to increase money in his treasury.[78] In December, the sultan contracted a loan from a European company.[79] Moulay Abdelaziz's concern for the royal treasury did not supersede his fear of urban instability during a drought that threatened food shortages, though. Providing sustenance to starving indigents quelled social unrest in his administrative and commercial centers. During the drought of 1905, even as fighting with the upstart Abu Himara strained the royal treasury, the sultan purchased wheat in Marseilles. The historian Edmund Burke III suggests that the arrival of this order prevented massive riots in Fez.[80]

The sultan exercised control over the price of flour through the *muhtasib*, the royal official charged with oversight of commerce in a specific city. The muhtasib was technically subordinate to two other urban officials. In the first rank of a city's bureaucratic hierarchy, there was the sultan's *khalifa*, a direct representative of the ruler. In the second rank, there was the *basha*, who managed a city's administration. The superior of the muhtasib, however, did not influence the discharge of his ordinary duties. The muhtasib verified weights and measures in a market, and regulated the quality of goods and set a price for them. In forging links between the market and the state, the sultan intended to allay the everyday concerns of his most disadvantaged subjects. For this reason, the kingdom's commercial laws prohibited the sale of wheat outside a *rahaba*, or designated market for trade of cereals. As explained by one jurist, the muhtasib ensured that the sale of wheat would be public so that "the poor and the old can see it."[81]

The muhtasib set a price for flour based on the going rate for wheat. Commercial laws, however, prevented the muhtasib from establishing the price of wheat, since he could verify neither the cost of production nor the fees of transport for this rural commodity.[82] In Fez, there were four rahabas where merchants sold wheat. If the muhtasib ascertained a change in the price of wheat at these markets, he would announce his intention to establish a new price for flour within three days. This interim allowed commercial millers to sell their existing stock of flour at the price for which they had purchased their wheat, whether higher or lower than the anticipated change.[83]

The muhtasib's lack of jurisdiction over prices in the wheat markets threatened urban food security when crops failed. If drought caused famine to loom, some wealthy Moroccans hoarded wheat. They bought large amounts during the harvest and sold it when wheat's rarity caused its price to rise. During the drought of 1905, Charles René-LeClerc insisted that speculators had caused the cost of cereals in Fez to attain a "more than exaggerated price."[84] His local informants accused the muhtasib Mohamed Tazi and the principal tax collector Omar Tazi of hoarding wheat. Like many royal officials, these brothers belonged to a family of successful merchants transacting business in England. Their brother Abdeselam was minister of finance. René-LeClerc counted their opulent house—along with that of the Moqris—as one of the five most ornate examples of Moroccan architecture in Fez.[85] Neither Moroccan nor French archives readily substantiate the allegation against them. Still, the claim demonstrated the extent to which urban residents held the government responsible for providing affordable wheat and also hinted at underlying class tensions.

Legally, the muhtasib had the authority to force speculators to sell their stock, but it was not easy to gauge this illegal activity. The kingdom's commercial laws permitted Moroccans to stock enough wheat to feed their households for a year.[86] In Fez, a wealthy household included twenty people or more. The heads of such households, as in the case of Tazi or al-Moqri, were often successful merchants engaged in a lucrative long-distance trade. Their homes sheltered not only their own wives and children but also the families of one or more of their sons as well as numerous slaves and other down-on-their-luck relatives, especially unmarried women. Since the average Moroccan consumed 330 grams of flour each day, a wealthy resident might store, as a conservative estimate, 2,555 kilograms of wheat without prosecution.[87] In Fez, rich families living in a courtyard house set aside a room on the mezzanine level for storing staples, while the wealthiest built an annex for the express purpose of storing wheat.[88]

If private individuals hoarded wheat, the sale of royal stocks offered a means of counteracting the resulting inflation. In 1882, for example, the third year of the Great Famine, Fez offered an ideal playing field for speculators intending to reap the rewards of their hidden stocks. In May, two months before the summer harvest, Moulay Hassan wrote to the muhtasib and expressed his concern for wheat's scarcity in Fez.[89] To identify speculators, the muhtasib ordered grain merchants to assemble at the Qarawiyyin Mosque with their entire stock of wheat.[90] The summer harvest did not resolve the crisis since drought again destroyed Moroccan crops.[91] Thus, in October 1882 Moulay Hassan ordered the muhtasib to sell royal wheat damaged by weevils.[92] When the sultan earmarked the revenue from this sale to buy fresh wheat, his act offered more than a means of turning a quick profit. In flooding the market with wheat, the sultan forestalled the inflation caused by an urban shortage. Rich notables would not purchase this wheat, so commercial millers could buy it for a fair price and deluge shops with the cheap flour sought by working families and the destitute. Moulay Hassan issued a similar order in February 1894, after a drought ravaged the kingdom's crops.[93] His successors engaged in similar transactions. In 1906, the French consul in Fez reported that Moulay Abdelaziz sold spoiled wheat "to the misfortunate at a low price in order to appease them."[94]

The sultan's direct communication with confirmed speculators reflected his concern for the political stability of his kingdom. During the fifth year of the Great Famine, Moulay Hassan wrote to Taib ben Hima, who, according to the sultan's informants, had sent his sons and associates to the northwestern region of Abda, where they purchased large amounts of wheat and barley. At this time, the sultan informed ben Hima that "the famine has reached an extreme stage." According to Moulay Hassan, peasants there had fled to coastal Safi in search of anything edible. Ben Hima's wholesale purchase of wheat, which the sultan deemed "illicit," had caused a sharp increase in the price of cereals. Moulay Hassan warned ben Hima to buy no more than needed for his own use, also informing him that his officials would prevent any wholesale purchases in the future. As if a royal order alone could not convince this charlatan, the sultan reminded ben Hima that God threatened to inflict leprosy on those who monopolized food supplies. Citing a verse of the Qur'an, the sultan warned against ill-gained wealth: "The one offering charity after cornering my community's food market for forty days will not find his gesture accepted."[95]

During a drought, the sultan forced the rich to provide for rural migrants, who were not embedded in existing patron-client networks. The sultan created structures of assistance to care for this group until the weather permitted their return to their rural holdings. In 1879, for example, Moulay Hassan ordered the muhtasib of Fez to collect money from the rich as "a consolation for those in straitened circumstances." The sultan intended to use this money for rural migrants, not for impoverished urban residents. He also ordered this market official to contact an administrator of religious endowments who could designate a site for their care.[96]

Throughout the environmental crises of this period, the sultan required that Fez's wealthy residents aid destitute rural migrants. When drought destroyed the wheat harvest in 1905, an official representative from each of Fez's neighborhoods collected money to feed dislocated peasants. Initially, these funds provided sustenance for eight hundred people, but their numbers grew to four thousand as the drought continued. Each day, they received bread, oil, figs, and water. The placement of their assigned lodgings suggests that established residents wanted to keep rural migrants at a distance. At first, administrators provided them with two buildings near the southeastern gate of Bab Ftouh. This undeveloped area had neither potable water nor sewage canals for human waste, so disease spread among the refugees. They were then sent to a site outside Fez's walls and prohibited from entering the medina. Some of the refugees scaled these walls each night, surreptitiously entering Fez. A report by the French consul in Fez reported an increase in theft. When he expressed a fear that violent crimes might follow, he undoubtedly repeated the concerns of his local informants in the city.[97]

Faith and Food Provisioning

Fez's wealthy residents feared urban instability, so they, like the sultan, had a vested interest in helping the poor. In a densely populated city like Fez, however, influential Moroccans, even rich ones, could not help everyone. For this reason, affiliation with specific religious groupings within the city often served as a means of defining urban networks of food supply. By feeding the poor, the rich reaffirmed their own social influence within the highly personal patron-client networks that defined the kingdom's political system.[98]

The most obvious religious division in any Moroccan city was that of Muslim and Jew. Residents of Fez's mellah represented the range of urban society's socioeconomic milieus. Notables included the families of ten different merchants engaged in overseas commerce as well as fourteen rabbis who each led a synagogue. Workers accounted for the largest socioeconomic group just as among Muslim residents. Rabbi Hassarfaty, for example, identified three hundred families depending on fees paid for twisting golden thread for clothing, which, given the small number of wealthy Jews, craftsmen must have sold to the royal family or other wealthy Muslims. Some Jews assisted Muslim workers, combing out, for example, the fibers of wool before it was spun. Other Jewish workers in the mellah included jewelers, saddle makers, and tailors.

The mellah's poor included the old and infirm who had no family to provide for them. Jews established special funds to provide for them. Revenue from community properties paid ten old men to read psalms as a public service every day. A charity also cared for the sick. With seventy people divided into seven groups, this society ensured their care each day of the week.[99]

When crops failed, starving Jews sought assistance from other residents of the mellah. In the past, some Jews who did not receive aid converted to Islam in order to get help. As recorded in a register in Hassarfaty's possession, one thousand Jews in Fez became Muslim during the famine of 1724. As this register also recorded that two thousand Jews died of hunger, it must be assumed that their conversion offered a means of gaining access to food.[100] A century and a half later, religious affiliation continued to offer the best means of ensuring a regular food supply. During the Great Famine, the mellah's residents created a fund for feeding the hungry, each resident contributing according to his financial ability. Moreover, Jewish notables assured the daily collection of bread and flour from individual houses, which was then given to the poor.[101]

The Jewish community did not count on help from Muslims but did rely on the sultan's assistance. Moroccan sultans demonstrated equal consideration for their Muslim and Jewish subjects. In fact, the sultan's exclusive right to sign a contract of protection with notables of the Jewish community highlighted his role as the kingdom's imam. The Jewish community paid an annual tithe in return for royal protection, which reinforced the sultan's political legitimacy.[102] In 1878, when the Great Famine began, Moulay Hassan provided the wheat necessary for the survival of Marrakesh's Jewish community. The sultan offered this wheat in the form of a loan requiring eventual payment, but he forgave the debt ten years later, a benevolent gesture for which the city's rabbis expressed gratitude.[103]

Institutionalized charity by rich Moroccans offered one means of providing for the poor among Muslim residents. *Hubus* was a legal institution by which the rich bequeathed income-generating properties in perpetuity in order to preserve Islamic culture. A benefactor might specify that revenues from his bequest be used to pay a prayer leader in a particular mosque. Or, he might stipulate that income from his property be used to purchase food for poor Muslims. There were many funds of hubus properties in Fez, and this institution played an important role in urban development. When the French inventoried Fez's properties after setting up the protectorate, they found that 80 percent of all commercial and industrial facilities were hubus properties.[104]

A strict interpretation of Islamic law dictates that an independent governing body should manage this religious establishment, but in Morocco, the sultan directly oversaw hubus properties. Moulay Hassan chastised Fez's administrators of hubus for their lethargic collection of rents and appointed an administrator for religious endowments legated to the Qarawiyyin Mosque.[105] Ever wary of bureaucratic inertia, his successor, Moulay Abdelaziz, assigned two outside observers the task of updating one register in order to verify the viability of properties. His appointment emphasizes the economic significance of this legal institution. Rather than religious scholars, he assigned the task to the long-distance merchants Hadj Mohamed Benjelloun and Hadj Abdelaziz Benkirane.[106]

Hadj Abdelghani ben al-Said al-Taib al-Tazi provides an example of an urban notable in Fez who made a hubus bequest to provide care for the poor. Hadj Abdelghani exemplified the elite group of merchants that developed in the nineteenth century. Hadj Abdelghani possessed properties not only in Fez but also in Egypt, where he conducted business. Even after 1882, when British colonization of Egypt closed some eastern markets, it continued to be a major trading outlet for Moroccans, who found in particular buyers for the leather shoes produced by craftsmen in Fez.[107] Hadj Abdelghani must have been one of the more successful merchants in Egypt, for the sultan Sidi Mohamed made him representative of Moroccans there.

By 1855, this wealthy merchant realized that he would never have children, a sorrowful fate because, as the North African proverb goes, "The one who leaves a son does not die."[108] That year, he ensured that future generations would remember him by legating in perpetuity one-third of his property as a charitable endowment, or the maximum legally permitted.

He died twenty-two years later, just as the Great Famine began, and this endowment immediately began generating funds for the poor. According to his nephews, who managed the endowment, his properties provided the poor with 24,000 kilograms of wheat each year.[109]

Hadj Abdelghani designated specific urban groups as recipients of his charity. Half of the income generated by his endowment provided bread for the poor who begged in the areas surrounding the mausoleum of Moulay Idriss.[110] Their numbers included not only the conjunctural poor found during periods of drought but also a permanent group of crippled or blind residents.[111] In this way, Hadj Abdelghani sponsored poor Muslims who could not work and had no family to provide for them.

In contrast, the second half of his bequest indicates the importance of lineage—and not just wealth—in establishing urban status. Hadj Abdelghani earmarked the rest of the revenue for indigent shurafa'. In Fez, eight branches of shurafa' claimed descent from the Prophet's grandsons Hassan or Hussein. In recognition of their privileged position in society, the sultan exempted them from taxes. Nevertheless, the social prestige of shurafa' did not guarantee wealth. For this reason, Fez had two houses set aside to care for poor shurafa', and a member of the royal family managed each of them.[112]

Rich Muslims often designated one branch of shurafa' as recipients of perpetual charity. Thus, administrators of the hubus properties of the mausoleum of Moulay Idriss collected flour, not money, as rent for a mill with two waterwheels located on the Oued Fejjaline. The prayer leader of the Sidi Yʻali Mosque received half of this flour as part of his salary, while impoverished members of the Husseini shurafa' kept the rest.[113] Hadj Abdelghani's support of the shurafa' was a demonstration of his piety that enhanced his social prestige.

Although the ranks of notables consisted of wealthy merchants like Hadj Abdelghani and his beneficiaries the shurafa', these groups did not form a homogeneous class with shared interests. The lineage of shurafa' gave them legitimate claims to power, so the sultan did not often appoint them to official posts.[114] In this way, their opportunities contrasted with the merchants increasingly incorporated into the makhzan. The shurafa' had socioreligious prestige without political power, while merchants had political power without socioreligious prestige. In the nineteenth century, some shurafa' began to marry the daughters of rich merchants. Expressing concern for the fate of spinsters, Moulay Hassan ordered their official historian, who recorded and verified their lineage, to strike from his list any shurafa' who did not take a paternal cousin as a wife.[115] Lineage was passed down through the father, so this policy blocked the consanguine creation of a social group with both wealth and religious prestige.

The shurafa' were not the only urban group in which individual wealth did not necessarily reflect status. Charitable endowments often assisted students, who, although respected for their study of religious sciences, could not always provide for themselves. At the turn of the twentieth century, seven hundred students came to Fez to study at the medina's six madrasas. The revenue generated by some hubus properties fed students who had no family in Fez, with each receiving one loaf of bread per day.[116] Rich Moroccans sometimes designated revenue to help students when legating properties as hubus. Rent from a plot of land in the northern outskirts of the city paid for bread for students at al-Guissa Madrasa at the turn of the twentieth century.[117]

Cults honoring local saints also offered a critical means of self-preservation during periods of famine. In 1899, the scholar Mohamed ben Ja'far al-Kittani published a hagiography of Fez's holy men. The entries in this book suggest that providing food was one important task of local saints. Before his death in 1720, Abou al-Hassan Sidi Ali had miraculously provided a couscous for his followers during a famine.[118] When a French sociologist mapped the Keddan quarter of Fez in 1909, he found that residents continued to maintain the saint's tomb.[119] In some instances, distinct groups of workers honored a specific saint, thereby reinforcing professional ties with religious rites. Eight hundred potters, for example, worked in Fez at the turn of the twentieth century.[120] During a drought, they all prayed for rain at the tomb of Sidi Mimoun el Fekhkhar.[121]

Al-Kittani's hagiography also points to the prestige of workers who supplied the masses with a staple food. Mohamed ben Ja'far described at least three saints who sold flour before receiving a higher calling, and their disciples commemorated their occupation. Followers of Abou Abdallah attached a title of respect to the Arabic term for flour, calling him Sidi Daqiq.[122] In like manner, Abdelmalek Arouifi, who died in 1750, was known simply as Daqiq.[123] One saint continued to sell flour even as his reputation as a religious leader grew. Abou Hamid Sidi al-Arbi had kept a shop even while calling to prayer followers of Sidi Mohamed ben Abdeselam Bennani.[124]

During drought and looming famine, a wealthy merchant might offer exceptional assistance to indigent followers of a specific brotherhood. In contrast to the saint's cult, brotherhoods cultivated disciples beyond a single given city. In 1874, the region surrounding Fez experienced a bad harvest.[125] That year, Hadj al-Barnoussi Benjelloun hosted a feast to help feed hungry residents in the city. Benjelloun used this collective meal as a means of building his own clientage within a defined constituency. He only invited the disciples of the Kittaniyya, a religious brotherhood that had just begun to form in honor of the saint Taieb ben Moulay Mohamed al-Kittani.[126]

The identity of guests at this meal reveals an alliance between two distinct groups of urban notables. On the one hand, the Kittanis represented one branch of shurafa' who, arriving in Fez in the sixteenth century, became renowned for their scholarly works. On the other hand, Benjelloun exemplified the new mercantile elite. In this instance, the merchant's lack of socioreligious authority was particularly acute since his Jewish forebears had converted to Islam around the time that the Kittanis first arrived in Fez. Benjelloun made sure that those receiving his charity recognized his beneficence by hosting this meal at his palatial home, which was located at the end of a cul-de-sac near the Qarawiyyin Mosque. Benjelloun served bread dipped in clarified butter, followed by tea, a beverage that members of his own extended family had helped introduce to Morocco. Abdelkabir ben Hachim al-Kittani was one descendant of the saint Taieb ben Moulay Mohamed who attended the meal. Fifty years later, he would still remember his amazement at Benjelloun's ability to feed so many hungry people.[127]

Benjelloun's charitable act had significant political implications. As each of his guests departed, they kissed the hand of their host, a gesture that demonstrates allegiance and continues today when Moroccans are presented to their ruler. In return, Benjelloun pressed a coin into their palms. Given the gender segregation marking this society, he surely intended for them to purchase food for the women in their families, who would not have come to the meal. Benjelloun's generosity must have reflected favorably on the Moroccan monarch, for the sultan appointed him to oversee the royal treasury.

Such acts of charity increased the independent strength of this nascent brotherhood. Within thirty-five years, the Kittaniyya brotherhood would establish lodges throughout Morocco. In Fez, members included not only the scholarly colleagues of Mohamed ben Abdelkabir al-Kittani, founder of the brotherhood, but also artisans and the poor.[128] During the early twentieth century, Mohamed ben Abdelkabir would fault the sultan for permitting a European takeover of the Moroccan economy. Eventually, this popular leader would ban followers from drinking tea, suggesting a break with some long-distance merchants.[129] Moulay Abdelhafid, for his part, wanting to eliminate centrifugal forces from the political arena, denounced brotherhoods as an aberration of Islam. By 1909, the opposition of the Kittaniyya was so strong that the sultan would execute its leader and close its lodges.[130]

## Conclusion

Moroccan rulers considered the stability of their kingdom's commercial and political centers as their highest priority. When famine loomed, the sultan took great care to ensure a supply of wheat in urban markets. The wealthy mercantile elite could purchase their own supply of this staple, but workers and the poor depended on royal largesse. To provide restless masses with a filling starch, the sultan redistributed some of his subjects' wealth. By assisting hungry Moroccans, the sultan reinforced his political legitimacy, thereby hampering the development of popular movements aimed at the dynasty's overthrow. If the scale of an environmental catastrophe sometimes made it impossible for him to feed all of his starving subjects in the city, it was not for lack of trying. Drought and locusts may have destroyed many of the forty-five harvests preceding the protectorate's establishment, but royal policies in the kingdom ensured that most urban residents had access to the flour considered necessary for their survival.

In Morocco, food provisioning and political stability have long been intertwined, and the government's responses to environmental crises manifest the sultan's sensitivity to the lot of the impoverished majority. In the nineteenth century, the political economy of drought and looming famine revealed a new gap between the rich and the poor. The former consisted of the mercantile elite, who, though having a preponderant economic influence in the kingdom, represented a small urban minority. Moroccan rulers recognized a need to protect workers and the poor from the avarice of their social superiors, so they ensured them a supply of staple foods. Alaouite sultans implemented fiscal and commercial policies that equitably distributed wheat to all urban residents regardless of wealth or status. Although Alaouite rulers may have used their highly centralized power to prevent uprisings that might have threatened their rule, such institutional procedures addressed the needs of the majority.

# 2

# Industrialism and Participatory Politics at the Water Mill

In 1905, Charles René-LeClerc issued a report on the economy of Fez for the Comité du Maroc, a French association lobbying for the colonization of this North African kingdom. He visited Morocco's precolonial capital seven years before the establishment of the French protectorate and his own appointment to its Department of Economic Studies. Envisioned as a guide for foreign entrepreneurs, his report evaluated business opportunities according to contemporary French commercial practices.

For René-LeClerc, the adherence of Moroccans to premodern technology offered one argument for colonization by an industrialized and, thus, superior France. When he visited Fez, drought had impoverished many of the city's residents. Nevertheless, René-LeClerc considered flour production a lucrative business opportunity for insightful financiers. "Some well-equipped industrial mills," he declared, "will advantageously replace the 160 small water mills spread along the banks of the Oued Fas."[1] The adverb in this statement offers an overly optimistic assessment of the productive superiority of modern machines in relation to the traditional hydraulic technology used by the city's millers. In assuming that the French could transplant a Western model of total industrialization to these semiarid regions, he advanced an evaluation of Moroccans as a backward people who had not yet proved capable of modernizing on their own.

Contrary to René-LeClerc's statement, Moroccans had knowledge of steam mills as well as the financial means to establish them. Indeed, René-LeClerc should have known this, for he had ample opportunity to see Morocco's steam mills in action while traveling to Fez through Tangier and Larache. Tangier had six steam mills, including one established by the sultan as early as 1862.[2] And in Larache, he had met a Spaniard operating a steam mill. René-LeClerc counted only a handful of Europeans living with Larache's six thousand Moroccan residents, so this machine served a local clientele. Throughout the late nineteenth century, private entrepreneurs, often Moroccan, set up other steam mills in Casablanca, Oujda, Marrakesh, Essaouira, Rabat, El Ksar, and Tetouan. Such entrepreneurial endeavors, however, did not always succeed. At least two steam mills in Fez had closed down by the time René-LeClerc visited the city.

The simultaneous flourishing of traditional technology and modern machines may seem, at first, a curious paradox. In René-LeClerc's homeland, mills powered by wind or water definitively closed down after 1843, when French engineers invented a hydraulic turbine that quadrupled flour production. Fifty years later, Parisians would designate the rare vestiges of their city's sixty-five wind and water mills as historic monuments.[3] Fez was also the political and financial center of a unified polity, so a Western model of modernity dictates that traditional technology becomes obsolete once machines begin operating in the kingdom. If Moroccans introduced mechanized milling to their country nearly a half century before René-LeClerc's visit, why did water mills continue to produce all of the flour consumed in Fez?

As the ruling sultans between 1873 and 1912, Moulay Hassan, Moulay Abdelaziz, and Moulay Abdelhafid never left an explicit statement of their industrial policy. In like manner, neither Fez's millers nor their clientele manifested overt opposition to mechanization. Nevertheless, the combined activities of the sultan and Moroccan workers perpetuated a continued reliance on the water mill. People of differing socioeconomic status opposed the industrialization of flour production, and their consensus in turn reveals the successful pursuit of shared interests in an absolute monarchy.

Investments in Fez's Water Mills

In Fez, the Oued Fas flowed through Fez's eight principal canals as well as through myriad secondary channels, with the Oued Sebou's tributary thereby creating a strong source of hydraulic energy that could be harnessed to water mills. During the dry summer months, the water's current decreased, but it never disappeared altogether. To compensate for the Oued Fas's seasonal decrease, urban officials used numerous lock gates to shift the medina's water supply. The assurance of an equitable distribution of water meant that some urban quarters lost their use of water for twelve hours a day during the four driest months of the year.[4] Some mills were located on the canals that conveyed human waste and sewage beyond the medina's walls, for their current was just as strong, if not, in the case of the Oued Bou

Kherareb, stronger than the canals transporting clean water.⁵ This shrewd management of water allowed mills powered by hydraulic energy to operate throughout the medina.⁶

Fez's water mills consisted of a horizontal waterwheel housed in a single-story building of approximately thirty square feet. These mills resembled the Norse-type direct-drive mill of Scotland, not the French model, which had a large vertical waterwheel affixed to the building's exterior.⁷ The building's foundation lay beneath the medina's water canals, so millers descended two or three steps when they entered their mills. A wooden flume diverted water from these canals. By constructing flumes at a downward slope, the mill's grinding capacity increased, since water fell onto the twenty-six planks of wood that made the subterranean waterwheel turn. A wooden pole from the waterwheel led up to the grinding stones on the ground level. A small iron bar at both ends of this pole secured the equipment in place. The grinding stones had a diameter of three feet and a thickness of ten inches. A square hopper, attached to the ceiling with cords, funneled wheat through a hole in the top stone. As wheat poured into this hole, the top runner turned, crushing the grains against the stationary bedstone.⁸

The grinding capacity of a given mill depended on the strength of the current and the number of waterwheels in it. If the water current was strong, a mill might have two waterwheels, each turning a separate set of grinding stones. In one instance, a French traveler reported that the current permitted the construction of one mill on top of another one, with each powered by water from a different canal.⁹ In a few cases, the strength of the current allowed a mill to have three waterwheels. The average water mill produced 15 *mudd*s of flour a day, equivalent to 600 kilograms, although some produced as much as 40 mudds (1,600 kilograms). In this way, Fez's 160 water mills annually produced at least 350,000 quintals of flour, which adequately served the needs of the medina's 100,000 residents.¹⁰

Most water mills in Fez were hubus property. The Maristan fund, for example, was one of Fez's four largest endowments of hubus property, and it contained at least thirty-six water mills in the early nineteenth century.¹¹ Bequests by wealthy notables increased the fund's influence over flour production as the century progressed. When Sherif Sidi Mehdi ben Sidi Hassan Alami died in 1884, the final year of the Great Famine, he left no children to inherit his vast properties, and so he bequeathed a third of his possessions to the Maristan. His two wives, his half sister, and his brother's son split the rights to one of his mills, but the Maristan assumed exclusive control of two mills, one in the Bayn al-Madun quarter and the other in the Laayoune quarter. Since the miller al-Said Hadj Balqacem Baraicha notarized the documents allotting the mills to hubus, which permanently removed them from private ownership and development, it seems that practitioners of the milling trade endorsed a system of ownership that allotted mills to hubus funds.[12]

Hubus was a legal institution that fostered a system of property ownership allowing as many as five individuals or institutions to participate in the production of flour at a single water mill. The *asl*, or structure, of the water mill consisted of walls, ceilings, columns, and water canals. The *galsa*, or site, corresponded to the floor and its whitewashing. The *i'qamat al-mal'ab*, or tools, included sieves, brooms, chairs, and a scale and its weights. The *i'qamat min al-zayri ila al-wadi*, or equipment, indicated the mill's apparatus from the flume flowing from a canal to the hopper into which millers poured grain. The only tangible indication of the *miftah*, or use of the mill, was the door and its key. Private individuals usually possessed the tools, equipment, and use of a mill, while the hubus fund's managers collected rent for the site and its structure. In this way, private investors assumed the greater responsibility for the maintenance of these properties and their transfer from one person to another.[13] The administrators of hubus properties benefited from the system because they collected rent without spending the money on the personnel or materials required to maintain the water mill.[14]

Even Fez's most important millers purchased no more than the right to a water mill's use. Hadj Abdesselam ben Sidi Mohamed ben Moussa was an influential miller appointed by the basha to a water committee at the end of the Great Famine. In 1882, he purchased the use and the equipment of a mill on the Oued Zerhoul in the medina's northeastern quarters. In this way, he owned the rights to use sixteen sieves (*gharbil*) as well as a sifter for removing pebbles from wheat (*bousayyar*). He also possessed three straw baskets with which to pour wheat into the hopper (*zayr*). This mill also had a pulley (*berniqa*) for lifting millstones, as well as a flat iron hammer (*manaqish*) and a pointed chisel (*minqar*) for dressing them. It possessed measuring cups for a quarter-mudd, or sixteen liters (ten kilograms), and a half-mudd, or thirty-two liters (twenty kilograms), along with a number of canvas sacks. Flour was weighed, not measured, and this mill came with a scale with weights ('*amudd bi-sarufihi*).

The tools were inalienable from the mill. When ben Moussa sold his rights sixteen months later, he transferred the tools, with the exception of two lost sieves, to the new owner.[15] Ben Moussa did not sell his rights to another miller but rather to a private investor, a member of the shurafa', the city's religious elite, who would then sublet to another miller.

Millers often sublet from a wealthy resident who possessed the right to the miftah of a mill, and this fostered cross-cutting social relations based on shared economic interests. In 1900, the millers Ahmed ben al-Saghir al-Missouri and Mohamed ben Idriss al-Draoui sublet a mill with two waterwheels from Sidi Mohamed ben Sidi Abdelaziz al-Kittani. Other millers with the same surnames had also served the Kittanis, suggesting that al-Draoui and al-Missouri came from interrelated milling families. Mohamed ben Abdeselam al-Draoui, for example, was a custom miller who died in 1890, and he worked with Mohamed ben Abdallah al-Missouri. Together, they ground the flour of the family of Abdelkabir al-Kittani.

Investments made by Mohamed ben Idriss al-Draoui underscore the vitality of this trade even during periods of drought and bad harvest. The year 1883 was the fifth year of the Great Famine, but al-Draoui was able to purchase the portion of a house inherited by his wife.[16] These millers, however, were not inordinately wealthy men. They offset their financial obligations by grinding three mudds of wheat (120 kilograms) each month for their landlord. In signing a contract with him in 1900, they also made sure that it was their landlord, and not they, who purchased two new waterwheels.[17]

Investments by royal officials underscore the cross-cutting socioeconomic relations fostered by water mills and demonstrate the flour industry's growth during periods of environmental crisis. At the start of the Great Famine, the public and private business activities of Fez's basha illustrate this official's anticipation of profits gained from the millers' trade. By February 1878, the absence of winter rains would already have led most Moroccans to foresee an economic decline. Nevertheless, the basha Abdallah ben Ahmed criticized his assistant (also his son) because he had not raised rents on the mills that they controlled in their official capacity. He stated that private investors had already increased their rents, suggesting that they foresaw the millers' continued prosperity despite signs of a poor summer harvest.[18]

The private investments of Fez's basha confirm milling's profitability during environmental catastrophes. The following year, Morocco was fully into the period later known as the Great Famine. So many malnourished individuals crowded Fez's narrow streets that foreign consuls had begun to send their doctors to deal with the resulting epidemic.[19] And yet the basha proposed to his son the purchase of some private properties in Fez, among them being one-third of a mill.[20] In identifying a water mill as a worthy investment for his own private funds, the basha made it clear that the increased poverty in Fez generated by rural drought only enhanced the profits of urban flour production.

Fez's muhtasib also had a public and private interest in the perpetuation of water mills. As a public servant, the salary of this royal official was based in part on a fee collected from each mill in Fez.[21] And since the muhtasib oversaw and controlled the city's commercial transactions, his private investments provided a sure indication of the profitability of the miller's trade. In 1894, the muhtasib, Mohamed Chami, purchased the miftah of a mill from the miller Mohamed ben Ahmed al-Mazglidi al-Shra'i. Drought had followed the swarms of locusts that invaded the region in 1892, and the region had suffered poor harvests for three years.[22] Despite the environmental crisis—or, as argued here, because of it—al-Shra'i made a 25 percent profit on his investment. Chami controlled the mill for two years and then sold the right to its miftah to the miller Allal ben al-Hadj Mohamed Bennani.[23]

The investments of protégés also indicate the profits of flour production, while revealing yet another socioeconomic group investing in the traditional water mill. Protégés were commercial agents who had a formal association with a Western country for which they theoretically rendered services.[24] In working for Europeans, these Moroccans were no longer subject to the kingdom's laws, so they operated beyond the sultan's jurisdiction. Their business contacts gave protégés knowledge of developments in Europe and the United States, while their legal status fostered opportunities for increasing their wealth.

In 1894, the British protégé al-Mekki ben Hadj Madani ben Zakour rented a mill to a miller. The muhtasib, Mohamed Chami, however, accused ben Zakour's tenant of theft. Such a charge meant that ben Zakour's tenant was most likely a custom miller, one who skimmed off the top some of the wheat brought to him by wealthy households. The muhtasib ordered the miller whipped. Ben Zakour made an effort to protect the man. He told the muhtasib that he had no right to punish the miller, who was protected by his own association with a protégé. Ben Zakour publicly insulted the muhtasib, provoking Chami to demonstrate his authority by ordering the miller whipped a second time.[25]

Ben Zakour lost his case but did not stop investing in water mills. In Fez, there were at least two protégés who eschewed investments in modern machines and instead controlled water mills as landlords. When the French established the protectorate in 1912, one Moroccan protégé in Fez sublet three water mills from hubus funds.[26] The American protégé Mohamed ben Mohamed ben al-Arbi Bennis also exploited several parcels of hubus property, including the right to the miftah of a water mill in Ras Djenan quarter.[27]

## Mechanized Responses to Looming Famine

Drought and looming famine led both public and private investors in Morocco to establish mechanized mills powered by charcoal, petroleum, and, by the start of the twentieth century, electricity. It was a sound investment since mills lacked neither wheat nor customers even when a failed harvest led to economic decline. The sultan, after all, made every effort to supply urban markets with wheat, whether imported from Europe or released from royal silos. Further, the poverty caused by a failed harvest only acted to increase the number of people demanding flour, a staple food of the poor. A steam mill quickly ground massive amounts of wheat, which, when provided by the sultan, often arrived in a city all at once, just like destitute rural refugees seeking a filling starch. For the sultan, a mechanized mill provided a means of soothing restless masses; for the savvy businessman, it offered an opportunity to turn a quick profit.

The sultan Sidi Mohamed (1859–1873) established the first mechanized mill in Morocco, and he did so in order to provide flour for the poor in Tangier. In 1862, the sultan imported a steam mill from England, a country then represented by John Drummond-Hay. By that time, the north had experienced drought and mediocre harvests for seven years.[28] Foreign diplomats had collected money to help starving Moroccans as early as 1857, but these funds "only saved those who were able to reach Tangier."[29] Corresponding with Tangier's basha ten years later, Drummond-Hay insisted that the sultan had "intended for this machine to be a kindness for the weak of the city and its immediate hinterland."

Having already served twenty-six years as British consul by the time he wrote that letter to the basha, Drummond-Hay was extremely knowledgeable about Morocco's social and political conditions. He wanted the basha to repair the broken furnace of the steam mill. To convince the royal official to authorize the necessary expenditure, he pointed to its efficacy in alleviating the lot of the poor. In 1867, when he wrote the letter, Morocco was experiencing a drought. "All of the people of the city and its immediate hinterland," Drummond-Hay stated, "have reached the utmost limit of deprivation, especially since the weak do not have a place for grinding food."[30]

Moulay Hassan's establishment of a steam mill in Marrakesh emphasized the role that environmental crises played in the adoption of mechanized mills. In the late nineteenth century, this southern capital had one hundred horse mills and a dozen water mills.[31] A single horse mill could treat 240 kilograms of wheat a day, while a water mill ground as much as 300 kilograms. During the Great Famine, drought prevented some mills from working, for the sultan restricted grinding in Marrakesh as early as 1878. Even Moussa ben Ahmed, the sultan's chamberlain and one of the kingdom's most powerful officials, needed to order his personal supply of flour from Fez.[32]

Four years after the Great Famine began, Moulay Hassan commissioned the construction of a steam mill in Marrakesh.[33] It was formally established to serve his household, the largest client in any of Morocco's four imperial cities. At the turn of the century, 1,200 people were attached to the palace in Marrakesh.[34] In imperial cities, however, the sultan's standing order included not only the finely ground flour preferred by the royal family and their retainers, but also a roughly ground product distributed as charity.[35] In this way, the royal steam mill produced flour that alleviated hunger among the poor.

The hyperurbanization experienced during periodic droughts led some savvy entrepreneurs to predict profits in urban flour production. As Morocco's major port, Casablanca was the headquarters of many European merchants. The city's economic vitality attracted large numbers of rural migrants, leading to sustained urban growth. Between 1860 and 1914, the urban population grew from five thousand to forty thousand.[36]

Casablanca's rapid growth promised to create fortunes for resourceful investors. Two Moroccans began operating mills as a private venture in the late nineteenth century. Royal officials did not specify the establishment of a *makina*, or mechanical mill, when describing these endeavors, but their terminology implied it. In one case, Abderrahman Benjedia rented a property in 1887 with the intention of installing new equipment (*al-atiha*) for a mill.[37] In a second case, a Jewish resident named Tadghi operated a mill (*tahuna*).[38]

By 1902, a mechanized mill in Casablanca was putting horse mills out of business. In this instance, the shady practices of the operators of horse mills propelled mechanization. According to a British traveler, Moroccans preferred to custom grind their wheat at the mechanized mill because its operator did not keep the bran. This byproduct of flour milling had a high market value when drought destroyed pasture necessary for grazing pack animals. As their business fell, traditional millers sent out town criers to announce their intention to "be honest in the future."[39] Private investors established mills, but their success depended on the patronage of Moroccan consumers.

Flour production attracted European investors in other ports. As the population of ports on the Atlantic Ocean nearly doubled between 1885 and 1905, increasing from 170,000 to 230,000 people, there was a proportional rise in the demand for flour.[40] In El Jadida, ninety-two miles southwest of Casablanca, an Italian set up a mill powered by petroleum by 1902, producing four thousand kilograms of flour each day as well as pasta and bread.[41] In southern Essaouira, the French consulate identified two industrial millers (*minotiers*), Antoine Sandillon and his son, among nineteen nationals there in 1906.[42]

The establishment of a steam mill in Oujda leaves no doubt that private entrepreneurs established steam mills in urban centers in order to make money from the influx of peasants desperately seeking flour for their survival. Oujda is a northeastern city bordering Algeria that the French had colonized in 1830. Its residents usually ground wheat at a water mill located in an oasis outside of town.[43] During a drought, however, such as that occurring in 1897, this mill was unable to operate. At that time, Moulay Abdelaziz sent to this city one thousand sacks of flour, not wheat, imported from Marseilles.[44]

Within ten years, a French officer reported on the development of a mill powered by petrol in Oujda. By 1907, a Tlemcen native crossed the Moroccan border. He imported machinery for a mill in Oujda, harnessing an engine to grinding stones. French officers writing for the procolonial journal *Afrique Française* did not often celebrate activities in independent Morocco, but, in this instance, a certain Captain Mougin praised "our Tlemcani," whose enterprise earned him a fortune. "He succeeded beyond all hopes," wrote this French officer, adding that this man "is today one of the commercial notables of Oujda." This mechanized mill explains a decrease in the flour imports during a drought between 1902 and 1907. In 1904, Oujda imported 42,678 kilograms of flour, but it imported less than half that amount the following year.[45]

The longevity of at least one venture indicates the financial success of entrepreneurs who established mechanized mills as crop failure spurred urban growth. In 1878, the first year of the Great Famine, a Belgian merchant named Clarembaux set out to establish a mill in Larache, a port on the Atlantic Ocean. The failure of local crops had caused the city's population to double in a matter of weeks.[46] As the urban population grew, Moulay Hassan agreed to cede royal property to Clarembaux, who, acting as his country's vice-consul, also exercised a non-negligible political influence.[47] Finding it difficult to come to an agreement with a royal official on a site for his mill, Clarembaux delayed construction. By 1886, however, a Spanish miller moved to Larache, and his consulate lent him the start-up funds for the establishment of a steam mill.[48] Despite the existing competition, or, perhaps noting this Spaniard's profits, Clarembaux pushed forward with his initial plan in 1888.[49] His steam mill still operated sixteen years later.[50]

The profusion of steam mills in a single city also provides tangible evidence of the profits of mechanized flour production. Located on the Mediterranean Sea, Tangier attracted rural migrants from the southernmost regions of Morocco as well as merchants and workers from Europe. The royal steam mill established in 1862 might have had difficulty keeping up with the demands of the local population, which doubled over the course of a decade. In 1884, 18,000 people lived in Tangier, but the population reached 36,000 by 1895.[51] The establishment of steam mills testifies to this city's demographic growth. By 1888, three privately run steam mills were operating in Tangier.

That summer, however, an influx of rural migrants sparked increased demand for flour. A severe rainstorm destroyed wheat crops in Tangier's hinterland just before the harvest, and the khalifa reported that his region would be unable to contribute to royal silos.[52] At that time, and despite existing competition, Printemps, a successful French company, not an independent risk taker, considered the construction of a new facility to be a sound investment.[53] Moroccans began competing for the flour market the next year. In 1889, the Jewish merchant David Azulay imported a boiler from a British company with a branch office in Tangier.[54] By 1890, yet another European company established a steam mill, and a local newspaper reported that it produced two thousand kilograms of flour each hour.[55] Consequently, six steam mills operated in Tangier before the turn of the twentieth century.

The sultan did not want all of the kingdom's mills in the hands of foreigners, for his ability to supply flour offered a means of expressing his political legitimacy. Moulay Hassan specified that he would permit Europeans to install mechanized mills only in coastal cities, where the foreign presence was strongest, while mandating that Moroccans establish such facilities in cities of the interior.[56] Moulay Hassan ceded royal property in coastal Larache to the Belgian merchant Clarembaux in 1878. For his steam mill in Marrakesh, however, an imperial city located inland, he not only invested royal money in the project, but he also appointed two Moroccan brothers as foremen of the site.[57] His successors would continue to patrol steam mills, even coastal ones. When a British entrepreneur in Safi established a steam mill in 1909, Moulay Abdelhafid thanked the royal official who informed him of the venture, expressing his intention to oversee the exploitation of property for "important works."[58]

In avoiding direct confrontation with foreign powers when implementing this policy, Moulay Hassan manifested his fear of colonial incursion. In 1886, a British citizen established a steam mill in Rabat. Rabat, though a port, was an imperial city, and therefore a critical component of sultanic structures of power. Royal officials blocked access to the materials needed to construct a building for the mechanized mill. They also prohibited Rabat's Moroccan laborers from working at the site, forcing the owners to import construction workers.[59] Once in operation, the governor banned local bakers from buying flour at it.[60] Rabat was one of several cases in which the sultan blocked the industrial ventures of foreign financiers.[61]

The sultan, however, did not intend to prevent his subjects from making a living; rather, his intention was that they not become dependent on foreigners. Royal policies favored and fostered the development of traditional mills. According to a French officer, there were thirty-four horse mills in Rabat.[62] In 1886, as a direct response to this foreign steam mill, Rabat's basha promised residents that he would build even more.[63]

The sultan, Moulay Abdelaziz, also restricted foreign steam mills by putting pressure on his subjects. Two Englishmen established a steam mill in Fez in 1897, and they did so in partnership with Moroccans Mohamed Ibn Idriss al-Tazi and al-M'feddel al-Qabaj. These local partners were Muslim residents of Fez, but their acquisition of protected status from the American consul allowed them to conduct their affairs beyond the sultan's jurisdiction. The four entrepreneurs rented a property at the periphery of Fez al-Jadid, in land set aside for the Jewish cemetery. After two years of drought, this area had already filled with the huts that later gave the *Nawa'il* quarter its name. For unknown reasons, the owners of the mechanized mill clashed with the Jewish merchant Ibn Yamin ben Samhoun.

According to accounts collected by royal officials, al-Tazi and al-Qabaj lured ben Samhoun to the mill and beat him mercilessly on 3 January 1898. When nearby residents, also Jewish, heard the merchant's screams, they broke down the walls of the mill to save him. The crowd set fire to the grinding machine. One of the foreigners then fired on the crowd, wounding at least one person. When royal officials investigated the incident, they took the side of ben Samhoun, who, unlike al-Tazi and al-Qabaj, was a loyal subject of the sultan. The sultan's officials, however, could not prosecute either the foreigners or the Moroccans with protected status. So they jailed—on trumped-up charges, according to the British vice-consul—three Moroccans working at the steam mill.[64] In this way, incidents with political overtones pushed the sultan to impede the use of some steam mills in his kingdom.

The Milling Lobby

In pursuing professional interests, millers also tried to block the mechanization of the flour industry. In the late nineteenth and early twentieth centuries, Fez's millers acted to maintain a strong current in the medina's canals, thereby preserving the infrastructure needed to operate their mills. They also pressured officials to establish high prices for flour that ensured maximum returns for the practice of their trade. This group of individual practitioners proved able to organize as a group in order to pursue their professional interests and subsequently shape public policy affecting Morocco's technological development.

The production of flour was a skilled trade, and a master miller, or, as Moroccans called him, a *ma'allam*, provided financial security for a large number of workers. A ma'allam usually assumed responsibility for a single mill, and he needed the assistance of at least two journeymen and two apprentices for each waterwheel in it.[65] Mills usually operated day and night, so a ma'allam hired two teams of workers.[66] If only half of Fez's 160 water mills worked twenty-four hours a day, flour production employed a minimum of 960 people, or 2 percent of the medina's male population.

These workers cleaned wheat at a shallow pool next to the mill and then let it dry on the mill's flat roof. A worker then sifted the dry wheat to eliminate pebbles before grinding it.[67] After the wheat's first passage through the grinding stones, the journeymen sifted the ground wheat. Sieves of four different sizes hung on the walls of the mill. The workers extracted the chaff and semolina, setting aside the rest for a second turn through the mill. Sitting on short stools, they placed their elbows on their knees to manipulate the sieve more effectively. Once sifted, flour was put in canvas sacks, and the youngest apprentice delivered it to its final destination on the back of a mule.[68]

A ma'allam knew more than the intricacies of transforming wheat into flour, for operating a water mill required extensive technical skills. Millers worked with heavy millstones on a daily basis, and these stones, though lasting for twenty years, needed regular dressing so as to grind flour at the desired consistency. Each mill had a pulley on site that permitted workers to lift the massive stones, and the ma'allam refreshed the stones' grooves with a pointed chisel. Millers also needed to clean equipment in the subterranean cavity (*sajan*) when garbage or weeds got caught in the waterwheel. A lock gate (*masrah*) permitted the miller to cut off water flow, and he kept leather slippers on site to protect the feet of the man descending into the cold hollow.[69] As recorded by a scholar in the late nineteenth century, milling was such a dangerous trade that the local saint, Sidi Ali ben Abi Ghalib, had passed master millers his secrets for healing wounds.[70]

Millers were an endogamous occupational group. Flour production occurred through millers born to "dynasties of flour families," signifying that several members of a family often practiced the miller's trade through successive generations.[71] At the turn of the twentieth century, for example, al-Arbi Ouali learned the miller's trade at his father's mill in Bzam Barquqa, a neighborhood near the central Rsif market. He married the daughter of another miller in Fez, afterward establishing his own mill in the western quarters of Laayoune. It was there that his eldest son, Abdelwahed, learned the miller's trade.[72] The family ties shared by millers contributed to making them a tightly bound social group.

The veneration of patron saints also fostered social cohesion among millers. Custom millers honored Sidi Hamamoush, while commercial millers venerated Sidi Abdelwahed al-Ghandour al-Saghroushni.[73] Disciples of Sidi Hamamoush had constructed a mausoleum in a cemetery outside of Bab Ftouh, while those of al-Ghandour buried their spiritual leader in the floor of his house when he died in 1761. Both commercial and custom millers held an annual festival honoring their respective patron saint. The *arif* representing the trade collected money from master millers to pay for a ram sacrificed for the festival.[74] Besides meeting on such special occasions, millers also regularly congregated at a saint's tomb in order to discuss the problems of the day.[75]

As demonstrated in Tetouan, millers might call upon local saints to promote their prosperity as entrepreneurs introduced modern grinding machines. When a French traveler visited this northern city in 1906, he found twenty-nine water mills producing flour for Tetouan's residents. At that time, between twenty and thirty thousand people lived there, which, being equivalent to approximately one-fifth of Fez's population, suggests that these water mills had an adequate capacity for serving the city's needs.[76] According to local informants, a Spanish entrepreneur had once established a steam mill in their city, but millers had found him unwelcome competition. To put an end to this modernizing project, the millers made a collective pilgrimage to saints' tombs in the area. Only a few days afterward, the Spanish mill miraculously broke down beyond repair.[77] This tale highlights the use of the cult of saints as a means of pursuing occupational interests.

In Fez, there is no ready evidence of such overt anti-industrial opinion, but millers pursued their collective desire to maintain water mills by ensuring the hydraulic infrastructure necessary to operate them. In this endeavor, the sultan was an undeclared ally of the millers, for, as seen in 1882, he privileged urban water supply over irrigation in the hinterland during a drought. That year, after four years of drought, Fez's muhtasib reported a decrease in the urban water supply, and one that hindered the operation of the city's water mills.[78] The sultan ordered his officials to investigate, and they blamed rich landlords and their sharecroppers, who built dams to siphon off waters from the river through irrigation canals. Moulay Hassan ordered the destruction of these dams in order to return the water to its original course.[79] In this way, Fez's water mills could continue to produce flour at maximum capacity.

The millers of Fez made sure that local officials maintained the sultan's policy. The following rainy season did not improve the lot of rural farmers, whose life and livelihood depended on their crops. As the dry summer months approached, urban notables drew attention to a continued decrease in the urban water supply. Fez's millers insisted on going to the source of the Oued Fas to rectify the problem, just as the sultan had ruled the previous year.[80] Once again, the sultan ordered his officials to destroy illegal dams. And no notable was exempt from this ruling, no matter his wealth, rank, or even bloodline. Accordingly, Moulay Hassan wrote to his brother, whom his officials identified as one of the landlords authorizing the construction of dams. The sultan informed him that any subject caught rebuilding the dams would be subject to a fine as well as a prison sentence.[81] In this way, the sultan appeased urban residents at the expense of rural peasants.

In 1884, urban notables called upon the sultan to rectify yet another decrease in Fez's water supply. This time, royal officials ascertained that the problem originated within the walls of the medina, and not the hinterland. Some urban residents had apparently diverted water from existing canals. To resolve the situation, the sultan ordered the basha, Ahmed ben Abdallah, to form a committee that would restore the distribution of water to its previous levels. Again, the sultan made it clear to a top official that he would privilege none of his subjects. Consequently, the basha ordered his assistant to form a committee that would "tour all places where water flows, even if it is in my house."[82]

The basha insisted that his son appoint millers to this committee, thereby giving members of this trade a privileged position in defining urban water rights. These three milling ma'allams joined an elite group of thirty men, most of whom either formally represented the authority of the state or, by virtue of their wealth and social influence, exemplified urban notables. As for the former group, the committee included two representatives of the sultan, one being from the shurafa', two notaries, two administrators of hubus properties, and one jurist. As for the latter group, their numbers included one student and nine merchants. The assistant basha also appointed two farmers as well as four workers specializing in the maintenance of Fez's canals.[83] Water mills were an important part of urban life and provided some millers with an opportunity to attain social status and to influence public policy.

Hadj Mohamed ben Qasm Baraicha was one of the millers appointed to this committee, and his family represents one of Fez's most successful milling dynasties.[84] The Baraicha family had practiced the miller's trade in Fez since the second half of the eighteenth century, when the brothers Hadj al-Khat and Hadj Abdeselam had moved from Tetouan to Fez. Bouaza Baraicha was a grandson of Hadj Abdeselam who became rich. Though fathering ten sons, he legated a house and agricultural land as hubus property. Qasm Baraicha, the father of Hadj Mohamed, was a grandson of Hadj al-Khat. He had been not only a miller but also a notary legalizing property transfers.

When the basha formed the water committee, the Baraicha family operated mills throughout the medina. Hadj Mohamed ben Qasm Baraicha had a reputation for excellent milling, and the muhtasib chose him and his nephew to produce the palace's flour, a full-time job for both millers.[85] Ahmed ben al-Mekki Baraicha, a great-great-grandson of Hadj Abdeselam, operated a mill in the Cherabliyyin quarter.[86] Hadj Mohamed's son Houmad would continue his father's work, becoming, according to one of his contemporaries, a "rich miller." Adding to their influence, this family maintained contacts with their relatives in Tetouan, where some members of their family worked as royal officials.[87]

The findings of the water committee strongly suggest that the number of Fez's mills increased during the Great Famine, since its members identified three mills built on recently constructed canals. In one instance, three residents had set up the Sidi Amine mill on a brand-new canal, then exploited it as private property. Perhaps fearing to establish a legal precedent, the committee closed the new canal. As a result, the Sidi Amine mill was left with only half its capacity for flour production.

Despite royal orders to return water to its original course, members of the committee did permit two mills on new canals to remain. When the committee found two new flumes leading to the al-Daouia mill, its members did no more than order the lock gates moved downstream in order to prevent them from cutting off their neighbors' water supply. In the second instance, private residents, who also wanted maximum access to water, helped millers. Thus, residents near a mill on a new canal convinced the committee that a notable, both a judge and a member of the shurafa', had ascertained authorization for this hydraulic innovation before his death.

The water committee ultimately strengthened the infrastructure needed for the operation of water mills. It corrected a blockage to the water flowing through the city, repairing a defective dam that lost water to a nearby sewage canal. The committee also provided direct assistance to specific mills. At the al-Jalil mill, the committee ordered the removal of rushes, the presence of which weakened the water's current. The committee privileged the millers' water rights. In past centuries, crop failure had led to urban dearth, and jurists ensured that agriculture took precedence over mills.[88] During the Great Famine, however, the committee ordered the destruction of a canal leading to a new garden, specifying that it took water from a neighboring mill.

The price of flour was a second issue that led millers of Fez to join together in pursuit of their shared occupational interests. A poor harvest in 1893 caused a food shortage in the fall and spring, but rains in December augured a bountiful summer harvest.[89] As new wheat began appearing in Fez's markets, the muhtasib, Mohamed Chami, recorded a 25 percent decrease in the price of wheat, and he adjusted the price of flour accordingly. At that time, Mohamed ben Mohamed ben Hadj Mahdi Bennani was the millers' arif, meaning that he represented the interests of their trade vis-à-vis the state. He convinced the men working in mills and selling flour to ignore the decrease in flour's price.

Bennani's colleagues readily did so, and they told the notaries sent by the muhtasib that they continued to sell flour ground from the more expensive wheat. The notaries discovered the ruse. Chami believed that the millers were artificially inflating the price of flour. Bennani, however, would not accept the changes ordered by the muhtasib. Instead, he hired a public crier to announce the price desired by millers in the name of the muhtasib. Chami was irate, but the sultan's more conciliatory response to this situation demonstrates the millers' influence on royal policies. According to the sultan, Bennani had acted with the knowledge of his khalifa in Fez. The sultan warned Chami to show "respect to men in the largest mills."[90]

Grinding fees were another component in the sale of flour that influenced the millers' profits. The muhtasib established grinding fees every year, and both commercial and custom millers needed to adhere to them. He would set these fees at the end of the summer harvest. At that time, usually August, the muhtasib ordered the grinding of sixty mudds of three different qualities of wheat. This amount of wheat would represent about four days of work for the average mill in Fez. This exercise took place at the Cherqaoui mill, which was a royal property sublet to a miller.[91] It was located upstream, at the fork of two major canals, and the current there allowed four grinding stones to operate within a single building.[92] In the late nineteenth century, Hadj Mohamed Masanou operated it. His skill as a miller was such that the muhtasib appointed him to produce flour for Ba Ahmed, grand vizier and protector of the young Moulay Abdelaziz. Both the muhtasib and the miller's arif presided over the annual exercise at the Cherqaoui mill, from the initial washing of wheat to the final sifting of flour.

These men watched as Masanou measured the amount of flour, semolina, and bran produced by the new wheat. Most wheat passed through the grinding stones at least two times. *Zrif* referred to the very fine flour produced in this process, while *quwayshi* indicated the coarsely ground leftovers. Sixty mudds of wheat produced about the same measure of both zrif, about twenty-six quarts, and quwayshi, about twenty-four quarts, although the latter was heavier and so accounted for more of the wheat.[93]

In Fez, no one consumed the finely ground zrif. Instead, millers mixed two parts zrif with one part quwayshi to create *khalis*, the type of flour sent every month to the sultan's palace. Through grinding and sifting, a miller had some control over the amount of semolina produced by his wheat. Most of the product emitted from the grinding stones was bran, with the partially ground husks making an excellent animal feed—and one with a significant market value during periods of drought. A skilled miller carefully rehumidified his flour, increasing its weight by at least 10 percent.[94] The muhtasib cut in half the established rates for six months out of the year, presumably during the dry summer months when water did not flow as freely.[95]

In their effort to generate maximum returns, millers engaged in a collective demonstration to raise the grinding fees established by the muhtasib in 1897. Drought had ruined that summer's harvest, just as it had the previous year.[96] On 1 September, millers decided to protest the grinding fee established by the muhtasib, Mohamed Chami. They closed their mills and filed into the sanctuary of Moulay Idriss, an ideal site to express opposition to the government since local custom prohibited arrests there. Fez's basha, Benchaqroun, opened negotiations with them, and the millers told him that the grinding fees set by the muhtasib forced them to operate at a loss. Benchaqroun convinced Chami to raise the fee, but the increased rate, despite the good intentions of Chami, did not satisfy the millers.

So the millers filed once again into the sanctuary the very next day. At this point, Benchaqroun "spoke rudely to them," but the millers still refused to work. Shops kept only a three-day supply of flour on hand, so the second day of the work stoppage must have frightened Fez's residents and administrators. Benchaqroun presented this problem to the sultan's khalifa, who proved far less recalcitrant than the muhtasib. He raised the grinding fees as proposed by the millers.[97] Once again, the millers had joined together and successfully exercised a collective influence on royal policy, one that maintained the profitability of operating water mills.

Consumers and Royal Price Controls

The very year that Fez's millers protested the grinding fees, a British national established a steam mill in their city. He rented a water mill from a private resident and set up his modern engine at a site already endowed with millstones. The sultan ordered the Moroccan landlord to break the lease in order to stop his endeavor. The British consul then intervened, preventing what he considered an illegal eviction. This foreigner, however, never attracted enough customers to stay in business. Since the owner of the steam mill was a British national, the muhtasib could not obligate him to adhere to the established price for flour. As this foreign entrepreneur imported grinding equipment and eschewed the free energy provided by the Oued Fas, his flour must have sold for more than his local competition. Within months of the sultan's effort to close down the steam mill, the basha reported that its owner had gone bankrupt.[98] Despite the demonstration of collective solidarity, one that increased the millers' profits, it seems that the price of flour produced at the water mill remained less than that of this mechanized venture.

The failure of this mechanized mill points to the cost of production as a final factor hindering the industrialization of flour production. The production of one hundred kilograms of charcoal required five hundred kilograms of lumber. Morocco's vegetation, however, differed from René-LeClerc's industrialized homeland. France consists of temperate forests, while Morocco is composed of desert, savanna, and temperate grasslands. Given the scarcity of forests, Moroccan rulers had, throughout the nineteenth century, periodically banned the felling of trees and the collection of roots for firewood.[99] Moulay Hassan had prohibited Europeans from exploiting the kingdom's forests for charcoal in 1876 because he wanted to reserve these forests for his subjects, who needed wood for cooking and for heating public baths, as well as for the state, which needed to construct boats and weapons.[100]

Wood became a precious commodity during periods of drought, and its price rose astronomically during the Great Famine.[101] Moulay Hassan needed to create a special budgetary fund for purchasing fuel for his steam mill in Marrakesh, chastising an official who slowed down flour production due to its cost.[102] Yet he ordered this machine used only when extenuating circumstances prevented the water mills from functioning.[103]

The sultan tried to develop alternative sources of fuel, but his efforts had limited success. In Marrakesh, the official overseeing the royal budget purchased not only firewood for Moulay Hassan's steam mill but also olive pits. Using olive pits as fuel became problematic when the olive crop was meager, as in 1879.[104] In Essaouira, the sultan set up a paper factory powered by esparto grass.[105] The sheer volume of grass necessary to heat water in a boiler created an obvious impediment to wide-scale mechanization using this alternative fuel. Some entrepreneurs powered their machines with the bark of the Mediterranean cork oak, a renewable resource regenerating every ten years.[106] As early as 1848, however, the sultan feared the degeneration of cork trees by opportunistic foreigners intent on exporting the bark.[107] Finally, Moulay Hassan made plans—never implemented—to dig a coal mine near Tangier.[108]

Without cheap alternatives to charcoal, mechanized milling inevitably led to higher prices for impoverished Moroccan consumers. In 1872, a British engineer from Gibraltar came to repair the royal steam mill in Tangier that Sidi Mohamed had set up to grind wheat for the masses. Upon his arrival, he also proposed replacing the furnace—then ten years old—with a more efficient model. Afterward, the furnace would burn 30 percent less charcoal than its predecessor, an important consideration for a ruler interested in the management of his kingdom's natural resources. The cost of updating the steam mill, however, proved prohibitive, more than doubling the cost of the engineer's work. Recognizing this facility's importance in the lives of poor people, Drummond-Hay believed that the modernization of the mill's equipment was critical to the long-term well-being of people in Tangier. Still, in writing to the city's basha, the British consul proposed increasing the fee for grinding so that, in conjunction with the reduced use of charcoal, the mill would eventually pay for its own modernization.[109] In receiving this proposal, the sultan's official confronted one conundrum of technological innovation in Morocco. Mechanized milling could serve increasing numbers of urban poor in the cities, but only if they paid more for flour than required by standard processes.

Given the scarcity of Moroccan forests, industrialization threatened to create dependence on costly imports. Moroccans needed to import not only a steam mill's equipment but also the fuel to make it run. Thus, in 1888, two years after an Englishman began operating a steam mill in Rabat, a British newspaper reporting on national commerce in this port boasted that coal "appears for the first time in the list, being an import for the use of the Steam Flour Mill."[110] The sultan had the funds for grinding wheat at his steam mill in Marrakesh, but he realized that his impoverished subjects did not. In 1894, two steam mills operated in Larache. When residents complained of the high cost of milling to their muhtasib, the sultan ordered the restoration of two existing mills that had fallen out of use. Although he did not specify whether water or horses powered these mills, he made clear his intention to fund traditional technology.[111]

Mechanized milling offered a means of helping victims of famine, who needed a lot of wheat ground quickly, but the sultan promoted the use of traditional technology when Morocco experienced favorable harvests. When a second bountiful harvest confirmed the end of the Great Famine in 1886, the sultan reverted to grinding royal wheat at water mills. At that time, many rural migrants in Marrakesh would have returned to their fields, leading to a decreased need for the mass production of flour. The sultan rented out his steam mill. He chose a tenant who, completely dependent on royal patronage, would pose no threat to his jurisdiction. As reported in one local newspaper, the new operator proved to be "the chief of his slaves, a rich and influential man."[112]

The next year, Moulay Hassan ordered the construction of two new water mills in Marrakesh's royal gardens, sending a miller from Fez to oversee the project.[113] The benefits ceded to this miller reflect the import of the project. The sultan paid for the transport of the man's family from Fez to Marrakesh and provided them with wheat and oil for their new home.[114] In total, the sultan constructed six new water mills in Marrakesh.[115] Coinciding with the rental of the steam mill, this hydraulic endeavor suggests Moulay Hassan deliberately replaced modern machines with traditional technology.

The use of water to operate a mill did not deplete the kingdom's natural resources, for steady winter rains usually replenished Morocco's rivers. In 1898, eleven years after his father replaced his steam mill in Marrakesh with water mills, Moulay Abdelaziz ordered the construction of a special water mill to provide flour for the palace in Fez. The construction of this mill coincided with previously described efforts to rid the city of two steam mills. The muhtasib oversaw the mill's construction, noting that its grinding capacity permitted the supply of flour for the royal household as well as for "charity, both old and new."[116] Officials chose to locate the mill in the eastern Douh quarter, which, situated upstream, allowed for the construction of three waterwheels in a single site. If each set of grinding stones milled three hundred kilograms of flour a day, then the mill could deliver nine thousand kilograms of flour each month to the palace, a capacity that would adequately serve the estimated minimum of three thousand members of the sultan's household in that city.[117]

In 1907, one of Fez's wealthiest and most influential merchants decided to establish a mechanized mill, and this project confirms famine's role as a catalyst for the mechanization of the flour industry. In the fifth year of a drought, dislocated peasants were flocking to the city. The concomitant revolt of Abu Himara heightened the need for flour, since it led the sultan to station troops in Fez. Omar Tazi signed a contract with Gabriel Veyre by which they became equal partners in a project to set up a mechanized mill in Fez. They also intended to establish a sawmill, a mechanized olive press, and an icemaker. Veyre assumed responsibility for importing the machinery and technical expertise, while Tazi agreed to provide the labor and land necessary for the facilities. As these partners discussed, but ultimately rejected, putting streetlights in the medina, it must be assumed that they intended to power their mechanized mill with electricity.[118]

The relationship of Tazi and Veyre to Moulay Abdelaziz made them different from other entrepreneurs establishing steam mills in Morocco. Tazi had, perhaps more than any other Moroccan, the means to appraise the worth of business opportunities in his hometown of Fez. He belonged to a family of successful merchants, and his family's political influence gave him insights into economic trends in the kingdom. His brother Abdeselam was minister of finance, and his brother Mohamed was Fez's muhtasib. As for Tazi, his loyalty to the Moroccan monarch was beyond question, for Moulay Abdelaziz appointed him responsible for tax collection in Fez, arguably his most important imperial capital. As for the French photographer Veyre, he too differed from other foreign entrepreneurs. During his extended stay in Morocco, he had become both the confidant of Moulay Abdelaziz and his engineer, setting up an electric generator for the palace.[119]

Since flour production was closely linked to politics, the project ultimately failed to get off the ground. In 1908, Moulay Abdelaziz ceded power to his brother Moulay Abdelhafid. The new sultan did not engage in a retributive political purge, but he did want his predecessor's prominent supporters to leave public life. After Tazi retired, the sultan did not question his private ventures, for he made a considerable fortune through commerce and real estate transactions in the four years preceding French colonization of Morocco.[120] Tazi, however, did not pursue the installation of his mechanized facilities as a private resident, highlighting the sultan's desire to maintain control of modern machines.

When Moulay Abdelhafid commissioned Giuseppe Campini to construct a mechanized mill in 1910, the sultan proclaimed his intention to adapt European modernity to a Moroccan context. Campini was an engineer who had come to Fez in 1902 as an officer in the Italian army. At first, he managed the Makina, the name given to the royal arms factory that Italy had helped to construct between 1888 and 1891.[121] By the time he signed the contract with Moulay Abdelaziz, however, Campini had settled down, bringing his wife and seven children to Fez with two more sons born after their arrival. Rather than linking his fortunes to the opportunistic extraction of Moroccan goods for export, Campini relied on a prosperous local economy. He rented from a hubus fund the rights to an olive grove outside

Bab Ftouh, next to the sanctuary of Sidi Hamamoush.[122] By 1912, when the French set up the protectorate, he controlled urban real estate and agricultural lands.[123]

As a state-sponsored project, Campini's mill highlights the sultan's desire to modify new technology to suit the Moroccan environment. The sultan ceded Campini an existing mill located at the city's largest waterfall.[124] Campini designed a hydraulic turbine to power his mill, thereby harnessing the new facility to a limitless source of energy. Thus, the success of his project depended on the creation of a more efficient water mill that, in straddling a waterfall, worked with a higher volume of water. The establishment of the protectorate hindered the completion of this project, but it would produce 15,000 kilograms of flour a day in 1920, when Campini finally opened the mill. Without setting up an electric generator, which had by then replaced steam and gas as the dominant form of energy for mechanized mills, the forty Moroccans working with the hydraulic turbine produced fifty times more flour than all of Fez's water mills together.[125]

## Conclusion

The drive to colonization skewed Charles René-LeClerc's understanding of modern development in Morocco, for he interpreted the political and religious culture of this North African kingdom as innately flawed. When analyzing the relative absence of modern industry in 1905, René-LeClerc explained to French readers that "the Muslim mentality is resistant to all attempts at progress; further, political despotism and insecurity in Morocco do not allow (native) industrialists to commit to costly expenses in order to transform their equipment and its use." For this reason, he added, Fez's workers, including millers, "continue to work according to traditional methods."[126] In this way, René-LeClerc provided one excuse for establishing European tutelage over Morocco.

Though differing from the more familiar Western model, the restrained industrialization in precolonial Morocco served the purpose of its private and public sponsors. Private entrepreneurs established steam mills to make money, and patterns of investment indicate that they achieved their financial objective. Tangier had six steam mills by 1890, and Clarembaux's steam mill in Larache operated for at least sixteen years. Moroccan sultans established mechanized mills to provide flour for their starving subjects, thereby quelling potential unrest. Despite an abrupt transfer of power from Moulay Abdelaziz to Moulay Abdelhafid in 1908, the perpetuation of the

Alaouite dynasty during this difficult period suggests that the government attained its political goals. As for millers, an influential albeit undercapitalized group of workers, they continued to practice their trade at water mills, which produced flour more cheaply than mechanized facilities. For these reasons, and despite Rene-LeClerc's negative evaluation, Morocco's thwarted industrialism should be evaluated as an unqualified success.

In Morocco, the adoption of machines did not issue from structural changes in the society and economy, as in René-LeClerc's homeland, but rather from a need to address environmental crises. In the late nineteenth century, France experienced sustained urbanization, with a proportional increase in demand for manufactured goods, including flour, fostering the creation of a group of powerful industrial capitalists who aimed to ruin merchant notables dependent on artisan labor.[127] In Morocco, however, urban growth was primarily episodic and cyclical, based on the annual harvests, and merchant notables continued to invest in water mills. Further, the sultan implemented policies that prevented industrialization, and he often did so at the prodding of either millers or the ordinary consumers that they served. In this way, the obstruction of industrial development in precolonial Morocco reveals a participatory aspect of the political life of this absolute monarchy, in which policy emerged through a combination of interests that cut across any one specific socioeconomic group in the kingdom's urban centers.

# 3

# Commerce and Class Tensions at the Butcher Shop

Sultan Moulay Abdelaziz uttered "Bismallah" as he slit the throat of the sacrificial ram on a cold January morning in 1903. His actions did not distinguish him from the butchers of Fez, but the eight thousand onlookers assembled to watch him certainly did. Spectators gathered early for the public celebration of ʿId al-Kabir, when Muslims reenact the offering made by Abraham in place of his son. The Great Sacrifice took place between the first and second of the five requisite daily prayers, so the sun had risen but not yet achieved maximum strength. The crowd included royal officials, urban residents, soldiers, tribal delegations, and Eugène Aubin, the French chargé d'affaires.

A cannon announced the completion of the royal sacrifice, and private residents then repeated the ceremony at home. The head of a household assumed the sultan's role as he sacrificed a ram before his family. During eight days of festivities, Aubin estimated that Fez's residents feasted on the meat of fifty thousand sheep.[1] The plethora of private sacrifices curtailed meat sales, and butchers did not work for more than a week afterward.

Meat consumption and the workaday practices of butchers provide a means of gauging the economic and political situation of a society. In France, Aubin's homeland and the eventual colonizer of Morocco, industrialization led to a rise in the demand for meat as lower classes earned steady wages at factories and then bought more meat.[2] As meat consumption increased, the state began supervising the butcher's trade. Parliament passed a law prohibiting butchers from slaughtering animals behind their shops, and the government collected a nominal tax on meat in order to maintain a municipal slaughterhouse.[3] In France, the modern era brought about the social expansion of meat consumption, and a bureaucratic administration to oversee the work of butchers.

The flourishing of water mills demonstrated that Moroccans rejected full-scale industrialization, and the Great Sacrifice reflects a further complication in the adoption of a Western model of modernity. The Great Sacrifice reflected meat's role as a consumable luxury and an expression of power by the elite. Such authority is linked to religion, for Islamic and Jewish law regulates the sacrifice and slaughter of animals as well as meat consumption for the Muslim majority and Jewish minority. For this reason, butchers of different faiths should have embodied religious divisions. Instead, their efforts to render meat a staple reveals an economic struggle within the sultanic state, with class interests, not religious belief, shaping the political action of Muslim and Jewish workers.

The Great Sacrifice

The celebration of 'Id al-Kabir transformed the workaday practices of butchers into a demonstration of faith, power, and prosperity. Islamic law promotes knowledge of the technical aspects of choosing animals for slaughter. Fez's Muslim residents purchased their sacrificial ram at Suq al-Khamis, a biweekly livestock market held outside Fez's northern walls. Other bought their ram from peasants who set up temporary markets outside the medina's gates two weeks before the holiday.[4] A sacrificial animal needed not only to be free from visible defects, such as a missing eye or a limp, but also in good health, able, for example, to maintain its balance when a prospective buyer shook its horns. Rams needed to be a year old, which residents verified by looking at their teeth. The purchase of a large ram offered a more elaborate display of wealth. The rich purchased several rams, while two or three working households pooled their resources to sacrifice one ram.[5]

The Great Sacrifice also diffused knowledge of the rites for transforming the flesh of a slaughtered animal into that which is *hallal*, or permitted for Muslim consumption. The patriarch of a household placed the ovine offering on its left side with its head facing northeast, toward Mecca. Muslims slit not only the trachea and esophagus, as required by Jewish law, but also the animal's entire throat from ear to ear. They dedicated the sacrifice to God with the words *"bismallah allahu akhbar."* Most Muslims in Fez sacrificed a ram as the Prophet had done.

Finally, the Great Sacrifice provided experience in dressing a slaughtered animal. After the sacrifice, a member of the family detached the skin from the flesh of an animal by blowing into the leg after the hoof was cut off. The skin had to be removed delicately in order to avoid damaging cuts. Many residents dried the skin and kept it as a mat. Others sold it to a tannery, although the glut of the market meant that prices offered after the holiday were relatively low.[6] The liver, lungs, and stomach would immediately be removed and eaten on the first day of the celebration. The flesh was consumed on the second day, when the blood had drained from the suspended carcass.[7] A household parceled out meat, giving between one-third and two-thirds to the poor. The rich had a set of clients to whom they gave meat, so a holiday sacrifice publicized benevolent prosperity while fostering relations of dependence.[8]

The sultan sacrificed publicly in the *musalla*, or "place of prayer." Islamic law requires the prayers of 'Id al-Kabir to be held outdoors because a mosque could not hold a city's entire Muslim community. Fez's royal musalla was on a hill beyond the northern walls of Fez al-Jadid. In praying outdoors, Moroccans paid homage to the Prophet, who had prayed in the desert. Jurists prohibited the construction of any features found on an ordinary building, like a ceiling or a door.[9] Nevertheless, the domed tomb of the saint Sidi ben Qacem embellished the site, accenting its sacred nature. A whitewashed wall marked the front of the musalla. Two feet high, it had a prayer niche pointing the assembly toward Mecca. Once oriented, however, the crowd directly viewed the palace, reminding them of the religious underpinnings of the sultan's temporal authority.[10]

In designating a prayer leader for the ceremony of 'Id al-Kabir, the Alaouite dynasty rendered the al-Fassi family a permanent fixture in the royal musalla.[11] The sermon of 'Id al-Kabir takes place after, not before, requisite prayers, as in the weekly services held in mosques, so this ceremony draws special attention to the prayer leader. During the reign of Sultan Abderrahman (1822–1859), Abdallah al-Fassi presided over the celebration of 'Id al-Kabir. His son Allal took over this role in 1855. Allal led the annual ceremony until his death in 1896. In leading the prayer of 'Id al-Kabir, the al-Fassis lectured on behalf of the sultan to the kingdom's most powerful notables. And, further, the prayer leader sacrificed a second ram in the royal musalla, just after the sultan.

When Aubin observed the sultan's sacrifice in 1903, Abdallah ben Abdeselam ben Allal al-Fassi led the prayers of 'Id al-Kabir in the royal musalla. Abdallah's father died young, so Abdallah assumed the function of prayer leader after his grandfather Allal passed away. Then twenty-two years old, Abdallah taught at the Qarawiyyin Mosque. He also led prayers at the Fez al-Jadid Mosque, where the sultan often attended Friday service. Abdallah played an active role in the royal administration after assuming the position of prayer leader. He administered hubus properties of the Fez al-Jadid Mosque and the Qarawiyyin Mosque. Moulay Abdelaziz appointed him a royal secretary. In 1905, he traveled to Paris with a Moroccan diplomatic mission. By that time, he was one of Fez's magistrates, interpreting the laws to which the sultan's subjects must adhere.

The ceremony for 'Id al-Kabir highlighted the political significance of the sultan's sacrifice. The sultan usually celebrated this holiday in Fez, the kingdom's most important political and economic capital as well as its spiritual center. Key members of the sultan's government, or the makhzan, meticulously organized this ceremony. When the sacrificial rams arrived late in 1904, the grand vizier personally sent two panicked letters to speed up matters.[12] Important Moroccan officials witnessed the sacrifice, so Aubin rubbed shoulders with Driss ben Aich, the royal chamberlain, and al-Mahdi al-Menehbi, the minister of war.[13] Since local custom prohibited non-Muslims from entering mosques, the presence of Europeans in the musalla reinforced the political overtones of the ceremony.[14] One anthropologist refers to the Alaouites' institutionalization of a public sacrifice on behalf of their subjects as "the most powerful ritual support of the Moroccan monarchy."[15]

Given the holiday's political import, royal officials ensured that Moroccan notables acknowledged dynastic succession before the Great Sacrifice. In 1894, Moulay Hassan died seven days before 'Id al-Kabir, while on a military mission to the south. As chief of protocol, Ba Ahmed rushed the late sultan's fourteen-year-old son Moulay Abdelaziz to Rabat. He hid the sultan's death from accompanying troops in order to avoid publicizing a power vacuum before his charge reached an imperial city. He did not go to Marrakesh, the closest center of sultanic power, since Moulay M'hamed, Moulay Hassan's son and his khalifa there, might have claimed the throne.[16] Once in Rabat, Ba Ahmed dictated an oath of loyalty to the new sultan. He sent it to Moroccan notables and officials on 9 Dhu'l-Hijja, the date on the Islamic calendar marking the eve of 'Id al-Kabir.[17]

'Id al-Kabir provided an opportunity for royal contenders to demonstrate power, effectively strengthening their challenge to the sultan's rule. When Aubin attended the sultan's sacrifice, Abu Himara was celebrating 'Id al-Kabir in Taza, headquarters for his rebellion. The historian Edmund Burke states that this pretender to the throne celebrated the 'Id "with great pomp," specifying that he "received tribal delegations in an effort to establish his legitimacy in the eyes of the tribesmen."[18]

In this way, Abu Himara replicated the trappings of royal authority, for, 120 kilometers away in Fez, Moulay Abdelaziz also received delegations representing different subjects from most regions of Morocco. Every year, a ceremony called the *hadiyya* followed the public sacrifice. At this time, urban notables and representatives of rural tribes gathered on the royal parade grounds, where they offered a tangible demonstration of their allegiance to the monarch. Foreign observers recognized the political stakes in attracting a large crowd to this ceremony, and Aubin attributed a moderate attendance to the sultan's failure to defeat Abu Himara in 1903.[19]

Transfers of power were likely to occur during the celebration of 'Id al-Kabir. By the end of 1907, Moulay Abdelhafid's challenge to the rule of his brother Moulay Abdelaziz had begun to gain popular support. In December 1907, peasants joined urban workers in rioting against a tax on staple goods. Collected at the gates of the city, this tax decreased the profits of peasants and increased the workers' cost of living. The unrest led Fez's notables to take a stand in the fratricidal struggle between Moulay Abdelhafid and the reigning sultan. On 4 January 1908, ten days before the celebration of 'Id al-Kabir, Fez's religious authorities declared loyalty to Moulay Abdelhafid. By the end of the week-long celebration of this holiday, authorities in Sefrou, Meknes, and Ouezzane also declared loyalty to Moulay Abdelhafid, effectively ending his brother's reign.[20] Despite the abrupt transfer of power, the new sultan emphasized dynastic continuity, retaining Abdallah ben Abdeselam al-Fassi to lead prayers for 'Id al-Kabir.[21]

Moroccans recognized their role in validating royal authority when the sultan sacrificed on their behalf. Moulay Abderrahman Ibn Zaydan was born in Meknes in 1878, but he spent his formative years studying at Fez's Qarawiyyin Mosque. While later working as the official archivist for the shurafa', he published a history of his hometown that described tensions surrounding the Great Sacrifice in 1727. That year, Moulay Abdelmalek claimed the right to succeed his father, Moulay Ismail, who had ruled Morocco for fifty-seven years. Royal slaves did not approve of Moulay Abdelmalek's management of state money. The term 'slave' here signifies men from families who served the sultan from generation to generation. These officials refused to accept the sultan's public sacrifice on 'Id al-Kabir, and the Beni Hassan and Oudaia tribes joined them. As a result, Moulay Ahmed ascended the throne.[22] Two hundred years later, Moulay Abderrahman's interpretation of these events underscores the fact that Moroccans of his generation considered 'Id al-Kabir as an opportunity to endorse or renounce a ruler.

The presence of foreigners with colonial ambitions created tensions in Fez that sometimes erupted on 'Id al-Kabir. On 7 July 1892, the diplomatic blunderings of a British mission led by Sir Charles Euan Smith caused riots in this city. Smith, then negotiating a commercial treaty, refused to send an official delegation to the sultan's public sacrifice and to the hadiyya ceremony, a slight interpreted by some Moroccans as a challenge to Moulay Hassan's rule over an independent kingdom.

Worse, some members of his diplomatic mission decided to spend the afternoon of this holiday transporting a flagpole to the offices of the British consul in the medina. The basha Bouchta al-Baghdadi prevented the completion of their task by closing the gate to Fez al-Bali. Moroccan onlookers assumed that their attempt to raise the Union Jack augured British colonization, and they pelted the diplomats with stones as they returned to their local abode. When stone-throwing crowds continued to gather outside the British mission's headquarters, the sultan arrested the rioters in order to avoid an international incident. This event forced the sultan to uphold the privileges of foreigners at the expense of his subjects less than twelve hours after sacrificing on their behalf.[23]

Uneasiness with the foreign presence sometimes was revealed in a less violent manner. In December 1909, the Finnish anthropologist Edward Westermarck spent 'Id al-Kabir in Fez. The French army had already taken over coastal Casablanca and Oujda, a city on the Algerian border. Westermarck attended a popular form of street theater organized by bakers. One performance satirized Europeans, portraying an ambassador barking orders at his cowed servants while reading his mail. The actors mocked this character, but the performance revealed popular concerns over foreign encroachment. When the ambassador climbed onto the back of a mule, the animal promptly died.[24]

The fear of colonial conquest took a new form the next year. On the eve of 'Id al-Kabir, a rumor circulated that Moulay Abdelhafid would come to the musalla wearing a European suit, a tacit endorsement of the French influence in his kingdom. A French diplomat reported marginal attendance at the royal sacrifice, placing the blame on rainy weather.[25]

As tradition required practicing Muslims to attend a collective prayer, it seems more likely that some urban residents went to Fez's second musalla. This musalla was located on the opposite side of the city, outside Bab Ftouh. A photograph by Westermarck shows that the musalla of Bab Ftouh did not physically differ from its royal counterpart.[26] It consisted of a field given definition by a low, whitewashed wall with a prayer niche. Nevertheless, where olive groves, a sign of national wealth, surrounded the royal musalla, the tombs of saints and urban notables enclosed this second musalla, closely linking it to urban life. A local prayer leader sacrificed a ram in the sultan's stead. In this way, the residents of Fez "the city" stood apart from the officials of Fez "the capital."

Debates on the role of this second musalla suggest that Moroccans officials had become uncomfortable with popular celebrations of 'Id al-Kabir. During Moulay Abdelaziz's reign, Moulay Ahmed ben Mohamed Ibn al-Khayat al-Zakar al-Housseini addressed concerns that Fez's residents disrespected the sultan by sacrificing their ram "after the prayer leader in Bab Ftouh, [but] before the sultan in the royal *musalla*." Born in 1836, Moulay Ahmed was both a member of the shurafa' and an alumnus of the Qarawiyyin Mosque. He belonged to the Darqawiyya, a numerically important brotherhood that would take up arms against French colonial troops in 1912.[27]

Moulay Ahmed's training and bloodline exhibited the criteria of an influential notable, but he, much to the chagrin of royal officials, exhibited distinctly populist leanings. At one point, Moulay Ahmed took a vow of poverty, wandering through Fez's urban markets in rags and calling out for charity. In a century marked by an increasing gap between the rich and the growing numbers of poor, officials found this a problematic gesture. A magistrate banned him from this practice, but Moulay Ahmed refused to stop. The magistrate threw him in jail, where he would, as put by one biographer, eventually "see reason."[28]

Moulay Ahmed argued that the prayer leader in the musalla of Bab Ftouh had always had the authority to sacrifice on the sultan's behalf. He chastised those who thought that Fez's residents could not sacrifice a ram until the sultan completed his sacrifice in the royal musalla.[29] Moulay Ahmed was not alone in defending the independent authority of private individuals. The scholar Mohamed ben Mohamed ben Abd al-Qadir Bennani defended "the legality of numerous collective prayers for Aid." In this way, he recognized the right of Fez's private residents to sacrifice a ram before the sultan's public sacrifice.[30]

Status and Sites of Slaughter

Although causing meat to be a symbol of high status and piety, the celebration of 'Id al-Kabir did not increase esteem for butchers. Since all Muslim men learned to slaughter a ram and dress its meat, butchers rendered a nonessential service, and not a specialized trade like millers. For this reason, many rural migrants with no training in urban occupations often took up this trade when they arrived in Fez. In 1905, Charles René-LeClerc counted fifty butchers in Fez, identifying most as migrants from the southern region of the Oued Draa.[31]

These migrants passed down the trade from father to son. Said Rabani practiced the butcher's trade when René-LeClerc visited Fez. His dark skin revealed family origins in sub-Saharan Africa. He learned the trade from his father, Gilalli, who had moved to Fez from the Oued Draa in the late nineteenth century. Said in turn would work with his son Mohamed.[32] Ahmed Sefrioui's fictional description of a butcher in Fez suggests that residents stereotyped these migrants as uncultured and fierce. Born ten years after René-LeClerc's visit, Sefrioui later described "Selam, the Negro" as torn "between the desire to hurl [the axe] at the head of a disagreeable client and the need to continue serving the people."[33]

Some butchers did come from Arab families with a history in Fez. Mohamed Tazi "al-Guezzar" was one such man. The designation "al-Guezzar" means "the Butcher," and it was surely used to distinguish him from a merchant of the same name, one with royal connections who would be appointed Fez's assistant basha when the French arrived. Tazi al-Guezzar was born in 1869, and he, like Gilalli Rabani, would teach the trade to his son M'hammed, born in 1891.[34] Tazi's prestige and social connections set him apart from other practitioners of this trade. When a French sociologist mapped some areas of Fez in 1906, his guide pointed out Tazi's house in the neighborhood of Zeqaq al-Roumane.[35] Since Tazi owned a house, he must have been relatively well-off, and he must also have had social influence, since Fez's residents identified this house as a landmark.

Tazi al-Guezzar cultivated business connections with foreign merchants and urban notables in order to supplement his dealings in meat and advance his personal interests. He became a protégé of the Compagnie Marocaine, a financial powerhouse offering loans to the sultan in exchange for contracts to build the kingdom's ports.[36] This French company opened an office in Fez at the turn of the century.[37] Tazi might have earned his status by virtue of his dealings in the livestock market, for this company wanted to exploit Morocco's agricultural lands.[38]

As a second sideline, Tazi became the legal proxy for Lalla Nafissa, Moulay Abdelhafid's aunt. In this capacity, he would watch over her house once the family moved to Rabat in 1912, ensuring the sale of some belongings left behind. He also managed two large agricultural plots that her family owned outside of Meknes, for which he found tenants and sold the harvest.[39] In this way, butchers differed from millers like Hadj Mohamed ben Qasm Baraicha, who rubbed elbows with elite members of the water committee by virtue of his occupational skill. Tazi al-Guezzar did not rely on butchery to raise his status, engaging instead in other supplemental business activities.

Whether of Arab or sub-Saharan African descent, all butchers slaughtered livestock at a *gurna*, a local term for the city's designated site of slaughter.[40] The gurna of Sidi Bou Nafa exemplifies this building type.[41] It was nestled in a small depression in the southeastern corner of Fez al-Jadid.[42] The only feature deliberately constructed on site was a canal, ensuring water supply. Measuring approximately twelve meters by twenty meters, a fortress in the medina's walls bounded this gurna on its eastern side, while a row of houses bordered its northern side.[43] In the late nineteenth century, dirt lined Sidi Bou Nafa's floor, although other sites of slaughter had a whitewashing of lime and sand.[44] The sewage canal carried away blood and intestinal contents, the only parts of an animal not eaten or otherwise used. A photo of a "military slaughterhouse," taken by France's chargé d'affaires in 1902, illustrates the open space that physically defined the gurna.[45]

Fez had four gurnas where butchers prepared meat for public sale. Sidi Bou Nafa was one, and commercial butchers there shared their workspace with the royal butchers serving the palace. The gurna of Bayn al-Madun was located in the center of Fez al-Bali, on the left bank of the Oued Bou Kherareb, which, as the city's major sewage collector, quickly washed away their refuse. The gurna of Bab Mahrouk was outside the city's northern walls, near the city's biweekly livestock market. Jewish butchers prepared meat for public sale at a gurna in the mellah. There, a pious shohet, a person trained in the rites of ritual slaughter, rendered meat licit for Jewish consumption.[46]

The butchers worked as independent artisans. They purchased livestock at Suq al-Khamis on Mondays and Thursdays and kept their sheep in a special pen near the livestock market, bringing it to the gurna as needed.[47] Once the animals entered the gurna, butchers paid a fee to an imam, a practicing Muslim of high standing designated to make the sacrifice.[48] Butchers also paid administrators of hubus properties for the use of their work site, with this fee earmarked for maintaining canals leading to and from the gurna.[49]

The commercial activities of Fez's butchers began at the gurna, where local peddlers purchased the viscera of slaughtered animals. The viscera comprised hooves, spleen, testicles, brains, and intestines. In some instances, the peddlers cooked these scraps and sold them to hungry travelers. At a market, the cry "Smells bad, but delicious!" may have advertised the sale of testicles boiled with chickpeas, just as it does today. Some peddlers sold grilled sheep heads at a market near the Qissariyya.[50] Other peddlers sold the raw viscera to residents, who then prepared meals at their own homes. Moroccans cooked the fatty hooves of cattle or sheep in a sauce of chickpeas. These organs and appendages, however, were not as valuable as the meat. They were sold at temporary stalls on the street, not shops, an indication of the minimal profits for the peddlers.[51]

Butchers sold the meat at shops that they usually rented from hubus funds. As illustrated by an Italian artist visiting Fez in 1875, a butcher shop was a small square room of five square meters.[52] Customers ordered meat while standing in the street. The butcher did not offer specific cuts of meat. Instead, he hung out a dressed carcass and cut meat according to weight. In Fez, the weight used for meat was the *ratal*, the equivalent of half a kilogram.[53] Every customer wanted the best cut of meat. In the drawing, a man at the back, perhaps noting the shrinking carcass, shouts his order, attempting to be served before other customers. "The butcher, low status by definition," notes anthropologist Ianthe Maclagan, "has it in his power to decide the quality of every man's dinner."[54]

Clusters of butcher shops operated in specific urban markets. Many butchers sold meat at the Talaa market near Boujeloud, while others worked at Ain Allou, where Talaa Kabira veered north toward Bab Guissa.[55] Butchers retailed their own meat, so they slaughtered only what could be sold in a morning. Commercial laws required them to transport meat to these markets in a clean container, one that prevented the spilling of blood in the streets or, worse, on the pedestrians walking along them.[56] Fez's butchers wrapped meat in cloth and transported it in a basket on the back of a mule.[57] Morocco's commercial laws also held a butcher responsible for clearing debris caused by the practice of his trade.[58] Butchers operating a shop in Fez's markets paid part of the muhtasib's salary. Every day, butchers gave him either a kilogram of meat or its monetary equivalent.[59]

The muhtasib oversaw the sale of meat in urban markets. He set a price for meat based on the price of livestock, performing the task in consultation with this trade's arif.[60] Just as in the case of wheat, this official did not control prices in the livestock market because he could not verify the cost of raising animals in a village and then transporting them to the medina. In setting a price for meat, commercial laws prevented the muhtasib from doubling the costs entailed in purchasing and slaughtering livestock, which favored butchers, or forcing the sale of meat at cost, which favored consumers.[61]

Butchers did not earn a lot of money. In 1901, the butcher Moulay al-Hadj Alaoui moved from Fez to Casablanca with the intention of starting a new life. It is hard to imagine a butcher better positioned to earn his keep. His title and surname suggest that he was not only shurafa' but also a member of the sultan's extended family. This may account for his writing Morocco's grand vizier, even congratulating him on his recent appointment. Requesting financial support, Alaoui informed this official that he did not have enough money to feed his children during a period of "insufficiency." Referring to the butcher's trade, Alaoui insisted that "the industry is in crisis."[62] A local proverb suggests that most butchers shared Alaoui's lot, earning so little that they could not afford to eat meat. North Africans described a paradoxical situation by noting that "the butcher eats turnips for dinner."[63]

The guidelines set down for the muhtasib by the scholar Abou al-Abbas Ahmed ben Said do not immediately reflect the small returns for the sale of meat, for he advised what may seem extreme leniency in exercising authority over butchers. He counseled this market official to turn a blind eye if a butcher mixed the meat of a lean animal with the meat of a fattened one. In like manner, ben Said also recommended ignoring butchers who mixed some goat with the more valuable sheep's meat.[64] Ben Said even advised tolerating, for a day or two, a butcher who sold meat above set prices, especially if he was saving for a marriage. In this way, the scholar advised the muhtasib to make a significant distinction between meat and flour. If bakers raised the price of bread, ben Said proposed punishing them because their act negatively affected "the masses."[65]

Nevertheless, there was one scheme that ben Said would not tolerate. The muhtasib, he insisted, must not allow a butcher to sell his meat for less than the official prices. If a butcher undercut competitors, ben Said advised the muhtasib to ban him from the marketplace.[66] Since this jurist believed that a decrease in meat prices posed a greater threat to market stability than an artificial increase, the logic informing the commerce of butchers clearly differed from that of millers.

### Everyday Expressions of Wealth and Status

Household budgets and consumption strategies demonstrate why officials treated a decrease in meat prices as an economic threat. Meat consumption offered a means of distinguishing the rich from the poor. In the sixteenth century, Leo Africanus observed that wealthy residents in Fez ate meat twice a day, while the urban majority ate meat no more than twice a week.[67] By the turn of the twentieth century, a local proverb identified meat as a consumable luxury. "If you pass the night without meat," North Africans advised, "you wake up without debt."[68]

When the cost of living rose, Moroccans stopped buying meat. In 1910, the price of sheep's meat doubled just as the price of staples—wheat, clarified butter, oil, and sugar—spiked. As described by one merchant, also a religious scholar who worked as a royal official, all butcher shops in Fez closed down as a result.[69] Clearly, butchers served a smaller and less steady clientele than millers, who provided a dietary staple.

Drought caused urban meat sales to decline. When drought struck, starving peasants sold their dying herds for rock-bottom prices. At first, this might have seemed a boon for consumers of meat. In 1878, Europeans living in Essaouira expressed amazement at livestock's low prices, especially since wheat prices had increased 300 percent.[70] During the next six years, however, half of Morocco's cattle and two-thirds of its sheep and goats died for want of grazing ground.[71] By 1880, livestock sold in Fez must have traveled long distances, for the hinterland could not supply urban markets. One British diplomat found this out as he traveled from Tangier to Fez. Passing through a village near Fez, inhabitants made the following appeal: "Give us some meat! In God's name, we have nothing to eat but grass."[72]

Drought increased the price of staple foods, and urban residents curtailed their consumption of meat, a consumable luxury. In 1878, the first year of the Great Famine, a tax collector in Meknes reported a 63 percent decrease in revenue collected from meat, while taxes collected at the wheat market increased by 170 percent.[73] In Fez, the sultan periodically auctioned off the collection of taxes to the highest bidder. By 1880, however, Moulay Hassan felt compelled to lower by one-third the payment of Sharif Sidi Ahmed Dagga, who had purchased the right to collect taxes from Muslim butchers. It seems that Dagga had not anticipated the length of the drought when he purchased this right, so he did not take into consideration a decline in meat sales. Moulay Hassan found no fault in the arrears, expressing instead a desire to "help him back on his feet."[74]

Meat was not a dietary staple, so the sultan did not provide it to impoverished subjects. Instead, he used the income generated from its sales to assist indigent Moroccans. In Meknes, Moulay Abdelaziz granted a Jewish subject the right to operate a royal property as a butcher shop. According to this man's heir, the sultan exempted him from paying any taxes as long as he set aside some profits to help poor Jews.[75]

The sultan only distributed meat on special occasions, when he wanted to highlight his authority. Moulay Hassan visited Tetouan in 1889 for the first time since ascending the throne sixteen years earlier. He entered this city on Ashura, forty days after 'Id al-Kabir, when Moroccans commemorated the death of the Prophet's grandsons by performing charitable acts. The day after entering this northern city, the sultan toured religious shrines, performing a sacrifice at each stop. A foreign journalist reported the sacrifice of fifty bulls, suggesting that the sultan bequeathed as much as five thousand kilograms of meat to urban residents.[76] The distribution of meat reinforced the sultan's political legitimacy. It demonstrated the sultan's benevolent prosperity and fostered loyalty among the masses. Distribution of meat on a Muslim holiday also emphasized the religious underpinnings of the sultan's temporal rule.

Islamic jurisprudence specifies that practicing Muslims of sound mind can perform a ritual sacrifice not only for the feast of 'Id al-Kabir but also for daily sustenance.[77] Muslims eat the meat of sheep, cattle, goats, fowl, and camels. In this patriarchal society, a private sacrifice was an assertion of masculine power. Some Islamic jurists acknowledged a woman's right to sacrifice, but they termed this practice *makruh*, an undesirable state falling between licit and illicit.[78] North Africans believed that men should sacrifice their own livestock. "If a man cannot slaughter his sheep or discipline his wife," they declared, "then it is better for him to die than to live."[79] To show authority, residents with the means to purchase livestock did not always buy meat from a butcher.

A wealthy household purchased livestock for private slaughter when it prepared a *mashwi*, a sheep roasted on a spit. The head of a household may have sacrificed this animal, but he hired a butcher to prepare it as a meal. It was a long and involved process. First, the butcher cut off its feet and removed its stomach, heart, intestines, and liver. He left the kidneys, which Fassis considered, along with the shoulder, the most delicious part of the barbecued animal. Then, the butcher roasted the dressed carcass over an open flame for five hours. If the flame was too low, the butcher added charcoal; if too high, he threw dirt on it. Turning the animal as it roasted, he coated it in butter, salt, and pepper. The butcher prepared the extracted organs as brochettes and grilled the feet, later serving them on the same platter as the barbecued carcass. Once roasted, the meat fell off the bone at the touch of a finger. A skilled butcher knew which medicinal plants to add in order to prevent the bouts of diarrhea that often incurred after overindulgence in ram's meat.[80] This mashwi did more than demonstrate respect for the large numbers of guests who ate it; it also advertised a host's wealth and status.

*Khali'a* is dried meat conserved in fat and spices, and its annual preparation also led well-off families to slaughter livestock at home. Fez's weather gave rise to the stocking of khali'a. Winter rains prevented the arrival of livestock in Suq al-Khamis. Animals sold between November and February were gaunt, suffering from the seasonal lack of pasture. For this reason, urban residents prepared khali'a in the summer, when livestock was fat. Families prepared khali'a with the meat of camels or cattle. The rich purchased more than one animal, with one Fassi remembering his grandfather buying three camels every summer, each intended for the preparation of khali'a.[81]

Preparing khali'a was labor intensive, so a butcher assisted with this annual endeavor. Camels were too big to pin to the floor, so they required a special sacrifice on the upper chest. The butcher tied a camel's front and hind legs to prevent it from moving. After a ritual sacrifice, the butcher left the carcass in this prone position. Khali'a consists of long strips of meat, so a butcher did not cut through the bones and cartilage. Instead, he peeled the meat from the bone, leaving the skeleton intact.[82] A family hung this meat on the flat rooftop of their house. They placed it high and covered it with oil so that neither cats nor flies could get to it. The hot summer air dried the meat. Afterward, a family stored it in clay pots with coriander, pepper, and the grease from the hump of a camel.[83] Khali'a would last one year without spoiling.

The preparation of khali'a advertised wealth and status. Women greeted the livestock's arrival with ululations and the banging of tambourines, publicly announcing their household's preparation of khali'a. Descendants of established Fassi families draw attention to this delicacy's social meaning. Abdelali al-Ouazzani grew up near Bab Guissa in the 1940s, and he records that meat drying on a terrace "gave authority to the house."[84] In a fictional and highly nostalgic account of this tradition, he describes the head of one household worrying that his neighbors were covertly taking khali'a from his clay pots.

In this sense, al-Ouazzani captures the popular envy aroused by the possession of khali'a in the precolonial era, especially when the cost of living rose. In 1873, tanners protesting a gate tax pillaged the tax collector's house, taking, along with other transportable valuables, his stock of khali'a.[85] Khali'a also delineated social divisions between notables and the masses, for the sultan annually granted money to destitute shurafa' so they could prepare it.[86]

Residents from a modest background also developed a consumption strategy involving private sacrifice. In Moroccan dialect, the term *luzia* signified that several households had pooled money to purchase a sheep and share its meat, which totaled about twenty kilograms. The people making this collective purchase need not be from the same family, leading a foreign observer to refer to it as a "temporary association."[87]

This collective purchase of a sheep addressed the technological limitations of an era that predated modern refrigeration. Temperatures in Fez often surpassed one hundred degrees Fahrenheit, making spoilage a constant threat. Residents often stored meat overnight by covering it in salt, a technique used by commercial butchers when they underestimated the day's sales and so had leftovers. If the house had a well, a family hung leftover meat above the cool fresh water.[88] If meat began to turn, some Moroccans covered it in onions, lemon, and salt.[89] The absence of storage facilities led urban residents to eschew the consumption of fresh beef since cattle provided too much meat to store readily.

Many households slaughtering collectively called on butchers to divide up the slaughtered sheep. A butcher was more adept at this than the men who had purchased the animal, able, for example, to cut a single hoof into seven equal pieces.[90] There was also less chance of tensions arising over the distribution when an impartial butcher parceled out the meat. The butcher placed the meat into piles, one for each household, and he then collected from each participant a ring, a coin, or some other personal item. The butcher randomly placed these items on the piles of meat. Participants entering the room collected their personal item and the meat beneath it. In this way, the services of the butchers ensured that no individual got "the lion's share."[91]

Service, not sales, defined the practice of the butcher's trade, and the sultan's employment of a cadre of royal butchers underscores this fact. The Palace bought flour, but it did not buy meat. Instead, it provided butchers with money to purchase livestock at Suq al-Khamis, which they then slaughtered.[92]

Food preparation was a critical part of the royal butcher's tasks. Butchers prepared the sultan's breakfast every day, as well as the couscous served to him.[93] If royal butchers had too much work, the Palace contracted commercial butchers to help them. Each year, for example, the Palace slaughtered as many as thirty bulls in order to prepare khaliʻa.[94] Fez's muhtasib hired local butchers to prepare this delicacy.[95] The sultan also employed butchers specializing in the preparation of mashwi. In 1901, six days before the month of Ramadan, when daylight fasting ends with an elaborate feast, the head of the royal army requested the immediate dispatch of a royal butcher because he feared that "people here don't know how to barbecue meat."[96]

Royal butchers accompanied the sultan on military campaigns, but they served ranking officials and not the troops. In the late nineteenth century, the Moroccan army consisted of as many as twenty thousand soldiers.[97] It was logistically impossible to bring supplies for these soldiers when the army traveled. Two hundred camels, after all, could carry enough supplies to feed eight thousand men—but only for one day. Instead, the sultan gave each soldier a daily allowance for purchasing food from the local population. The soldier's daily food budget was comparable to that of the lowest stratum of urban society, which meant the soldier's diet consisted primarily of cereals. Burning thousands of calories as they marched each day, soldiers craved meat. One French doctor accompanying a military campaign to the Souss witnessed soldiers sacrificing cattle that he believed already dead.[98] Malnourished soldiers often deserted, a danger for a sultan trying to consolidate power.[99]

In return for their services, the sultan's butchers gained access to royal favors. At times, the sultan's government helped royal butchers to cover the cost of special events. When one royal butcher decided to marry, Moulay Hassan's chamberlain agreed to use money from the treasury to help pay for the celebration.[100] The sultan's government also cared for royal butchers when they were sick. When nine sick butchers could not accompany the sultan on a military expedition in the south in 1882, this same chamberlain ordered daily provisions for them.[101] As evident in Fez, twenty years later, the sultan could be extremely generous. Moulay Abdelhafid authorized the royal treasury to give the following items to a butcher: 12 1/2 kilograms of flour, 12 1/2 kilograms of couscous, 4 1/2 kilograms of clarified butter, 3 kilograms of oil, 12 chickens, and a ewe.[102] Royal butchers did not reap the monetary rewards of selling a commodity, like their milling counterparts, but the Palace offered other forms of compensation for their services.

## The Commercial Objectives of Butchers

The scheming of one butcher shows that practitioners of this trade preferred earning their keep by selling meat, and not by relying on favors granted for services rendered to the Palace. In 1904, Fez's muhtasib contracted with a local butcher to prepare mashwi for the sultan's household. The butcher then requested a shop, saying he needed it to barbecue for the royal household.[103]

The placement of this shop near Bab Silsila reveals the butcher's ulterior motives. To bring a barbecued carcass to the palace, he would have traveled from the center of Fez al-Bali, through the Talaa and the Boujeloud quarter, and finally into Fez al-Jadid. This route was entirely uphill, making transport through the narrow streets difficult. The shop, however, was located in a major meat market, just a few minutes from the Bayn al-Madun gurna. At the very least, this strategy indicates that the butcher felt a need to supplement income earned for services rendered to the Palace. It also seems highly likely that the butcher used favors provided for these services as a means of claiming prime real estate for the sale of meat. Since the muhtasib identified this butcher as the trade's arif, his commercial objective indicates the orientation of the trade.

To increase profits from meat sales, butchers needed to resolve a dilemma. Meat held a secondary place in most household budgets, so lobbying for increased prices, as millers did for flour, caused their sales to decline. Forty-five butchers in Meknes protested the high price of meat set by the muhtasib in 1887, forcing him to decrease the price from fourteen *ouguiya*s per *ratal* to thirteen and one-half ouguiyas.[104]

Cows and ewes sold more cheaply than their male counterparts, so slaughtering female animals was one way to decrease expenses and so the price of meat. A Moroccan preference for the meat of male livestock partially explains this price differential. The Prophet had sacrificed a ram, leading scholars to propose that it was better to sacrifice male animals than females.[105] Further, Moroccans did not like the taste of the female animal's flesh, which, in their opinion, contained too much fat. Taste, of course, is subjective, and at least one European found the preference for uncastrated ram "bizarre."[106]

The environmental crises of this period increased the number of female animals for sale at the livestock market. Herders sold off cows and ewes after eight years, the age after which they could no longer increase herds or provide milk for home consumption. When drought struck, however, peasants sold all animals, even fecund females. During a drought, butchers could purchase female livestock for the proverbial song.

Wanting to safeguard his kingdom's livestock, the sultan prohibited butchers from purchasing female animals for most of the drought-prone late nineteenth and early twentieth centuries. After the Great Famine, the northern peoples of Beni Mguild presented Moulay Hassan with 665 head of cattle and 9,129 sheep. The sultan wanted to rebuild Moroccan herds, and he ordered the basha of Fez to sell the livestock in that city. The sultan specified, however, that the basha should find buyers who intended to breed livestock, explicitly prohibiting him from "selling female livestock to the butchers."[107]

A Jewish butcher in Marrakesh illegally slaughtered female livestock in 1879. The subsequent disruption of the market proved that consumers purchased meat based on low prices, not high quality, even when Muslims found the most advantageous prices at Jewish butcher shops, for Muslims frequented Jewish butcher shops if they had the most advantageous prices. Judaism is a monotheistic religion, so Islamic law permits Muslims to eat the meat of animals sacrificed according to Talmudic rites. Many Moroccans must have done so, for one jurist felt compelled to remind readers of his treatise on commercial law that Muslims should seek meat from animals sacrificed according to Islamic rites.[108]

In this case, the Jewish butcher counted on the protection of a Muslim magistrate whose sister, probably a seamstress, was a frequent visitor to his home. After speaking with three rabbis, the muhtasib concluded that the butcher's relatives, and not a shohet, had sacrificed a cow butchered that very day in the mellah. If true, the meat would have been impure for both Jewish and Muslim consumption since a trained religious specialist had not performed a ritual sacrifice.

The muhtasib's determination suggests that the commercial activities of this butcher threatened the stability of urban markets. According to the muhtasib, the butcher "did not sell meat according to the fixed prices." He did not specify that the butcher undercut competitors, but, since this charlatan had nothing to gain in artificially inflating the price of inferior meat, this meaning was implicitly conveyed. The Jewish butcher slaughtered a cow, an animal that provides five times more meat than ewes, so he counted on large numbers of customers.

The muhtasib raided the shop of this Jewish butcher and shut him down. The city magistrate, however, then complained that the muhtasib had usurped his authority to implement laws in the mellah. The muhtasib acknowledged that he had overstepped his jurisdiction, but he believed that his actions were necessary to carry out his responsibility to preserve stability in the markets frequented by the Muslim majority. The Jewish butcher's sale of inferior, low-cost meat had stolen the customers of his law-abiding Muslim competitors. The muhtasib otherwise would not have provoked the magistrate by raiding a shop outside of his established jurisdiction.[109] The Jewish butcher sold meat for less than his competitors, ultimately counting on increasing his profits by attracting more customers.

This was not the only instance of Jewish butchers stealing customers from Muslim competitors in Marrakesh. The prohibition on female slaughter remained in place in 1881, but two Jewish butchers sold the meat of cows. Being protégés, they were beyond the jurisdiction of the sultan's officials. The muhtasib reported that they sold the meat of female livestock "without [adhering to] the established price." Consequently, the butchers "undermined buying and selling by their colleagues in the aforementioned trade." The muhtasib expressed concern for law-abiding butchers in Marrakesh, who might try to engage in a similar strategy.[110] Once again, butchers selling inferior meat for a cheap price attracted more customers than their competitors, who slaughtered male livestock.

In responding to the muhtasib, Moulay Hassan revealed his concern for his kingdom's livestock during a drought. He told the muhtasib to meet with the Grand Rabbi, who would order the shohets working with Jewish butchers to stop sacrificing female livestock. The sultan intended to contact representatives of the foreign countries sponsoring the butchers to demand that they order the protégés to adhere to the law.[111]

Muslim butchers in Fez also tried to decrease prices by making a concerted effort to slaughter cows and ewes. In 1879, the sultan expressed concern that butchers there were falsely claiming foreign protection to avoid the ban on female slaughter. Moulay Hassan asked the muhtasib for a list of butchers asserting protected status so that he could verify it with foreign representatives.[112] Since the rich would not eat low-quality meat from a female animal, the butchers wanted to attract customers considering cost before quality.

Most butchers in Fez managed to transcend the ban in 1890. The winter had been unusually cold and dry, causing a high mortality among herds. The spring did not bring relief, for swarms of locusts struck the hinterland in March.[113] Many peasants must have brought cows to Suq al-Khamis, hoping to sell them before they died of starvation. To leave the livestock market with a cow, butchers needed special authorization verifying it was too old to bear young. According to the basha, the official charged with verifying an animal's fertility was accepting money in exchange for proper documentation. The basha did not use the word "bribe," but he made it clear that he found this payment of dubious legality. Most butchers must have been slaughtering female animals, since the basha ordered their arif to stop his colleagues from engaging in this illegal practice.[114] Again, the consistent and concerted effort of butchers to oppose the sultan suggests that they predicted sizable profits in providing meat of an inferior quality to urban consumers.

The butchers' sale of viscera to European entrepreneurs confirms their intentions to expand their clientele. By the late nineteenth century, byproducts had become big business in the West. In Europe, increased meat consumption generated massive amounts of offal, which industrialists processed as other commodities. The albumin of animal blood was used to refine sugar and to set the color of fabrics. The neck, shanks, bones, and entrails of slaughtered animals were boiled into tallow that in turn was used to make candles and soap. Fat was transformed into margarine, a substitute for butter invented in 1870. An animal's bones, horns, and hooves were used to make glue or fertilizer. In some slaughterhouses, as in Chicago, the sale of byproducts brought in more money than the sale of meat.[115]

In Morocco, drought was a catalyst for the development of the trade in offal. With herds dying during the Great Famine, the sultan permitted Europeans to export bones. Unlike other exports, the trade in bones increased during the Great Famine, and two million kilograms of bones passed through the port of Casablanca in 1878.[116] As the sultan built up herds after a famine, he stopped authorizing the export of bones. The logic informing his decision to authorize (or not) this trade was not lost on Europeans. A British newspaper published in Tangier pointed out that "this permission is only availed of to any great extent in years when the crops are poor."[117]

One German merchant came to Fez in 1887 with the express intention of buying intestines from butchers. A German representative complained to the foreign minister that his compatriot's business was in jeopardy. The basha rescinded his predecessor's authorization for this trade.[118] Trade in offal would only have been an attractive venture for the buyer and the sellers if there was a consistent and relatively high consumption of meat. If meat consumption was low or unstable, there would not have been enough livestock slaughtered to guarantee a profit. Thus, the advent of this commercial activity confirms that butchers slaughtered females in order to increase meat sales by expanding their clientele.

## The Guerjouma

Moroccan sultans jeopardized the butchers' efforts to attract more customers by implementing the *guerjouma*, a new tax that increased the price of meat. The guerjouma, signifying "the neck," was collected on each animal slaughtered by commercial butchers. The sultan set fees based on the amount of meat an animal provided. Thus, butchers paid more for the slaughter of camels than for cattle or any class of ovine. The sultan placed this fiscal burden on butchers, declaring that he would not collect fees for the feet, spleen, testicles, brains, intestines, and horns sold to peddlers or foreign merchants.[119] By the turn of the twentieth century, the guerjouma was collected in Casablanca, Essaouira, Tangier, Larache, and Fez.

The sultan intended for this tax revenue to serve what he explicitly termed "public interest" by ensuring the regular cleaning of a city's streets. In 1879, Moulay Hassan explained to an official in Essaouira that removing garbage from city streets eliminated the bad odors that caused disease.[120] The germ theory of disease was not yet accepted in either Europe or Morocco, so his statement represented standard medical theory. By specifying the guerjouma's purpose, the sultan distinguished it from other tax revenue that he controlled as he saw fit.

When Moulay Hassan instituted the guerjouma in Essaouira during the Great Famine, he addressed the epidemics of typhoid, cholera, and smallpox fostered by drought. Malnourished peasants migrated to the city, where they proved susceptible to disease. Essaouira's population doubled in a matter of weeks after the failed summer harvest of 1878. At least five thousand people in this city succumbed to cholera between July and January.[121] Observers agreed that the epidemics took the highest toll on the malnourished poor. Thus, the guerjouma did more than fund a public service enjoyed by all residents. It also acted as a program of social assistance by which the sultan redistributed income from privileged Moroccans, those who could afford meat, to his poorest subjects, who, living in the streets that needed cleaning, were wracked by disease.

The scheming of Idriss al-Harishi suggests that butchers in Essaouira did not want to incur extra costs. A Muslim, al-Harishi had been given the status of protégé for services rendered to the Spanish embassy. Spain did not accord him a salary, so al-Harishi, a recent migrant to the city, needed to earn money. Since he had no training in a trade, he became a butcher. To maximize profits, al-Harishi took advantage of his protected status by slaughtering female livestock despite the sultan's prohibition. To avoid paying an imam, he also sacrificed the animals himself. The basha complained that al-Harishi refused to sell meat according to the official price. As done in Marrakesh or Fez, he must have undercut competitors, for it made no sense to sell inferior meat for an inflated price. Al-Harishi not only used his protected status to avoid taxes at the gurna, he also passed his exemption to other butchers, pretending that their animals were his own.[122]

Butchers in Essaouira had a very shrewd understanding of costs and benefits in relation to their tax obligation, for al-Harishi was not the only protégé avoiding the guerjouma. When Moulay Hassan first implemented this tax, other protégés paid it. One week later, however, a royal official raised the tax by nearly a third, from twenty-nine ouguiyas to forty ouguiyas. It was only at this moment that the protégés refused to pay the guerjouma.[123] For this reason, the refusal to pay the higher tax suggests a fear that this financial burden, once factored into the final cost of meat, would decrease sales.

The strategizing of a protégé in Meknes confirms the notion that taxes collected at the gurna caused a decrease in meat sales. Samuel Akoulid was a Jewish butcher. His status as a protégé of Italy meant that Akoulid paid fewer taxes than his colleagues. When approached by notables in the mellah who collected a tax for the coffers of the Jewish community, he agreed to assume the same fiscal burden as other butchers. Once he began paying these taxes, the butcher claimed that he "suffered damage." As he would have known the financial burden when acquiescing to the request, it can only be assumed that he had not anticipated a drop in the sale of meat once he factored the taxes into the price of meat. An Italian diplomat wrote to the foreign minister on Akoulid's behalf, suggesting that parity between Akoulid and his colleagues might be best achieved if the Moroccan government decreased the butchers' tax burden.[124]

Because of a drought-induced influx of malnourished migrants, the sultan also collected the guerjouma in Fez. By the fall of 1878, thirty people a day were dying of cholera in Fez.[125] Foreign diplomats in Tangier sent a doctor to this city, and Moulay Hassan's chamberlain ordered the basha to facilitate public access to his services.[126] The sultan paid the doctor's salary, thereby showing his concern for public health as well as his faith in Western medical practices.[127]

By 1882, Fez's muhtasib expressed concern for the increasing amount of garbage in the streets. The city had several canals designated as *al-ma' al-mudaf*, or water to which residents added refuse and waste. Residents also counted on winter rains for an annual drenching that refreshed the entire city. By the time the muhtasib wrote to Moulay Hassan, however, the drought had lasted four years. In damming the Oued Fas, peasants had decreased the city's water supply. As a result of this decrease, the muhtasib explained to the sultan that there was "a lot of garbage, which will bring a bad odor and cause an epidemic among the people." Water's relative scarcity raised the cost of street cleaning. Moulay Hassan hoped that the razing of rural dams combined with a favorable rainy season would eliminate the need to pay extra for street cleaning.[128] Apparently it did not, for within four years, butchers in Fez also paid a tax earmarked for street cleaning.[129]

The sultan's refurbishment of the Sidi Bou Nafa gurna facilitated the collection of this tax. In 1888, Moulay Hassan ordered the physical separation of royal butchers, who did not pay taxes, from those serving the "rest of the people." He ordered a separate entrance for his butchers, constructed inside the city walls. In compliance, his officials purchased a room in a house controlled as a charitable endowment by the neighboring mausoleum of Sidi Bou Nafa. The room was ten feet above the gurna's floor, so builders created a ramp from the new entry. Commercial butchers continued to enter the gurna through a door in the southern walls. The sultan ordered a clay wall constructed in the middle of the gurna, with its height equal to that of a man. The sultan modified the canals serving this gurna so that both royal butchers and those serving the public had access to water.[130] In this way, Moulay Hassan prevented commercial butchers from passing their animals off as nontaxable royal livestock.

When builders completed this work in May 1889, butchers refused to work there for four days, insisting that the construction was defective. As Fez's muhtasib, Mohamed Chami called upon two representatives of these butchers, asking them to convince their colleagues to work at the refurbished gurna.

The butchers agreed to his request, but their first day of work justified their complaints. The builders had provided the royal gurna with a rod for hanging carcasses, but they failed to provide it with a solid foundation. When butchers hung the thirty sheep required for royal consumption, the entire structure crashed to the ground, wounding several workers. Since the butchers could not serve the sultan meat covered in blood and intestinal contents, another thirty sheep were then slaughtered. Without this rod, the butchers spent the better part of a day dressing the meat, hanging the carcasses one by one from a wooden joist in the wall. They nearly needed to repeat the slaughter a third time because the builders had measured the width of the door according to the size of livestock, rather than that of mules with loaded sidesaddles. The baskets filled with dressed meat nearly tumbled to the ground as the pack animals squeezed through the gurna's new entry.

After describing the day's events to the sultan, the muhtasib suggested building improvements. Since Chami was from a family of merchants and scholars, and not butchers, his comments reflected the standards of the men working at the gurna. The butchers wanted the sultan to provide two strong rods at the gurna, one for skinning animals and one for suspending carcasses. They also recommended the building of a wooden structure on the site to dress the meat beyond the sun's rays. Further, they wanted the entire gurna paved with wide and flat rocks to prevent dust from soiling the meat.[131] By making suggestions that would increase efficiency and improve hygiene, the butchers pushed the state to assume more responsibility for maintaining their work site.

Butchers in Fez were not the only ones advocating for an improved work site. A diplomat in Tangier proposed constructing two new sites of slaughter for Muslim and Jewish butchers there. Writing to Morocco's foreign minister, he proposed building larger sites for slaughter outside the city's walls. Jewish merchants agreed to provide the capital for the project if they could collect a fee on each head of cattle slaughtered in order to recoup their outlay. More importantly, Jewish butchers had agreed to the fiscal conditions of the new gurna.[132] Moroccan butchers would only have agreed to such a fee if they perceived that a larger facility would permit increased meat consumption.

## Conclusion

Issues of class were inextricably linked to meat consumption. As represented by the sultan's public sacrifice on 'Id al-Kabir, meat symbolized status and wealth. Urban notables regularly consumed meat, often sacrificing an animal at home, but working families and the poor did not eat a lot of meat. To earn money, butchers wanted to lower the price of the commodity that they sold, thereby enlarging their base clientele.

Their economic scheming, however, obstructed the sultan's efforts to care not only for his kingdom's livestock but also for his poorest subjects.

To safeguard herds of sheep and cattle, he prohibited the slaughter of female animals, compelling butchers to sell the meat of the more expensive male animals. To assist the urban poor, the sultan created a tax on slaughter that further increased the price of meat. Moroccan butchers—both Muslims and Jews—constantly tried to escape royal regulations in order to keep prices low and profits high.

There was an unstated but significant struggle over social and economic policy transpiring in the interactions of butchers and the state. Butchers acted as unintentional advocates for expanding access to a commodity heretofore limited to the richest and most influential residents of Fez. The sultan, however, implemented policies expressly designed to retain meat's role as a consumable luxury, in order to ensure the well-being of his poorest subjects. Given that Muslim and Jewish butchers engaged in the same strategy and that Muslim consumers bought meat slaughtered according to Talmudic rites, class, not religion, defined public interests in the urban marketplace.

**PART II**

# . . . the More They Stay the Same

# 4

# The Economic and Political Order of Colonial Morocco

Impending colonization provoked anxiety among all Fassis, regardless of income or social rank.[1] Merchants had assumed that the presence of French troops would increase their business dealings, but the colonial army did not award them contracts. And military activities blocked trade routes, which decreased commerce in the hinterland. As for religious scholars, French officers abolished their tax exemptions, which threatened their social privilege and economic standing. Workers and the poor also suffered. The presence of colonial troops increased local demand for food, which aggravated an inflationary trend that had already rendered staples costly. Then, in March 1911, some resistant tribes blockaded Fez, the colonial army's regional headquarters, causing a food shortage that lasted three months.[2]

The sultan formalized a colonial relationship with France on 30 March 1912. Rural tribes expressed discontent with establishment of the French protectorate by blockading Fez. In the medina, looting was rampant. A rumor spread that the French would undertake a house-to-house search for stolen items, which inadvertently disrupted flour production. Anticipating the search, so much loot was thrown into water canals during the night of 13 April that mills could not operate.[3] The French hoped that the colonial order would stabilize the city, but concerns for food security instead reached new heights.

Three days later, a military announcement set fire to this urban tinderbox. French officers in Fez wanted to improve the military diet and, thereby, the efficacy of the army. On 17 April, French officers informed 3,200 Moroccan soldiers that they would establish a mess hall. To cover the cost of their food, an officer explained to his troops, the army would decrease their daily stipend from five francs to two francs. Angry at the cut in pay, the announcement sparked a mutiny. As the first French officer fell, one soldier called out: "We don't want your provisions!"

The soldiers' discontent over the interconnected issues of wages and food supply must have resonated with many urban residents. Within three hours, a riot broke out in Fez's streets, forcing merchants to close their shops. Foreign observers heard the ululations of women on rooftops accompanying rioters in the street.[4] The participation of this sequestered population demonstrated popular alienation from the French, while also implying that the riot did not stem solely from concerns expressed in the male-dominated sphere of formal politics. According to the British vice-consul, some women even stoned a French soldier crossing their flat rooftop.[5] Administrators of the nascent protectorate blamed workers for this urban disorder. One French officer identified butchers, tanners, and day workers as participants in the insurrection.[6]

The riot lasted for two days. Urban masses killed thirteen French civilians and fifty-three soldiers. Popular frustrations, however, focused on Jews. Angry crowds killed forty-two residents of the mellah. The sultan offered his Jewish subjects refuge on the palace grounds, but a mob razed their neighborhood, leaving ten thousand homeless. By the time the French quelled the riot, six hundred Muslim residents had been killed.

The head of the colonial army afterward exacted punitive measures. General Moinier imposed marshal law. He levied reparations of 200,000 francs, a financial burden that fell on merchants even though they had not participated in the riot. A French firing squad executed seventy-two Moroccan soldiers and civilians after a peremptory judgment by a military tribunal.

The newly appointed resident-general of Morocco arrived in Fez the day after this unlawful sentence. Hubert Lyautey abhorred Moinier's repressive rule. He freed imprisoned rioters and canceled reparations. To forestall further opposition to French rule, he gave a salary to Islamic scholars and offered stipends to students who promised to avoid political activities. He met personally with urban notables in order to assuage their fears. He also reopened lodges of the Kittaniyya brotherhood, which, closed by Moulay Abdelaziz in 1909, had once attracted many urban workers. From the first, Lyautey sought conciliation with groups from all ranks of the city's social hierarchy.

Lyautey instituted a policy of association, which signified colonial rule through customary institutions and in partnership with a local elite.[7] Urban notables in Fez mainly consisted of merchants and scholars. Given this system of indirect rule, they would continue to play a key role in the formal institutions of the protectorate's central and local government.

The French counted workers and the poor among rioters, so they also recognized a need to address the concerns of the restive urban majority. As in the precolonial era, ordinary Moroccans were constantly threatened by conditions outside their control. Drought struck Morocco twice during the first eighteen years of French rule. Monetary instability caused rampant inflation between 1919 and 1921. Tribal unrest in the mid-1920s led to the Rif War, which also threatened the workers' cost of living. To forestall economic disaster and political unrest, the French put into action new opportunities for workers and the poor. Ultimately, the protectorate defended the economic interests of the struggling majority against initiatives by the very elite with whom the protectorate had formally forged a political partnership.

The Formal Influence of Fez's Notables

To further the policy of association, Lyautey maintained the institution of the monarchy as well as the Alaouite dynasty. Moulay Abdelhafid, however, proved an unwilling partner in the colonial venture, refusing to sign laws drafted by the French. Lyautey offered the sultan a financial settlement in exchange for his peaceful abdication, appointing his younger brother Moulay Youssef as successor in August 1912. Since Moulay Youssef had been the sultan's khalifa in Fez, Lyautey's choice highlights his desire to reach out to the elite who lived in the kingdom's political and economic center. Religious scholars in Fez would send an oath of loyalty to the new sultan within a week, suggesting that Lyautey succeeded in this task.

The French maintained the precolonial trappings of royal authority. Lyautey moved the capital of Morocco to Rabat, but Moulay Youssef continued to live in Fez for the first three years of his reign.[8] The protectorate retained a chamberlain and a chief of protocol, and families long serving the Alaouites continued to hold a place of honor in the colonial makhzan. The son of Driss ben Aich was chief of protocol, just like his father under Moulay Abdelaziz. The French assumed financial responsibility for the royal family and their retainers; the protectorate's budget included 3,550,000 francs for the upkeep of Moulay Youssef's household.[9] These colonial funds supported at least twelve hundred servants in four imperial cities.[10]

The French appointed Ahmed Djai to head the new Ministry of Religious Endowments, thereby demonstrating the extent to which Fez's notables continued to hold positions of influence. Born in 1839, Djai had trained at the Qarawiyyin Mosque and then at al-Azhar Mosque in Cairo. Djai had intimate knowledge of the urban economy since he had been Fez's muhtasib under Moulay Abdelhafid.[11] In Fez alone, 80 percent of commercial and industrial property was hubus property.[12] Under Djai's guidance, administrators standardized regulations regarding the use of hubus property. Eleven Moroccans, including two scholars from Fez, participated in establishing regulations on the rental of such properties.[13] Besides these higher-ups, there were three hundred Moroccans making all the daily decisions shaping this organization in specific locales.[14]

The social and economic role of religious endowments expanded under Djai and his French counterparts. Djai increased the value of hubus properties by repairing them.[15] In 1920, Moroccan officials allocated 730,000 francs for the repair of Fez's mosques, sanctuaries, and houses.[16] Djai's ministry also invested in the creation of income-generating properties. On Rue Boukhessissat in Fez al-Jadid, the Ministry of Religious Endowments would construct 106 shops, 46 houses, and 2 public baths.[17] As a result, the profits generated by hubus properties grew. In 1913, the ministry collected 1,870,000 francs from its properties.[18] Within four years, this figure quadrupled.[19] Twenty years later, income from hubus properties would reach 16,800,000 francs.[20] In this way, and despite French colonization, the Moroccan elite maintained their influence over Morocco's political economy.

The colonial makhzan also included Mohamed ben al-Hassan al-Hajoui.[21] Si Mohamed was the son of a merchant who did business in Manchester. He studied at the Qarawiyyin Mosque and then assumed oversight of royal expenses in Meknes in 1900. Two years later, Moulay Abdelaziz sent him to Oujda, where he supervised the collection of custom duties. There, al-Hajoui served on a commission to regulate the frontier between Algeria and Morocco. Despite his cosmopolitanism and his contacts with Europeans, al-Hajoui retained, in Lyautey's view, his adherence to Islamic principles and Moroccan traditions, thus representing an ideal colonial associate. In 1912, Lyautey made him the delegate for public instruction. Al-Hajoui was not the only resident of Fez in the colonial makhzan. One historian counts fifty notables from Fez in the central government, with only three Moroccans *not* from the precolonial capital.[22]

Some of these Fassis caused Lyautey more of a headache than others. Mohamed al-Moqri was grand vizier at the start of Moulay Youssef's reign, but Lyautey relieved him of this duty in 1913, replacing him with Mohamed Guebbas. The grand vizier directly supervised all local officials, making his power second only to that of the sultan. Both al-Moqri and Guebbas were natives of Fez, so Lyautey's choice did not necessarily indicate a geopolitical preference for residents of this imperial capital. Rather, Lyautey idealized Guebbas as a Muslim traditionalist, belittling al-Moqri as a religious skeptic and "very Parisian."

Lyautey made a serious effort to break al-Moqri's power base. He dismissed his son Mokhtar from his post as basha of Tangier and his son Taieb from his duties as minister of finance. A third son, Ahmed, had been basha of Fez in 1912, but French officers had already ousted him, claiming that his slow response to the April riots reflected anticolonial leanings. Lyautey further damaged al-Moqri's reputation when he condemned his construction of a house on illicitly gained hubus property.

Al-Moqri outmaneuvered Lyautey. Lyautey may not have liked the Western pretensions of this rich Fassi, but al-Moqri had acquaintances in the French government who held him in high esteem. After Lyautey relieved him of his duties, al-Moqri went to Paris for two years. He connected with French supporters and paved the way for his reappointment as grand vizier in 1917. From this position, he manipulated the ascension of Mohamed V in 1927, after Moulay Youssef's death. He would remain grand vizier until 1956, when Morocco regained its independence.[23]

Notables could also exercise influence through local structures of governance. The French managed Moroccan cities through a system of municipal government.[24] The municipal government structure in Fez came into existence six months after the April riots. The Department of Indigenous Affairs appointed a French chief of municipal services to head this administration, and he exercised political and fiscal independence from his superiors in Rabat. Thus, the chief of municipal services balanced the municipal budget, spending on personnel and public works only as much money as collected through local taxes.[25] Further, a colonial decree vested this official with exclusive control over issues relating to a city's public works, security, and health.[26]

To promote political stability, the French maintained a basha as the Moroccan counterpart of the chief of municipal services. The French appointed Mohamed ben Bouchta Baghdadi to this post in October 1912. Baghdadi was born during the reign of Sultan Moulay Abderrahman and belonged to the Ouled Jamai, a tribe cultivating hard wheat twenty kilometers north of Fez.[27] His family also owned property in Fez, a royal gift that acknowledged the family's loyalty to the Alaouites.[28] Baghdadi's father, Bouchta, had been basha of Fez between 1888 and 1896. As for Si Mohamed, he was a seasoned urban administrator, having acted as basha of southern Taroudant under Moulay Hassan.

The French first took notice of Baghdadi in 1911, when his troops subdued tribes in Fez's hinterland. In April 1912, he assisted in quelling urban riots. Given Baghdadi's experience as a local official, as well as his proven loyalty to the colonial partnership, he was a logical successor to the alleged malcontent Ahmed al-Moqri. To cultivate good relations with him, the protectorate paid Baghdadi a salary, while also perpetuating his family's traditional privileges. For this reason, neither Baghdadi nor his clients paid taxes.[29] Baghdadi would remain basha for twenty years, until his death in 1932.[30]

Baghdadi exercised substantial independence from his French counterpart. He implemented local regulations, such as building codes and urban security, while also enforcing national laws. Colonial officers feared provoking unrest with a visible French presence in the medina, so Baghdadi headed a Moroccan police force. In order to put a prisoner to death, the signature of the French commissioner of the Sharifian government was required, the only limitation on the basha's policing power. In some respects, the protectorate expanded the basha's formal powers. In the precolonial era, a royal official auctioned off the right to collect taxes, but the French made the basha responsible for this duty, thereby increasing his hold on residents.[31] As noted by a French scholar in 1931, "His regulatory power is more extensive than that of mayors in France."[32] Since the French trusted Baghdadi, he exercised his power with few restrictions.[33]

The French also retained a muhtasib to oversee exchanges in urban markets. The French appointed Driss al-Moqri as muhtasib of Fez in October 1912, a position that he would hold for twenty-six years.[34] The brother of Mohamed al-Moqri, Si Driss had been Fez's principal tax collector in the precolonial era. At that time, this post must have provided a lucrative salary, for Si Driss constructed a palatial courtyard house in the medina's eastern quarters during Moulay Abdelhafid's reign.[35]

The municipality paid the muhtasib, making him an agent of the chief of municipal services. And yet, he was the official setting the price of staples sold in Fez's markets serving Moroccan consumers. (The muhtasib could not enforce prices on goods produced and sold by Europeans, such as margarine, a situation that overcharged French residents in the Ville Nouvelle wanted to change.) Si Driss also verified weights and measures, which, despite a law requiring change to the metric system, were still transacted according to premodern standards, such as the mudd (equivalent to twenty-one kilograms of wheat).³⁶

As one French officer admitted, the influential Si Driss retained most of the precolonial functions associated with this royal official.³⁷ Si Driss enforced laws prohibiting fraud. In 1913, he caught a spice seller diluting red pepper. He destroyed seven sacks of the fraudulent product and sent the spice seller to prison.³⁸ Apparently Si Driss did not lose his penchant for excessive prison sentences, for the French counselor for the Sharifian government would complain twenty-one years later that Si Driss had not only fined two merchants for the sale of bad butter but also sent them to prison for three months.³⁹ Ultimately, the director of political affairs endorsed Si Driss's punitive innovations, arguing for a similar extension of the Moroccan muhtasib's powers in all of the kingdom's cities.⁴⁰

To foster the consensus of colonized Moroccans in the municipality, the French created the *majlis*, a consultative body of urban notables.⁴¹ The majlis consisted of notables elected by their peers, with each representing one of four electoral districts in the medina. These elected representatives served with five permanent members: the muhtasib, the basha, and the basha's three assistants. Members of the majlis did not receive remuneration, so notables must have sought election only to increase their influence on public policy. Their term lasted two years, but they could serve indefinitely. Ahmed Benchaqroun, for example, a merchant elected in 1912, remained in office until 1924, when his appointment as assistant to the basha disqualified him from holding elected office.⁴² In a city of nearly 100,000 residents, the majlis represented an oligarchic democracy. Only six hundred notables—all men—participated in the elections.⁴³

The chief of municipal services met with the majlis once a month. This body oversaw public health, sanitation, prisons, and medical facilities. Its members also approved the municipal budget. A municipal services official explained:

> It would have been bad policy to push aside the Muslim city dweller from municipal deliberations. From the beginning, it was necessary to give him the impression that we wanted him to participate actively in all the technical and administrative works that would transform the life and the form of urban centers set up as municipalities.⁴⁴

Within the first year of its existence, the majlis prohibited the consumption of alcohol in Muslim quarters, banned gambling in Suq al-Khamis, set up a program to combat ringworm, and organized lighting for the medina's streets.⁴⁵ The majlis issued opinions without the power to enforce them, but the chief of municipal services, wanting Moroccans to acquiesce to French rule, made a serious effort to address their concerns.

This new institution cultivated the support of merchants, for at least nine members elected in 1912 imported goods from Europe.⁴⁶ Hadj Tahar ben al-Amine, who represented the Lemtiyyin quarter, frequently traveled to Marseilles and owned a house in London. The other representative from this quarter was Hadj Hadi Ghallab, who, trading primarily in Algeria, had long-standing ties with the French. Representing the Andalous quarter, Hamza Tahiri was the thirty-two-year-old son of a cloth merchant. His father had also managed the hubus properties of the Qarawiyyin Mosque.⁴⁷ Tahiri was a British protégé. He had lived for fourteen years in Manchester and worked as interpreter at the British consulate upon his return to Fez.⁴⁸ Most of these men, it is important to note, had not previously served the makhzan. In this way, the majlis offered some members of the mercantile elite a new means of exercising political influence.

Perpetuating Premodern Trades

Merchants and religious scholars were the elite minority with whom the French forged a formal political partnership, but workers represented the preponderant majority. After fifteen years of colonial rule, French officers would count 81,172 Muslims in Fez as well as 8,000 Moroccan Jews.⁴⁹ If the average family consisted of five people, then the active male population represented only 20 percent of this figure, or about 17,800 men. According to Fez's muhtasib, the Moroccan population then included 9,000 artisans and 3,150 day laborers.⁵⁰

Two-thirds of the men in Fez earned a living by producing a good or performing a service, so Lyautey implemented policies to improve the lot of colonized workers. As pointed out by one historian, his administration wanted "to avoid repeating the shortcomings and faults that contributed to unmaking indigenous society in Algeria and to provoking the emergence of a mob of uprooted and proletarized men."⁵¹ An official later identified a study of local industries in 1913 as a first initiative to provide economic security for urban workers in Morocco.⁵²

When Lyautey ordered this study, the French conquerors were facing the socioeconomic fallout of an environmental crisis. Drought had destroyed crops, and the price of wheat and barley shot up by midwinter. The chief of municipal services reported that "for the lowest classes, the conditions of existence remain extremely difficult." Fez's malnourished residents proved susceptible to disease, and smallpox that winter led to a high mortality rate. The chief of municipal services identified the weak purchasing power of workers as a factor contributing to the crisis, stating: "The elevated cost of all sorts of staples reduce people of the poor classes to a semifamine and put them in a state of least resistance in relation to this malady."[53]

The basha banned the growing numbers of beggars from sleeping in Fez's streets, particularly those near the Moulay Idriss mausoleum. This edict mentioned only a fear of spreading smallpox, but, given the sanctuary's proximity to the Qissariyya market, where Fez's wealthiest merchants plied their wares, it seems likely that a fear of theft may have grounded the policy. Administrators of hubus funds constructed temporary housing for beggars on land between the western gates of Bab Ftouh and Bab Sidi Bou Jida. Within a month, the huts sheltered thirty men, thirty-four women, and eight children. Baghdadi tried to protect influential residents from the riffraff, ordering these beggars to return to their extramural huts by sunset, when, coincidentally, merchants closed their shops. Income from hubus property provided food for beggars unable to walk to the medina.[54]

The French provided food to keep the urban poor alive. By February 1914, municipal administrators ordered one thousand sacks of semolina for distribution.[55] That winter, the French also provided a daily allotment of flour to 1,842 poor Muslims. Twice a week, they also distributed flour to 700 poor Jews in the mellah.[56] Following the lead of his royal predecessors, Moulay Youssef distributed two thousand loaves of bread to Fez's poor in February and March.[57] The French assumed responsibility for the medical care of malnourished Moroccans by having a doctor in the colonial army visit the huts of beggars twice a week.[58] The chief of municipal services lauded this doctor's voluntarism and ensured that the budget included money for the shelter's hygienic upkeep.[59] During the crisis, the Ministry of Religious Endowments distributed bread to 1,500 poor Moroccans.[60]

The drought lasted another year, and the rising price of basic foods led to a decrease in the demand for nonedible goods. In January 1915, the chief of municipal services counted 5,000 unemployed workers in Fez. Some workers sold their belongings, while others begged in the street.[61] When the drought increased the cost of primary materials, consumers could no longer afford the higher price of finished products. The chief of municipal services blamed the high price of skins and wool for rendering unemployed many of Fez's 1,700 tanners. In blocking maritime commerce, World War I aggravated their woes, since they could not export shoes to Egypt or

Senegal. Weavers also experienced an economic downturn, as did bronze workers, many of whom had not worked for months on end by December 1915.[62]

Fearing political unrest, the French pushed forward with public works in order to provide wages to unemployed workers. Two-thirds of Fez's cobblers were unemployed.[63] The municipality paid 150 of them each day to break the stones needed to pave city streets. Their wages were abysmally low, but the municipal coffers still did not hold enough money to hire all workers demanding a job. The chief of municipal services asked his superior to negotiate the sultan's purchase of shoes from these cobblers, with the makhzan then taking responsibility for their sale. He also requested 100,000 francs from Rabat's offices. This French official intended to use the money to create work programs, which were, in his opinion, better than charity. "Inactivity and hunger," noted the chief of municipal services, "make bad advisers."[64]

To address this crisis, Lyautey appointed Prosper Ricard as Fez's inspector of indigenous arts in April 1915. Ricard had already devoted fifteen years to improving the lot of craftsmen in Algeria. There, he had established a training program for carpenters in both Tlemcen and Oran. After, he had spent five years as inspector for artistic and industrial training, overseeing programs in all Algerian schools.[65] Lyautey wanted this new officer to address "the future of our indigenous industries and the preparation of indigenous manpower of which Europeans will have need in this country."[66]

Ricard intended to preserve handiwork. Handiwork signified a system of labor based on individuals producing one specific good from beginning to end. In his opinion, Fez's economic crisis had not sprung from environmental catastrophes but rather from "the mass of foreign products that compete with local industries and paralyze them."[67] He later clarified that "the use of the machine and some hybrid innovations, which encourage mass production and the counterfeiting of Moroccan art, degrade it [art] very quickly while also leaving without employ the most interesting main d'oeuvre in the country."[68] Ricard's statement pointed to a policy preference for workers crafting goods, and not for consumers wanting cheap commodities.

Ricard set out to revive 126 trades in Fez, ones that "give us a close idea of European crafts before innovations that began in the eighteenth century."[69] After his arrival, Ricard informed Fez's chief of municipal services that they must re-create styles from the fifteenth century. "To maintain and restore the worthy tradition of indigenous industries," the latter summed up, "it is necessary to examine ancient models and classic décor of Hispano-Moorish art, which will provide exemplars to artisans of tomorrow."[70] By re-creating past styles, Ricard hoped to temper the economic dislocation wrought by modern innovations.

Ironically, French officials set up programs that trained workers to satisfy the tastes of foreign buyers, not local consumers needing everyday items. As inspector of Moroccan arts, Jean Gallotti insisted that the artistic ability of potters had "degenerated toward the end of the last century."[71] Trade with Europe permitted the rich to purchase Chinese porcelain, constraining local potters to the production of cheaper wares for everyday use. Since potters provided only "common products at low prices," the chief of municipal services feared the reeducation of these workers would be difficult.[72] Ricard insisted that this industry "is still worthy of interest since it presently employs 150 workers divided into thirty workshops."[73] In 1919, the colonial administrator Alfred Bel expressed his intention of rectifying "this degradation" through the re-creation of styles popular in the sixteenth century.[74]

The French established programs and policies that ensured the production of luxury goods reflecting medieval styles. First, they funded schools to train potters. The Department of Fine Arts gave the municipality 1,500 francs to establish a laboratory for ceramics so that the French could create shades of black, blue, and yellow reflecting "ancient tones of enamel."[75] In Dar Batha, the palace constructed by Moulay Hassan, French officials set up a museum displaying ancient pottery and other crafts. Fez's first chief of municipal services donated his collection of antique pottery.[76] The French then awarded monetary prizes to workers who copied these exemplars.[77] By 1923, these programs provided artisans with a financial incentive for visiting the museum, and Ricard reported that "artisans parade through the halls in clusters."[78] Finally, the French mediated purchases overseas, putting Fez's potters in touch with buyers in Paris.[79]

Ricard believed that the perpetuation of a system of production relying on handiwork would foster political stability. In his view, Moroccan craftsmen were lynchpins of political quiescence. Describing the social hierarchy in densely populated cities, Ricard stated: "If one accepts that makhzan officials, scholars, religious or otherwise, and merchants constitute the upper class of Fez's society and that the crowd of small tradesmen, retailers, and workers form the people, then the artisan belongs to a type of middle class which, without being too prominent, occupies an honorable social rank."[80] In equating craftsmen with a middle class, considered the lynchpin of stability in European states, Ricard's social analysis highlights the political aims of his programs. "As comfort increases with work," he stated, "the moral benefit of an action so spread in the middle classes or laborers of indigenous society was as appreciable as the pecuniary advantages that it earned for them."[81]

The protectorate promoted handiwork, even when machines had led a trade to verge on extinction. Ricard, for example, identified only two specialists in bookbinding in 1915. A printing press did not operate in precolonial Fez, but Moulay Abdelaziz had ordered texts copied by lithography.[82] Fez's literate population also purchased books from Syria and Egypt. Ricard disparaged local patterns of consumption, stating, "Seduced by the cheapness of mechanically produced goods, students and men of letters have lost their taste for calligraphic books that are richly protected. In this case, as in so many others, a destructive decadence has exercised its ravages on sound traditions."[83] Bookbinders had once practiced their trade near the mausoleum of Moulay Idriss, but the two men identified as master craftsmen worked at home. According to Ricard, they used the cheapest skins on the market and let their tools fall into disrepair.[84]

Ricard created programs to increase the number of workers depending on a demand for bound leather books.[85] Using a text describing the art of bookbinding in 1610, he trained new workers in this medieval craft.[86] He set up two workshops, one in Rabat and the other in Fez, each headed by one of the two bookbinding experts identified in 1915. In Rabat, the Department of Fine Arts funded the bookbinders' workshop, while the municipality took charge of the one in Fez. The municipality then provided "monetary encouragements" to workers so that they would make an effort to improve current practices of the trade and to re-create "beautiful models of ancient times."[87] By December 1915, the workshop in Fez included not only the master craftsman but also two journeymen and two young apprentices.[88]

Ricard's appointment of Mohamed al-Arbi Lahlou as head of Fez's bookbinding workshop promoted his vision of workers as a harbinger of urban order. Lahlou's family had long supported the Alaouites. According to Ricard, one of his forebears had been grand vizier in the eighteenth century. In the nineteenth century, the bookbinding Lahlous completed orders for Moulay Hassan and Moulay Abdelaziz.[89] In return, Moulay Abdelaziz had given Si Mohamed a regular salary as well as gifts of wheat, butter, and clothes.[90] Si Mohamed al-Arbi had trained his six sons to bind books. He also had four cousins, three second cousins, one nephew, and two great nephews trained in this trade.[91] Further, his sister married a bookbinder from another family. In fact, Ricard appointed Lahlou's brother-in-law Haha to head the bookbinding workshop in Rabat.[92] Pointing to living testimony of Fez's past, Ricard counseled foreign tourists reading his *Guide bleu* to visit Si Mohamed's workshop.[93] When Si Mohamed al-Arbi died, his son took over the state-sponsored workshop.[94]

The protectorate became a promoter of this trade as well as a major client. Once the bookbinding workshop began its operations in February 1916, Ricard informed the Department of Fine Arts that it could begin placing orders with it.[95] When Lyautey visited Fez the following year, he stopped by the workshop and publicly complimented their craftsmanship.[96] Ricard promoted the sale of bound books among French tourists "looking for artistic bookbinding in Fez."[97] Further, the protectorate and the municipality budgeted money to purchase bound books.[98] Ricard sent bound books from Fez to industrial fairs in Casablanca, Fez, and Rabat.[99] Fez's chief of municipal services insisted that these public displays stimulated demand for the bookbinders' products. Since he recognized that the buyers were foreigners, not Moroccans, this official also sent the wares of bookbinders and other artisans to fairs in Paris and Lyon.[100] By 1919, Ricard reported that orders for bound books from France and Algeria were such that "the workers are overloaded."[101]

By the end of 1917, the municipality opened a second bookbinding workshop that provided a salary for four journeymen and six apprentices.[102] Some workers broke free from state sponsorship. In April 1918, Ali Slaoui, one of Lahlou's first apprentices, established a private workshop and hired his own workers.[103] By 1919, the chief of municipal services reported that this trade employed fifteen people.[104] The following year, the sales of bookbinders, now sixteen in number, reached 100,000 francs.[105] By 1923, Fez's muhtasib counted forty shops selling the wares of bookbinders.[106] The growth of this trade shows that colonial patronage improved the economic lot of workers.

The French invested in the perpetuation of premodern trades in order to guarantee wages for Moroccan workers. The municipality patronized craftsmen, paying the wages of an unspecified number of weavers and potters working at eight workshops as well as fifty-one apprentices of bookbinding, illumination, painting, carpentry, brass work, and embroidery.[107] In 1918, the municipality distributed 6,000 francs to support the production of local goods.[108] By then, French officials were beginning to see that their efforts were bearing fruit. The chief of municipal services counted 1,183 objects constructed according to colonial standards, with a market value of

39,940 francs. The following year, in 1919, Fez's chief of municipal services requested permission of his superior in Rabat to offer a monetary prize to more artisans.[109] He used this money to reward three bookbinders, a weaver, two potters, a carpenter, an illuminator, a wood carver, and a stone carver.[110]

Social Mobility of Workers

The French provided workers with opportunities to earn money, and this fostered social mobility. Ricard would extol the carpenter Ahmed Bennani as one worker who took advantage of the colonial economy.[111] Bennani was twenty-five years old when Ricard came to Fez. He practiced his trade in the Nejjarine suq, alongside other carpenters. His workshop was ten square meters, and only one apprentice worked with him. As Ricard passed this workshop one day, he saw Bennani decorating a walnut box with fragments of a lemon tree's blond wood.

The day of his encounter with Bennani, Ricard ordered a box from him. From the start, Ricard demonstrated a desire to foster a new aesthetic in carpentry. He asked Bennani to change the color scheme of the box so that it reflected his French perception of a traditional Moroccan style. Money was an inducement for change, and Ricard told Bennani that he would only pay him "on condition that some defects will be avoided."

Bennani completed this box to colonial specifications, so Ricard then encouraged him to make furniture. Moroccans did not make European furniture such as couches.[112] So, inspired by ornamentation of wood and plaster on medieval mosques, Ricard provided Bennani with designs for tables, bookshelves, chairs, and beds in a traditional Moroccan form. The director of the protectorate's Museum of Decorative Arts undoubtedly was referring to Ricard when he described "one of our compatriots" designing furniture based on "the best models of ancient art."[113]

Ricard promoted Bennani's wares in his capacity as a colonial official. He sent Bennani to the Franco-Moroccan Fair in Casablanca so that he could display his skill as a carpenter. Upon Lyautey's insistence that colonial offices adopt a Moroccan style, the protectorate became a principal buyer of Moroccan furniture. The Department of Education established schools in Fez, and Bennani supplied chairs and desks for its classrooms and offices. When the orders became too large for Bennani to fill on his own, colonial administrators established three workshops for carpenters. They produced tables, bureaus, seats, filing cabinets, bookshelves, armoires, and banquettes in 1915.[114]

In promoting tourism, the protectorate augmented Bennani's profits. The chief of municipal services insisted that foreign travelers be provided with comfortable lodgings. The municipality spent 330,000 francs on the purchase of a hotel in the western quarters of Fez, renovating the building's interior design.[115] The chief of municipal services commissioned most furniture for this hotel from Bennani. The development of tourism, however, also benefited Bennani by bringing foreign consumers to Fez. Even as this carpenter completed the furniture for the hotel, the chief of municipal services reported that he was receiving increasing numbers of orders from Europeans.[116] Responding to their travel needs, Bennani designed collapsible furniture for transport overseas. Ricard tried to increase this carpenter's foreign clientele. When he published the *Guide bleu*, he directed French tourists to Bennani's workshop.[117]

Bennani's business quickly grew. By 1920, the chief of municipal services reported that he had sold one thousand chairs, five hundred tables, and two hundred armoires, thereby bringing in 270,000 francs.[118] Such high demand for his products led Bennani to establish two more workshops in Fez. Since each workshop measured one hundred square meters, it seems that his volume of business increased twenty times over. In these workshops, he oversaw the work of more than ten employees. Bennani ordered business cards that allowed him to publicize his business and to increase orders.

As Bennani's profits increased, he acquired upwardly mobile social aspirations and assumed the trappings of urban notables. Bennani attended the Sultan of the Tolba festivities in 1916. This was a local celebration in which a student from the Qarawiyyin Mosque became sultan for a day, thereby having the power to make one demand from the government. Ricard reported that he appeared at this celebration "in the same apparel as the bourgeois of Fez, under a personal tent that he had been able to acquire with his economizing."

There were other signs of his social aspirations. As Bennani's business grew, he purchased property on the medina's eastern margins and constructed a house. This carpenter would eventually save enough money to travel to Mecca, thereby earning the title of "Hadj." Thus, the French officials who helped workers to increase their earnings also provided them an opportunity to claim a higher social status in the urban hierarchy.

In remembering his childhood, Abdelmajid Benjelloun reflected elite disdain for his family's upwardly mobile social inferiors. Born in 1919, Benjelloun spent his first ten years in Manchester with his father. Upon his return to Fez, he and his family lived next to a "self-made man" (*'asami*) who had earned a fortune through "hard labor." Benjelloun's description of this man suggests that notables linked their own status to intangible factors that money could not buy. He states:

> He dressed just like the Moroccan elite, but he was not concerned with his gestures and his conduct. He was always in new clothes, but he treated them like rags. He did not try to appear dignified and calm like his peers.[119]

Spotting the neighbor's wife in a satin gown deemed uncouth, a woman in the Benjelloun family declared that "her husband is a nouveau riche (*moustahadath ghani*), and she does not know beautiful clothes."[120] Given such comments, it seems notables did not laud the entrepreneurial spirit of workers like Bennani.

And Fez's elite feared the aggregation of the influence of individual workers. In 1919, some workers demonstrated in front of the sultan's palace in Rabat. A lack of surplus income contributed to this unrest. France's postwar monetary policy had caused rampant inflation in Morocco. A concerned official reported that the workers publicly objected to a tax on licenses that authorized them to practice their trades.[121] At that time, the grand vizier stated that the sultan knew that local workers had forged an alliance with their European counterparts.[122]

Shortly thereafter, Mohamed al-Moqri ordered all bashas to prevent Moroccans from joining trade unions composed of European workers.[123] He asserted that Moroccans did not have the right to seek the protection of French labor laws. They could neither give money to associations representing French workers nor ask them to seek redress on their behalf. In al-Moqri's opinion, the consolidation of European and Moroccan interests would make local workers too strong and so "help them to demonstrate against the makhzan." Al-Moqri wanted workers to present their affairs through an arif, a respected Moroccan practicing their trade.[124] Al-Moqri promoted the perpetuation of informal networks of patronage over independent organizations making demands of the government as equal power holders. Fez's basha promised to remain "vigilant to all that you explained."[125]

Al-Moqri visited France one month after sending this directive, and strikes there would have hardened his position against unionization in

Morocco. The grand vizier was one of eight Moroccans representing the makhzan at a celebration of the Great War's end. This group included the Fassi notables Mohamed al-Hajoui, delegate for public education, and Omar Tazi, then Casablanca's basha. During the voyage, they witnessed the disorder caused by France's unionized workers. "Every day," al-Hajoui recorded, "a new category of workers goes on strike." His vilification of these workers provides insights into the class interests of the mercantile elite in Fez.

For al-Hajoui, the social disorder and political disruption of the strikes verged on anarchy. In Paris, waiters struck, leaving the owner of al-Hajoui's hotel to serve food to guests. In Strasbourg, public transportation workers struck. When the army tried to ensure public order, striking workers killed a lieutenant in the army. After his trip to France, al-Hajoui visited Moroccan friends in England. There, miners in Manchester struck, blocking the distribution of coal. Al-Hajoui reported that manufacturing in England and the entire European continent stopped. Worse, in his opinion, the British police struck, abdicating their role as agents of national order.

A merchant exporting goods to Morocco, al-Hajoui exhibited no sympathy for the workingman's plight. He did not believe that the high cost of living justified the strikes in France and England. Instead, he blamed "the diffusion of bolshevist ideas in the inferior class of the general populace, which incite workers to claim a part of the profits from manufacturers." He condemned European patrons who acquiesced to demands for increased pay and a simultaneous decrease in the working day. Al-Hajoui believed that higher pay would cause a rise in the price of consumer goods, leading to a recession. "I do not know," this merchant-cum-public official warned, "where this situation is leading, since it is nothing more than disorder."[126]

In Ricard's opinion, the institutionalization of corporations in the colonial state would prevent disorder. To legitimize the formal organization of trades, he referred to them with the Arabic term *hanati*.[127] If a corporation represented each urban trade, the protectorate could control Moroccan workers. According to Ricard, "This organization should make it possible for public powers to oversee [it] and to make diverse enterprises submit to a collective discipline."[128]

In other words, Ricard advocated for a more conservative association than radicalized trade unions. The corporation fostered stable relations among workers since its members were often related by blood and honored the same patron saints. The master craftsman's unquestioned supervision of his underlings meant that one member of a corporation could influence the actions of many workers. If a corporation's *amin*, or official representative, which Moroccans had referred to as arif, negotiated the price of finished goods, then the cost of living could be kept down. The amin could also delegate work, thereby minimizing unemployment. Since the corporation assumed responsibility for the care of its sick and old members, it would also forestall Moroccan demands for social insurance.[129]

Ricard began to push for the revival of the corporation in 1920. At that time, the protectorate upgraded the Office of Indigenous Arts and Industry into an autonomous department, and Lyautey replaced the acting director, the artist J. de la Nézière, with Ricard. The department adopted the full employment of Moroccans as a key objective, quickly publishing its intent to train adult artisans and find outlets for their goods.[130]

At the same time, the socialist Alexandre Millerand became president of France in September 1920.[131] Predisposed to consideration of labor issues, this president also had a strong interest in Morocco, visiting two years after his inauguration. That very year, France's National Printing Press finally published a study of Moroccan labor undertaken by Camille du Gast in 1914. Referring to the corporation, du Gast noted that Moroccan workers "already possess an organization which, although in an embryonic state, contains a number of dispositions which would be in our interest to preserve."[132]

To realize this vision of a harmonious colonial order, Ricard and his colleagues wanted to provide a legal statute for the corporation. In October 1920, George Hardy, director of the Office of Education, drafted a decree to institutionalize the corporation. Like Ricard, Hardy wanted to revive traditional trades at "Muslim schools of apprenticeship."[133] His decree called for collective decisions of the corporation to replace independent initiatives by artisans. The decree would transform a trade's amin into the head of a governing body run by four other master craftsmen. These men would have the authority to purchase materials and tools on behalf of its members. The drafted decree also gave them authority to sell goods and to set prices. Further, this governing body would have the right to sign for loans, thereby committing all members to help with repayment. Royal officials would directly influence each corporation representing a specific trade. The muhtasib would countersign all official decisions, with all documentation then passing to the chief of municipal services.[134] The director of the protectorate's Department of Commerce and Industry supported the decree, finding that it "should prove very useful for us."[135]

But the grand vizier vehemently opposed the decree. Communicating through the French counselor of the Sharifian government, al-Moqri insisted that the law contradicted Moroccan traditions. It decreased the power of merchants, he specified, while increasing the power of workers. The decree would lead to the formation of "commercial corporations," so al-Moqri foresaw a curtailing of the "liberty of commerce that the makhzan has always respected."

His real concern hinged on the rise of workers' rights. Groups representing workers, he noted, had never had a "civil capacity." In this sense, the French would "make them leave their normal course, transforming them into trade unions." Identifying formal recognition of corporations as a "political danger," al-Moqri insisted that it was in fact the absence of formal order among Moroccans that provided the sultan with the base of his power. He posed the following rhetorical question: "Are we going to fabricate organizations for workers and force them to obey elected chiefs, which would allow them to develop an awareness of their force?" He then asserted that "they would rebel against us one day, pretending to make professional demands that would quickly slip into political agitation." Referring to a protest among Moroccans, he prophesized doom. "In place of finding ourselves in the presence of an amorphous crowd," he predicted, "we would have before us disciplined groups that would have organized resistance."[136]

This decree never passed, so al-Moqri's opposition killed the effort. Three months later, de la Nézière insisted that the grand vizier had missed the significance of the decree. "The project presented by the Department of Education," he stated, "aims to give artisans and retailers sufficient advantages so that they will not dream of affiliating themselves, from one day to another, with trade unions."[137] The French shelved, for the moment at least, their efforts to legalize the corporation. The notables' shooting down of the corporation did not end French efforts to cultivate the loyalty of workers to the colonial state, but such efforts cannot be traced through formal legislation and institutions dealing with labor policy.

## Constructing Loyalty

City planning and building codes provided an indirect means of cultivating colonial loyalties among ordinary Moroccans. In Fez, as in other cities in Morocco and North Africa, colonial administrators fashioned and maintained a dual city, whereby Moroccans lived in the premodern medina and the French in the newly constructed Ville Nouvelle.[138] More than evidence of cultural imperialism, this ethnic segregation highlighted a concern for Moroccan workers. As new forms of transport and manufactured goods threatened upheaval, Ricard noted, "the economic shock would be very grave and of great consequence if it was not canceled, or at least lessened, by wise measures of precaution dictated from a high place: preservation of ancient cities, restoration of historic monuments, encouragement of indigenous arts, and the adoption of a Moorish style in the construction of a number of new edifices."[139] In this way, the director of the Department of Indigenous Arts and Industry underscores the colonial perception of a direct link between urban form and the well-being of colonized Moroccans.

Colonization required the construction of facilities for the foreign conqueror. Thus, the economic crisis of 1915, fatal for tanners and shoemakers, did not unduly affect those in the building trades, especially since most European workers in Fez returned to their country during World War I. In fact, there were so many construction projects that patrons competed for both skilled craftsmen and unskilled day laborers, leading to an average salary increase of 25 percent over a period of two years. To prevent increased building costs, colonial agencies "unionized," as ironically termed by the chief of municipal services, in order to institute standard wages.[140] This initiative does not mean that colonial administrators begrudged a living wage to Moroccans. To the contrary, the French privileged local interests even in coastal Rabat, where, with a large European population, the director of public works ensured that foreign companies hired Moroccans, not Europeans.[141]

In the medina, the restoration of Fez's madrasas provided a significant employment opportunity for some Moroccans. Many state-sponsored building projects focused on the preservation of historic monuments, for Lyautey intended to preserve the walled quarters of the medina as a medieval relic.[142] The protectorate set up a Department of Fine Arts and Historic Monuments, and its director had the power to classify historic monuments.[143] By 1915, this agency classified six madrasas, all but one dating to the fourteenth century.[144] Within eight months, the Department of Fine Arts and Historic Monuments began to restore the Bou Inania Madrasa and the Attarin Madrasa. The French charged a Moroccan official with oversight of the project's 10,000-franc budget.[145]

The restoration of madrasas permitted the French to train workers in a medieval building style considered appropriate to the medina. When Maurice Tranchant de Lunel became the director of fine arts and historic monuments in 1912, he found only two sculptors capable of carving a madrasa's plaster walls. Under his auspices, these sculptors trained thirty students, and they were all hired to renovate Fez's madrasas.[146] In like manner, the colonial architect Léon Dumas found only one worker able to carve wood, and he ordered this artisan to train other Moroccans working on the restoration of the Madrasa al-Saharidj.[147] Another French official noted that "the restoration of madrasas ... will be an excellent school for the indigenous industries."[148]

French officials recognized the economic impact of this training program. Advocating for such projects, the architect Henri Saladin argued that Moroccans should continue crafting *zallij*, or polychrome tiles, since the adoption of European designs and modern building materials "would reduce to misery worthy artisans who presently make a living from this trade."[149]

The restoration of the Attarin Madrasa and the Saharidj Madrasa provided for the financial survival of at least ninety-seven Moroccans by 1922. The Department of Fine Arts and Historic Monuments assigned a Moroccan foreman to each construction site, each working six days a week at thirty-five francs a day. The restoration of the Saharidj Madrasa required eight skilled craftsmen. Hamed Sarfaoui, for example, sculpted plaster for twenty-five francs a day. Mohamed Sattar, who crafted mosaics, earned only thirteen francs a day. The protectorate also paid the assistants of these craftsmen, who received between two and five francs a day. These projects required work by those supplying or transporting building materials, thereby generating more employment in Fez.[150]

French administrators also wanted to perpetuate a traditional style in new buildings, but rich notables proved all too willing to innovate. Ricard counted nine palatial residences constructed just before French colonization. Pointing to the exaggerated height of the two- or three-story structures as well as the use of marble, he condemned their "European elements."[151] Fez's well-traveled merchants were particularly irritating to French administrators. They wanted to build a subway system with a stop underneath the Qarawiyyin Mosque.[152] They expressed a desire to replace wood with iron in construction.[153] And in rebuilding the Qissariyya market after a fire in June 1918, Ricard reported that "the merchants of Fez were modernizing their installation too willingly; more than once, we needed to remove doors and windows with a much-too-European aspect."[154]

To ensure compliance with the colonial vision of Fez as a medieval relic, the French regulated the design of private buildings. A law passed in 1923 explicitly aimed to prevent the development of "quarters where European houses were erected." It also enunciated the French intention "to maintain the city of Fez in its original aspect." To achieve this goal, the decree listed sanctioned "architectural elements," thereby regulating a house's external molding, chimneys, windows, awnings, doors, and grillwork. French administrators also set rules for decorative aspects of a house acquired through use of painted wood, sculpted plaster, varnished tiles, and wrought iron. To ensure that houses met the criteria of this "Fassi" style, the colonial government required all residents to apply for building authorization from French, not Moroccan, administrators.[155]

In establishing this law, the colonial government deliberately assisted Moroccan workers in the building trades. Advancing the interests of builders, the decree states: "Measures striving for the protection of the medinas must have as a direct consequence the protection of the trades of all those who make or employ elements of construction for which their character is indebted to local techniques; furthermore, they combine to provide for a large number of artisans and workers, by their accustomed means, work and the profits of production."[156] The French favored the producers of buildings, and not the elite clients who commissioned houses and other structures from them.

One month after the law's passage, the muhtasib completed a list of workers in Fez that specified the number of ordinary Moroccans assisted by this law. Al-Moqri counted 229 masons in Fez. These craftsmen purchased bricks from twelve different ovens in the medina. They bought stone from seventeen men who extracted it from local quarries. They purchased varnished tile for awnings from thirteen artisans in the western quarters of Bab Ftouh. As for the decorative elements of a house, al-Moqri counted thirty artisans who embellished a building's internal walls with multicolored mosaic tiles in varying shapes, referred to as *zallij*, with another thirty in Paris working on a mosque. In total, al-Moqri's list shows that this law directly influenced the economic security of 572 workers or, assuming each worker to be the head of a household, nearly three thousand residents of Fez.[157]

In regulating the design of houses, the French set a collision course with wealthy notables constructing new houses on the medina's western outskirts. The property values in the Batha and Boujeloud quarters increased because this area was closest to the Ville Nouvelle, which the French began constructing after World War I. Abderrahman Bennis was from a mercantile family, and he built a house in Batha in 1921.[158] Boris Maslow, an inspector for the Department of Fine Arts and Historic Monuments, blocked the completion of this project, at least until its owner eliminated architectural embellishment that did not represent a traditional Moroccan design. He asked the chief of municipal services to order Bennis to replace three external windows with "indigenous grillwork." Also, he wanted him to make sure that the door would be replaced with one of an "indigenous style."[159] Maslow's complaints revealed the French intention to make the rich conform to their vision of Moroccan building traditions.

The French also blocked the completion of a house by Taieb ben M'Feddel Bouayad, who, like Bennis, came from a family of merchants in Fez.[160] In 1924, he purchased a property just inside the Bab Boujeloud, a gate constructed in a traditional style by the French.[161] Referring to this quarter as the "vestibule of the medina of Fez al-Bali," administrators found that the building "hid a part of the tableau, of which is composed the terraces of Talaa and the minarets, along with the Zalaj mountains."[162] Demonstrating his family's business acumen, Bouayad agreed to tear down his second floor in exchange for two shops near his house. It was a savvy demand, for, by that time, the value of commercial space in the Qissariyya had decreased, while it had increased in Boujeloud.[163] Bouayad would take advantage of the protectorate's development of tourism. He set up a *maison de touristes*, selling goods to foreign tourists who shared the aesthetic vision of French officers.[164]

Colonial officials did not exempt any residents of Fez from these new building codes, even such influential partners as Mohamed al-Hajoui. In 1926, the grand vizier's delegate for education constructed a house in the eastern Douh quarter between the Batha and Boujeloud quarters. Ricard expressed concern that the well-traveled al-Hajoui would construct a house having "a character that is not indigenous." He asked the head of Fez's Economic Bureau to make a special effort to oversee the construction. This official assured Ricard that plans submitted met building codes established for houses.[165]

Mohamed Mernissi was one of Fez's most influential residents. His family came from a farming region near Taza, but his great-grandfather had made a home in Fez after studying at the Qarawiyyin Mosque.[166] Si Mohamed became a merchant who had earned protected status through his dealings with French companies.[167] His wife was the daughter of Mohamed Feddoul Gharnit, grand vizier under Moulay Abdelaziz.[168] For most of the 1920s, Mernissi served as president of the Indigenous Chamber of Agricultural and Industry, whose membership included Fez's richest landlords and merchants. At the same time, his brother El Ghali was assistant to Casablanca's basha.[169] If "association" signified the appeasement of notables, then French officers should have bent over backward for Si Mohamed.

Nonetheless, French officers conflicted with Mernissi when he developed several properties in the Batha and Boujeloud neighborhoods. Tensions between Mernissi and the French began in 1922, when Maslow found that Mernissi had painted the external walls of his house a nontraditional blue.[170] In 1927, Mernissi began to construct a house and shops in the Boujeloud quarter. Again, he colored the external walls, rather than leaving them white, and he built windows facing the street, ordering a framework outside one of them in order to build an iron balcony.

The director of the Department of Fine Arts and Historic Monuments expressed outrage with the design of a "dwelling that is not Moroccan."[171] Maslow designed an appropriate grillwork for external openings of Mernissi's house, but this wealthy Moroccan refused to change his building.[172] Mernissi would not make the requested changes until the French threatened legal proceedings against him.[173] The colonial oversight of the construction of private houses created tensions with the very notables who the French hoped would act as colonial collaborators.

Fez's population began to rise in the second half of the 1920s, so housing was an important issue not only for the rich but also for the poor. In 1925, the Rif War brought dislocated tribesmen to Fez.[174] The next year, drought destroyed local crops. During the first four months of 1927, the municipality spent 21,700 francs burying victims of the famine.[175] Temporary settlements sprang up, and concerns for public health led the Municipal Bureau of Hygiene to order the destruction of 141 *nawa'il*, or huts, in Fez al-Jadid.[176] Concerned for urban security, the chief of municipal services ensured that "rigorous surveillance is exercised, and it was demanded that the unemployed be returned to their country of origin."[177] The basha's police arrested 101 vagrants in February and March.[178]

Ever wary of unrest among the masses, French officials sought to improve the lot of migrants and workers. The municipality built a homeless shelter, specifying that the French contractor must use local workers and building materials.[179] Moroccan hubus administrators transformed an urban garden into a housing development. By renting houses, the Ministry of Religious Endowments could address a social problem, thereby serving its charitable purpose, and also increase its income. In accordance with colonial building codes, the inspector for the Department of Fine Arts and Historic Monuments guaranteed the "indigenous character" of the housing in this project.[180]

Fez's growth caused a need for more cheap housing in the medina. By 1928, the housing crisis was severe, and Maslow noted that "the overpopulated medina of Fez requires an enlargement in all senses." Three notables transformed their gardens in the western quarters of the medina into housing developments, a means, no doubt, of reaping profits from urban growth. French administrators oversaw the architectural style of this housing and marked the new settlement with a portal constructed "in the spirit of neighboring gates."[181]

As explained by one official, the new neighborhoods in the western medina created jobs for local workers, since the French insisted on "Moroccan dwellings as made by local craftsmen, not European entrepreneurs or architects." Equally important, in his view, the prohibition of "dwellings that were half European and half Moorish" ensured affordable housing for workers. Europeans, he stated, would never live in an authentic Moroccan dwelling unless modified for their use. This statement undoubtedly referred to the high ceilings of the courtyard house—difficult to heat in the winter—as well as the absence of private baths. Through a strict interpretation of building codes, this official intended to vouchsafe that new housing would be rented to ordinary Moroccans in need of shelter.[182]

As gauged by the number of building permits issued to Moroccans in the medina, private construction generated employment for a large number of workers—even during periods of crisis. In 1925, the French authorized 300 building permits. In 1926, they authorized 600 building permits. By 1927, as drought increased need for urban housing, the French authorized 1,150 permits. The following year, they issued 1,251 permits. And, finally, in 1929, French administrators issued 1,123 building permits.[183] In each case, the proposed project met colonial requirements established in 1923, ones that perpetuated the medina's medieval form. That law had expressed the protectorate's concomitant desire to generate work for Moroccans. Thus, in evaluating how colonial building codes improved the lot of those Moroccan builders trained in medieval craftsmanship, these statistics speak for themselves.

## Conclusion

The French perceived their role as guarantor of the wages of workers from the protectorate's start. In May 1913, Lyautey visited Fez for the first time since the riots thirteen months before. According to a French journalist, some participants in that riot assembled in the crowds that gathered to greet the resident-general. By creating work opportunities, Lyautey had earned the loyalty of these men now described by the journalist as "satisfied in having a regular pittance."[184] According to this French witness, Lyautey's efforts to impose French rule without harsh crackdowns met with instantaneous success.

The French hoped to eradicate the root cause of popular unrest by implementing policies that fostered full employment among Moroccans. Standard interpretations of the policy of association highlight a formal partnership between French officials and the Moroccan notables. A closer examination of relationships between the French and the urban majority, however, underscores the colonial consideration for workers and the poor. The French implemented policies designed to perpetuate premodern trades, and some workers had new opportunities to earn money and to assume the accoutrements of higher status. The French also wanted to create formal institutions representing workers and incorporating them into a system of colonial governance, although the Moroccan elite shot down their initiative to formalize the corporation. The French ultimately used historic preservation and building codes to protect workers from the avarice of their social superiors, with the perpetuation of a premodern medina acting to foster an economy based on the communal organization of manual labor. In this way, the French appeased the working majority by blocking the modernizing tendencies of elite notables.

# 5

## The Colonial Preservation of the Miller's Trade

By marking water mills on its map of Fez, the conquering colonial army immediately acknowledged the strategic significance of local flour production. Lieutenant Colonel Orthlieb began to map the medina seven months after the signing of the Treaty of Fez in March 1912. He placed seventy-five boxed Xs on his map, each representing a water mill. Orthlieb detailed only the mills in heavily trafficked quarters of the medina, and not those tucked away in residential quarters, so this total represented only a fraction of the mills in operation. In the northeast quarter of Mokhfiyya, for example, his map did not include nine mills on the Oued Masmouda, which separated this residential quarter from a cemetery.[1] Nevertheless, each water mill identified by this military cartographer ground between one and three quintals of wheat each day, thereby constituting a productive capacity of as much as 7,500 kilograms of flour. These seventy-five mills would have provided flour for at least 22,000 people each day.[2]

French officials identified the water mill as an extant feature of Fez's medieval heritage. Lieutenant Henri Gouraud was stationed in Fez in the protectorate's early years, and thirty-seven years later he still remembered that "everywhere we heard the noise of water and of mills; there are thousands of them."[3] Prosper Ricard explained to the French tourists reading his *Guide bleu* that the sultan Youssef ben Tachfine (1063–1069) had "brought numerous workers from Spain to construct hydraulic mills like the present-day type."[4] In the early sixteenth century, Leo Africanus had counted all mills operating in Fez.[5] Citing this same number four centuries later, the director of the Department of Indigenous Arts and Industry emphasized that "there were 360 [mills] at the beginning of the protectorate."[6]

Despite this ahistorical conception of the water mill's immutable role in urban life, practical concerns sustained Ricard's nostalgic commemoration. He did not want modern machines to replace the water mill. In 1918, he lauded "the multitude of small millers ... who caused the failure of an enterprise offering to install a modern mill with cylinders in Fez."[7] Ricard did not provide details of this incident, but his comment appeared in an article, "Moroccan Labor and the Economic Role of Morocco after the War." For that reason, his observation suggests that the preservation of the water mill would serve colonial policies designed to employ Moroccans and to protect them from the dislocation of rapid modernization.

Water mills were a critical component of urban life, and so they were important to the French administrators in Fez. Precolonial attempts to mechanize flour production in Fez had not flourished. And yet, Charles René-LeClerc had predicted that machines would replace Fez's water mills seven years before the Treaty of Fez's signing. Once in power, however, French officials sustained the water mill, thereby ensuring local production of a dietary staple with traditional technology. If France was an industrial country, why did its colonial administrators preserve Fez's water mills? An analysis of flour production during the protectorate's first two decades highlights the advantages of preserving the urban reliance on the water mill, a more efficient means of employing and feeding Moroccans than industrial factories.

Wartime Investments in Water Mills

When statesmen in Paris mobilized French troops against Germany in August 1914, they inadvertently contributed to the preservation of the water mill in Fez. World War I blocked maritime trade, thereby impeding the delivery of goods from Europe. The war prevented the importation of flour from France, so some industrial mills in Morocco increased production between 1914 and 1919.[8] Fez, however, did not yet have an industrial mill when the war broke out. Until the signing of the Treaty of Versailles in June 1919, Moroccan millers produced flour for all residents of Fez, including European civilians.

From the outset of the war, the French implemented policies that revealed their intention to rely on Fez's water mills. It seems that some millers used sewage water not only to make their waterwheel turn but also to clean wheat before its passage through the grinding stones. The chief of municipal services passed a law that required all wheat to be cleaned in potable water. Ahmed Tazi, who oversaw Fez's hubus properties, then ordered any owner of a mill's miftah to construct canals that would bring clean water to a small pool outside a mill.[9]

Colonial administrators also repaired water mills, ensuring flour production at water mills for a long time to come. In the northern quarter of the medina, the Oued Zerhoul's strong current destroyed a column and an arch supporting a mill with two waterwheels in September 1914. Hubus controlled most shares of this property, with its Moroccan officials overseeing the mill's repair. The chief of municipal services visited the damaged mill with a French engineer, and the two officials agreed to cut off the neighborhood's water supply in order to expedite repairs. During the course of these repairs, workers restored a lock gate that had fallen into disuse, thereby improving the mill's productive capacity. The repairs cost 500 riyals (2,500 francs). Since the administrators of hubus property rented the mill for 30 riyals (150 francs) a month, they would not recoup the initial outlay for these repairs for one and a half years.[10]

This repair was not an isolated case. An arch supporting a mill on the Oued Rashasha fell in May 1915, damaging one mill's walls and ceiling. Once again, hubus officials oversaw repairs, and the chief of municipal services cut off water to facilitate them. When the municipal engineer discovered that the mill's foundation lay on a stone in the process of disintegrating, the municipality invested in improvements that would indefinitely extend the mill's life. They set aside 200 riyals (1,000 francs) in order to build a new foundation.[11] Since this mill rented for 18 riyals (90 francs) a month, it would need to operate for three years and two months before turning a postrepair profit.

Royal officials certainly foresaw continued profits in flour production. In March 1916, the Moroccan administrators responsible for managing royal domains repaired the Eddiban mill, where the annual processing of sixty mudds (1,260 kilograms) of flour allowed the muhtasib to set up grinding fees. One of three mills on Zanqat al-Ratal, a street in the southern half of the medina, the Eddiban mill had two waterwheels.[12] Royal officials ordered the reconstruction of a wall and of the terrace, which had recently fallen. They charged the Ministry of Religious Endowments for one-eighth of the cost, since it co-owned the mill.[13] The Moroccans responsible for property controlled by the Alaouites would not have made this investment of state funds if they foresaw an imminent end of water mills in favor of mechanized flour production.

Private investments underscore the return of water mills during World War I. Thami Ababou was chamberlain to Moulay Youssef.[14] Ababou's position in the makhzan provided him with critical insights into the wartime economy and projected postwar developments. One and a half years after

World War I's start, Ababou purchased the Bennani mill on the Oued Fejjaline. Located in the eastern quarter of Douh, this mill had two waterwheels. Ababou intended to buy the six-tenths of this mill controlled by the Department of Royal Domains. A Moroccan mason and carpenter placed a value of 2,400 riyals (12,000 francs) on the mill. Ababou negotiated a decrease of 400 riyals (2,000 francs), and Lyautey consented to the reduced price. Assuming that the resident-general would not allow an important Moroccan collaborator to make a bad investment, the sale provides evidence that the highest echelons of the French administration actively participated in the perpetuation of water mills.[15]

The wartime flourishing of water mills was further advanced by the need to supply flour to Fez's French residents. These foreign consumers preferred bread made of a finely ground flour of soft wheat. Moroccans referred to this flour as *farina*, an adaptation of the French term, which emphasized its foreign origins. Moroccan millers, unlike their industrial counterparts in France, produced flour from hard wheat, which was better suited to the semiarid climate of North Africa. That said, colonial officials did convince some Moroccan farmers to cultivate soft wheat during the war, but the protectorate sent the crop to France in order to forestall food shortages there.

Consequently, the war forced foreigners in Fez to purchase *khalis*, which, produced by Moroccan millers, was a mixture of finely ground flour of hard wheat and coarse leftovers. With Fez's supply of soft wheat running out in July 1917, the chief of municipal services ordered European bakers to add it to "indigenous" flour. Serving six hundred Europeans in Fez, the bakers began to mix a dough that was 30 percent hard wheat flour and 70 percent soft wheat flour.[16] It was hoped that this mixture of farina and khalis would make bread suitable to European tastes. Certainly, it would keep bread's price down, for soft wheat's wartime rarity in North Africa had led to an increase in its price.[17]

Anticipating a further depletion of Fez's supply of soft wheat, European merchants traveled to coastal cities in order to find a stable supply of farina from industrial mills.[18] The merchants, however, failed in their effort, and municipal officials predicted "a sharp increase in the consumption of hard wheat." Luckily, abundant rains had fallen during the winter months of 1917, so the Moroccan crop of hard wheat would be ample.[19]

To ensure the provisions of French civilians, this official counted on the water mills operated by Moroccans. "The indigenous mills," reported the chief of municipal services, "are endowed with a productive capacity that will sufficiently satisfy the needs of the [European] population."[20] If a French resident ate as much bread as the Moroccans, than each one of them needed 330 grams of flour a day. For this reason, wartime penury led Moroccan millers to increase production by 200 kilograms a day.

Given the increased need for Moroccan flour production, it is not surprising that hubus administrators reopened a water mill located next to the makina in Fez al-Jadid. The mill had become a hubus property in 1711, but, for reasons not specified in the records, the mill had stopped operating at the beginning of the nineteenth century. It was still dormant when Moulay Hassan built his arms factory in the 1890s, so workers there constructed an interior entrance to the mill, effectively enlarging his new industrial facility. A little over twenty years later, the chief of municipal services authorized the restoration of the water mill as a functional property.[21]

Rich Moroccans also invested in water mills during the war. Ahmed al-Moqri was the son of the grand vizier and former basha of Fez, so he had his finger on the pulse of the local economy. He decided to purchase the miftah of three mills in the northern quarter of Ras Djenan in spring 1918. His brother Taieb owned a generator that produced electricity for the medina, so this purchase represents a deliberate decision to invest in traditional technology and not modern machines.[22]

At the very same time, a British merchant also invested in water mills. Salvatore Gallos paid 2,600 riyals (13,000 francs) for the miftah of the mill as well as for its *i'qamat min al-zayri ila al-wadi* (equipment) and *i'qamat al-mal'ab* (tools). These mills were on the Oued Fejjaline of the Douh quarter, next to the British consulate. When informed of the impending sale, hubus officials expressed concern that Gallos would set up a machine. Local officials believed that a modern grinding machine at this mill, located upstream on one of the medina's principal canals, would pollute water used for public baths or ablutions in mosques. The chief of municipal services proved sympathetic to this concern, informing Gallos that he must provide legal assurance that he would do nothing to jeopardize Fez's potable water. Gallos signed the paper and came into possession of his water mills on 3 September 1918.[23] This foreign merchant recognized that water mills were a more attractive investment than mechanized grinding machines.

The Predicaments of Industrialization

Giuseppe Campini's lot exemplifies the difficulties of industrialization in colonial Morocco, for this Italian engineer continued his precolonial effort to install a machine in Fez that would mass-produce flour. Moulay Abdelhafid had ceded a royal water mill to him in 1910, and Campini intended to build a hydraulic turbine that would increase its productive capacity. Located upstream on a waterfall on the Oued Hamia, the water mill straddled one of the three most important sources of hydraulic energy in Fez.

French officials, much like precolonial sultans, wanted to oversee the modernization of milling. The French did not honor the contract with the deposed Moulay Abdelhafid, even though Campini had already imported equipment valued at 20,000 francs.[24] Instead, they took bids from other entrepreneurs, ones who would guarantee the daily production of fifty quintals of flour. According to Campini, these French officials deliberately precluded him from bidding, for they accepted proposals when he was out of town. The French awarded the contract to Charles Sabathier, a French industrialist from Algeria who promised—in vain, it turns out—to begin production within six months.[25]

At first, a shortage of money slowed down work on this industrial mill. Sabathier's contract required him to compensate Campini for the equipment already installed in the mill. Sabathier did not have 20,000 francs in cash, so he invited Campini to form an association with him. Under the terms of their agreement, they became equal partners, each required to invest 100,000 francs in the Societé Sabathier & Campini.

Then, a shortage of land slowed down work. Processing large amounts of wheat each day, industrial mills required a large structure for the milling equipment as well as silos for wheat and a warehouse for flour. The partners claimed the right to construct buildings in the gardens next to their mill. The consul of Spain prevented the partners from building on this land, claiming that a Spaniard possessed the rights to it.[26]

To avoid construction in these gardens, Campini and Sabathier asked for—and received—authorization from French officials to divert the *oued*, or river. By January 1914, when winter rains replenished the oued, they had changed the course of the water passing through the medina's canals. This deviation increased the water current upon which their mill depended, but it was not a well-planned venture. It also amplified the water flow against the mill's foundation to such an extent that the entire structure crumbled to the ground within a month.

Afterward, the mill needed substantial repairs, and the need for large amounts of money once again became an impediment to industrialized flour production. Since the municipality was responsible for Fez's water supply, Campini and Sabathier argued that it should pay for the oued's deviation and the subsequent damages to the mill. Citing faulty workmanship, French administrators insisted that the owners pay for the damage. Six months later, still waiting for a resolution, Sabathier informed Lyautey that the cost of repairs proved prohibitive for the partners, requiring the government to pay for the damage.[27] Lyautey was unmoved by the industrialist's arguments. In December 1916, he ruled that the protectorate would not pay the 150,000 francs demanded for repairs, especially since it seemed to him that the requested sum included money spent on the construction of Campini's private house.[28] Six years after Campini's initial contract with Moulay Abdelhafid, the mill had yet to produce any flour.[29]

Given this delay, the mill's equipment began to suffer from disuse. Campini had purchased many of the needed machines before the protectorate's establishment. The moisture of a major river like the Oued Fas is not conducive to storing anything metal, meaning that the equipment of water mills—made primarily of wood and stone—had an advantage over industrial mills. The machines purchased by Campini began to rust only six months after the foundation collapsed, leading the argumentative Sabathier to seek compensation from the protectorate.[30] Thus, industrial flour production required equipment susceptible to degradation, which, because the equipment was imported, proved difficult to replace.

Three years later, Fez's infrastructure again manifested itself as a factor inhibiting modernization. By 1919, Sabathier had died fighting in World War I, leaving Campini as the mill's sole owner.[31] After Sabathier's death, the Department of Public Works modified a contract between Campini and the Department of Royal Domains. The new contract awarded Campini the right to exploit a waterfall of seven meters for a period of twenty years—provided that the mill began operations within two years. Campini failed to fulfill this condition, which meant that his right to exploit the waterfall could be called into question.

The French Compagnie Fasi d'Electricité set its sights on Campini's waterfall. By 1919, it had begun to plan facilities where it could produce electricity for the burgeoning Ville Nouvelle. The Department of Public Works decided to modify the distribution of water in the medina.[32] In doing so, it confined Campini's mill to the use of a waterfall of only four meters, thereby breaking, at least in Campini's opinion, the contract with royal officials.[33] Anticipating a reduced milling capacity, French officials decreased Campini's annual rent from nine thousand francs a year to four thousand francs.³⁴ Campini, however, had already adjusted equipment for a waterfall of seven meters, so he prepared for yet another legal battle with the protectorate.

Other industrialists began to set up mills in Fez, although they experienced obstacles similar to those of Campini. Moïse Levy had received authorization to construct the Minoterie Levy in 1918. He ran out of cash in August, forcing a temporary halt on the construction of the industrial mill.³⁵ When he started work once again, he ordered equipment from an industrial mill in the French Alps.³⁶ This equipment would allow his mill to grind two hundred quintals of flour a day.³⁷ Like Campini, Levy counted on selling flour to the colonial army, and the director of military supplies agreed to provide wheat in order to ensure flour for troops in Fez.³⁸ Although Levy had set up his equipment and received an order, he could not operate his mill for another year. Levy's mill required electricity, so he could not begin operations until January 1920, when the Compagnie Fasi d'Electricité would open its electrical power plant on the oued.³⁹ And so, two years after he first received authorization to build his mill, Levy had yet to begin producing flour.⁴⁰

A certain M. Peres and M. Mohring built their industrial mill in Fez's Ville Nouvelle.⁴¹ Hoping to avoid difficulties in establishing the necessary infrastructure for their industrial mill, they set up their own turbine on the Oued Fas in order to produce their own electricity. Although the protectorate authorized this turbine, Campini opposed their use of a waterfall on the Oued Fas.⁴² Once again, lawsuits by Europeans threatened to slow down industrial flour production in Fez.

Above and beyond Campini's legal threats, the mill's projected launch did not go smoothly. Peres and Mohring planned to construct a building of four floors, which would certainly have been the tallest structure in Fez at that time. Such a large construction, however, required a lot of wood. This building material was in short supply in April 1919, and the partners needed to stop work until the municipality organized a delivery from the protectorate's forest service.⁴³

The importation of milling equipment also proved problematic. The partners purchased machines that produced three hundred quintals of flour a day.⁴⁴ In July 1919, however, striking dock workers in Marseilles caused an unanticipated delay in delivery of the machines.⁴⁵ The stevedores finally loaded the machines onto boats four months later. Unfortunately, the boat sank in the Mediterranean Sea.⁴⁶ Given all the difficulties in setting up industrial mills, it seems that an exclusive dependency on the mass production of flour would prove a risky venture for protectorate officials.

As was apparent in Campini's business strategy, these entrepreneurial endeavors did not affect local millers. In January 1920, Campini's mill began producing fifty quintals of flour a day, thus operating at one-third its capacity. Campini, however, made no effort to sell mass-produced flour to Moroccans who shopped in local markets. "Fez possesses indigenous grinding stones," he explained to Lyautey, "which are able to grind about three hundred quintals of wheat a day." Flour, he added, was found in "a quantity that is nearly sufficient for the city's needs." The colonial army, however, had grown from 84,000 soldiers in 1916 to 100,000 in 1919.[47] And the director of military supplies wanted all major cities in Morocco to have an industrial mill that could serve colonial troops.[48] Thus, the litigious Campini asked the resident-general to order fifty quintals of flour a day for colonial troops.[49]

## The Wheat Crisis, 1919–1920

The end of World War I brought on a new set of difficulties that obstructed the supply of wheat to Moroccan markets. Insufficient rains in December 1918 and January 1919 augured a poor harvest. Since the French had encouraged the cultivation of soft wheat in 1917 and 1918, colonial policy contributed to the wheat deficit. Soft wheat, after all, is less drought resistant than hard wheat. The signing of the Treaty of Versailles in June 1919 should have signaled the end of wartime penury, but instead the commandant of the region of Fez warned that the harvest was "very average."[50]

Massive purchases by the colonial army aggravated the wheat crisis. French officers got first choice of the new wheat, buying in bulk before any merchants or public officials. Sensitive to the lot of civilians, the officers avoided purchasing wheat in Fez's hinterland that year.[51] Their purchases, however, decreased the wheat supply of other regions, meaning Fez's officials could not find a supplier when their own region's wheat proved insufficient for the needs of urban residents.

France's wartime policies aggravated the wheat crisis long after the ratification of the Treaty of Versailles. France had addressed the high cost of staples on the continent by issuing more paper money. The resulting inflationary spiral decreased the value of the French franc in relation to its Moroccan counterpart, the peseta hassaniyya. Until 1919, these currencies had existed in relative parity to each other. By October 1919, however, due to the franc's instability, Fez's chief of municipal services reported that some Moroccan tradesmen refused the franc, accepting payment only in the peseta hassaniyya. Peasants and merchants alike feared losing money on the sale of wheat. Monetary instability, he specified, led to "a profound discontent [that] is appearing in the population."[52] The chief of municipal services blamed an absence of wheat in local markets on the "crisis of the hassaniyya."[53]

Just as in the precolonial era, a poor harvest led some Moroccans in Fez to hoard wheat. By spring 1919, wheat in Fez cost seventy francs a quintal, twice the price found in the markets of other Moroccan cities. Alfred de Tarde, the protectorate's director of civil affairs, blamed rich merchants for this inflated price, some of whom, he insisted, clung to a false hope that the protectorate would authorize its export to France.

To offset the resulting penury, the French purchased wheat with municipal funds. By filling the stalls of Fez's four rahabas, the municipality hoped to convince speculators that the price of wheat had leveled out and induce them to sell before losing money. Wheat from the harvest would usually appear in urban markets at the start of the summer, provoking the municipality to purchase wheat from the colonial army in June. Merely the rumor of this order's imminent arrival caused the price of wheat to drop forty francs a quintal.[54] Once in Fez, the chief of municipal services reported that "the sale of this wheat by the municipality was welcomed by the part of the population earning an average income, who felt that this initiative was an appropriate measure for defending them against speculators."[55] By September, wheat sold for only 32.50 francs a quintal.[56]

This purchase proved to be a temporary solution. By November, the chief of municipal services again expressed concern for Fez's diminishing wheat supply. The municipality had stocked 12,320 quintals of wheat, while wealthy residents, those with the means to purchase wheat in bulk, possessed another 8,300 quintals. To supply residents with flour, it was necessary to grind 400 quintals of wheat a day, so this stock would last only fifty-one days.[57] Fearing a shortage, the chief of municipal services asked his superiors to organize delivery of 20,000 quintals of wheat.[58]

The wheat shortage led French officials to impose new regulations on rich notables. In December, they inventoried wheat stored not only by merchants but also by private residents. The protectorate required the latter to make an official declaration of their wheat if they stocked more than one hundred mudds (2,100 kilograms).[59] After completing the inventory, officials congratulated wheat merchants for their honesty, but they condemned some private residents who harbored undeclared wheat stocks.[60] To manage the urban wheat supply more effectively, the chief of municipal services ordered all cereals to pass through four designated gates before transport to a rahaba.[61]

Afterward, the municipality helped working families and the poor to secure a supply of flour at a reasonable price. The municipality had found eight thousand mudds (168,000 kilograms) of wheat at the home of a resident identified only as a "Muslim notable." French officials set a fair price for it and then sold his stock to ordinary Moroccans. The chief of municipal services declared his desire to "calm the apprehensions of the indigenous population." He ensured a supply of cheap flour to designated shopkeepers who then retailed it to "people having only weak purchasing power and living from hand to mouth." The French sold wheat to workers and the poor for twenty-one francs per mudd (21 kilograms), nearly 20 percent less than its market price. Once again, these measures served more than a humanitarian purpose, for the French recognized "the political repercussions of the wheat crisis." In the opinion of the chief of municipal services, these initiatives decreased potential unrest by "sustaining the laboring class and the poor."[62]

Making a conscious effort to employ Moroccan millers, municipal administrators stocked wheat, not flour, during this crisis. The winter rains between November 1919 and January 1920 had again been insufficient. Anticipating a poor harvest, the chief of municipal services placed an order with the customs service for two thousand quintals of wheat in spring 1920. The customs service countered with an offer to send instead eight hundred quintals of flour and eight hundred quintals of semolina. To convince his immediate superior to intervene on his behalf, the chief of municipal services criticized the delivery of a preprocessed product. "This decision," he wrote, "deprives an interesting category of local industry of the benefits that it would have been able to earn by grinding 2,000 quintals of wheat."[63] In this way, municipal officials strove to maintain the water mills' profits.

The needs of French residents continued to increase the sales of Moroccan millers. The city's three European bakers ran out of farina in December 1919, compelling them to bake bread with khalis, or flour of hard wheat.[64] French residents wanted to import soft wheat from the United States, but the price, an exorbitant 165 francs, proved prohibitive, for it would have doubled the price of bread. Hearing this price, one French resident sang the praises of flour produced by Moroccan millers. "I make my own bread with indigenous flour," he boasted, "and these samples [that I brought with me] demonstrate that my bread is better than that of the [European] bakers." It is not clear if his swagger swayed the French commission, but its representatives did agree that "we will go without flour of soft wheat and be content with indigenous flour."[65] The next month, bakers in the Ville Nouvelle arranged to visit millers in the medina in order to secure access to flour of hard wheat.[66]

Moroccans invested in the construction of water mills during this wheat shortage, demonstrating its beneficial effects on local milling. In February 1920, a religious brotherhood decided to restore a dilapidated water mill in its possession. This mill was located on the Oued Draa el Djenan, outside of the southwest gates of Bab Hadid and Bab al-Jadid. The repairs cost 8,000 francs. Since the brotherhood did not have enough liquid assets to cover this investment, its administrators sold the rights to half a house in the southeastern Keddan quarter. Valued at 3,375 francs, the sale would cover only half of the required expenses, so the members of this brotherhood donated another 4,625 francs to settle the rest of the cost. Once renovated, they intended to sublet the mill for 150 francs a month, meaning it would operate four years and five months before turning a profit for the brotherhood.[67]

One advocate for foreign industrialists accused French officials of favoring Moroccan millers. An editorial in a newspaper expressed the resentment felt by French civilians:

> Turn, turn, little mill! This refrain that cradled our childhood no longer belongs to us. Here, the natives alone have the right to sing it in their language.[68]

In defending French civilians, the newspaper editorial revealed tensions between French officials and their civilian compatriots. The author believed that French officials favored Moroccan workers, a belief that highlights the productivity of water mills. "There is an absolutely unjust regime that we protest," sums up the author, "in asking the protectorate if there is some protection for French interests here." The protectorate, he continued, imposed regulations on industrial mills and vigilantly oversaw their business ventures, but Moroccans operated water mills without any restrictions.

The wheat crisis aggravated tensions between French industrialists and colonial officials. Since industrial mills ground between 150 and 300 quintals of wheat each day, their owners needed access to massive amounts of wheat. Colonial officials had earmarked 40,000 quintals of imported wheat for industrial mills, certifying their continued operation. But the cost of wheat from this stock was nearly a third more expensive than that found on the open market in July 1920, when prices dropped during the annual harvest. Thus, a French industrialist needed to grind wheat that cost 148 francs a quintal, even though the market price for wheat had fallen to 100 francs a quintal. The protectorate would not allow industrial mills to grind this cheaper wheat until the colonial stock was exhausted. For French industrialists, this policy created a vicious circle. The cost of wheat made their flour expensive, which, in turn, decreased sales, thereby forcing them to extend the period in which they used the stock.

Unlike French industrialists, Moroccan millers never needed to purchase massive amounts of wheat to ensure their mills' viability. Indeed, the undercapitalized Moroccan would have been hard pressed to do so. "There are hardly more than ten [millers]," noted one French traveler, "who have the necessary resources to make their purchase at an opportune moment and prepare reserves."[69] Such a commercial system, though clearly not based on surplus income, did offer nonnegligible benefits to craftsmen running a small-scale operation in a land prone to drought. Moroccan millers may not have bought massive amounts of wheat when its price fell, but, unlike industrial mills, they were not confined to stocking expensive wheat in order to ensure the continued operation of their mill. A number of Moroccan entrepreneurs recognized this advantage. Thus, the author of the editorial records that "many local facilities for processing palm fiber have been hastily transformed into mills operating at top speed, whereas our industrial mills are stopped."

Moroccan millers played an important role as agents of colonial stability. To forestall unrest, the French wanted to convince Moroccans that colonial rule did not change the fabric of their daily lives. In August 1920, when it seemed that the wheat crisis would continue for another year, the chief of municipal services purchased forty thousand quintals of hard wheat "for providing fresh supplies to indigenous mills and bakeries." In placing this order, this official did more than just guarantee the basic survival of Moroccans. He wanted to make sure that Moroccans could continue to prepare *kasra*, the round flat bread consumed by residents of the precolonial capital. By allowing Moroccans to perpetuate their food traditions, he pursued the protectorate's "political and economic interest in making sure that nothing changes in the customs of the Fassi population."[70]

By November 1920, the municipality had stocked 37,000 kilograms of wheat, while rich households possessed another 8,051 kilograms. Given the rate of consumption, this supply would last only until February. The four months that precede a harvest are a dangerous time because existing wheat supplies often run out before new crops mature. To allay popular concerns, the French earmarked more funds for wheat purchases.[71] In February 1921, the French gave them 60 kilograms of wheat each day.[72] The next month, they provided them with 100 kilograms of wheat, or 25 percent of Fez's daily need.[73] Commercial millers supplied flour to shopkeepers, who, in turn, retailed it to people without the means to buy wheat in bulk. By purchasing and distributing wheat, officials forestalled concerns over urban food supply and so forestalled popular unrest.

The Wheat Distribution of 1921

The municipality stocked a massive amount of wheat, so the plentiful winter rains that fell between November 1920 and January 1921 caused an unanticipated problem. Anticipating an end to the wheat shortage, speculators opened their storerooms. Wheat flooded the market, and the prices in the rahabas fell dramatically below those offered by the municipality.[74] To avoid a costly surplus, the chief of municipal services tried to sell 10,000 quintals of municipal wheat to the colonial army, which had a reputation for squandering money. At 160 francs per quintal, even the army found the price of the wheat too high. The director of military supplies wanted the municipality to reduce the price by 25 percent, to 133 francs per quintal. Fearing a budgetary loss, the chief of municipal services refused the offer.[75] Thus, the harvest led to a new problem, budgetary in nature, since Fez was left with 29,000 quintals of wheat.[76]

To resolve a costly miscalculation, French officials sought the support of Moroccan notables. The chief of municipal services wanted to force Fez's millers to buy the stock, even though market prices were now far below those of the municipal wheat.[77] Lyautey sent the director of customs to the majlis in order to explain the reasons for imposing this purchase. At that time, six members of the majlis were merchants, while another three made their living by farming rural properties.[78] For this reason, their initial opposition to the protectorate's plan does not seem surprising. Members of the majlis complained that "the closing of [market] doors would be a hindrance to commercial exchanges." In response, Lyautey's representative reminded urban notables that the municipality had purchased this wheat in order to place a cap on rising prices in the rahabas, an act that had improved the living conditions of Fez's residents. Given the unanticipated rains, the municipality was now in danger of losing money by selling its stock of wheat on the open market. After hearing his arguments, the majlis voted in favor of a temporary closing of markets to wheat from outside Fez.[79]

The director of civil affairs wanted European industrialists and Moroccan millers to grind the wheat. To convince them to operate at a loss, he argued that the municipality "had set up a stock of wheat with the goal of supplying European and indigenous mills of the city," further pointing out that "it would have been more convenient to deliver manufactured products." In other words, the protectorate had helped them to maintain their profits during the crisis, so this official called upon millers to grind the wheat stock despite its high cost. The distribution of municipal wheat was to be "proportional to the productive capacity of mills."[80]

In April, the chief of municipal services invited millers to discuss the situation. Campini and Levy attended the meeting, as did a representative of the Minoterie Oranaise. These industrialists met with Mohamed Mekouar and four other commercial millers from the medina. Mekouar came from a "dynasty of flour families." He had learned to be a master craftsman from his father and would in turn pass on this knowledge to his son Abdelaziz.[81] At that time, he was the millers' arif, and so represented the interests of the members of his trade. Fez's muhtasib, Driss al-Moqri, also attended. Just as in the precolonial era, the operation of water mills provided millers with the ability to consort with the city's political elite.

Municipal officials worked out an agreement to get rid of Fez's wheat stock between 15 April and 15 June, during which time millers would make no purchases at the rahabas. The Minoterie Oranaise had the greatest productive capacity of Fez's three industrial mills, so its representative agreed to grind 5,200 quintals of municipal wheat. Levy promised to grind 3,000 quintals of wheat at his mill, while Campini took responsibility for 2,000 quintals. Mekouar agreed that commercial millers would grind 7,200 quintals of municipal wheat. The muhtasib proposed selling the remaining 11,600 quintals of wheat to Moroccan households, which would ultimately go to custom millers. Charged with grinding 1,880,000 kilograms of wheat, the water mills of Fez had a productive capacity that surpassed their industrial counterparts by a ratio of two to one.[82]

The majlis split the wheat stock for sale in the medina's different quarters.[83] During the first week of June, the forcible sale of this wheat to private residents began in Fez al-Jadid. It was not only the Muslim residents who needed to purchase this wheat but also Jewish inhabitants of the mellah.[84] Moroccan officials could not finish the distribution before the ʿId al-Fitr holiday.[85] The chief of municipal services expressed concern that this pause would not allow them to complete the distribution before 20 June.[86] By that time, wheat from the harvest would begin streaming to urban markets.

French officials considered the distribution of municipal wheat an important initiative, but they did not want it to supersede programs of social welfare. Residents paid 35 francs for each mudd of wheat, the equivalent of 166 francs a quintal.[87] This price was more than twice the rate in the open market, where a mudd cost no more than 14 francs.[88] When the chief of municipal services learned that Moroccan officials were forcing all residents to buy at this price, regardless of their income, he went before the majlis to prevent further sales to indigent residents. He ordered representatives of each of the medina's neighborhoods to divide residents into four categories based on income. Afterward, they could exempt the poorest category from the purchase of municipal wheat.[89]

Due to this exemption, four thousand quintals of municipal wheat remained after the distribution.[90] Fearing unrest, the majlis indicated that "it would be bad policy to obligate the population of Fez to accept a new distribution." French officials, however, refused to lose money on the wheat. They implemented a fee of 5 francs on each quintal of wheat ground by Moroccan millers, allowing the municipality to collect 1,700 francs a day. The municipality would then recuperate the outlay for the wheat stock over the next seven months.[91] In this way, Moroccan millers proved critical in balancing the municipal budget and preserving urban stability.

In sharp contrast to Moroccan millers, European industrialists in Fez failed to fulfill their municipal obligations. The medina's water mills served a clearly defined local clientele who purchased flour on a daily basis. Given the small European population in Fez, it seems that industrial mills struggled to find buyers, especially since their mass-produced product was too expensive. By July 1921, the chief of municipal services reported that the Minoterie Oranaise refused to meet its obligation in regard to the 5,200 quintals of municipal wheat that its representative had promised to grind in April. Worse, in the eyes of the director of indigenous affairs, a representative of this industrial mill tried to strengthen its position against the colonial state by trying to convince Moroccan millers to protest the protectorate's costly policies.[92]

Campini also failed to fulfill his obligation. The owner of the Minoterie Campini insisted that the forced distribution of municipal stock hurt his business. At the end of July, he explained to the chief of municipal services:

> The perturbation of the flour market caused by the distribution of wheat caused me to suspend grinding at my mill on 1 June. Since I have yet to surmount difficulties in selling its flour, my mill has not yet begun to grind wheat once again.[93]

Campini, as the Minoterie Oranaise, could not grind the municipal wheat. His failure to do so provides more evidence that industrial mills were less efficient than water mills.

Campini operated his mill at a loss. The municipality stocked 4,312 quintals of its wheat in one of Campini's silos. French officials considered this a boon to the foreign entrepreneur, for he could freely use this stock and so avert the need to amass capital for large purchases in the wheat market.[94] Between 8 December 1920 and 1 June 1921, Campini ground 2,232 quintals of this wheat. His principal client was the department charged with the care of prisoners, which bought one-third of the flour produced during those months. The value of the wheat used by Campini was 233,083 francs, but he paid less than half of this sum by July 1921.[95] Apparently, the operational costs of Campini's enterprise exceeded his profits.

Campini mismanaged the wheat stock, increasing his debt to the municipality. During the municipal distribution, a French official found 458 quintals of wheat missing from his silo. Campini insisted that the discrepancy stemmed from an undue amount of stones in the wheat as well as a normal decrease in wheat's weight after it had been stored for a certain time. French officials, whether in the municipality of Fez or the capital of Rabat, did not find his excuse very persuasive. They charged him 75,318 francs for the missing wheat. By July 1921, Campini owed the municipality 250,596 francs, a substantial sum that the industrial entrepreneur insisted he could not pay.[96]

By the end of the wheat crisis, French officials lost patience with industrial entrepreneurs. Addressing Campini's excuses for his debt, the chief of municipal services extended his criticism to all industrial flour producers in his jurisdiction. He stated:

> I can no longer tolerate European millers, with whom we have played enough games this past year. With the presence of the municipal stock, they continue to believe that the municipality must support rather significant losses, as if it was itself a merchant.[97]

The need to grind massive amounts of municipal wheat should have given Fez's industrial mills a chance to demonstrate their worth, but they did not prove up to the task. The wheat crisis thus highlighted the advantages of water mills over machines.

## The Prosperity of Moroccan Millers, 1922–1929

By the end of the wheat crisis, another European discerned profits in the sale of flour to Fez's Moroccan population. In September 1921, the chief of municipal services reported that a foreigner had set up a mill in order to custom grind wheat for a local clientele. In seeking Moroccan customers, his enterprise differed from that of most European industrialists, who ground wheat for bulk orders. The Campini mill and the Minoterie Oranaise charged 10 to 12 francs per quintal for custom-ground wheat. The Minoterie Levy charged 8.75 francs. This European charged a more reasonable 8.40 francs per quintal.[98] In creating a small-scale business, he avoided the costly setup and operational pitfalls of industrial mills that mass-produced flour.

It proved difficult to operate industrial mills as a profitable venture in Fez. The cultivation of soft wheat grew from 24,000 hectares to 275,000 hectares in the course of the 1920s, which should have boded well for industrial mills. In 1923, however, France established a quota system that permitted soft wheat from Morocco to enter it duty free. Market prices in France proved more advantageous than those in Morocco, increasing the export of soft wheat. The rarity of soft wheat in Moroccan markets inflated its price, augmenting production costs at industrial mills. That year, a quintal of soft wheat flour sold for five francs more than hard wheat flour produced at a water mill.[99] The protectorate set up subsidies to prevent the collapse of industrial milling, demonstrating, once again, the heavy cost of modernization for the colonial state.[100]

Nevertheless, the foreign entrepreneur who custom ground wheat did not offer Moroccans a financial incentive for having their wheat ground at his mill. Custom millers in the medina charged 7.35 francs for each quintal of wheat ground at a water mill. Part of this payment was in kind, not cash, proving advantageous for struggling Moroccan consumers. Custom millers collected 2.90 francs in cash, but the rest of the payment was the chaff, which weighed as much as eighteen kilograms per quintal.[101] When a miller ground wheat that was damp, not dry, he increased the yield of chaff by 20 percent.[102] In grinding three quintals of wheat each day, a custom miller could count on receiving payments of at least 661.50 francs each month.

Commercial millers purchased their own wheat, with their profits reflecting the difference between the cost of wheat and the market price for products produced from it. When millers ground wheat, they produced chaff, semolina, and two grades of flour. The two grades of flour were the finely ground *zrif* and the roughly ground *quwayshi*. Most residents of Fez preferred to prepare bread with khalis, a mixture of two parts zrif and one part quwayshi. The remaining quwayshi could be sold as inferior flour. To evaluate the rate of extraction, the muhtasib and the miller's arif oversaw the grinding of sixty mudds (1,260 kilograms) of wheat each summer. This wheat generated approximately 190 kilograms of chaff and 120 kilograms of semolina. It produced more of the rough flour than its finer counterpart. In this instance, there were approximately 494 kilograms of quwayshi and 456 kilograms of zrif.[103] Thus, the rate of extraction was the following: 15 percent chaff, 10 percent semolina, 39 percent quwayshi, and 36 percent zrif. To sell it, the commercial miller paid a fee to the shopkeeper, who sold his flour to Moroccan consumers in the medina.[104] Based on the price of hard wheat in May 1923, commercial millers could count on a return of between 17 percent and 25 percent from the sale of these various milled products.

The number of Moroccans practicing the miller's trade reflected the water mill's ability to provide jobs for local residents. Protectorate officials counted 320 millers in Fez in 1923.[105] Each master craftsman would need at least three workers in his mill, so this trade employed about 960 men. Industrial mills could not ensure the same number of jobs for Moroccans. Campini's mill, for example, even when grinding its maximum capacity of 150 quintals a day, employed only forty Moroccans.[106] Milling more than 31,000 kilograms of wheat each day, commercial transactions (not profits) made by Moroccan millers would surpass six million francs that year.[107] Thus, the protectorate recognized the milling trade as being among "a few that conserve their social importance by virtue of their members' civic value [*qualité*] and the situation of their fortune."[108]

French officials made no significant changes in the nature of milling in the medina, enabling dynasties of flour families to continue grinding wheat at water mills. In the mid-1920s, Abdelkabir ben Hachim al-Kittani wrote that the Bou Taher family "is known in Fez for milling," specifying that his contemporaries in this family were the third generation of millers.[109] In a like manner, al-Arbi Ouali passed down the miller's trade to his sons. Ouali learned this trade at his father's mill in Bzam Barquqa in the late nineteenth century. He would set up his own mill in the Laayoune quarter, training his son to be a miller.[110] The Baraicha family also continued to practice the miller's trade as they had done since the mid-eighteenth century. Abdelwahed Ouali identifies the Baraichas as one of the most important families practicing this trade as he was growing up.[111] Three members of this family operated different mills in the Laayoune quarter, each with a single waterwheel.[112]

The milling industry provided employment opportunities for rural migrants in the 1920s. Hadj Mohamed Filalli "Terras" was born into an Arab-speaking tribe near the southern city of Rashadia. His mother died when he was young, and his father afterward moved the family to Fez. His family arrived in 1927, when Hadj Mohamed was seven years old. His father worked as a porter in one of Fez's rahabas. Immigrants from the southern region of Tafilalet monopolized this trade in Fez.[113] Working in grain markets, his father must have met many millers. One of these millers, Hadj Djilalli al-Fayda, ran a mill at Bayn al-Madun. Al-Fayda was training his two nephews, but he also took on Hadj Mohamed as an apprentice.[114] By investing time and money in training these three boys, it seems that al-Fayda not only did a brisk business but also anticipated the trade's growth.

Incidents of crime draw attention to the value of the agricultural commodity with which Fez's millers worked. The price of hard wheat had stabilized by 1923, selling for eighty francs a quintal, nearly half its cost at the height of the wheat crisis.[115] That year, abundant winter rains promised a good harvest.[116] Despite the favorable prices, the chief of municipal services reported several cases of wheat theft in the medina. Some thefts occurred as the harvest approached, when wheat was plentiful and relatively cheap. In May and June, this French official reported two incidents of stolen wheat.[117] The thefts also occurred in the winter months, when wheat's relative rarity made it more expensive. In December and January, he reported three more incidents of stolen wheat.[118] Wheat was always a sought-after commodity with a value for ordinary Moroccans.

In fact, some street children formed gangs targeting peasants who sold the fruits of their labor in Fez. Lahcen ben Ahmed Sanhadji had left his village to sell his wheat in Fez's urban markets, but he took a nap at Bab

Rabiba before returning to his village. While sleeping, one hundred francs were stolen from his money purse. Sanhadji did not report the theft until he learned that several other peasants were targeted in a similar manner. According to testimony given to the basha, Sanhadji had seen children watching him before he fell asleep. After an investigation, the basha ordered the arrest of two young "hoodlums," who, according to this neighborhood's Moroccan representative, "would spend all their time in the street."[119]

The basha found at least one Moroccan miller complicit in a conspiracy to launder stolen wheat. In July 1925, a fight over a sack of wheat raised the suspicions of the Moroccan representative of the Taala quarter. At that time, the Rif War, then only forty kilometers from Fez, threatened the transport of wheat to the city. Recognizing his distinctive sack, a merchant identified the wheat as part of his stock. He accused an employee guarding his warehouse of stealing the wheat. The employee admitted his guilt and identified three accomplices, including the miller El Hadi ben Mohamed Slaoui. Apparently, the men responsible for stealing wheat brought their ill-gotten gains to him for grinding, so Slaoui must have been a commercial miller who managed his own mill. In this way, he could grind the stolen wheat without notice and then sell it at a shop in the medina. In fairness to Slaoui's posthumous reputation, Rabat's Court of Appeals overturned the basha's ruling.[120] Still, the accusations—and the basha's willingness to believe them—highlight the role played by millers in the stabilization of the wheat market, a key component of the local economy.

Whether or not these accusations were accurate, the fallout from misconduct at a water mill could not compare with the effects of an industrial mill's mismanagement. Giuseppe Campini died on 23 January 1924, and his son Umberto took over his business. By 1925, this mill had incurred a large debt to various offices of the protectorate, owing 239,000 francs to the municipality for the mill's failure to fill contractual obligations during the wheat crisis. Umberto also needed to pay 73,549 francs for back taxes and rental of a royal property as well as 400,000 francs to private lenders. These debts made it more difficult for the mill to operate at a profit, which, in turn, made it impossible to pay off the debts. Umberto did not have ready cash, so he could not stock wheat when its price was lowest.[121] Much like Moroccan millers, he purchased wheat as needed. His industrial mill, however, produced fifty times more flour a day than a water mill. This difference in scale meant that he needed to sell a larger volume of flour and in a market where other industrial mills had purchased wheat at more advantageous prices. This case of industrialization provided no obvious benefits either for consumers, who paid too much for flour, or for the state, an implicit partner through loan defaults.

Under Umberto's management, the Campini mill continued to demonstrate the disadvantages of relying on industrial facilities in a semiarid land, especially when managed by Europeans with a propensity for lawsuits. The Rif War led the colonial army to increase troops in the region of Fez. The military had wheat custom ground at Campini's mill, which should have been a piece of good fortune. That summer, however, was dry, and the flow of water through the medina's canals decreased. Campini's mill could operate no more than six hours a day.

Umberto blamed the Compagnie Fasi d'Electricité for his mill's productive woes. This company was planning to construct a thermoelectric couple, a device producing electrical force by heating metallic conductors.[122] Once realized, it would increase the production of electricity over the turbine then being used and concomitantly decrease the need for the water. In the meantime, the dry summer meant that Campini's water current was being utilized by the electric company. In contrast, water mills did not require as strong a current, and they continued to operate without problems. The decreased water current led Campini to inform the military that he could not custom grind the wheat that it had stocked in his silo. Campini threatened to sue both the electric company and the municipality, claiming a loss of two thousand francs over the course of four months.[123]

Fire destroyed Campini's mill on 10 September 1925.[124] A water mill serving urban residents ground only 3 quintals a day, but Campini's mill processed 150 quintals. If this industrial mill had been serving urban residents, the fire would have caused a severe flour shortage, especially since its silos, which also burned to the ground, stocked 320,000 francs worth of wheat.[125] If the industrial mill had been a water mill, repairs might have cost only 2,500 francs. At Campini's mill, even with insurance, the damages caused by the fire made its repair prohibitive, for the building and stored wheat was valued at 1,720,000 francs.[126] The mill's destruction revealed the danger of industrializing flour production intended for urban markets, for the absence of flour would surely have led to economic chaos and political unrest.

The danger of a flour shortage was brought home the next year, when drought led to rural famine and an influx of indigent migrants in Fez. By summer 1925, flour of hard wheat cost 290 francs a quintal, two and half times its price three years earlier.[127] The French estimated a need for 175,000 quintals of wheat during the winter and the spring.[128] There was an absolute absence of wheat, as opposed to the wheat crisis, at which time urban, not rural, dearth had caused high prices in Fez. For this reason, the chief of the economic office reported that "it is necessary to envision the replacement of semolina and flour of hard wheat for the indigenous population in the cities."[129] Much like precolonial patterns of consumption, drought caused a conjunctural reliance on industrial mills. Fez's chief of municipal services reported that "the indigenous population consumes, beside flour coming from local indigenous mills, some flour sold by European industrial mills of Fez and Meknes."[130]

The purchase of soft wheat flour from industrialized mills, however, did not supplant the work of Moroccans operating water mills in the medina of Fez. Paul Odinot highlighted this commercial reality in his book *Le monde marocain* (The Moroccan World). As an officer in the French army, Odinot had come to Morocco in 1912, working for the Department of Indigenous Affairs. He had a somewhat unique perspective on the social and economic conditions of this colonized kingdom, for his wife was Moroccan. Even if some Moroccans relied on flour of soft wheat during the drought, he did not predict the demise of the water mill. "I hardly see," he asserted, "that indigenous millers must capitulate little by little before the large modern mills." He based his observation on the fact that "nearly all European industries in Morocco are only installed to respond to the needs of Europeans," identifying this commercial strategy as a "great danger." Recognizing the numeric superiority of Moroccan consumers, he believed that "the European industries only have a chance at prosperity if they win over the indigenous clientele."[131] Local markets remained a key to commercial success, so the water mill remained a profitable venture.[132]

The owners of industrial mills did not heed his advice, so the protectorate needed to implement policies designed to protect flour production at their facilities. Once the drought ended, France's quota system still led most farmers in Morocco to export their crops of soft wheat to France. Between January and August 1928, 1,400,000 quintals of Morocco's tender wheat entered French markets.[133] Thus, the operational costs of industrialized milling remained high in Morocco, as did the price of mass-produced flour. Two years later, a global wheat surplus threatened to cause new problems for millers in Morocco, both European industrialists and local craftsmen. This surplus threatened to cause a flood of imported wheat and flour, leading French officials to ban the import of wheat, flour, and semolina.[134] In this way, local consumers would not be tempted to favor cheap products from abroad. Favoring producers over consumers, this policy maintained an equilibrium between European industrialists and Moroccan millers, an equilibrium that would last until the global recession and local drought of the 1930s.

## Conclusion

During the first seventeen years of the protectorate, water mills outperformed the industrial facilities operated by European entrepreneurs. Running a small-scale business, the medina's Moroccan millers produced on a daily basis as much flour, if not more, as any one industrial mill in Fez. The water mills transformed the existing water supply of this semiarid land into an effective source of energy, while industrial mills, powered by electricity, required substantial changes to the urban infrastructure. Water mills, unlike industrial mills, operated at a profit and without state subsidies. Further, Moroccan millers were unofficial agents of colonial stability. If Moroccans consumed flour of hard wheat, they would not, or so the French hoped, associate colonial rule with drastic change. The water mill also generated jobs for some Moroccan workers. Some modernizing efforts under the protectorate may have been inevitable since France was an industrial country. And yet, the French established policies that preserved flour production at water mills. In this way, their adaptation of industrial modernity to a Moroccan context built upon precolonial policies. In both the precolonial and colonial periods, the state implemented policies that allowed traditional technology to flourish alongside modern machines.

# 6

# Fiscal Politics at the Municipal Slaughterhouse

Methods of French butchery threatened to create political tensions in colonial North Africa. At the turn of the twentieth century, seventy years after the French colonized Algeria, Morocco's eastern neighbor, the lyrics of a popular folksong denounced the colonial overlord because its rulers forced Muslims to use the byproducts of animals that were not slaughtered according to Islamic law. Algerians recounted:

> They will flood our market with their impure products. The sugar they will sell us will be bleached through a process using bones of forbidden animals [such as pigs, and animals not killed according to the Muslim ritual]. They will mix lard with their butter. The candles we light to our saints are made with pork [fat] and wax, and the soap they sell us is adulterated. We can no longer live in a state of purity; our prayers are no longer valid. Our body, soiled in more than one way, is but a mass of impurities.[1]

In this way, slaughter became a means for some Algerians to advance a persuasive cultural argument against French rule.

As demonstrated by a group of merchants living in England, Moroccans also hesitated to consume meat or animal byproducts that were not licit for Muslim consumption. Mohamed al-Hajoui traveled to Manchester in 1919, where he visited friends from Fez. As the grand vizier's delegate for public education, al-Hajoui oversaw all schools in Morocco teaching Islamic law. He was a respected legal scholar, and these wealthy merchants plied him with questions regarding their consumption of meat from livestock slaughtered by British butchers. They were concerned because this foreign city had no Muslim butchers to recite "bismallah" before sacrificing an animal.

One of al-Hajoui's interlocutors refused to buy meat from Christians, frequenting instead kosher butcher shops. Al-Hajoui was knowledgeable on the issue of sacrifice and slaughter, having published an essay entitled "Why It Is Permitted to Slit the Throat of Animals Even Though This Action Is Against the Principles of Humanity and Compassion."[2] He assured this man that Islamic law permitted Muslims to eat meat from animals slaughtered by Christians because they, like Muslims and Jews, were monotheists. Making an oblique reference to modern slaughterhouses, he also remarked that meat from livestock slaughtered by Christians, unlike that of Jews, who adhered to premodern rites and practices, was "clean and good for the health." Despite the esteemed jurist's arguments, this resident of Fez was not convinced that Islamic law permitted him to eat meat sold by foreign butchers. Favoring concerns for his spiritual well-being over his physical health, al-Hajoui's interlocutor henceforth refused to eat any meat at all.[3]

French administrators in Morocco wanted to allay the cultural concerns of consumers of meat in local markets. By the time al-Hajoui visited Manchester, the French had constructed a municipal slaughterhouse in Fez. To forestall resistance to colonial rule, they ensured that this new facility adhered to standards established by Islamic law. The purchase of *hallal* meat by Muslims would do more than further the policy of association that facilitated political calm. Because the municipality collected a tax on each animal slaughtered by butchers, the purchase of meat in local markets increased colonial revenue.

French policies had repercussions far beyond their administrative and fiscal intentions. Administering public facilities and collecting taxes were seemingly trivial accoutrements of bureaucratic modernity. Nonetheless, the colonial regulation of the meat industry transformed the way that the social classes of Fez conducted daily life. During the first seventeen years of the protectorate, colonial policies allowed increasing numbers of Moroccans to consume meat, historically a luxury item that simultaneously embodied power.

## Legitimizing Lyautey's Colonial Regime

Through the celebration of the Great Sacrifice, meat played a central role in legitimizing the French protectorate. In August 1912, Resident-General Lyautey forced the abdication of Moulay Abdelhafid, appointing his brother Moulay Youssef as sultan in his stead. Three months later, Morocco celebrated ʿId al-Kabir for the first time as a colonized kingdom. To prevent political discontent, Lyautey drew upon models of sultanic leadership in order to generate a sense of continuity with the precolonial past. The resident-general expressed his intention to celebrate this holiday "with an unaccustomed brilliance and following the traditions abandoned since the death of Moulay Hassan."[4]

Despite Lyautey's intentions, Moulay Youssef's initial celebrations of ʿId al-Kabir highlighted the sultan's weak claim to political legitimacy. In November 1913, Moulay Youssef sacrificed on behalf of the Moroccan people for the second time. He performed this sacrifice in Rabat, which Lyautey had designated as the capital of the French protectorate. It seems that the new sultan had yet to win popular support among the urban masses, for few local residents attended his public sacrifice. Moulay Youssef also failed to gain the support of the kingdom's political elite. A delegation of urban notables from Rabat, for example, attended the sultan's public sacrifice, but they skipped the hadiyya, when the presentation of gifts provided tangible evidence of their loyalty to the sultan. Notables from other regions in Morocco did attend this ceremony, but a French official later reported that the gifts offered by them were "insignificant in cash and kind." The sultan expressed particular disappointment that he had not received any horses.[5]

The celebration of this holiday in October 1914 did not strengthen Moulay Youssef's hold on the popular imagination. According to Lyautey, "The holiday of Aid took place in Rabat with a distinct lack of brilliance and even of standard formalities."[6] The public turnout was even lower than the previous year. Several dozen cavaliers showed up, but Lyautey described this military presence as "the most miserable." Moulay Youssef received six horses, but, in Lyautey's opinion, they were all "in such a pitiful state that they should not even have been offered." Embarrassed by his subjects' disregard, Moulay Youssef used a rainstorm as an excuse for canceling the ceremonies. According to the resident-general, this public celebration "gives rise to differences of interpretation and uncertainties that led to such an abstention of the indigenous population and such a decrease in the *hadiyya* that the sultan felt a considerable disappointment and a serious discontent."[7]

Lyautey decided to amplify future celebrations of ʿId al-Kabir in order to strengthen the sultan's tenuous claim to the Moroccan throne and to give the appearance that an Alaouite continued to rule Morocco, now a colonized kingdom. The day after the disappointing celebration, Lyautey stated, "Given the reduction of the sultan's political attributes, it is all the more necessary to maintain his representative side and the brilliance of demonstrations of a religious order, of which the most important is 'Id al-Kabir. It is the only means of safeguarding his prestige and his moral authority in the eyes of natives."[8]

Lyautey believed that these celebrations would legitimize not only the sultan whom he had appointed but also France's role in this North African kingdom. It would, in his opinion, "show to the indigenous population our respect for traditions."[9]

When Moulay Youssef sacrificed on behalf of the Moroccan people the following year, French and Moroccan officials choreographed the public ceremonies. Lyautey ordered Henri Gaillard, the secretary-general of the Cherifian government, to meet with Si Kaddour ben Gharbrit, an Algerian whom the French had appointed as the sultan's chief of protocol. Three weeks before the Great Sacrifice, these two officials would begin planning the royal celebration of 'Id al-Kabir.[10] The resident-general expected each city and tribe under French control to send a delegation of notables to witness the royal sacrifice.

The gifts presented to the sultan were supposed to demonstrate fervent support for Moulay Youssef. For this reason, the resident-general passed a decree that forced municipal administrators to allocate the funds necessary for the presentation of gifts offered to the sultan at the hadiyya ceremony following the sultan's public sacrifice. Lyautey even chose the gift that each delegation would offer to their ruler. Fez's representatives needed to give Moulay Youssef four horses. To foster a more ostentatious display of loyalty, Lyautey wanted four hundred cavaliers to accompany this equine tribute.[11] One French official had argued that Moroccans would attend the public sacrifice in greater numbers if these horsemen performed tricks.[12] In case people did not attend, the basha of Rabat began ordering urban residents to attend the sultan's sacrifice.[13] In this way, the protectorate's officials ensured an appropriate display of loyalty by the political elite and the masses.

Fez was still an imperial capital as well as Morocco's spiritual center, so French officials declared an intention "to enhance the prestige of the *khalifa* and the *basha* when they participate in public ceremonies."[14] There, the sultan's khalifa sacrificed a ram in Moulay Youssef's stead. Fez's three magistrates accompanied the khalifa from Fez al-Jadid to the royal musalla. Representatives of the Qarawiyyin Mosque called the faithful to the prayer of 'Id al-Kabir. The French chief of municipal services attended the ceremony next to urban notables and tribal delegations. In 1915, the Department of Indigenous Affairs reported that "everyone swore that they had not seen the like in past years."[15] The subsequent distribution of funds to religious scholars led another official to claim that "the generous gesture of the sultan, which should be repeated at each religious festival, was highly appreciated by the population of Fez, which sees anew a proof of the return to the old traditions of Moulay Youssef's ancestors."[16]

The al-Fassi family had been responsible for preaching the 'Id sermon since the reign of the sultan Moulay Abderrahman (1822–1859), so their participation in this ceremony was critical for the legitimization of Moulay Youssef's authority. When the French established the protectorate, Si Abdallah al-Fassi had already preached in the royal musalla for sixteen years, sacrificing a ram next to both Moulay Abdelaziz and Moulay Abdelhafid. In fact, Si Abdallah penned the oath of loyalty to Moulay Youssef after Lyautey deposed his brother, so he proved amenable to yet another fraternal transfer of power. Recognizing Si Abdallah's influence, Moulay Youssef promoted him to the position of Fez's assistant khalifa, and as such he would work directly under the sultan's brother Moulay al-Mehdi.[17]

This new position might require him to sacrifice in Moulay Youssef's stead, so Si Abdallah stopped leading prayers for 'Id al-Kabir. The colonial government then passed this job to Si Abdallah's brother Si Abdelwahed, also a religious scholar, thus continuing a tradition of having a member of the al-Fassi family lead the prayers of 'Id al-Kabir.[18] By ensuring that a member of the al-Fassi family led the holiday prayers, the ceremony downplayed the political change wrought by the colonial regime.

Moulay Youssef returned to Fez for 'Id al-Kabir in 1916, when Moulay Ahmed Al Raisuni questioned his authority as sultan. A religious scholar as well as a member of the shurafa', Al Raisuni had already challenged the sultan's three predecessors. Moulay Hassan had jailed this royal contender, who remained in prison until 1899. Moulay Abdelaziz freed him, but Al Raisuni then engaged in activities that destabilized the sultan's reign. He kidnapped foreigners, including an American, which led the United States to threaten military intervention. To win over Al Raisuni, Moulay Abdelaziz made him basha of Tangier. Al Raisuni, however, supported his brother's bid for power in 1907. Once sultan, a grateful Moulay Abdelhafid made Al Raisuni basha of Asilah.[19]

Al Raisuni still held this post in 1913, when Spain conquered the northern region and set up a system of direct rule. It was this system of governance that caused Al Raisuni to take up arms against the foreign conqueror, for it curtailed his power. The Spanish released prisoners placed in Asilah's jails by Al Raisuni, who responded with a reference to Christian modes of slaughter. "You have no more right to meddle with our traditions and our customs," he told the commander of Larache, "than I have to tell you that the food you eat is unclean."[20] Preparing for war against Spain, he began stockpiling weapons.

By 1916, Al Raisuni established himself as not only an opponent of the Spanish but also a contender for royal authority in the French protectorate. His supporters had designated him "Sultan of the Jihad."[21] As he later explained to his British biographer Rosita Forbes, many Moroccans wanted him to take control of the kingdom because they believed that Moulay Youssef was "in the hands of the French."[22] Al Raisuni seemed willing to accept the royal mantle and thus to act on behalf of his Moroccan subjects. As he told Forbes, he wanted to protect "the rights of the people, for they were my people."[23]

In 1916, Al Raisuni did not celebrate 'Id al-Kabir on the same day that Moulay Youssef sacrificed on behalf of Moroccans. Al Raisuni insisted that Moulay Youssef had failed to distinguish the beginning of the lunar month of Dhu'l-Hijja, which, according to his calculations, should have begun a day later, on 30 September. By accusing the sultan of sacrificing on the ninth rather than the tenth day of Dhu'l-Hijja, Al Raisuni undermined the sultan's religious authority, the lynchpin of his temporal power. Five days before 'Id al-Kabir, one French official predicted that most people in the north would not sacrifice their ram until the day after the sultan's public celebration.[24]

Moulay Youssef parried this political challenge by sacrificing in Fez, not Rabat, just like his forebears. Moulay Youssef's representative in Tangier advised the sultan to publicize his sacrifice in Tangier's Great Mosque. He told the sultan to send a letter to be read there that "would inform the inhabitants of Tangier, according to the custom practiced by his predecessors, of his entry in Fez."[25] According to one French administrator, thirty thousand Moroccans witnessed the sultan's sacrifice in Fez, including ten thousand cavaliers loyal to Moulay Youssef.

The celebration of 'Id al-Kabir in Fez communicated Moulay Youssef's control not just over his Moroccan subjects but also over the protectorate's French officials. The French diplomatic agent in Tangier celebrated the holiday in Fez, afterward making a very public appearance at Moulay Youssef's palace. There, the sultan welcomed him as "our principal collaborator in the northern region of this empire." Lyautey also went to Fez in order to pay his respects to the sultan. He told Moulay Youssef: "It is the first time in recent memory that this holiday is celebrated in Fez among such a show of highly placed persons and a population coming from all points of the empire."[26]

The following year, Tangier's population again celebrated the Great Sacrifice a day later than the sultan. At that time, colonial authorities adopted a different strategy for dealing with the opposition. Moulay Youssef celebrated 'Id al-Kabir in Rabat that year. The French, however, made sure that Tangier's basha attended the sultan's sacrifice. Lyautey understood the significance of this notable's presence. When he hosted a dinner for Morocco's political elite, he announced to his guests that "the sultan had to be particularly sensitive to the presence among you today of the basha of Tangier."[27] To avoid similar recriminations in the future, French administrators invited regional authorities to inform the sultan's chamberlain of their sighting of the moon that marked the first day of the month of Dhu'l-Hijja.[28] The strategy was successful. Al Raisuni would never again make a strong claim to Moroccan leadership, and the Spanish defeated his forces in 1922.[29]

In 1925, Moulay Youssef again celebrated 'Id al-Kabir in Fez, with his public sacrifice then highlighting his power in face of a challenge by Mohamed ben Abd al-Karim. Originally from the Rif mountains, Abd al-Karim was a disillusioned magistrate in Melilla who, arguing for a stricter interpretation of Islamic law, began to organize a revolt against the Spanish protectorate in 1921. Indeed, the beginning of the Riffian revolt diverted Spain's attention from Al Raisuni, inadvertently saving the remnants of his forces. Abd al-Karim led a very large military force. During the first year of the revolt, his army defeated foreign troops near Melilla, an engagement that left dead more than ten thousand Spanish soldiers. As Abd al-Karim extended territorial control throughout the northern regions, he appointed officials to manage a new state administration.[30]

In organizing the Great Sacrifice in 1923, colonial officials revealed a fear that this rebel, looking to secure supply routes, had already gathered supporters in the region of Fez and Taza. The French insisted that Moulay Youssef invite the sons of Si Mohamed ou Belkacem Azeroual to his public sacrifice in Rabat.[31] Officials identified this member of the shurafa' as the most important religious authority in the region of Taza. The French wanted to retain Azeroual's support, so they ordered the sultan to give his sons a private interview. They also advised the sultan to present each of them with a *burnus*, a cape worn during the winter months.[32] In highlighting royal esteem for Azeroual, the French hoped to prevent the defection of this holy man, whose loyalty would legitimize Moulay Youssef's rule.

By 1924, this rebel adapted one of the sultan's honorary titles to suit his role in the nascent polity. Sultan Moulay Youssef was the Amir of the Believers, and Abd al-Karim styled himself as the Amir of the Rif.[33] The next year, an American reported that Abd al-Karim's followers referred to him simply as "the Sultan."[34] The use of this title led Lyautey to acknowledge the religious threat to Moulay Youssef's temporal power:

> 'Abd el Krim is overtly regarded as a sultan, the first sultan of Morocco since Abd el 'Aziz [because] Moulay Hafid has sold his country to France through the protectorate treaty and Moulay Youssef is no more than our puppet. ['Abd el-Krim's] name is said in prayers ... in the Rif, for the first time since the [establishment of the] Protectorate they have ceased mentioning the name of Moulay Youssef in prayers.[35]

In this way, the revolt led by Abd al-Karim, much like that of Al Raisuni, did more than challenge the foreign conquerors; it also questioned the very foundation of Moulay Youssef's rule.

As Fez prepared for 'Id al-Kabir in 1925, Abd al-Karim's claim to sultanic power threatened Moulay Youssef's control over Fez, the city considered the seat of royal authority. By June, the rebel's army was camped only forty kilometers from its gates. In Rabat, rumors circulated that Abd al-Karim would synchronize his offensive with 'Id al-Kabir, entering Fez in time to carry out a public sacrifice on behalf of Moroccans.[36] Abd al-Karim's diplomatic overtures to Fez's religious scholars substantiate this rumor. Two days before the public sacrifice would take place, the Riffian commander directed an open letter to the head of the Qarawiyyin Mosque. In this letter, he argued that "since all other Moroccan leaders had failed, he, bin Abd al-Karim, was the only one who was entitled to be sultan."[37]

Given this challenge, Moulay Youssef informed Lyautey that he would celebrate the Great Sacrifice in Fez that year.[38] Fez's religious scholars, so keenly courted by Lyautey and Moulay Youssef since 1912, did not rally to Abd al-Karim's cause, and the sultan's public sacrifice went off without a hitch. Since Lyautey wanted this ceremony to reinforce the pretense that France served the Moroccan sultan, he and his military commanders attended the ceremonies, saluting the sultan on the parade grounds where his father, Moulay Hassan, had once received foreign emissaries.[39] The sultan Moulay Youssef demonstrated to all, whether residents of Fez or rebels in its hinterland, that he was the one to exercise authority over the city considered to be Morocco's historic center of royal authority.

The sultan's presence in Fez may have reassured his Moroccan subjects, but in Paris, French politicians failed to perceive the larger significance of the celebration of this holiday. In a city prone to protest, Moulay Youssef's peaceful sacrifice in Fez strongly suggested that Abd al-Karim's defeat was only a matter of time. He failed to gain the support of either the urban masses or religious scholars, showing the limitations of his revolt. French politicians, however, did not understand the social and political significance of meat in Morocco. Looking for more tangible evidence of a military defeat, of which there was little that summer, they condemned Lyautey's military strategy. French politicians replaced him with Jules-Joseph Theodore Steeg three months after the Great Sacrifice, so Lyautey did not witness Abd al-Karim's surrender on 24 May 1926.

## The Municipal Slaughterhouse

Clearly, the Great Sacrifice was loaded with layers of political and social meaning for Moroccans. And the French, though wanting to improve standards of Moroccan butchery for everyday meals, did not want to repudiate completely the cultural specificities of Moroccan sacrifice and subsequent meat consumption. The director of the protectorate's municipal services highlighted the conundrum facing officials who wanted to modernize the meat industry without undermining the Islamic practices of 'Id al-Kabir:

> One of the municipal administration's first concerns, from the very start of the protectorate, consisted of prohibiting all private slaughter, with an exception made for 'Id al-Kabir, when all Muslims must slaughter the traditional sheep at home. At the same time, the old slaughterhouses—usually consisting of no more than an esplanade that was more or less paved—would be modernized and rendered healthier.[40]

Colonial officials expressed an intention to improve public health by forcing Moroccans to eat meat slaughtered at a municipal slaughterhouse. And yet, they allowed colonized Muslims to eat the meat of an animal butchered at home once a year. The protectorate administration's desire for political stability would often trump expressed intentions to improve modern standards of hygiene and public health.

Certainly, the construction of a new municipal slaughterhouse at Bayn al-Madun's gurna in Fez did not meet basic standards of public health. The regional director of health services opposed the plans for the municipal slaughterhouse because Bayn al-Madun was in a residential neighborhood located one hundred meters before the medina's northwestern gate. Fez's municipal engineer complained that the offal dumped into the Oued Bou Kherareb caused a health hazard because residents downstream used the water for their vegetable gardens. One doctor in the colonial army testified that the site, as a basin in the foothills of the Atlas Mountains, would trap the odors of slaughtered livestock, which, attracting flies, would cause disease. Indeed, Morocco's director general of health services refused to endorse the project.[41] The military officer commanding the protectorate's northern regions suggested that conditions at the proposed slaughterhouse broke "rules in France which have the force of law."[42] In fact, these laws also existed in the protectorate, for, only four days before the commandant's complaint, the protectorate had banned "unhealthy" industries, including slaughterhouses, from all of Morocco's urban centers.[43]

Municipal administrators deliberately ignored these dire warnings, deciding instead to locate the municipal slaughterhouse at Bayn al-Madun. They made this decision in consultation with local residents, thereby highlighting their concerns for political stability. The Moroccans with whom they spoke endorsed the creation of a municipal slaughterhouse in Bayn al-Madun. In regard to hygienic conditions, it was enough that they told the chief of municipal services that they could not remember a time when meat slaughtered there had caused an outbreak of disease.[44]

Besides fostering political stability, the construction of a new slaughterhouse at Bayn al-Madun would also advance the municipality's goal of fiscal responsibility. The municipality needed to balance the city's budget, so it could only spend as much money as was collected through taxes.[45] For this reason, the commandant of the region of Fez opposed locating a slaughterhouse outside of the medina. He informed the French experts who issued warnings about Bayn al-Madun that the placement in another area was far too costly. It would require the construction of a building, the purchase of land, the development of water canals, and the laying of a new road.[46] The protectorate would pay for only half of Bayn al-Madun's renovation, leaving the municipality to pay 100,000 francs.[47] In this instance, fiscal concerns outweighed good hygiene.

The municipality's renovation of Bayn al-Madun centralized the butcher's trade. Administrators replaced three gurnas with a single facility. In April 1914, the majlis closed Bab Mahrouk's gurna because it did not have sufficient access to water. They put money earmarked for its renovation toward the municipal slaughterhouse.[48] The city rented the gurna of Sidi

Bou Nafa from administrators of hubus properties until 1916, when Bayn al-Madun's municipal slaughterhouse was inaugurated. The butchers of Bayn al-Madun continued, of course, to work at the same site, but they slaughtered at a warehouse downstream during the year in which the municipality was constructing the new facility.[49]

To accommodate an increased number of butchers at the site, the municipality enlarged the area of the gurna at Bayn al-Madun. The Oued Bou Kherareb bordered one side of it. There were private gardens on two other sides, and the walls of a private house marked the remaining boundary.[50] To enlarge the area, the municipality acquired one garden from the Ministry of Religious Endowments.[51]

Though intended to centralize the butcher's trade, colonial officials displayed excessive sensitivity to the dietary regulations of the Muslim majority and the Jewish minority by maintaining a separation between butchers of different faiths. Such a separation differed from the organization of the meat industry in France, for Jewish butchers in Paris had worked alongside Christian colleagues since the inauguration of the La Villette slaughterhouse in 1860.[52] In Fez, however, French administrators designated the municipal slaughterhouse of Bayn al-Madun for the "exclusive use of the Muslims of Fez al-Bali."[53] At this facility, they formalized the position of imam, a practicing Muslim, often an aging butcher, whose sacrifice according to religious prescriptions ensured that meat was licit for Muslim consumption.[54]

The French constructed a separate slaughterhouse in the mellah for Jewish butchers. In 1914, they closed the mellah's existing gurna and moved its butchers to a nearby facility.[55] The French permitted a rabbinical tribunal to oversee work there. Its members made decisions based on religious concerns and not hygienic criteria, thereby preventing several butchers from working because they were not practicing Jews.[56]

Muslim butchers began working in the new slaughterhouse in May 1916. The physical changes wrought by the French to their worksite were apparent even before they entered the colonial facility.[57] Butchers purchased livestock at Suq al-Khamis, afterward driving the animals through the southeastern Keddan quarter. In this way, they followed the newly extended length of the slaughterhouse's walls from the opposite bank of the Oued Bou Kherareb.[58] Crossing the Bayn al-Madun bridge, an iron gate on the right marked the entrance to the renovated facility.

As the butchers entered the municipal slaughterhouse, they passed through an underpass linking two administrative buildings.[59] The municipality paid several administrators either to assist the butchers or to oversee their work. The municipality provided a tax collector with a book of receipts so that he could record payments received.[60] The municipality also paid a Moroccan to brand the livestock, thus preventing disputes between butchers claiming the same animal as their own. It paid a concierge to watch over the slaughterhouse after the butchers had left it. Further, it paid a Moroccan to stamp meat before it was sold to the public, thus allowing market officials to verify that it came from the slaughterhouse. The municipality also hired a male nurse to provide butchers with some emergency care.[61] Bayn al-Madun's municipal slaughterhouse heralded a new bureaucratic era for practitioners of the butcher's trade.

For butchers, the municipal veterinarian was the most important official making use of the administrative offices. The butchers slaughtered at night, and a French vet came every morning to inspect meat in order to ensure that it did not threaten public health. In this way, a butcher's purchase of a gaunt animal might have unanticipated consequences. In January 1919, for example, when the veterinarian identified a cow as cachectic, or emaciated due to ill health, and not merely suffering from a seasonal lack of pasture, he ordered its 93 kilograms of meat destroyed.[62]

The colonial government did not reimburse butchers for money spent on such meat, and butchers worried about the financial repercussions of these new state controls. One year after the municipal slaughterhouse's inauguration, Fez's butchers formed an association as protection against an overly meticulous veterinarian. These butchers, representing about 80 percent of the trade, contributed a set fee to a collective fund for each animal that they slaughtered, whether ovine, bovine, or camel. The association then used this money to reimburse its members who had meat rejected by the veterinarian.[63] Other butchers used a more corrupt means to get around the municipal veterinarian. In at least one instance, the municipality jailed the concierge and the stamper, presumably for allowing condemned meat to leave the slaughterhouse with a stamp of approval.[64] Whether by lawful means or not, butchers wanted compensation for the financial risks wrought by France's modernizing project.

Jewish butchers in the mellah also engaged in questionable activities in order to avoid unfavorable inspections. The municipality paid the Moroccan Jew David Attar to help the French veterinarian. On 12 August 1924, all fifteen of Fez's Jewish butchers went on strike, demanding Attar's removal. They accused him of soliciting bribes in exchange for approval of their livestock and denounced him for impious behavior, such as courting a married woman and smoking on the Sabbath. After the muhtasib's representative met with members of the rabbinical tribunal, Attar was condemned to three months in prison.[65]

When Fez's basha reviewed the case, he found evidence that the butchers were in fact guilty of fabricating their charges. They had tried to get Attar to accept their bribes in exchange for the authorization of the slaughter of unhealthy livestock. When he did not, a clerk for the rabbinical tribunal, a man who counted several butchers as friends, advised the butchers on the best means of getting Attar fired from his job. Facing condemnation, Jewish butchers revealed the truth of the basha's claim, for they "assumed an insolent attitude toward the municipal veterinarian, who was obliged to call the municipal police to the slaughterhouse." The basha not only exonerated Attar but also fined the butchers twenty-five francs for their "refusal to slaughter and [causing] a scandal."[66] Attar continued to work at the Jewish slaughterhouse for at least thirteen more years.[67]

Once Muslim butchers passed Bayn al-Madun's administrative offices, including that of the dreaded veterinarian, they turned right, toward the complex of functionally specific buildings that now filled what had previously been the gurna's empty space. Veering north, the butchers walked fifteen meters toward the holding pen for livestock. The pen for animals was a free-standing building on the right, and the slaughtering chamber was located across from it. Between these two buildings, a narrow passage led to the Oued Bou Kherareb. From the end of this passage, butchers could look downstream and see the drain used to flush intestinal contents into the sewage collector.

The design of the slaughtering chamber demonstrates the care taken by colonial authorities to construct a facility merging modern building codes with the local architectural style. This structure's principal façade, as well as its facing side, was an iron grill. The open façade ventilated the main chamber, while also facilitating administrative oversight of the butchers' work. The two solid walls of the slaughtering chamber consisted of bricks baked in local ovens, and they were lined by a series of windows. A delicately etched arabesque embellished the exposed wooden lintel, diminishing the inherent gloom cast by the site's functional purpose. These windows had iron grillwork over them, which, much to the chagrin of French administrators, butchers found more convenient for hanging carcasses than the hooks on the ceilings.[68] The floor of the chamber was a patchwork of square stones drawn from the local quarry that must have rendered clean-up difficult.[69] The beamed ceilings of the three wings of the slaughtering chamber called to mind Fez's courtyard houses. The light and air of the slaughtering chamber was considered critical in providing healthy meat, and these elements contrasted with the gloom of the temporary pen used for holding animals.

Municipal administrators hired the French architect René Canu to complete this slaughterhouse, a choice that emphasizes their desire to respect traditional building design. The municipality paid Canu to repair the slaughterhouse's water canals, paving, and grillwork.[70] These tasks seem like mundane work for an architect who was gaining renown for his modern adaptation of Fez's historic architecture. By then, Canu had designed the Collège Moulay Idriss, where the French educated the sons of notables. In hiring Canu rather than an engineering technocrat, municipal administrators ensured the maintenance of the traditional veneer of the slaughterhouse, despite their transformation of this facility's managerial content. In this way, the slaughterhouse, much like the Collège Moulay Idriss, was intended as architectural evidence of the protectorate's political goals.

French officials took pride in the municipal slaughterhouse. It is not often that tourists find slaughterhouses marked on maps in their guidebooks, but Prosper Ricard did just that when describing Fez in the *Guide bleu* for Morocco.[71] Ricard was well versed in the architectural traditions cultivated by colonial officers, for he worked as a local inspector for the Department of Fine Arts. In his guidebook, he advised readers to walk southeast to the Bayn al-Madun bridge after viewing the thirteenth-century Seffarine Madrasa. To the right, Ricard pointed out a panoramic view, and, to the left, "the slaughterhouse, inaugurated in 1916."[72]

Despite efforts to integrate the slaughterhouse into the traditional fabric of the medina, butchers recognized the transformation of their gurna, thereby adopting the French term *l-battoir*. Born in 1928, Hamid Aouad learned the butcher's trade from his father, Ahmed, who told him about sites used for slaughter before the arrival of the French. At seventy-four years old, Aouad makes a precise distinction between the l-battoir of Bayn al-Madun, where he learned the butcher's trade, and its precursor at Bab Mahrouk, which "we call a gurna."[73] In like manner, Gilalli Fakhir, born in 1920, began working for the butcher Mohamed Slaoui when he was sixteen years old.[74] When Gilalli's neighbors asked him where he was going, he always referred to his workplace as "l-battoir." He worked a lot, so people began to call him Gilalli Fakhir "l-Battoir," a name still used to identify him.

The term *l-battoir* is now used not just by butchers, but also by Moroccans speaking the local dialect.[75]

Colonial Taxes on Meat

Omar Tazi was one of the richest residents of Fez, indeed of all of Morocco, and his investment in this new type of slaughtering facility demonstrates the financial aims of colonial administrators overseeing the meat industry as well as the confidence of influential Moroccans in it. Tazi was very familiar with the meat industry, for Moulay Abdelaziz had charged him with tax collection in Fez, including the guerjouma. Tazi had retired to private life when Moulay Abdelhafid deposed Moulay Abdelaziz in 1908, but this wealthy merchant rejoined the sultan's government six years later when Lyautey appointed him basha of Casablanca.[76] Tazi's experiences as a public official and a private businessman gave him insight into the economy and the funds to take advantage of new investment opportunities.

When the French built a slaughterhouse in Casablanca in 1917, they provided Tazi with just such an opportunity. Casablanca was Morocco's principal port, so the French wanted to construct a municipal slaughterhouse to supply meat to local markets as well as an industrial facility where butchers could dress meat for export overseas. Since the project cost 3,000,000 francs, the city contracted a private company to build the slaughterhouse, ceding the right to collect taxes on meat for the first twenty years of its operation. To generate capital, the Société Générale des Abattoirs Municipaux et Industriels allowed private investors to fund one-sixth of the new slaughterhouse. Tazi invested 500,000 francs in the project, buying all shares allowed to private investors, which underscores the potential profits of the meat industry.[77]

In Fez, the municipality, not private investors, ran the meat industry, but the French officials organizing it still intended to make a profit from the sale of meat. Thus, the very first municipal decree passed by them on 28 October 1912 institutionalized the guerjouma. As with its precolonial precursor, French officials collected a fee for each head of livestock slaughtered by Muslim butchers. The class of livestock determined the fee, resulting in butchers paying less for slaughtering sheep than for cattle.[78] The French, however, did not designate the guerjouma for street cleaning, but instead placed it in the municipal treasury with other budgetary funds.

The rabbinical tribunal overseeing Jewish butchers also used taxes on meat to generate revenue for the mellah. In the Jewish quarter, the protectorate vested religious notables with responsibility for collecting taxes and then creating a budget. The Jewish notables taxed meat, much as for the medina's Muslim butchers, but they based the fee on the kilogram. They used the revenue to pay the shohet who performed the sacrifice and also for the maintenance of the Jewish cemetery.[79]

The success of this fiscal policy depended almost exclusively on the purchase of meat by Moroccans because Fez, unlike coastal Casablanca, did not attract a lot of foreigners. In 1916, 600 Europeans lived in Fez.[80] Five years later, French officials counted 1,500 Europeans in Fez, of whom two-thirds were French.[81] Their numbers would peak in 1926 at 4,923 Europeans. These Europeans lived alongside 81,172 Muslims and approximately 8,000 Moroccan Jews.[82] Since two-thirds of the active Moroccan male population earned their living by either producing a good or performing a service, the raising of colonial income via a tax on slaughter would require increased meat consumption in the households of workers.

The renovation of Mohamed al-Qadmiri's butcher shop in 1914 highlighted the French intention to increase meat sales among Moroccans. Al-Qadmiri came from a family of butchers that had practiced the trade for at least three generations.[83] The muhtasib oversaw the renovation project on behalf of the municipality, and he ordered the tiling of the shop's walls so that suspended carcasses would no longer brush against bare brick. He also made sure that the butcher's block was marble, not wood, so that it could be wiped free of dust and coagulated blood. This shop was at the center of the medina, and not its outskirts where foreign residents made their purchases, so it would have been frequented by a Moroccan clientele. Municipal administrators decreed that the owners of all butcher shops—usually hubus funds—must undertake identical renovations by March of that year.[84]

Jewish notables also decided to invest in butcher shops. In May 1914, the administrators of Jewish endowments constructed butcher shops on the site of the precolonial gurna, recently moved to a nearby location. These shops adhered to the hygienic standards recently implemented in al-Qadmiri's butcher shop in the Rsif market.[85] In exchange for funding these shops, Jewish notables would collect rent from butchers. In this way, they too demonstrated confidence in the meat industry's growth under French rule.

The chief of municipal services tempered proposals to increase taxes on kosher meat, suggesting a desire to make meat a dietary staple for workers. In response to a Jewish notable's proposition to raise taxes on kosher meat, the chief of municipal services asserted that "Israelites consider meat a vital foodstuff," continuing:

> The tax does not distinguish between poor craftsmen and rich usurers. Further, the need for the Israelites to buy fatty animals in order to cook the meat without butter regularly causes meat in the mellah to be more expensive than meat in the medina. The disparity will increase more from the implementation of the new tax.[86]

Although he authorized this tax, he did so for far less than recommended by Jewish notables. Nevertheless, by 1918, it would be one franc per kilogram of meat, thereby raising the price of beef by 25 percent.[87]

And yet, the chief of municipal services still identified taxes collected from butchers as "one of the most important budgetary funds."[88] The muhtasib counted ninety Muslim butchers in Fez and fifteen Jewish butchers in the mellah.[89] The fiscal responsibility of these workers surpassed their demographic significance. Representing .001 percent of Muslim residents, butchers provided 10 percent of Fez's municipal income.[90] The budget for the Jewish quarter presented a nearly identical situation. Jewish butchers, though representing only .0018 percent of the population, also generated 10 percent of the mellah's income.[91] The municipal budget funded employment programs, so taxes on meat provided some workers with the wages that allowed them to buy more meat.

The butchers' interpretation of colonial regulations rendered their commodity less costly, which made meat even more accessible to workers. Every day, the veterinarian decided if meat was of first or second quality, and the butchers then sold it according to the prices established by the muhtasib. The municipal veterinarian wanted butchers to purchase livestock that would furnish first-quality meat. Toward this end, the municipality gave butchers the right to purchase livestock at Suq al-Khamis before private residents, to allow them to choose the best animals.[92] Nevertheless, the butchers made a deliberate effort to provide the public with cheap meat, for they usually purchased tired and thin animals, which, having just arrived in the livestock market, provided meat of a cheaper second quality.

The veterinarian expressed frustration that most of Fez's butchers "don't follow the example of a small number who keep sheep purchased at the suq in order to properly feed them in the stable."[93] The butchers were not avoiding the expense of feeding animals. Even when Suq al-Khamis contained animals that would provide first-quality meat, the veterinarian still complained that "the butchers tend to buy young and thin [ones]."[94] Deeming this meat second quality, the muhtasib would set a price lower than that for fattened animals. Thus, butchers continued to pursue their precolonial strategy of decreasing the price of meat in order to expand their clientele and their concomitant profits.

Colonial tax laws provided butchers with enough leeway to pursue their goal of selling cheap meat. When the French institutionalized the guerjouma, administrators created monetary penalties for the commercial slaughter of cows and ewes. They doubled the guerjouma paid by butchers for slaughtering females. Butchers paid ten pesetas for slaughtering a cow and five pesetas for slaughtering a bull.[95] It would seem that the government tried to prevent the slaughter of female animals.

But in fact, the tax on female animals did not prevent butchers from slaughtering cows and ewes. For this reason, the majlis proposed a tax increase during a period of drought. As recounted by the chief of municipal services in May 1915, the merchants and landlords on this consultative body argued that it was "necessary to increase the rate of the guerjouma for female animals in order to diminish as much as possible the slaughter of these animals, which, despite the dispositions of the decrees passed, occurs on a grand scale."[96] The city's butchers preferred to slaughter cows over the age of eight years because, no longer fertile, they sold more cheaply than bulls and yet provided the same amount of meat.[97] A prohibition on female slaughter would force butchers to slaughter bulls and rams, and the price of meat would increase.

French administrators proved amenable to the tax hike proposed by the majlis, for they wanted to pay for Fez's new slaughterhouse.[98] After the French raised the guerjouma in May 1915, butchers paid 7 francs 50 for slaughtering a bull and 15 francs for a cow.[99] In maintaining a higher tax for females, this official expressed an intention "to encourage butchers to curb their neglect of bulls."[100] Nevertheless, female livestock still sold much more cheaply than the male. At that time, a butcher could purchase the average cow at Suq al-Khamis for 187 francs, while a bull sold for about 325 francs.[101]

To make up for this price differential, the French would have had to implement a fourteen-fold tax hike on female animals, which they did not do. For this reason, the butchers, even in paying the higher tax, still saved a great deal of money when they bought a cow. Two months after the tax increase, in July 1915, when butchers prepared khali'a for public sale, the municipality recorded the slaughter of 728 cows at the city's slaughterhouses, compared with only 203 bulls.[102] In a sense, it was a win-win situation. Butchers flooded the market with inferior meat purchased by working households. At 15 francs each, the tax on females provided Fez with an extra 5,460 francs of revenue.

After the drought, municipal administrators decreased the guerjouma with the express intention of helping butchers to increase meat sales. Henceforth, butchers paid five francs for slaughtering either male or female cattle and camels and one franc for goats and sheep.[103] The guerjouma, the chief of municipal services explained to urban notables, was higher in Fez than in other cities, and he believed that the high tax rate decreased transactions at Suq al-Khamis.[104] He informed Lyautey that the tax decrease would help in the sense that "it [slaughter] is rendered more accessible to the small-scale butchers."[105]

The chief of municipal services also believed that a decrease in the guerjouma would help the butchers' working-class clientele. He informed Lyautey that this decision helped in "the struggle against the constant augmentation of the price of meat." In lowering taxes on meat, he continued to tax the rich, thus drawing fiscal distinctions between workers and the wealthy. The chief of municipal services told Lyautey:

> I only demanded upholding the tax for slaughter undertaken at home by individuals who sacrifice choice livestock for the preparation of dried meat. As this exception only affects the well-off part of the population, it can be accepted without inconvenience.

This statement revealed an intention to help Moroccan workers purchase more meat. The chief of municipal services argued that the lower guerjouma would increase slaughter, making up for the 100,000 francs of lost tax revenue caused by the wheat crisis.[106]

Lyautey rejected this reorganization of Fez's tax system, clearly preferring to maximize revenue in the shortest period of time. The resident-general refuted his subordinate's logic, informing him—correctly—that a tax on livestock had no real bearing on meat's retail price. Lyautey's rejection of the proposal does not mean that he was indifferent to the plight of Moroccan butchers. He blamed the decrease in transactions at Suq al-Khamis on illegal commerce with the Spanish protectorate, and he proposed new measures to stop it.[107] Given the resident-general's opposition to the tax increase, the municipality returned the guerjouma to the higher rates.[108]

Fez's European population, though relatively small, still increased the profits of some butchers and the municipality. The French would not construct a ville nouvelle until after World War I, so most Europeans shopped in the mellah during the first eight years of the protectorate. When butcher shops there could not serve the growing European population, the municipality sponsored the construction of more.[109] Thus, the municipality invested some tax revenue in the meat industry, providing Jewish butchers with more outlets for meat sales.

Even as the Ville Nouvelle developed, Moroccan butchers, both Jewish and Muslim, reaped the rewards of the European presence. In 1919, two European butcher shops were established in the nascent Ville Nouvelle.[110] Within three years, it would have at least two more butcher shops.[111] The owners of these shops purchased meat from butchers working in the mellah or at Bayn al-Madun's slaughterhouse, so the Ville Nouvelle's growth allowed some butchers to wholesale meat.[112]

In the medina, some Moroccans also retailed meat provided by butchers at the municipal slaughterhouse. A shopkeeper on the outskirts of the Rsif market transformed his hardware store into a butcher shop in 1921. This transformation occurred during a building boom in the nearby quarters of Bab Ftouh, which, since construction materials would have been in high demand, highlights meat's rising importance as a commodity.[113] This is especially true since the Rsif market served a Moroccan clientele. The owner of this shop wanted to lure as many customers as possible, digging up the floor in order to open a door into the market itself.[114] This was not the only case of an entrepreneur retailing meat at butcher shops. By 1930, Hadj Abdelmalek Anoun operated several butcher shops in the medina.[115]

French residents identified meat as a staple food, badgering municipal administrators to ensure an affordable supply of meat.[116] Members of the French Municipal Commission complained that European shopkeepers did not post the price of meat, assuming that their clientele would buy from them without regard to cost.[117] They accused these tradesmen of inflating the price of meat, which sold for 60 percent more than in the medina.[118] Noting the disparity between prices in the European and Moroccan quarters, one member wanted "to safeguard the interests of the European population and, in particular, that of the Ville Nouvelle, by making them apply fixed prices." The French, however, could not force European businessmen to sell their products at prices set by the muhtasib for Moroccans.[119]

The chief of municipal services proposed a solution to this problem that benefited Moroccan butchers. He informed the French Municipal Commission that the municipality would sponsor more Moroccan butcher shops at the markets of Bab Smarine and Bab Boujeloud, which, on the medina's outskirts, were most accessible to Europeans. He also intended to establish Moroccan butcher shops at a market then being constructed for the Ville Nouvelle.[120] Since Moroccans sold meat according to the prices established by the muhtasib, French consumers would be guaranteed access to affordable meat. It was a favorable situation for both the butchers and the municipality. The former sold more meat, while the latter collected more taxes, which, once invested in programs of social welfare, allowed more Moroccan workers to purchase meat from Fez's butchers.

Meat and Social Status

Some French policies reinforced meat's use as a marker of social status, but others, such as prohibitions on the right to private slaughter, removed a prerogative of the urban elite. When the municipality of Fez institutionalized the guerjouma in 1912, it enacted rules designed to stimulate the sale of commercially butchered meat among rich notables. "It is formally prohibited for butchers," stated the decree, "to kill outside the municipal slaughterhouses." Despite the threat of punishment to butchers, this regulation also called on wealthy residents slaughtering at home to modify their behavior.

The penalties imposed on law-breaking butchers underscored the colonial desire to ensure maximum municipal returns on meat consumption. In the case of a first infraction, the French made butchers pay a double tax on the illegally slaughtered livestock. For a second infraction, the municipality sold the meat of illegally slaughtered livestock, with the proceeds then placed in the city's treasury.[121] Since the French did not destroy meat butchered in places without sanitary oversight, the law did not aim to improve public health. Instead, the French designed a law that would increase municipal funds, whether or not butchers adhered to it. If butchers followed the law, the rich would buy meat at shops, which would augment the number of animals butchered at the slaughterhouse. In so doing, the municipality increased taxes collected there. And if butchers broke the law, the penalties also increased municipal revenue.

Two years later, the French created legislation that aimed directly at consumption strategies in elite households. In October 1914, they banned the slaughter of cattle in private houses.[122] The commandant of the region of Fez acquiesced to a request by notables serving on the majlis who insisted on preserving the right to prepare khaliʻa at home. If a resident wanted to slaughter cattle at home, the municipality allowed him to apply for a permit. In this way, the French honored local expressions of wealth and status. Nevertheless, this official warned them not to abuse this "legal indulgence."[123]

The penalties established for lawbreakers reinforced meat's role as an indicator of wealth and status. The French ordered the confiscation of meat illegally butchered in private homes. Colonial administrators would sell it and donate the proceeds of the sale to Sidi Frej, a hospice caring for Fez's indigent population.[124] Thus, the French did not treat meat as a staple in the diet of the low-status poor. The state, after all, much as in the precolonial era, did not donate meat to charity but rather the revenue generated from its sale.

Other colonial policies aiming to help the poor reinforced meat's significance as a social marker that created a tangible distinction between impoverished residents of low and high status. When a drought in 1914 increased poverty, the French made charitable distributions of food to the poor. The French distributed 560 kilograms of meat each week, but only to religious students and shurafa'.[125] These colonial officials did not treat meat as a staple in the local diet, using meat instead to distinguish between high- and low-status poor.

In like manner, the French institutionalized the royal distribution of meat to the most financially disadvantaged members of the royal family. The French guaranteed that the sultan's unmarried female relatives received one kilogram of meat every day, or more if close ties to Moulay Youssef rendered them "important." Since these women had no income, some of them requested the monetary equivalent of the meat two out of every three days. In this way, they had the means to purchase clothes or pay expenses. The French ensured a meticulous oversight of this program. Thus, in 1927, when French officers of the Ministry of Cherifian Affairs heard rumors that the sultan's chamberlain was cheating these women at the palace in Meknes, they interceded on their behalf.[126] The French honored the sultan's extended family by guaranteeing distributions of meat.

The French wanted all Moroccans to sacrifice for 'Id al-Kabir, regardless of their social station. Just before the holiday, the French offered a tax break to residents of Fez holding a *carte d'indigence*, a declaration of poverty provided by a representative of their neighborhood.[127] The French did not usually permit the slaughter of a young ram, but they lifted these prohibitions two weeks before the holiday in order to "permit poor families to buy the sheep intended for the sacrifice."[128] A resident could purchase a ram even if it did not yet have the two replacement teeth that signified it was between eighteen and twenty-four months of age.[129]

Struggling residents sought to sacrifice even if they could not afford it. One servant working for the director of the Department of Fine Arts did not, as his employer readily admitted, earn enough money to purchase a sacrificial ram. Nevertheless, he pawned his mother's silver bracelets in order to sacrifice on ʿId al-Kabir.[130] By encouraging the poor to participate in the Great Sacrifice, French officials undoubtedly raised popular expectations in regard to daily meat consumption.

Although French officials honored the Great Sacrifice, they demonstrated equal enthusiasm in preventing the elite from sacrificing at home for ordinary meals. In October 1915, the commandant of Fez found evidence that a resident had privately sacrificed three cows—even after the municipality had denied him authorization. The commandant did not criticize the slaughter of female animals or the hygienic conditions of the house. Instead, he complained that this man had slaughtered "without paying the guerjouma." In this instance, the city's financial concerns outweighed the protectorate's political consideration for urban notables. The commandant wanted to prosecute the resident, even though he described the lawbreaker as "one of the most well-known Fassis, probably justifying himself on the good relations that he maintains with the municipality."[131] As a result of this incident, the municipality banned the slaughter of cows at home, threatening butchers who abetted private sacrifice with prison sentences and the removal of their license to practice the trade.[132]

The concern for municipal revenue led the French to curtail private slaughter intended for the preparation of khaliʿa. In July 1920, French officers caught one resident of Fez slaughtering two young cows at home.[133] French prohibitions, however, threatened not only ordinary urban residents but also some of Morocco's highest royal officials. In 1922, municipal administrators in Rabat even threatened to bring action against Driss Zemrani after he slaughtered two bulls at home.[134] A native of Fez, Zemrani was the sultan's assistant chief of protocol. In Fez, municipal administrators explicitly associated khaliʿa with "clandestine slaughter," thereby denying a request in 1924 by the wealthy merchants and landlords of the Indigenous Chamber of Commerce to eliminate a tax on the livestock brought to the city from their rural holdings.[135]

The following year, municipal administrators enacted a regulation permitting residents to apply for special permission to sacrifice at home, but in doing so, they revealed their concern for the emerging meat industry as a source of revenue. A resident of Fez could apply for permission to slaughter at home as long as he promised not to sell the meat and paid a tax.[136] Municipal administrators in Fez remained vigilant in their search for abuses. In July 1927, during a drought, municipal officers caught at least one recalcitrant resident who sacrificed two cows at home without authorization.[137] By prohibiting private slaughter, the French suppressed a mode of meat consumption associated with elite prerogatives in Fez.

The majlis reinforced the institutional framework supporting meat's use as a social marker. In 1925, the Riffian war was at its height, and refugees from the hinterland were fleeing to Fez.[138] The chief of municipal services permitted notables serving on the majlis to institute a new tax on meat designated for the care of orphans, the most deserving victims of this crisis. The majlis required butchers to pay two francs for each head of cattle slaughtered and fifty centimes for each sheep. Basha Si Mohamed ben Bouchta Baghdadi announced the measure and appointed himself president of this new charitable organization. The director of the Maristan hubus was its secretary-treasurer. France's municipal administrators considered the fee nominal, for it would raise the price of meat by two and half centimes a kilogram.[139] Still, the tax embodies the quandary of this era, for, even if certain programs helped more people to work, meat was not treated as a staple food.

Notables deliberately emphasized the links between meat and social status when they enunciated a policy to improve the diet of their social inferiors. In 1926, the majlis requested the removal of a municipal regulation that prevented the city's fishermen from casting their lines in the Oued Fez. The majlis wanted to improve the lot of these fishermen, who, according to its members, were unable to earn a living. Equally important, however, they wanted to lift the restrictions "in order that the working class is able to improve its standard fare by obtaining small fish cheaply."[140] Fish differs from meat in Islamic law, for it does not require a special sacrifice before its consumption. In this way, the notables on the majlis raised the price of meat, thus confirming their belief that meat was a consumable luxury of the rich, while ensuring workers' access to fish, which they considered a staple in the workingman's diet.

## The Chevillard

By the 1920s, Mohamed, M'hamed, and Ahmed Slaoui were the largest purveyors of meat in Fez. The Slaouis learned the butcher's trade from their father.[141] Nevertheless, Hadj Alami, who grew up across the street from them, insists that the brothers never sullied their expensive clothing by slaughtering livestock.[142] Between 1912 and 1929, the Slaouis became *chevillards*, meaning that they sold meat wholesale. Awarded military contracts by French officers, these butchers represented the social mobility fostered by colonial opportunities, and the brothers would transform their new wealth into a symbolic claim for the status of traditional notables.

The French made sure that colonial soldiers found fresh meat on their table every day. Given the importance of this dietary policy, they built a separate military slaughterhouse in the Ville Nouvelle. Every six months, the army called for bids on a contract to slaughter there and supply meat to Fez's troops. French officials announced bidding for this lucrative contract in *Akhbar talagrafiyya*, the Arabic newspaper distributed by the Department of Indigenous Affairs and read only by local residents.[143] The winner of the contract supplied meat to about five thousand soldiers.[144] Mohamed ben Larbi Tazi "al-Guezzar" worked with the Slaouis to secure the contract until the 1920s, afterward conducting his business activities independently.[145]

The Slaouis purchased livestock and hired workers to slaughter it, then sold the meat and offal. The butchers serving the military slaughtered only bulls and rams, never female animals. The French purchased only the animal's flesh, liver, and heart. The butcher's assistant took home the spleen.[146] Some byproducts were sold to the French industrialists who established a factory for processing bones, blood, and intestines. The Slaouis sold the skins to tanneries in Fez, also collecting hides from other butchers in Fez, which proved a lucrative side business.[147] In this way, the winner of the military contract never had face-to-face contact with those who ate the meat that he supplied. Moroccan dialect provides evidence of the newness of this type of commercial activity, for the French term *chevillard* signifies the wholesale meat trade.[148]

The French exempted the purveyor of military meat from many policies implemented in the municipal slaughterhouse. The military chevillard did not need to hire an imam to perform a sacrifice, even though the colonial army included Muslims from Senegal, Tunisia, and Algeria. Instead, the Slaouis employed a Muslim butcher named Ibba. He performed the sacrifice, but, as noted by Gilalli Fakhir "l-Battoir," who worked for him as a boy, he was not an imam.[149] Tazi al-Guezzar hired the French butcher Jacinthe Delphin to oversee the slaughter.[150]

Demonstrating concern for the final cost of meat, protectorate officials exempted the winner of the military contract from the fiscal responsibilities of their colleagues at the municipal slaughterhouse. For the first twenty years of the protectorate, neither the Slaouis nor Tazi al-Guezzar paid the guerjouma.

The quantity of livestock slaughtered and subsequent profits set this chevillard apart from butchers at the municipal slaughterhouse. In May 1919, 228 bulls and 116 rams entered the military slaughterhouse, providing the winner of the military contract payment for approximately 29,100 kilograms of meat.[151] That same month, 290 bovine animals and 5,722 ovine animals, both male and female, entered the municipal slaughterhouse, with the medina's Muslim butchers then selling approximately 119,430 kilograms of fresh meat.[152] Butchers in the medina provided the public with nearly five times as much meat as the chevillard serving the army, but the profits were divided among ninety-one men. The winner of the military contract profited not only from the volume of slaughter but also from the stability of the military demand. Military demand did not suffer seasonal fluctuations, whether for winter, when some residents stocked khali'a, or holidays, when they sacrificed rams at home.

Tazi al-Guezzar and the Slaouis multiplied their profits by investing in private property in the burgeoning Batha and Boujeloud quarters of the medina. In 1919, Tazi al-Guezzar bought a house and a warehouse in the Boujeloud quarter with Si Mohamed ben Larbi al-Mernissi.[153] Then, seven years after the protectorate's establishment, these partners catered to the housing needs of Europeans. Thus, they renovated the building as four self-contained apartments. Other Moroccan landlords rented out rooms in a courtyard house to workers, who shared space for cooking and washing. These units, however, had three separate rooms as well as a kitchen and a bathroom.[154] By introducing private apartments designed for a nuclear family, Tazi and Mernissi demonstrated an innovative spirit as well as a desire to reap rewards from colonial circumstances.

The Slaouis also invested in real estate in the Batha and Boujeloud quarters. In 1922, Mohamed Slaoui and Tazi al-Guezzar became partners in the purchase of a house and garage. The partners in this real estate venture included members of Fez's mercantile elite, specifically Ahmed ben

Tahar Mekouar, Taieb Bennani, and Mohamed ben M'Feddel Benjelloun. Through the purchase, these chevillards also cultivated contacts with Driss al-Moqri, another partner. Driss was brother to the grand vizier as well as Fez's muhtasib. These men purchased the property at an auction of real estate confiscated from Germans during World War I.[155] This venture must have been speculative in nature, for they sold the property to a tobacco company the next year.[156]

The Rif War proved a boon to the military chevillards. In 1925, forty battalions were stationed in Fez. Despite these numbers, Lyautey requested a 25 percent increase in troops in order to combat the twenty thousand tribesmen fighting with Abd al-Karim. This increase would include nine infantry battalions, three cavalry squadrons, and three artillery batteries.[157] The war benefited the Slaouis in particular, since Tazi al-Guezzar was disqualified from bidding on military contracts after a French officer accused his son of tampering with the scales at the military slaughterhouse.[158] The Slaouis translated their financial success into another real estate venture. One week before Abd al-Karim's surrender, the Slaouis purchased a warehouse in Boujeloud, which they rented out for five hundred francs a month.[159]

After the Rif War, the Slaouis publicized their wealth through the purchase of a huge house in the Boujeloud quarter. The house and its property had a value of 1,000,000 francs, which the brothers seem to have paid in cash.[160] At that time, they sold their warehouse for 67,500 francs, thus making a 12.5 percent return on their initial investment.[161] The enormous courtyard house was situated on a property measuring 62,500 square meters, which included an expanse of walled gardens.[162] Together, the house and its land took up five lots, numbers 44 through 52, on Derb Ben Aich. From their home, the Slaouis could walk up Talaa Saghira to the Boujeloud Gate in less than five minutes.

These butchers purchased a house that exuded prestige. It had originally been owned by Driss ben Aich, who, as chamberlain to Moulay Abdelaziz, once was one of the most influential men in Morocco. The Slaouis would entertain guests in the main courtyard, a space that publicized their social ascent. Its walls were embellished with polychromatic tiles, with the geometric pattern bequeathing a distinctly Fassi identity on the house. The elaborate praises of God and the Prophet carved in plaster above this green and gold faience emphasized the household's religious devotion while also presenting its owners as members of the city's educated elite. A massive fountain in the middle of the courtyard emitted a constant murmur of fresh water, which, as a valuable resource in Fez, subtly announced their influence.[163]

Tazi al-Guezzar lived in the less fashionable neighborhood of Souikat ben Safi, but he too translated his residence into social capital. In 1924, he was elected to the majlis as a representative of the Lemtiyyin quarter of the medina.[164] Except for Hadj Tahar ben al-Amine, a wealthy merchant probably living in his London home when the French arrived, Tazi was the first representative of this quarter who had not appeared on a master list of notables drawn up by colonial officers in 1912.[165] At first, Tazi struggled to prove that he belonged in this consultative body of notables. In 1924, Tazi won the election with a simple majority, with only two votes separating him from defeat. Six years later, he won with a plurality, awarded the seat despite having the support of fewer than 33 percent of his constituents.[166] His ascension to this body of notables signified the rising fortunes of Fez's butchers.

## Conclusion

The colonial regulation of the butcher's trade transformed meat's social and economic significance, democratizing meat consumption between 1912 and 1929. Prohibiting routine slaughter at home, the French suppressed a time-honored prerogative of the elite. In addition, they financed employment programs with revenue generated in part from the municipal slaughterhouse, thereby allowing workers to consume more meat. The increasing number of butcher shops in the medina reflected a rising demand for meat. And some butchers, particularly those supplying the colonial army, came to be counted among Fez's wealthiest families, even entering the ranks of urban notables. Thus, the colonial development of the meat industry in Fez decreased the ability of notables to exhibit traditional prestige, while increasing access to meat among working households, a consumable luxury that signified their rising influence.

# PART III

# Continuity and Change

# 7

# Struggles for Scarce Resources in the 1930s

On 16 May 1930, Resident-General Lucien Saint traveled to Fez, hoping that his presence would quell the unrest brewing there.[1] This date marks the passage of the controversial Berber Dahir, a law that effectively removed the non-Arab minority from sultanic jurisdiction, but Saint did not go there to address concerns over the judicial system. Residents of Fez had already been demonstrating against the colonial administration for more than a week.

Fez's residents opposed a project proposed by the Department of Public Works that would shift the distribution of water in the medina. This issue mobilized Moroccans of all socioeconomic milieus, from wealthy merchants to impoverished beggars. Even royal officials counted as colonial allies expressed dissatisfaction with the project. According to a British diplomat, ten thousand Moroccans had assembled in six mosques to express their anger with the colonial administration.[2] The resident-general needed to assuage the concerns of Fez's residents, who, once again, proved restive and prone to protest.

This crisis over Fez's water supply was the first sign of a popular struggle to increase the access of Moroccans to basic necessities. In the 1930s, drought led to the worst food shortage since the nineteenth century's Great Famine. At the same time, a global recession decreased the wages of workers and the profits of merchants, aggravating hardship in urban centers. Building upon precolonial policies during the first seventeen years of the protectorate, the French had fostered a social contract with Fez's working majority, guaranteeing a minimum standard of living in exchange for political quiescence. But given the extent of the crisis in the 1930s, the protectorate no longer had the means to uphold its end of this undocumented agreement.

Drought and global recession made workers and even rich notables less capable of ensuring their own access to the basic resources needed for survival, such as water and food. Moroccans learned that neither the colonial state nor global networks of exchange could ensure their well-being, and the resulting economic and political strategies of this period of crisis reaffirmed the central place of the local economy and of the personalized sociopolitical networks that intersected there. The survival strategies of workers and notables in the 1930s would facilitate the forging of a conservative form of popular nationalism.

## The Struggle for Control of Local Resources

In September 1929, the director of public works announced a plan to improve Fez's water system. Expressing a benevolent intention, this French official wanted to ensure the production of electricity throughout the year, even if rainfall proved deficient, as in 1926 and 1927. The director negotiated an agreement between the entrepreneurs Perez and Coudert and the Compagnie Fasie d'Electricité. Perez and Coudert ceded the Compagnie Fasie the rights to exploit the waterfall that had previously produced electricity for their own industrial mill. Further, the department devised a plan to divert some water from the medina's three principal canals to this company's turbine. The project, however, as the director was quick to point out, would not decrease local access to water for drinking or irrigation, for the department would compensate for the loss of water from the Oued Fas by redirecting the nearby Oued Nja. The project would actually increase the medina's rate of water flow by 30 percent, even in the summer.[3]

Nevertheless, the majlis expressed strong opposition to this colonial project. Three months later, notables provided French administrators with a history of water rights in Fez that began with the city's tenth-century foundation. This report also expressed concern that the project would affect the quantity and quality of urban water. Members did not believe that the project would increase the water supply, which, in Fez, ran through most houses. And, anyway, as they argued, the taste of the Oued Nja was not as "sweet" as the Oued Fas. Further, they suggested that the copper turbines producing electricity would pollute public drinking water. And finally, they expressed a fear that the French intended to set up meters, which, by forcing the payment of a fee for water, would cause financial hardship for private individuals and public institutions. In such a case, the decreased access to water would cause the hubus funds to lose money on their properties, making it difficult to care for the poor. Concluding the report, the majlis demanded that the government "end all discussion on the subject of the water of the Oued Fas."[4]

Focusing on the projected benefits of this project, French technocrats ignored the objections of the majlis. In February 1930, the director of public works acknowledged a modification of customary rights to water, but he insisted that the project would increase water supply. He advocated standing firm against the notables' complaints.[5] Five days later, a colonial engineer concurred, arguing that this project would do no more than formalize a series of small changes already implemented. Opposition to the project seemed illogical to him, and he wondered "if the people of Fez are aware of their own interests."[6] At the same time, the chief of municipal services advised the protectorate's secretary-general "to ignore, for the moment, the opposition that has manifested itself."[7]

It seems that the director of indigenous affairs was the only official who recognized the extent of the political unrest caused by this project. In mid-April, he acknowledged his inability to judge technical aspects of the project, but he warned: "Whatever the value of arguments of a technical order presented to counteract the reasoning invoked by the Fassis, we collide with their psychology and their traditions, which date to the far past."[8] His warning fell on deaf ears. Three days later, the protectorate passed a decree that officially opened a study of the project. In setting a closing date of 20 May, this decree was a first step toward changing water rights.[9]

Even the staunchest allies of French officials opposed this colonial project. Mohamed Tazi was the basha's assistant, a loyal French ally who would be promoted to basha after Mohamed Baghdadi's death in 1932. Validating elite complaints against this project, he urged the commandant of the region to contact notables in order to assuage popular concerns. Hadj Mohamed Benjelloun was president of the Indigenous Chamber of Commerce and Agriculture, thereby leading a group consisting of Fez's wealthiest residents, and he also advised the commandant to negotiate a conclusion to this affair.[10] As the grand vizier's brother, Taieb al-Moqri represented the upper echelons of Fez's notables. He warned the chief of municipal services that the project threatened to reduce access to water on his property.[11] In recounting a visit with one resident of Fez, an official with the Department of Indigenous Affairs recorded the French shock at the negative response by their Moroccan allies. He described his interlocutor as "a bourgeois Fassi with good sense and a remarkable spirit of moderation, and who is sincerely attached to us." This ally expressed support for a tax increase, but he unequivocally refused to consider paying for water because he considered it collective property.[12]

The Department of Indigenous Affairs identified the cotton merchant al-Arbi Bouayad as one firebrand instigating popular unrest. The Bouayads had long been among Fez's mercantile elite.[13] By 1930, however, the onset of a global depression had bankrupted most merchants importing cotton from England. To keep his business afloat, al-Arbi had used private property as collateral for a loan from the West Africa Company. This last-ditch effort to save his business proved a costly mistake. By the time the French opened the inquest on the water project, al-Arbi had begun liquidating his holdings in Manchester. Al-Arbi was not the only disgruntled merchant accused of fomenting unrest. The Department of Indigenous Affairs identified three other bankrupt merchants who opposed the water project.[14] The global depression forced them to rebuild their fortune in Fez, so they had a strong interest in protecting local rights to urban resources.

By May, these elite merchants began to discuss a strategy for blocking the project. Hassan Bouayad was the son of the bankrupted al-Arbi.[15] According to a colonial informant, this British protégé led a delegation of twenty-two merchants protesting the transformation of Fez's water supply. A French official with the protectorate's security services described members of this group as "notables," not seditious radicals. Si Hamza Tahari also participated in these discussions. Raised in England, this merchant represented the Andalous quarter in the majlis between 1912 and 1927. The participants Mohamed Chami and Sidi al-Ghali al-Amrani were current members of the majlis. The wealthy landlord Mohamed Mernissi also contributed to these discussions. According to French officials, he held a personal grudge against the Compagnie Fasie, which had accused him of stealing electricity.

Whether motivated by altruism or ill will, the French could not ignore a group amalgamating the influence of Fez's wealthiest residents. To engage in a legal fight for water, this group immediately provided a retainer of 20,000 francs to a lawyer. To continue the struggle, one half of this group took responsibility for raising another 180,000 francs to enable them to take their case to La Haye's world court. Hoping, it seems, that legal maneuverings would act as a bargaining chip, the other half of the group agreed to set up a meeting with the commandant of the region of Fez.[16] In deciding to change the distribution of water, the French put themselves at odds with the lynchpin of "association."

As the closing date for the inquest loomed, more Moroccans began to condemn the colonial project. Claiming popular rights to the Oued Fas that dated back 1,156 years, nearly five hundred men signed a petition by 10 May, protesting this project. The organizers of the petition included not only Mohamed Mernissi but also Ahmed Tazi, an official working for the Ministry of Religious Endowments.

The signatures suggest that the petition enunciated the interests of disparate socioeconomic milieus, not just the elite merchants and scholars who wrote it. The script ranges from the trembling hand of a man with little education, even, in one instance, a thumbprint, to the more sophisticated penmanship of the educated, with two signatories even transcribing their names in French.[17] The Office of Land Titles received a similar petition signed by 130 men.[18] As the 20 May deadline approached, a formal request to put an end to the water project continued to circulate in Fez. Within ten days, the protectorate's security services reported one thousand signatures on a petition protesting the project.[19] The French then counted 90,279 Muslims in Fez, assembled in roughly 15,046 households.[20] Assuming that each signature appeared only once, nearly 10 percent of Fez's active adult men made their personal animosity to this project a matter of public record.

Some residents did more than sign letters of protest. On 11 May, the French Security Service counted eight hundred men gathered at the Sidi Ahmed ben Nasser Mosque as a public protest against the water project.[21] The next morning, an unspecified number of Moroccans gathered at the mausoleum of Moulay Idriss, a sanctuary where Fassis historically gathered to protest.[22] Fez's elite did not appear at these gatherings, but the French still blamed them for the unrest. The commissioner of regional security insisted that they should have tried to calm the crowds, interpreting their nonintervention as tacit support for the protest.[23] In like manner, the Department of Indigenous Affairs accused Sultan Sidi Mohamed of complicity in these protests, for he neglected to warn the resident-general of increasing tensions.[24]

By 14 May, a French woman living in Fez felt compelled to write the resident-general of her fears. Fez, she noted, had been "bubbling" for three days. Believing that this unrest might spread to other cities, she advised him and his officials to give in to local demands as a demonstration of their "enlightened rule."[25]

Millers had an obvious interest in guarding their right to a free source of energy. Mohamed Mekouar was this trade's amin, and he went every morning to the mausoleum of Moulay Idriss, where he met with the merchants Mehdi el Laraki, M'hamed Youbi ould Hadj Tahar, and Tahar Mekouar.

Before discussing measures to prevent the project advocated by French administrators, they forced suspicious characters to leave the building, especially gallicized Algerians. The candle makers' amin attended the daily meetings, signifying that other workers were involved in this action.[26]

A letter sent to the president of France underscores the material interests at stake while also highlighting the intersection of the concerns of workers and the educated elite. At the end of May, the French president received a letter signed by "A Group Discontented with French Policy in Morocco." According to its authors, Moroccans had permitted the protectorate to pass new taxes and expropriate lands. Drawing attention to a need for water in homes and mosques, they asserted that they would not accept a project stripping them of their water rights.

The letter also highlights the plight of workers. Referring to employment programs set up by Prosper Ricard in the protectorate's early years, the authors noted: "Water is the driving force behind large establishments of industry and arts. Now, the protectorate has already decided that one could not introduce any machines in the city in order to conserve traditional arts. How are they able to endure without water?"[27] In this way, the authors referred to an implicit understanding between workers and colonial authorities. During the first seventeen years of the protectorate, the French had, in effect, guaranteed a minimum wage to Moroccan workers through policies predicated on the development of artisans trained in traditional crafts—and not mechanized vocations.

By June, Moroccans from other regions had begun to show signs of sympathy with Fez's residents. A merchant in Rabat expressed a sentiment that must have seemed dangerously radical to his French interlocutor. "French policies have never been just," al-Alou informed the commandant of the region, "but it is only now that Moroccans see with clear eyes."[28] In the Spanish zone, one French official reported a demonstration supporting the water rights of Fez. Two notables from this northern region visited Fez to evaluate the lay of the land. In fact, the French official thought that agitators of the unrest manipulated popular sympathies in regard to water distribution in order to incite a movement aimed at liberating the Riffian zone from foreign rule.[29]

After the resident-general visited Fez on 16 May, French administrators worked hard to resolve tensions between urban residents and the colonial government. Speaking with the majlis, French resident-general Jules-Joseph-Théodore Steeg extended the deadline for the inquest's completion in order to foster a negotiated solution to the crisis.[30] The commandant recommended rewriting the initial decree opening the project, thereby acknowledging formally the Moroccan right to water.[31] To appease notables, the French invited Moroccans to sit on the committee that would decide the fate of Fez's water.[32]

Despite efforts to appease Fez's residents, the water project fostered the formation of a society advocating increased Moroccan participation in colonial governance. Mohamed Hassan al-Ouazzani was a founding member of this nationalist group. He was educated at the French Collège Musulman, and his surname links him to one of Morocco's most influential shurafa' families. Fellow cofounders of this secret society were the merchant Hamza Tahiri, as well as al-Arbi and Hassan Bouayad, so its core group included several opponents of the water project.[33]

Now remembered as the driving force behind Moroccan independence, Allal al-Fassi was also an original member of this group. Born to the family that had long led prayers in the royal musalla, Allal was the son of a scholar at the Qarawiyyin Mosque and the nephew of the sultan's assistant khalifa in Fez. His signature is found on the petition of 10 May. As he later recounted in his memoirs, the water crisis gave Allal his first taste of political activism. Then twenty years old, Allal spoke before angry crowds gathered at municipal offices. He also worked with Hassan Bouayad on a letter of protest, which, detailing popular complaints, they submitted to colonial authorities.[34] Thus, the founders of the nationalist movement represented a cross section of Fez's mercantile and religious elite, all of whom actively opposed the colonial water project.

This group tried to build upon the momentum of the water crisis. In June 1930, they protested the juridical system set up by the Berber Dahir. Legal rights, however, unlike the distribution of resources, did not foster a united front. Disenchanted youth with little economic or social influence rallied to their cause, but workers and the elite did not. By October, when protests finally died down, Fez's basha had arrested seventy-five men, all between the ages of fifteen and twenty.[35] Nationalists wanted to represent popular aspirations, but legalistic issues did not spark mass support. Most Moroccans would not heed nationalists until drought and recession caused a sharp decline in the standard of living.

Patronage and the Poor

Between 1929 and 1935, Moroccan exports dropped 49 percent, while imports fell by 57 percent.[36] The decline of foreign trade harmed not only merchants but also the workers producing goods for them. Between 1915 and 1929, the French had sought foreign buyers for goods produced by artisans practicing traditional trades. During the recession, the purchasing power of this Western clientele declined. And overseas governments, hoping to protect the economic well-being of their own citizens, erected prohibitive tariff barriers that rendered Moroccan goods costly. By 1934, one French official asserted that the demand for goods produced in Fez had dropped to 10 percent of previous levels. As a result, he counted thousands of unemployed workers, including weavers, carpenters, blacksmiths, spinners, and embroiderers.[37] By that time, the wages of most workers had dropped by 60 percent.[38]

Moroccan crop failure aggravated economic hardship. In 1930, locusts destroyed southern crops for a second year running, and the lack of pasture caused the death of a third of this region's cattle and one-fifth of its sheep.[39] Northern Morocco also experienced unfavorable weather patterns. In 1931, rainfall was below average, and the resulting drought killed crops. Two years later, torrential rains destroyed the harvest.[40] After scanty rainfall in 1935, the average farm in northern Morocco lost half its wheat.[41]

Nevertheless, Moroccans had not yet faced the worst of the environmental crisis. The following year, in 1936, farmers harvested only three million quintals of wheat, approximately 27 percent of the already dismal harvest of the previous year.[42] By 1937, the protracted drought threatened severe famine, and Steeg, now acting as consultant for the protectorate, estimated that death by starvation threatened 1.4 million Moroccans, or 25 percent of the population.[43] The price of wheat and other cereals sold in urban markets skyrocketed as a result not only of poor harvests but also the price of transport. The purchase of barley, a cereal normally consumed by the very poor, proved nearly impossible, as its original price in the field tripled to ninety francs a quintal by the time it reached the city.[44]

Municipal programs reflected a rising numbers of Moroccans in Fez who could not afford food. As early as 1931, the chief of municipal services banned beggars from the Ville Nouvelle and the mellah, quarters frequented by European residents.[45] The majlis set aside two tracts of land for burying the poor.[46] Some homeless migrants found shelter in empty silos outside the medina's gates, poignant testimony of the food shortage.[47] Others found room at a shelter that the protectorate constructed in 1932. Poor men stayed in a shelter near Bab Ftouh, while women stayed in a rented warehouse near Bab Guissa.[48] As in the late nineteenth century, a rural exodus led to a sharp rise in Fez's population, from 98,205 in 1931 to 135,000 in 1936.[49]

Wages decreased as food prices increased, leading to the impoverishment of urban workers. On 18 June 1936, a colonial decree required enterprises contracted for public works to implement a minimum wage of 4 francs a day, but the skyrocketing cost of living rendered this return inadequate within less than a year. By April 1937, two French analysts asserted that "a minimum daily salary of 7 fr. 25 would be absolutely essential."[50] In Fez, however, an ordinary weaver earned only 5 francs a day.[51] The average family numbered six members, so a head of a household needed to purchase at least two kilograms of flour each day. In July 1937, at the famine's height, flour of hard wheat sold for 1.95 francs a kilogram in Fez, thereby forcing a worker to spend about 80 percent of his wages on the filling starch required by members of his family.[52]

Circumstances constrained workers like Mohamed el Haiani to sell their belongings. El Haiani had been one of forty-five artisans making cauldrons in 1931. Five years later, this unemployed artisan walked the streets barefoot, having sold even his shoes.[53] El Haiani was not an anomaly. By 1937, a colonial officer reported that five out of six families in Fez went into debt in order to buy food.[54]

Deteriorating economic conditions augured political unrest among practitioners of urban trades. The tanners' trade employed 161 master tanners and 350 journeymen and apprentices, while also generating work for 500 men who provided materials and transported skins. Between 1930 and 1934, demand for leather dropped 80 percent. Prohibitive tariffs hindered the sale of shoes in Egypt and the Spanish protectorate. At the same time, Japan dumped 350,000 pairs of plastic shoes into Moroccan markets, which, selling for 10 francs each, cost 75 percent less than shoes produced by Fez's tanners. Decreased demand caused the tanners' wages to plummet. In 1930, an average tanner earned between 20 and 25 francs a day. Four years later, he brought home no more than 6 to 10 francs a day.

The arrival in Fez of indigent peasants aggravated the lot of tanners. Working for less than established residents, by 1934 nearly half the workers employed at tanneries were from southern Morocco. To maintain their standard of living, Fez's tanners appealed to municipal authorities to get rid of their competition. The French did not ban migrants from the tanner's trade. Instead, they prohibited the importation of foreign shoes in order to stimulate local demand for leather goods.[55]

The builders' trade also suffered. The regulations passed by the French in the 1920s failed to protect workers from the global recession and drought, fostering a sharp decline in construction. This crisis impoverished the elite, and creditors threatened foreclosure on the properties of heretofore rich men, like Mohamed Mernissi. He contracted a loan of 875,000 francs, using as collateral property valued at 3,150,000 francs.[56] Impending financial ruin forced him to stop construction on all buildings, including a courtyard house in the Batha quarter intended as a home for his family.[57] Mernissi would save his properties, but other landlords did not. Archived accounts of building permits suggest that residents infused no more than seven million francs into the local economy by 1936, a small fraction of the forty-nine million spent in 1929.[58]

As a result, the wages of builders dropped by half. Noting this trend in June 1933, the Department of Fine Arts decided to restore the medina's walls in order to employ some builders.[59] The carpenter Ahmed Bennani had previously sold furniture of a Moroccan design to foreigners, but the crisis led him to take a job repairing a collapsed wall near Bab Guissa.[60] This project did more than further the preservationist goals of the French. Alluding to "some troubles in the indigenous city," one Fine Arts inspector hoped that the repair of the walls would increase urban security. "Access to the city would be more easily controlled," he stated, "since there would only be the gates (which are guarded) as entrances and exits."[61]

The protectorate tried to help colonized workers, but it simply did not have enough funds to alleviate Moroccan poverty. The Department of Indigenous Affairs gave 95,000 francs to the municipality in 1936 to permit the hiring of Moroccans to clean and repair roads. To assist a maximum number of men, the organizers of this program rotated personnel every fifteen days. Nevertheless, it employed only 202 people at any given time, a miniscule fraction of Fez's indigent population.[62] That same year, a regional administrative council allotted 7 million francs to assist workers, an amount which, once shared among all Moroccan cities, also represented no more than a drop in the bucket.[63] The French, however, did not have the means to do more. After the harvest of 1936, they calculated the protectorate's budget deficit at 152 million francs.[64]

When Charles Nogues became resident-general in October 1936, he planned to improve the lot of urban workers. Nogues was familiar with Morocco, having periodically served as an officer there between 1910 and 1930. As highlighted by William Hoisington, Nogues was Lyautey's disciple, thus an advocate of state paternalism. To rule the protectorate effectively, he believed that the French needed to make Moroccans richer. "Poverty," he told France's Council of Government, "brings with it political illness."[65] He negotiated financial aid from French politicians in Paris before assuming his new post. In this way, he brought with him 123 million francs, with half designated for improving the lot of Moroccans.[66]

In Nogues's view, poverty led to dissatisfaction among workers, and this threatened colonial stability because it fueled the nationalist movement. Between 1930 and 1932, nationalists had attracted only forty adherents.[67] As the crisis continued, they increased their clout by assuming the role of spokesman for workers. When Nogues arrived in Morocco, nationalists, now organized as the Comité d'Action Marocaine, called for higher wages for workers and a weekly day off.[68] They also contacted Fez's shoemakers and gold workers, two trades hit hard by the economic decline.[69]

In November 1936, the month after Nogues's arrival, Fez's nationalists led a protest that proved that some workers accepted them as their advocate. On 17 November, five hundred people demonstrated after Friday prayers at the Qarawiyyin Mosque. They headed up Talaa Kabira and Talaa Saghira, the medina's principal roads, but then, after finding the basha's police force blocking the way, backtracked toward the Rsif Mosque. After three and a half hours, Moroccan authorities arrested 149 people.[70] Besides thirty-two students from the Qarawiyyin Mosque and eight other academics, the basha judged the cases of a representative cross section of urban workers, including thirty-two cobblers, twelve bronze workers, four gold workers, three blacksmiths, four leather workers, and three spice sellers. This list also included a belt maker, a tanner, a painter, a shopkeeper, a mason, a saddle maker, a potter, and a mosaicist.[71] At that time, an official with the Ministry of the Interior identified "the danger of a liaison, now complete, between nationalist intellectuals, who, until recently, were the only ones of their inclination, and the corporations [of urban trades] confined, for the most part, to the most extreme misery."[72] Visiting Fez eleven days later, Nogues expressed concern with the adherence of workers to the nationalist group.[73]

Nogues also considered trade unions a threat to the political stability of the protectorate. Under duress, he legalized them in December 1936, with the protectorate's French workers thereby acquiring the same rights as their metropolitan counterparts. To augment the impact of ensuing strikes, however, union leaders also courted Moroccan workers.[74] On 11 January 1937, for example, most of the six hundred construction workers that struck in Fez's Ville Nouvelle were Moroccans.[75] Five days later, Nogues came to Fez to resolve this strike,[76] which ended on 19 January. The next day, however, employees of a bus company occupied the business offices, demanding higher wages.[77]

Restive workers continued to threaten colonial stability. French unionists convinced workers at the Ville Nouvelle's industrial mills to strike in February. Municipal authorities would arrest nine Moroccans who had picketed outside the entrance of these factories.[78] Nationalists tried to unite with striking workers, for a Moroccan interpreter for two French union organizers later admitted that he put two striking workers in contact with Allal al-Fassi.[79] Throughout Morocco, strikes continued over the next six months, leading the sultan to prohibit Moroccan participation in trade unions in June 1937.[80]

Nogues set out to revive the corporation in order to block groups of organized workers with their own independent influence in relation to the state. French officials failed to institutionalize the corporation in 1920, but Nogues quickly passed a decree allowing the protectorate to approve loans to corporations representing urban trades—and not individual workers—in May 1937.[81] The decree also enlarged the powers of the amin and created a corporate council for each trade, whereby French officials named members after consultation with workers.[82]

At the same time, colonial officers set up a fund to ensure that artisans received money as quickly as possible. By September, the French had already distributed 60,000 francs.[83] By the end of the year, this sum grew to 600,000 francs.[84] "All this," as pointed out by Hoisington, "smacked of fascist corporatism with workers bound hand and foot to the state."[85] This decrease in the autonomy of workers fostered social harmony, but it also suppressed political demands that threatened the colonial order.

Once Nogues's decree regulated the corporation, his administration reoriented the production of workers to serve local, and not foreign, needs. Shoemakers and weavers were among the principal beneficiaries of state loans.[86] Under French direction, shoemakers began making sandals for soldiers, and weavers produced cloth for prison uniforms.[87] To further stimulate the economy, the French advertised clothes produced by local craftsmen, explicitly attempting to decrease an elite tendency to wear European outfits.[88]

Moroccan nationalists advanced similar strategies to improve the worker's lot. In 1937, women began boycotting foreign cloth in order to promote local textiles.[89] Allal al-Fassi later highlighted the success of this campaign, stating that "Maghrib textiles which had hitherto lagged behind on the market became the most popular attire."⁹⁰ By coordinating the demand of the elite with the production of workers, both French officers and Moroccan nationalists tried to stimulate the local economy and to be identified as protector of Moroccan interests.

## The Mechanized Moulin du Quartier

Drought caused poverty, making the price of flour a pressing political concern. Mohamed ben Larbi Tazi "al-Guezzar" had made a fortune selling meat to the colonial army and then used his new economic clout to lay claim to more traditional social influence. Advocating in the majlis on behalf of ordinary Moroccans, he drew attention to the "continual rise in the price of flour and the risk to the household budgets of natives." Serving their poor constituents, members of the majlis followed Tazi's lead. When drought fostered increased reliance on flour produced at factories, the majlis voted "to petition the resident-general to invite European industrial millers to sacrifice a bit of their profits for several months to take into account the difficult period before the harvest."⁹¹

By acting on behalf of the poor, the interests of young nationalists and their more conservative counterparts in the majlis converged, with both groups ultimately calling for increased colonial intervention. Between 1934 and 1936, nationalists made it clear that they considered the price of factory-produced flour an important issue, and they wanted the colonial government to fix flour's market price "so that workers obliged to buy it would not be harmed."⁹² In like manner, the majlis called on the chief of municipal services to assume, in effect, the traditional role of the makhzan, blocking the export of wheat and preventing sales outside the rahaba.⁹³ Shared conceptions of Islamic charity among nationalists and majlis members promoted interaction among various social groups in Fez.

There was a need for the mass production of flour, but the intersection of price and productive capacity continued to offer a strong argument against industrialization. As documented by a local newspaper, an entrepreneur purchased a quintal of wheat for 55 francs, which he would then sell as flour at the steep price of 105 francs. If an entrepreneur made a profit of 18.50 francs for each quintal of wheat ground at his mill, then the owners of the Minoterie Oranaise, which ground 300 quintals a day, would have made 5,550 francs a day even after paying overhead.⁹⁴ Colonial officials, however, estimated that industrial mills operated at only 59.09 percent of their capacity in 1933, a rate that would drop to 48.45 percent by 1937.⁹⁵

Although having a grinding capacity of 400,000 quintals a year, industrial mills ground only 172,000 quintals of wheat.[96] The industrialized production of flour was not efficient, and the price of the product precluded purchase by the poor.

The need for cheap flour led some Moroccan entrepreneurs to set up grinding facilities that mechanized the small-scale commercial operation of water mills. Grinding thirty quintals of wheat a day, the productive capacity of this type of mill, called a *moulin du quartier*, was one-tenth that of an industrial mill. Nevertheless, it rectified the inefficiency of the Ville Nouvelle's factories, which, despite large investments, never operated at full capacity. The moulin du quartier produced ten times more flour than water mills, which, given urban growth, were unable to meet market demand.

The set-up was simple and, relatively speaking, cost efficient. Entrepreneurs harnessed an engine to a water mill's equipment, but, since they had no experience in this trade, its owners were not millers. By December 1936, Ricard counted fifteen mechanized mills in Fez's medina grinding 420 quintals of flour each day.[97] Operating on a smaller scale than inefficient industrial facilities, the moulin du quartier permitted entrepreneurs to avoid costly investments in facilities that did not turn a profit.

The global economic crisis led some bankrupt merchants to develop the moulin du quartier. Hossein Lahbabi was the son of a cloth merchant. Born in 1912, he briefly attended the Collège Musulman. After his studies, he imported novelty items, such as fireworks and toys. To cut out French middlemen, Lahbabi traveled to Germany. Since Lahbabi's brother was a nationalist who imported seditious books in Arabic, colonial officials at first refused to authorize his exit visa. Lahbabi, however, was able to convince the French that his intentions were purely commercial. He arrived in Leipzig in time to witness Hitler's election as chancellor in January 1933.

Novelties were not in great demand in the 1930s, forcing Lahbabi to trade at a loss. As he later explained to his son, an item purchased in Germany for ten francs sold for only six francs and, later, for four francs. Lahbabi did not want to take out loans, like other merchants who then lost their homes. To cut his losses, he sold off his goods with the intention of using the proceeds to start a new business.

"Flour," he told his son, "is something that everyone needs."[98] In 1934, Lahbabi set up a machine to grind wheat.[99] He used a secondhand engine of one cylinder powered by electricity. He harnessed the engine to a water mill on the western outskirts of the medina. Within twenty years, this moulin du quartier would grind 150 quintals of flour each day. Though representing only half of the productive capacity of the Minoterie Oranaise, he still produced fifty times more flour than a water mill.[100]

Lahbabi was not the only bankrupt merchant with nationalist leanings who mechanized the medina's traditional trades. Referring specifically to European ventures, Allal al-Fassi stated that nationalists "demanded protection for old Moroccan industries against competition from without as well as from within, where large-scale modern enterprises pose a threat to the survival of these small-scale industries."[101] In this way, adapting machines to urban trades became a matter of national pride. The French would reject Lahbabi's petition for a permit to run a moulin du quartier until the 1950s. Thus, his business activities acted as a political statement about Moroccan rights. Referring to colonial authorities and the Moroccans to whom they gave special rights, he asserted: "If Frenchmen and Jews operate industrial mills, then why not a Moroccan?"[102]

And yet, entrepreneurs operating a moulin du quartier bid for the business of water mills, which put them in conflict with traditional millers. Mohamed Bedaoui Larachi established a moulin du quartier called the Minoterie Andalousia in 1936, when he was forty years old. Since he custom ground wheat, his clients must have been Moroccans who would otherwise have frequented water mills.[103]

Like Lahbabi, Larachi avoided costly start-up investments. He harnessed a gas engine to a water mill near Bab Ftouh, one rented from the hubus administrators.[104] Larachi applied for a permit to run his mechanized mill, but a French official with the Department of Fine Arts refused to authorize it, stating, "Combustion engines must be banned in the medina.[105] Undeterred, Larachi continued to operate his moulin du quartier without authorization. When he sold it to brothers Abdeselam, El-Ghali, Mohamed, and Abdelhamid Larachi in 1947, it was grinding thirty quintals of wheat each day.[106]

These brothers also helped initiate the moulin du quartier. Since 1936, they had operated a moulin du quartier on the Oued Fejjaline, grinding flour for sale at shops.[107] Then a teenager, Hadj Mohamed Filalli "Terras" had worked at a water mill for a decade. He identifies this Moulin Fejjaline as the medina's first mechanical mill, and the clarity of his recollection suggests its potentially harmful effect on millers.[108]

Indeed, workers in traditional trades made explicit their opposition to the use of machines in the medina throughout the 1930s. One entrepreneur had set up a mechanical sawmill near Bab Guissa. Located in the northern quarters of the medina, far from the Ville Nouvelle, its owner was surely

Moroccan. The carpenters' amin, Si Mohamed Belhassan Elmghari, sent two letters to the Department of Fine Arts, each requesting a ban on the mechanization of their trade. "This machine," he stated, "gets in the way of providing bread for our children."[109]

In like manner, workers in the garment industry also protested the mechanization of their trades. There had been 460 Jewish workers and 150 Muslim workers producing gold thread for clothing at the end of the 1920s. In the following decade, these workers blamed the establishment of several machines for the high rate of unemployment among them. In 1936, the Jewish majority demanded a special tax on products from these machines so that the artisans could compete with them.[110] The next year, artisans making silk and ribbons for Moroccan clothing demanded a ban on machines through the French League for the Defense of the Rights of Man and Citizen. Politicized workers, unlike some nationalists, pursued a traditionalizing agenda.

French officials did not want machines to replace the handiwork of artisans, making them tacit allies of workers. When the French built a housing development in the eastern quarters of Tamdert, they banned machines in order to encourage only "small Moroccan industries."[111] Milling was a key urban trade. In 1931, the protectorate counted 1,416 millers in Morocco, and more than half of them operated mills in Fez and its region.[112] The French expressed an intention not only to maintain the miller's trade but also to increase the number of water mills operating in the medina. Thus, one official added forty-three marks on a map of water mills in the medina, each indicating the future establishment of a new water mill.[113]

Despite colonial intentions, Fez's millers experienced a setback during the economic crisis that fostered the moulin du quartier. Some millers in Fez left the trade. In December 1936, Prosper Ricard counted three master millers and twelve workers "constrained to abandon a profession in which they had hoped to earn their livelihood."[114] The next year, in 1937, Abdelwahed Ouali also left the trade. Then twenty-one years old, Ouali traveled south as a *graisseur*, an assistant to a driver transporting goods.[115]

The protectorate charged Moïse Levy with evaluating the flour industry. Owner of the industrial Grands Moulins Fasis in the Ville Nouvelle, Levy counted only two hundred millers in Fez, approximately one-third less than at the start of the protectorate.[116] By 1938, a colonial report would count only ninety-one water mills in Fez. This number represented seventy-eight commercial mills with 113 sets of grinding stones, and thirteen custom mills with 18 sets of grinding stones.[117] These findings show the decrease in the number of millers practicing the trade.

In January 1937, a decree placed the moulin du quartier and the water mill on an equal footing vis-à-vis the colonial state. The French established the Office Chérifien Interprofessionnel Céréalière (OCIC) to ensure the production of flour at a fair price. Henceforth, mills producing more than 3,000 quintals of wheat each year would be under a central authority, and wheat would be guaranteed to them at a subsidized price.[118] Water mills produced no more than 1,095 quintals of flour a year, so Moroccan millers did not receive state protection from the vagaries of the market. The entrepreneurs operating the moulin du quartier produced at least 10,950 quintals of wheat each year, so they should have qualified, but the French refused to authorize them. Only European industrialists benefited from the OCIC, so the decree offered a basis for an uneasy alliance between this group of workers and entrepreneurial notables.

Nevertheless, Fez's millers lodged a complaint regarding the decline of their trade, one that alludes to a certain frustration with Moroccan entrepreneurs in the medina. The millers sent twenty representatives to the office of basha Mohamed Tazi. They explained to Tazi that their business was so bad that they could no longer pay taxes. They blamed this decline at least partially on the moulin du quartier. Thus, the Commissariat of Fez noted that "indigenous millers operating water mills are discontent with the competition of those having installed electric mills." To rectify this situation, the millers wanted "the suppression of electric mills." They also wanted subsidies, which simultaneously emphasizes their resentment of policies underpinning the creation of OCIC.[119] The class tensions revealed in these demands suggest that an alliance between workers and the elite was fragile.

## French Failure to Industrialize the Butcher's Trade

To care for the growing number of urban poor, colonial officials, both French administrators and Moroccan notables, perpetuated precolonial fiscal policies. They raised the taxes collected from butchers, elevating the price of meat. In July 1930, the majlis quadrupled taxes that it had originally implemented in 1925 as a means of raising funds for the Muslim Orphanage and the Muslim Charitable Society. Henceforth, butchers paid eight francs for each head of cattle slaughtered and two francs for each sheep or goat.[120]

As a commodity, meat was to be taxed as a luxury item that would help care for the increasing numbers of urban poor. Butchers also continued to pay the guerjouma, mainstay of municipal revenue.

As early as spring 1931, the crisis also led the Jewish Council to start collecting a special tax from butchers selling kosher meat.[121] Members based the tax rate on the kilogram of meat sold, not on the head of livestock slaughtered. Jewish consumers paid an extra 1 franc 50 per kilogram of meat. Of this sum, the Jewish Council collected one franc, and the muhtasib collected fifty centimes on behalf of the municipality.[122] Within two years, the chief of municipal services reported that the initiative proved "one of the most important taxes collected by the said committee for charitable endeavors."[123]

The response of Jewish workers to this tax reveals class tensions among Moroccans. One month after passage of this initiative, workers protested the tax on kosher meat in a petition sent to the chief of municipal services.[124] These workers wanted cheap meat, not social welfare.

For the next two years, the workers sought the repeal of this tax. In 1933, six hundred workers addressed the chief of municipal services as "protector of the poor and needy":

> You must not ignore that our food—of workers and needy artisans—is composed above all of meat and bread. Between the elevated price of meat and our shortage of money, we cannot assuage the hunger of our children.... Unemployment intensifies daily among practitioners of our ordinary occupations.... You must save us from the rich landowners and landlords who initiated this idea, for they do not put themselves in the place of the poor before judging if we should submit to this tax.[125]

Goldsmiths, tailors, carpenters, shoemakers, and ironworkers were among those who signed the petition. According to the chief of municipal services, Jewish butchers supported the protest against the new tax.[126] Within three weeks, the general commandant would receive another three petitions.[127]

The protest of Jewish workers forced the French to mediate between two sets of socioeconomic interests. Notables seated on the Jewish Council refused to consider meat a nontaxable staple. On 27 July 1933, they informed the general commandant that "to cede to the petitioners would amputate the community's budget of its most important revenue at a moment marked by a renewed outbreak of unemployment and poverty."[128] The meat tax then provided annual revenue of 360,000 francs, 54 percent of the mellah's budget. The general commandant did not want to deprive the Jewish community of its tax base, but he feared the ire of the working majority. He recommended a middle road: an initial tax decrease of 25 percent that would later fall to 50 percent.[129] Still, subsequent administrative action—or lack thereof—suggests that French officers tacitly sided with notables. Four years later, the tax on kosher meat remained one franc per kilogram, and the issue was again before notables for consideration.[130]

The French used Fez's fiscal policies as a model for charity taxes on meat in all Moroccan cities. By implementing this tax in April 1934, the French intended to combat the economic crisis within a tradition that they deemed "Muslim." As justified by one official, a tax on meat increased alms giving by the rich.[131]

Although the French considered meat a staple, colonial officers in Morocco treated it as an elite luxury. The director of indigenous affairs later explained:

> It is not a question, in effect, of levying a surcharge on other foodstuffs, like sugar, tea, cereals, oil, which are staples of first necessity and are consumed as much by the poor element of the indigenous population as by the rich element. It would be aberrant to make the poor support such a tax, no matter how small, when the conditions of their existence are so difficult. Many must regularly content themselves with a little tea, some flat bread [kasra] dipped in oil, fruit, and vegetables. They eat meat rather infrequently. The well-off element of the population, by contrast, regularly consumes meat, and a surcharge on slaughter, in reality very slight, would not be an obstacle for them. A decrease of a few centimes on meat would not have an appreciable effect on the indigenous poor. They would, however, be sensitive to an augmentation, even small, of the price of foods that serve as daily alimentation.[132]

With the French promoting tea and sugar as dietary requirements, the concept of staple foods was—and still is—a relative matter. The tax, however, seemed to serve its intended purpose of raising income. In 1935, the French collected nearly two million francs in seventeen cities.[133]

And yet, the new tax wrought unanticipated consequences, threatening to pit butchers and the workers who patronized their shops against the notables who supported the charity tax on meat. A year after its passage, the French members of the High Council of Livestock Breeding demanded "the suppression of price setting for meat in cities, the reduction of slaughtering taxes, and a readjustment of secondary taxes collected for the Muslim and Jewish charitable societies." The French farmers who made up the governing body of this consultative organization made clear that the new tax had led some butchers to revert to their strategy of flooding the market with inferior meat that sold relatively cheaply.[134] In this instance, the interests of urban workers converged neatly with those of French farmers in the countryside, and not with the notables ostensibly representing their interests. Both French farmers and Moroccan butchers wanted to increase meat sales in urban markets, which would democratize meat consumption. The Department of Indigenous Affairs asserted that the farmers "reckoned... that the superposition of this surcharge to the slaughtering tax, already heavy, has a regrettable consequence on meat consumption and contributes to checking the development of raising livestock."[135] Colonial officials, however, did not heed the plea of either French farmers or Moroccan workers, maintaining the charity tax.

Meat consumption in Fez noticeably declined as wages decreased and the cost of living increased. French analysts noted that meat was the first cost eliminated from household budgets.[136] One economist engaged in a study of the household budgets of a locksmith, a carpenter, and a construction worker. Earning between six and ten francs a day, these workers served meat to the three others in their household only twice a month.[137] Prosper Ricard suggested that meat consumption in Fez represented only 25 to 33 percent of its normal average, with butchers slaughtering ninety to one hundred animals a day, and not three hundred to four hundred.[138] The decline in meat consumption caused a modification of the municipal budget, for anticipated meat taxes fell short by 100,000 francs.[139]

To increase tax revenue, the chief of municipal services proposed modernizing Fez's meat industry. This French official had first proposed replacing Bayn al-Madun's municipal slaughterhouse with an industrial facility in the Ville Nouvelle in 1932. Similar to its municipal counterpart, the industrial slaughterhouse would include a common hall, administrative offices, and a temporary holding pen for animals. In addition, its grounds would contain a livestock market, a factory for processing byproducts, and refrigerated chambers for storing approximately 39,585 kilograms of meat.[140] Officials planned to construct a facility that allowed for the daily slaughter of at least 150 head of cattle, 1,150 sheep, and three camels.[141] Thus, the French intended to commission a slaughterhouse incorporating new technology and the latest design principles in the hope of expanding the sale of meat to recoup initial outlays and increase tax collection.

The French did not intend to displace Moroccan butchers or to eliminate hallal or kosher meat from markets. The chief of municipal services wanted one-third of all cattle and one-fifth of all sheep passing through the industrial facility to endure the ritual act of slaughter by a Jewish shohet or one of twenty-five Muslim imams in Fez. He also required the slaughtering hall for pork to be in a separate building so as "to avoid all possibility of argument between Muslims and Christians."[142]

Nevertheless, the enlargement of slaughtering facilities signified an important commercial transformation. Two-thirds of cattle and four-fifths of sheep would not undergo a ritual slaughter, making them unfit for local consumption. Further, the chief of municipal services wanted the industrial slaughterhouse established next to the Ville Nouvelle's train station. As lauded by the president of the French Chamber of Commerce, an industrial slaughterhouse would cultivate wider Moroccan markets and encourage exports to foreign countries.[143] Access to a major line of transport leading to other cities and ports would favor the rise of chevillards engaged in a wholesale trade in dressed meat. In this way, this French official advocated the technological modernization of the meat industry as a means of sparking commercial innovations.

French civilians in Fez welcomed the proposal for an industrial slaughterhouse. Public works promised building contracts for local firms while also offering jobs to unemployed Europeans in the Ville Nouvelle.[144] Fearing advantageous proposals from companies outside of Fez, the French Municipal Commission refused to accept public bids on a contract.[145] To ensure the use of local companies and manpower, its members authorized a loan of four million francs.[146] The fiscal import of meat justified the expense, for the new slaughterhouse would increase Fez's tax revenue. Further, French officers could maintain a closer surveillance of tax collection at a facility located in the Ville Nouvelle. Thus, the fiscal success of the slaughterhouse ultimately hinged on developing new markets and not on energizing the purchasing power of local residents.

When the chief of municipal services presented the project to the majlis, notables did not want to endorse it. Before acquiescing to it, members of the consultative council imposed conditions on the municipality. The first two demands suggest support for undercapitalized butchers and the local consumers whom they served. They insisted that the municipality divide the industrial slaughterhouse into three sections so that Muslims, Jews, and Europeans worked separately. They also wanted Bayn al-Madun's facility to remain operational even after the new slaughterhouse's inauguration. Two other demands focused on the livestock market. The majlis insisted that Suq al-Khamis remain Fez's sole livestock market, seeking assurances that animals slaughtered at the new facility would pass through it.[147]

Given this focus on Suq al-Khamis, the economic interests of notables shaped majlis opposition. Fez's elite had acquired a great deal of property in the hinterland during the nineteenth century, so they owned a lot of livestock. In the mid-1930s, one French official estimated that Fassis owned between 75 percent and 95 percent of the city's hinterland.[148] The urban notables wanted to make sure that a modern facility would not harm their interests.

When the majlis enunciated their conditions, Mohamed ben Abdelmajid Benjelloun had already represented the Andalous quarter for twenty years.[149] Based on his family's business dealings, it seems that the economic crisis increased the number of urban notables who raised livestock. Patriarch of a family of cotton merchants, Si Mohamed had weathered previous economic slumps. His son Si Larbi had moved to Manchester in 1919 to run their business. By 1932, however, he, too, returned to Fez, the last Moroccan cotton merchant to go bankrupt.[150] No longer able to maintain his vast courtyard house, Si Larbi replaced it with a modest dwelling, even renting a part of his new home to the widow of a former business associate.[151]

The Benjelloun family intended to rebuild their fortune through less costly ventures that served the basic needs of local consumers. Using equipment imported from Europe, Si Larbi constructed an oven and a public bath on his lands in the Douh quarter in 1931.[152] He also invested in cattle, which he regularly sold to local butchers.[153]

Like the bankrupt merchants who established the moulin du quartier, the Benjellouns' activities in the local economy seemed to foster a milieu favorable to the development of nationalism. When Si Larbi's son Abdelmajid studied at the Qarawiyyin Mosque in the 1930s, he became a committed nationalist. Given the commercial and political activities of the Benjellouns, Si Mohamed's opposition to the industrial slaughterhouse in the majlis indicates that his resistance to colonial intervention was based on the need to protect personal wealth during the crisis of the 1930s.[154]

Si Mohamed ben Larbi Tazi "al-Guezzar" also sat on the majlis. This butcher had made a fortune wholesaling meat to the colonial army, but his election as representative of the Lemtiyyin quarter in 1924 marked his rise as a notable. During the five years in which the debate over the new slaughterhouse took place, Tazi al-Guezzar had a vested interest in policies affecting the management of Moroccan livestock. During that time, as one

French officer later charged, he and his associate Si Mohamed Mernissi developed a business relationship with a Moroccan who was a British protégé. Their associate's protected status permitted him to act as front man in an otherwise illicit livestock trade in the Spanish zone.[155]

Certainly, his elected colleagues considered him an expert in issues concerning livestock. Fez's private residents needed to pay a tax on animals entering the medina, even if they were not for sale. In 1936, members of the majlis appointed Tazi al-Guezzar to a special committee charged with reviewing this tax.[156] As a result of this reevaluation, there was an across-the-board reduction of the tax.[157] Ultimately, this outcome suggests that Tazi al-Guezzar might support his elite colleagues over ordinary workers. The decrease in this tax would have created an even greater reliance on the slaughtering tax paid by butchers who sold meat to the public.

Tazi had worked as a butcher, so the chief of municipal services chose him as the sole Muslim on the committee investigating the placement of the industrial slaughterhouse.[158] As pointed out by an officer with the Secrétariat Général, "The indigenous population is incontestably hostile to the project of installing a slaughterhouse in the industrial quarter."[159] To address concerns over the displacement of Suq al-Khamis, municipal officials briefly considered putting the slaughterhouse in the Makina, which, first constructed by Moulay Hassan as an arms factory, was near this livestock market.

In regard to the slaughterhouse, Tazi al-Guezzar clung to a seemingly anachronistic vision of urban development. In regard to modernizing the meat industry, he insisted on "the maintenance of the present gurna for animals destined for Muslim butcher shops in the medina as well as the maintenance of Suq al-Khamis." Posturing as conservative champion of the status quo, he argued that "the indigenous slaughterhouse was created 1,100 years ago on the Oued Bou Kherareb, knowingly downstream from the city so as to avoid all pollution of the waters." Encouraged by the support of his colleagues in the majlis, he called the proposed slaughterhouse "a deplorable action that would cause pain in the heart of every Muslim in the city." This impassioned opposition led the chief of municipal services to promise that he would not force Muslim butchers to work at the new slaughterhouse until the elite "will themselves manifest the desire to adopt a similar installation."[160]

Concerned over the economic and political implications of the project, the resident-general ended plans to build an industrial slaughterhouse in spring 1937. As he explained to the president of the Chamber of Commerce and Industry, the municipality could not afford a loan. And even if the contractor constructing the new facility put up the funds, the municipality would need to transfer the collection of meat taxes, thereby losing critical revenue. Urban notables, he continued, had already ensured that Muslims would continue to work at Bayn al-Madun, so the industrial slaughterhouse would serve only European and Jewish butchers. "It seems then that the most important element of the urban population," noted Nogues, "is not directly interested in the construction of a new slaughterhouse." For this reason, he did not perceive a need to stretch municipal resources.[161] In maintaining Bayn al-Madun's slaughterhouse, notables proposed a vision of development that was similar to that of the moulin du quartier in eschewing large industrial facilities that mass-produced either flour or meat and advocating instead for a smaller facility that served only local markets.

## Conclusion

The local drought and global recession of the 1930s impoverished even heretofore rich Moroccans. As revealed by the water crisis of 1930, most Moroccans became politicized not in the hope of increasing legal rights but rather in the pursuit of tangible interests that had everything to do with their personal well-being. Within the context of a drought, there were more poor needing care, but the French, suffering from the economic crisis, could do little to help. The ensuing struggle for scarce resources revealed potential fault lines running through colonial society, and these included not only French against Moroccan but also the Moroccan elite against Moroccan workers.

This struggle, though potentially of seismic proportions, bred innovation and clarified shared ideals in regard to the future orientation of Moroccan commercial and technical development. Some bankrupt merchants set up a mechanized moulin du quartier, but these machines were a form of intermediate technology that served local markets, thereby leaving intact highly personal economic relations. In like manner, Moroccans of all social milieus rejected the industrial slaughterhouse proposed by French technocrats and officers, consequently blocking the creation of more wholesale chevillards and choosing instead to maintain the municipal slaughterhouse at the Bayn al-Mudun set up for Fez. In this way, drought and recession became a paradoxically fertile field for the emergence of a conservative form of nationalist networks aimed at ending colonial rule.

# 8

# Famine and the Emergence of Popular Nationalism

On 15 April 1937, thirty thousand euphoric Moroccans in Fez greeted Sultan Sidi Mohamed ben Youssef. The crowd expressed enthusiasm for the putative ruler of this North African kingdom despite the dislocation fostered by political and economic conditions of that time. The dearth of wheat and livestock in the countryside had inflated the cost of flour and meat in urban markets, doing so just as a global depression curtailed many employment opportunities. Responding to the distress of impoverished residents in the former imperial capital of the Alaouite dynasty, Sidi Mohamed ben Youssef prayed in Fez's royal mosque and then distributed food to the poor.

After completing this act of charity, he toured the medina. Highlighting the perpetuation of his dynasty's rule, the sultan stopped first at parade grounds built by a celebrated sultan of precolonial Morocco, his grandfather Moulay Hassan. A living memory for older residents, this ruler had also reigned during an environmental crisis, when locusts and a drought lasting six years destroyed the kingdom's wheat crops and half its herds.

Sixty-five years after Moulay Hassan's reign had begun, Moroccans, though now colonial subjects, still looked to the Alaouites for a solution to their economic woes. As demonstrated by one onlooker at the parade grounds, colonized Moroccans sought the patronage of their sultan. At the monumental gate of Bab Dakkakin, a man handed a letter to the sultan describing his lamentable situation. He was a worker, a tailor named Moulay Ahmed ben Driss ben Abdeselam. Like other urban workers, he found it nearly impossible to earn a living. Requesting royal benevolence, he informed the sultan that he could not pay for the food necessary for his family's survival.[1]

The sultan had by then allied with Allal al-Fassi, so this incident highlights the conservative nature of Moroccan nationalism. The French had ruled on behalf of the Alaouites for twenty-five years, yet this tailor continued to observe the traditions of sultanic rule. Given the rising cost of food, why didn't Moulay Ahmed and others in the crowd show signs of more radical mobilization? Why didn't they try to create new institutions, which, if not pluralistic, were not controlled by the traditional elite? The elite, after all, had initially consigned Morocco to French colonization in 1912. In identifying himself as Sidi Mohamed ben Youssef's subject, the artisan Moulay Ahmed proved loyal to a political system based on monarchal privilege. And the tailor's demands suggest that his support of the sultan should be approached through the issue of urban food supply, the most pressing concern for ordinary workers like him.

Grievances over the distribution of local resources sparked the movement that would eventually lead to Moroccan independence, and nationalist conservatism offered a rational response to food insecurity. As Fez's workers became less capable of buying flour and meat, the threat of sociopolitical unrest increased. The educated sons of the Moroccan elite courted these unhappy workers by reinvigorating personal networks of elite patronage, thereby organizing a popular movement that opposed the colonial state.

Addressing the misery of impoverished residents in Moroccan cities, these nationalists conveyed a vision of the kingdom's future that was, in fact, very similar to the past. Led by members of elite families, the nationalists were at best cautious modernizers, implementing instead programs of social welfare premised on patriarchy as a social value and divine kingship as a political system. At the same time, they fostered the maintenance of small-scale ventures that fostered highly personalized economic relations, thereby eschewing the dislocation of industrial economies. This contributed to the flourishing of the conservative political values that accounted in turn for the enduring stability of the Moroccan state.

The Nationalist Distribution of Bread and Meat

Allal ben Abdelwahed ben Abdeselam ben Allal ben Abdallah al-Fassi, or, as he is better known, simply Allal al-Fassi, was a logical choice to head a conservative nationalist movement. Under his aegis, nationalists in Morocco premised their political action on the preservation of the monarchy and the purification of Islamic practices. Allal came from a family of religious scholars who had already demonstrated loyalty to Alaouite sultans. His forebears had long led prayers in Fez's royal musalla. Allal's father, a professor at the Qarawiyyin Mosque, had led prayers there since the onset of French rule.

Despite his youth, Allal quickly became a leading figure in the nationalist movement that would begin in earnest during the water crisis of 1930. Allal joined Fez's secret society that year, when he was only twenty years old, although he had not yet completed his studies at the Qarawiyyin Mosque. At that time, his cousin Abdeselam, ten years his senior, led prayers at the royal mosque in Fez, so he, and not Allal, seemed destined to assume the mantle of al-Fassi influence. Allal, however, merged scholarship and politics in a public manner. After finishing his studies in the summer of 1933, he began to organize public lectures on the Prophet that also criticized colonial policies. Since these lectures drew large crowds, French officials began to consider Allal a threat to Morocco's political stability.[2]

French officers identified Allal as a radical, but his use of public holidays to exhibit loyalty to the Alaouite sultan reveals a conservative political vision. After completing his series of public lectures, Allal traveled to Tangier. Because Moulay Abdelhafid lived in this northern city, Allal's trip sparked a rumor that he would back the deposed sultan's return. Allal later claimed that the French started this rumor in order to undermine the nationalist movement.[3] If Allal's assertion was correct, then French officers revealed a sly knack for power politics *à la marocaine*. After all, the sacrifice by Allal's uncle in the royal musalla after Moulay Abdelhafid's revolution had legitimized an abrupt political transition in 1908.

Certainly, Sultan Sidi Mohamed ben Youssef felt uneasy with the rumor of this al-Fassi defection. During Allal's trip, the sultan sent Allal's father, Abdelwahed, to a rural outpost, which, though deemed a promotion, effectively exiled the al-Fassi patriarch from Fez, a center of Moroccan power.[4] Further, colonial officials prevented Allal from returning to Morocco after a brief trip to Spain in August.[5] In this way, the sultan and French officers indicated the serious nature of charges that a member of the al-Fassi family did not support the seated Alaouite ruler.

Responding to this rumor in September, nationalists began calling for a celebration marking the anniversary of the sultan's ascent to the throne. Nationalists celebrated this holiday on 18 November 1933. By that time, many students at the Qarawiyyin Mosque, like Abdelmajid Benjelloun, whose father was a bankrupt cloth merchant, were politicized nationalists. That day, they sent the sultan telegrams swearing their loyalty. In other cities, such as Marrakesh, nationalists distributed food to the poor, a time-honored holiday custom in Morocco.[6] This celebration eased the concerns of colonial officials, both French and Moroccan, who allowed Allal to return to Morocco six weeks later. Only one month after Allal's return, in February 1934, Sultan Sidi Mohamed ben Youssef (officially called "Mohamed V" after independence) personally met with this nationalist leader for the first time. In this way, it seems that the young sultan and Allal reconstituted a historic alliance between Alaouite rulers and the al-Fassi scholars who legitimized their reign.

In stipulating a celebration of the reigning sultan's rule, the nationalists put the French in a position where they could not reject their demands. Mohamed V was the son of Moulay Youssef, who, as Lyautey's hand-picked successor to the recalcitrant Moulay Abdelhafid, had been the lynchpin of colonial rule. In September 1933, the first Fête de Trône had taken the form of a spontaneous uprising in support for the sultan. The next year, the French passed a decree formalizing the holiday.[7]

The celebration of this holiday in 1934 seemed to bring nationalists closer to both notables and workers. In Marrakesh, a colonial officer reported that Thami al-Glaoui, the city's iron-fisted basha, and Abderrahman Ibn Zaydan, historian of the shurafa', had both attended public ceremonies.[8] In Tangier, nationalists marked the holiday by offering tajine to workers, followed by cakes and tea.[9] The conservative nature of this nationalist strategy fostered the appearance of a unified political movement that transcended a specific social class.

In June 1934, the sultan planned to visit Tangier for Mawlid, the holiday marking the Prophet's birthday, so nationalists planned a large celebration there. Because Mohamed V had not yet fully endorsed the nationalist movement, he canceled his trip. Nationalists from Fez still traveled to the northern city for the ceremony, sacrificing a bull in front of attending crowds. They called their act *al-hadiyya al-wataniyya*, "the national tribute," evoking the traditional ceremony after the sultan's public sacrifice for 'Id al-Kabir.[10] By making a public sacrifice, nationalists engaged a readily understandable symbol of power to the Moroccan masses.

Moroccan officials also understood the symbolism of this sacrifice, and so they identified it as a seditious act. The *mandub* in Tangier ostensibly represented the sultan in the Spanish protectorate, and he ordered police to round up the attendant crowds. Just as with the Fête de Trône, the crowds cut across different social classes. Thus, a French official reported that the mandub arrested the poor and the rich, sending the former to jail and banishing the latter from the city.[11]

Three years later, the Aisawiyya and the Hamadsha brotherhoods decided to offer a public sacrifice in Meknes to mark Mawlid. Mohamed V, however, had already banned religious brotherhoods in 1933.[12] In doing so, he supported the nationalist effort to purify Islamic practices, while also, much like his uncle Moulay Abdelhafid, who had disbanded the Kittaniyya in 1909, eliminating centrifugal forces from the kingdom's political arena. These brotherhoods in particular were the largest informal religious groupings in Morocco, and they attracted many workers, including Fez's butchers.[13] Having participated in riots during the reign of Moulay Hassan, these brotherhoods also had a history of radical political activity.[14]

In a tract written by Mohamed Lyazide and Ahmed Cherkaoui, the nationalists condemned the act as well as French support for it. Lyazide and Cherkaoui accused French officials of providing "these barbarians" with money to purchase animals for sacrifice. In identifying ewes and goats as the animals used for the public ceremony, the nationalists undermined the religious legitimacy of the sacrifice. Both types of animals, after all, provided meat inferior to the sacrificial ram preferred by the Prophet. According to the nationalists, the French offered these animals "to be massacred and devoured by these savages."[15] Thus, nationalists sacrificed for Mawlid to show their own power, as in 1934, but they simultaneously undermined sacrifices by other groups making claims of popular legitimacy with the Moroccan masses.

The nationalists did not object to the commemoration of popular saints as long as they exercised principal influence in ceremonies honoring them. Hadj Hassan Bouayad, who had helped organize Fez's water protest in 1930, would attend the festival for the saint Sidi Boughaleb in 1937. There, he distributed money collected specifically for impoverished parents who wanted to sacrifice a ram on behalf of their newborn. The French Commissariat referred to this charitable distribution as "an act of propaganda effectuated by nationalists with the aim of drawing the sympathy of the medina's poor classes."[16]

'Id al-Kabir also threatened to become a contested holiday, especially since the French raised taxes on sacrificial rams. The French wanted to ensure the maximum collection of taxes during the economic crisis of the 1930s in order to help the rising numbers of urban poor. The French placed a new tax on young rams raised at home for the sacrifice of 'Id al-Kabir in 1933.[17] The chief of municipal services made sure that the inspector of fine arts repaired holes in the medina's walls in order to prevent residents from smuggling sheep for this holiday.[18] This new tax was added to the ten francs already collected by the French for each ram purchased at Suq al-Khamis.

The French collected the tax to care for the poor, but this paradoxically highlighted the poverty of some residents, who, unable to pay the tax, could not sacrifice for the holiday. Previously, the protectorate had offered a tax exemption on sacrificial rams to residents identified as poor. Given the economic crisis, some officials insisted that this exemption caused "an excessive loss for the municipal budget."[19] One year after its implementation, it was clear that this new tax led some Moroccans to forego a sacrifice for 'Id al-Kabir.[20] In response, the chief of municipal services made sure that taxes were lightened ten days before the holiday in 1935, but this proved only a temporary measure.[21] By 1936, another French official again cautioned that such tax exemptions cost the municipality as much as thirty thousand francs.[22]

By 1937, the taxes collected by the French on sacrificial rams provided nationalists with an opportunity to demonstrate against the colonial system. By then, the French collected twenty francs for each sacrificial ram.[23] In January, only one month before the celebration of 'Id al-Kabir, nationalists formed the National Action Party, voting Allal president of the new organization. Led by a member of the al-Fassi family, the first act of this nascent political party was a boycott of the sacrifice of 'Id al-Kabir. In boycotting the sacrifice, the nationalists intended to publicize opposition to the collection of a tax by French officers on a ram intended for an Islamic celebration. Given the role of the al-Fassi family in sacrificing next to Alaouite sultans, Allal was the only nationalist who could have called for a boycott of 'Id al-Kabir. In doing so, he revealed the conservative nature of a nationalist movement that re-created premodern symbolism.

The nationalists insisted that "all taxation would nullify the religious significance of the sacrifice of the holiday."[24] In Fez, nationalists asked residents to donate money intended for the purchase of a ram to their treasury.[25] Some nationalists from Fez lived in Kenitra (then called Petitjean), and they also called on residents to boycott the purchase of a ram. Instead, they advised purchasing an equal amount of meat to distribute to the poor. Butchers normally experienced a decline in demand during this holiday, so they must have been ecstatic with the nationalist program. Ultimately, nationalists in Kenitra distributed two hundred kilograms of meat for the holiday.[26]

Nevertheless, the boycott of 'Id al-Kabir did not prove an immediate success as a political strategy. Although the political party headed by Allal had attracted six thousand new members, it does not seem that rich Moroccans joined it.[27] As recorded by the French, the nationalist boycott did not affect the number of sacrificial rams purchased for 'Id al-Kabir, so the members must have been too young to head a household or too poor to purchase a sheep. That year, French officials recorded the sale of 12,607 sacrificial rams, collecting 88,121 francs as taxes on them. One official remarked that there had not only been no noticeable decrease in the sale of sacrificial rams but also that officials had actually collected four thousand francs more than the previous year.[28] In this way, the boycott highlighted what would prove a momentary weakness of the nationalist movement.

Further, the boycott revealed social fractures among the Moroccan nation, for some notables vocally opposed the nationalist action. The nationalists had not intended to undermine the legitimacy of their beloved Mohamed V, but some Moroccans interpreted the boycott as opposition to the sultan. Concerned, Mohamed V canceled a trip to Fez that he had intended to make immediately after 'Id al-Kabir. Instead, he visited Marrakesh. According to the security services, religious scholars and other notables of Fez decided to contact the sultan to disassociate themselves with "the point of view of the youth."[29] At that time, the French, possibly pushed by a nervous Mohamed V, himself aware that such a boycott often preceded a sultan's overthrow, banned the nationalist party.[30]

The sultan finally arrived in Fez on 7 April 1937, and religious scholars, including rabbis, and royal officials greeted him on the palace's parade grounds.[31] One week later, he attended a commemorative service for his royal predecessor and paternal uncle, the late Moulay Abdelhafid. Afterward, he would meet the tailor Moulay Ahmed. Only five months before, workers like Moulay Ahmed had participated in a demonstration, but the crowds gathered to glimpse the sultan suggest that the French were the object of their anger, not Mohamed V. According to one French official, Moroccans crowded windows and rooftops just to catch a glimpse of the young sultan.[32] The visit must have included meetings with nationalist leaders, for the sultan would permit Allal's political party to re-form by the month's end.[33]

The next month, Allal attended a celebration of Mawlid at the home of the Slaoui brothers. Like Tazi al-Guezzar, these brothers had made a fortune selling meat to the colonial army. By inviting one thousand guests to this house for Mawlid, the Slaouis publicized their new social capital. Hadj Alami lived across from the brothers at that time, and he remembers the care which the brothers took in presenting themselves to the world, wearing, for example, only the best clothing.[34] Given his comment, the Slaouis would have made sure that their guests were respected members of Fassi society, thereby suggesting that nationalists had made headway with the new social classes formed during the French protectorate. The subsequent political activity of Driss ben Mohamed Slaoui confirms this statement. Only eleven years old when Allal attended this celebration, the son of the eldest Slaoui brother would later become a nationalist leader and, after Independence, a minister in the government.[35] In 1937, however, one French official demonstrated a surprising naiveté, calling Allal's visit to this celebration "of no political significance."[36]

The distribution of flour to the poor, like the public sacrifice, was also a means for nationalists to underscore popular legitimacy. In August 1936, nationalists submitted to the French minister of foreign affairs a demand for an increased supply of bread for workers.[37] Allal and his colleagues organized soup kitchens to immediately address poverty in Fez.

The nationalists also distributed bread to the poor. On Thursdays, they collected money from merchants for the purchase of wheat. Moroccan millers ground it at no charge. Bakers and the operators of public ovens volunteered to prepare the dough and cook it. The French estimated that nationalists distributed between four hundred and five hundred loaves of bread each day at the Fonduk al-Jadid in the Kettarine quarter.[38] Allal asserted that nationalists distributed bread in most Moroccan cities. He claims nationalists distributed 3,500 meals in Fez alone.[39] He also asserts that the French consistently obstructed nationalist charity, thereby preventing them from courting the urban poor.[40]

Allal's claims were not the trumped-up accusations of a man with a vested interest in condemning French officers; an archived colonial document supports his claim. A French official in the Direction de l'Intérieur asserted that the charity tax on meat provided a means of beating nationalists at their own game. In raising charity taxes collected from rich Moroccans, the French would decrease contributions to the nationalist treasury. He stated: "One is right to believe that the charitable works of the partisans of autonomy in political matters [*la bienfaisance particulariste*] undertaken by young Muslims, thus deprived of its principal resources, will quickly run out of steam."[41] The charity tax on meat offered a deliberate political act intended to stymie nationalist programs of social welfare.

The case of underemployed bookbinders highlights the political import of the nationalist distribution of bread. Between 1915 and 1930, colonial officials implemented policies that fostered the growth of this urban trade. From only two practitioners in 1915, the trade grew to ten master craftsmen and ten journeymen by 1935. During the 1930s, however, the earnings of master craftsmen dropped by 80 percent, falling from one hundred francs a day to twenty francs a day.[42] Nogues tried to assist them, guaranteeing the bookbinders' corporation a loan of thirty-five thousand francs in August 1937. Bookbinders did not consider this sufficient, and they began to protest their declining lot that month.[43] The protectorate created this trade, but it could not sustain its workers during the 1930s.

Nationalists seized the opportunity to assume the role of protector of destitute bookbinders. In August 1937, the members of the bookbinders' trade walked through the medina with signs signifying their desperate situation. Written in Arabic, not French, which reflected their reliance on Moroccan munificence and not on French assistance, one sign read, "We demand bread!" Another sign read, "The corporation of bookbinders, which does not have sufficient means to subsidize its needs, requests aid from its Muslim brothers."[44] According to the Office of Political Affairs, a charitable association headed by Allal distributed one or two loaves of bread each day to the unemployed of the corporation. In this way, nationalists slowly accrued popular legitimacy among the urban majority in Moroccan cities, which, in turn, allowed them to organize anticolonial demonstrations.

## The Water Riots of 1937

A qualitative shift in nationalist demands began in September 1937, when a struggle for water rights in Meknes sparked sympathy demonstrations throughout Morocco. At that time, residents of Meknes expressed a concern that the colonial administration would decrease the waters of the Oued Boufekrane. According to a rumor spreading throughout the city, the French would divert the river from Moroccans in order to irrigate European farms and to construct a municipal pool. As in Fez seven years before, the popular tale told in the streets did not accurately portray official intentions. Colonial administrators did plan changes to the city's canal system, but they did so to compensate for shortages caused by drought and disrepair.

Nevertheless, the nationalist Mohamed Ouazzani publicized the complaints of urban residents, focusing in particular on those expressed by millers operating the city's eighteen water mills. On 2 June, the millers accused the French of decreasing their water supply. This decrease, they asserted, did more than adversely affect their own commercial ventures. As highlighted in Ouazzani's newspaper *L'Action du Peuple*, this action hurt urban residents, for water mills "contribute in large measure to the city's provisioning, particularly of the poor."[45]

The tensions over water rights led to the first case of violence in a northern city since the French had established the protectorate. On 1 September, a crowd of five hundred impassioned Moroccans gathered outside the municipal offices, where local notables discussed the potential decrease in water with French officials. As discussion of the issue of the Oued Boufekrane began, the angry crowd chanted: "They have taken our water."[46]

Colonial officials, both French and Moroccan, cracked down on the demonstrators. The next day, the basha arrested the men who instigated the protest; as a consequence the nationalists called for shops to close and for a meeting at the Grand Mosque. The assembled crowds marched to the jail and demanded the prisoners' freedom. The irate crowds frightened the policemen guarding the jail. When a skirmish between the crowds and the policemen ensued, the police killed thirteen demonstrators. Fifty other demonstrators were wounded, as well as fifty-two policemen.[47]

Moroccans everywhere sympathized with demands for water rights, and this tragedy unified them and the nationalist movement spearheading the demonstrations. Residents of Marrakesh and Sefrou were predisposed to such sympathy, for they had already expressed fear that the colonial government might take their water. In a like manner, residents of northern Tetouan had already suffered when Spanish colonists seized a number of water springs in and around their city.[48]

Given the general concern for water rights, sympathy demonstrations spread to other cities. After the violence in Meknes, many urban residents in Morocco stopped working for one day, instead attending prayers at mosques commemorating dead protestors. In Fez, nationalists proved their increasing authority by making sure that everyone showed support for the people of Meknes. According to French informants, the nationalists coerced at least one Muslim butcher and one Jewish mill owner to close down their place of business.[49] Even the sultan protested the French response to the incident in Meknes. Mohamed V accused the French, albeit privately, of taking water, chastising them for ordering the arrest of demonstrators.[50]

The fallout from the Meknes demonstration aggravated living conditions. In Meknes, widespread panic led some residents to stockpile wheat, which, in turn, caused an urban shortage of this staple. Within a week, a food riot threatened to follow on the heels of the protests over water rights.[51] In Fez, the French superintendent of police reported that hoarding had led to a wheat shortage that threatened urban stability. Fava Verde indicated to his superiors that "you should not delay remedying the shortage of this critical staple. Otherwise, the turmoil might provoke some incidents—of which we would not be able to envisage the exact significance from hereon in."[52] The wheat shortage added fuel to the nationalist fire, and a French official warned that "nationalists in different Moroccan cities are prepared to spark—whether tomorrow, Sunday, or most likely Monday—a protest on the subject of water in Morocco, the cost of living, and especially the price of wheat."[53]

Elite nationalists assumed the role of spokespeople for the masses. On 14 October, they sent a note to the protectorate's French officials. This letter linked the workaday needs of impoverished workers to the interests of the educated elite. It insisted on freedom of the press and an improved school system, demands that specifically served educated members of a local bourgeoisie. At the same time, however, the nationalists condemned the low wages of workers and demanded the right for Moroccans to unionize, just like workers in France. Further, the nationalists protested "the constant rise in the price of staples, most notably, wheat, semolina, and sugar."[54] Given the low wages and the high cost of food to which nationalists drew attention, the subsequent protest fits into a historical pattern. In Moroccan cities, popular unrest loomed when ordinary households had difficulty acquiring provisions of food.

## The October Protests

On 25 October at 5 p.m. exactly, the French arrested Allal al-Fassi. One week earlier, the French had learned that he and his nationalist cadre planned a large protest in Fez.[55] When the French brought Allal to the police station, they also took the nationalists Omar ben Abdeljellil and Ahmed Mekouar. There, they learned of their impending exile. That night, the French sent Allal to Gabon and Abdeljellil and Mekouar to the Sahara.[56]

The abrupt arrest of these nationalists intensified brewing unrest in Fez. By 7 p.m., nationalists, including Mohamed Hassan Ouazzani, who had split from Allal's group in order to form his own party, grew concerned that their colleagues had not returned. Despite his competitive bid for Allal's position as leader of Moroccan nationalists, Ouazzani left the medina for the Ville Nouvelle, to speak with French officials in order to learn the fate of his erstwhile rival.

Concerned with growing unrest, colonial officials ordered police at Bab Boujeloud and Bab Ftouh to stop Europeans from entering the medina.

That night, crowds insulted the public criers who announced that the sultan had ordered everyone to remain calm. Nationalists sent other criers to proclaim that "those who want to die for their country and Islam should go tomorrow morning to the Qarawiyyin Mosque." At 10 p.m., a French informant reported that workers from several trades were sharpening knives at Bab Sansala, near the Rsif market. They were preparing for a major confrontation, for the informant noted that they hugged and bid each other a tearful adieu.[57]

At 9 a.m. the next day, nationalists forced shopkeepers to close for the day. They posted tanners near commercial centers in order to prevent looting of both Muslim and Jewish shops, so they did not intend to permanently damage urban commerce. Crowds at the Qarawiyyin Mosque recited the *Ya Latif* prayer, which, normally said during severe drought, indicated the gravity of the brewing demonstration. At that time, a nationalist gave a speech accusing the French of tyranny.

By 10:30 a.m., crowds at the Qarawiyyin Mosque began to march in the streets of the medina, protesting Allal's arrest and the general substance of colonial policy. According to the French, at least fifteen thousand men participated in this demonstration. After half an hour, they returned to the Qarawiyyin Mosque, where they said more prayers before leaving again at 11:30 a.m.[58] Heavy rains halted protests scheduled for the afternoon.[59] But in a semiarid land like Morocco, which had then suffered drought for nearly seven years, demonstrators must have interpreted inclement weather as tangible evidence of divine favor.

Throughout the day, workers, often youths, expressed support for the protest by closing down shops, even the ones near the police stations at the medina's margins. At 4 p.m., the French caught a cloth merchant, a shoemaker, and a weaver, all between sixteen and twenty-two years old, threatening shopkeepers near Bab Boujeloud who had decided against closing for the day. Three hours later, the French arrested a shoemaker and a tanner, also young, for threatening shopkeepers in this quarter.[60]

Butchers played an active role in propagating urban unrest. At 1 p.m., approximately two hundred youths, most between fifteen and eighteen years old, had gathered around the police station at Bab Ftouh, where, just as in Bab Boujeloud, some shopkeepers had remained open. According to the commissariat, a butcher, identified as Bachir ben Mohamed ben X, twenty-five years old, selling meat in Rsif market, emerged from the crowd and tried to strike a police officer with his knife. Later that afternoon, the French arrested the butcher Si Hamed ben Abderrahman ben X in the same place. The French accused them of carrying a dangerous weapon, although Si Hamed and his companion insisted that they carried their knives for occupational purposes. The French found this plausible, but the men were drunk so they arrested them anyway.[61] Roger Le Tourneau, then director of the Collège Moulay Idriss, blamed the high participation of butchers in this riot on the fact that the French had not established policies to help them weather the economic crisis.[62]

As demonstrated the next morning, elite nationalists and French officials engaged in a struggle to win over the Moroccan masses. Because workers and the poor did not have money for storing food, some nationalists pointed out that the forced closure of shops threatened to create bad feelings among urban residents.[63] At the end of the first day of protest, many Moroccans found it difficult to provision their households with bread, the mainstay of their diet.[64] Nationalists then permitted shops to remain open on the morning of 27 October. At the Qarawiyyin Mosque that morning, a nationalist publicly asked merchants selling food to keep their shops open until noon.[65]

As the same time, colonial officials, both French and Moroccan, met with workers in order to undermine the nationalists. The chief of municipal services and the muhtasib, Driss al-Moqri, met with ten representatives of each corporation in Fez. Hoping to persuade them not to participate in the demonstrations that day, he insinuated that their participation would hurt their interests because the makhzan made decisions regarding the distribution of financial aid. Once the meeting was over, however, these workers headed straight to the Qarawiyyin Mosque to join protests. According to a French informant, the representatives of the tanners led this procession, bragging all the way that they did so against the will of both the French municipal services and the muhtasib.[66]

That day, nationalists again met at the Qarawiyyin Mosque before leading marches through the medina. By 10:45 a.m., demonstrators left the Qarawiyyin Mosque. The French counted twelve thousand participants, all yelling, "Down with colonization!"[67] The number of men marching in the street, however, does not fully reflect the depth of popular support. Throughout the morning, the ululations of women on rooftops accompanied the cries of male protestors.[68] Just as in April 1912, the participation of sequestered women revealed widespread disaffection with the French, while also suggesting that the protest did not stem from concerns expressed only in the male sphere of formal politics.

Violence seemed imminent, an outbreak that would pit artisans and tradesmen against each other. A man stood at the door of the Qarawiyyin Mosque, calling: "The one who is a true Muslim should enter the mosque; the one who loves France should return to his occupation." Some disillusioned workers took it upon themselves to ensure that no Moroccans supported France, even shopkeepers. At 9 a.m., one group forcibly closed down the shops near Bab Sansala. In the quarters of Sidi al-Aoued and Nekharine, one hundred shoemakers also closed down nearby shops. Similar threats to shopkeepers occurred in the Fonduk al-Yahoudi neighborhood of the northern Cherabliyyin quarter. In the Seffarine quarter, bronze workers prevented shoemakers from working, forcing them to go to the Qarawiyyin Mosque. In like manner, forty men obliged shopkeepers at Bab Guissa to close. When a policeman from a nearby station tried to arrest this group's leader, the crowd threw rocks at him. By 12:15 p.m., the commissariat reported that looting had begun, with 150 demonstrators breaking the doors of shops in the Achabine quarter.[69]

With urban order breaking down, the French strengthened their response to the demonstration. On 28 October, the colonial army occupied the medina for the first time since 1912. By 9:30 a.m., soldiers had completed a search of nationalist headquarters, where they collected a series of political tracts. At the offices of Ouazzani's newspaper, the French arrested a twenty-five-year-old tanner who confronted soldiers with a knife.[70] French troops quickly secured the medina, with the exception of the area surrounding the Qarawiyyin and Rsif Mosques. Unfortunately, the legionnaires sent to the central rallying point of the nationalist demonstrations panicked when they encountered a hostile crowd of several hundred people. Soldiers threw two hand grenades, wounding six people.[71] Nevertheless, the commandant of the region of Fez proved able to walk through the medina for one full hour by 11 a.m.[72]

The next day, French troops neutralized the nationalist leadership in order to forestall further demonstrations. Nationalists had once again met at the Qarawiyyin Mosque, although crowds numbered only two thousand that morning. Most of the assembly dispersed quietly after noon prayers. By that time, the French placed guards at the mosque's seven doors. The policemen of the basha were Muslim, so they could enter this sacred building and then drive nationalists from it. Once outside, French soldiers captured 696 nationalists, eventually arresting 464 of them. By 3 p.m., the French had ended the largest anticolonial demonstration to date and seemingly crushed the nationalist movement.[73]

## Conclusion

The militarization of colonial rule signaled the death knell of the French protectorate of Morocco, although independence was still nineteen years away. Fez's protests quickly spread to other cities in the French and Spanish protectorates. In Port Lyautey, two demonstrators died in a fracas between police and Moroccan crowds. In agreement with Paris, Nogues forcefully blocked any nationalist activities in Morocco. French troops remained in Fez's medina for ten days.

On 31 October 1937, the resident-general traveled to Fez, hoping that his presence would calm restive spirits there. Nogues met with notables as well as with representatives from urban trades, promising aid to "hard-working, orderly people." The resident-general, however, had already decided that benevolent policies of full employment were not enough to maintain urban order. While in Fez, Nogues ordered the construction of two garrisons in the medina in order that soldiers could respond quickly to future protests.[74] Built near Bab Guissa, the garrison would house three French officers and thirty soldiers.[75] Though designed in a traditional architectural style, its presence offered a constant reminder to urban residents of the military force backing French rule.

By 1937, the distribution of scarce resources was a major concern for most Moroccans. The economic and environmental crisis of the 1930s had led to a breakdown of the social contract between French officials and Moroccan workers. As a means of asserting political legitimacy, nationalists began to provide flour and meat to impoverished workers in Fez.

Moroccan workers, fearing a shortage of water and food, began to align with the elite leadership of the nationalist movement because they advocated on their behalf. Born to a family of religious scholars that had long supported the Alaouites, Allal al-Fassi's leadership role in the nationalist groupings embodies the conservative nature of a political movement premised on the perpetuation of a monarchy—indeed, a divine kingship—integrating Islamic values of charitable works. Under Allal's aegis, nationalists, much like precolonial rulers and urban notables, distributed flour and sacrificed publicly in order to communicate their concern for workers and the poor.

In 1930, a demonstration for water rights in Fez had preceded protests against the Berber Dahir as a colonial policy. Seven years later, this pattern would be repeated, but, in the context of ever increasing poverty, on a larger scale and with a qualitative shift in demands. From an initial desire to participate more fully in the colonial system, nationalists in 1937 began to demand independence for the kingdom of Morocco. In the face of this unrest, colonial officers felt compelled to rely on the threat of a forceful response to urban unrest. The October protests of 1937 proved that the young nationalists, much like their forefathers, could gain wide support among urban masses by manipulating popular issues in regard to the distribution of key resources such as water and food.

# Conclusion

In October 1999, Mohamed VI came to the imperial capital of Fez for the first time since ascending the throne after his father Hassan II's death two months before. By late morning, crowds lined Fez's principal avenue, which ran through streets of the Ville Nouvelle and ended at the palace. Moroccans turned out in droves to show support for the new king, even those, like my friend Adil, who had struck me as politically apathetic.

Adil was a *shabab*, the term North Africans use to describe an unemployed young man. He frequented a café next to the Téléboutique where I used to call home for news. Under normal circumstances, I probably would not make friends with someone like Adil. One day, however, I learned that my father had fallen ill. Adil and his buddy Karim appointed themselves my neighborhood protectors after they saw me crying as I left the Téléboutique.

When the king visited Fez, Adil had only recently returned to his hometown. Apparently, the Greek authorities had sent him home after a ten-day stint in their jail as, in Adil's words, "a guest of the commissar." With his unkempt dark hair and goatee, Adil presented a grim front to the world. For this reason, I was surprised at his extremely warm reception of the king.

On that October day, he had woken up early and taken great care in writing a letter addressed to Mohamed VI. His letter explained his lamentable situation, and he asked this royal benefactor to help him find work in Morocco. Adil accompanied me on a brief tour of the main boulevard but soon excused himself so that he could jockey for position in the crowd. If he got up front, he explained, he could hand deliver his letter to the king.

If I had thought that Adil was exceptional in his loyalty to the king, my experiences the next morning proved me wrong. At that time, I, along with, it seemed, half of Fez, waited at the medina's monumental Bab Boujeloud in order to catch a second glimpse of Morocco's new sovereign. Strangers in the crowd chatted as they watched schoolgirls in brightly colored jellabas line up with baskets filled with flowers to be tossed in the king's path once he arrived.

As the king descended from his car in the square before the gate, urban notables greeted him, each bending to kiss his hand, a demonstration of their loyalty. The rules of sociopolitical hierarchy in Morocco, however, are complex. The young must sometimes bow to their elders, even if, like Mohamed VI, the young are richer and more powerful. To show respect for the men who had worked for his father, Hassan II, the new king gently stopped some of the notables from kissing his hand, a gesture favorably commented upon by members of the crowds.

As the king finished greeting people in the reception line, he walked purposefully toward the Boujeloud gate, intending, like many Alaouite rulers before him, to visit the Qarawiyyin Mosque. As he passed in front of me, the two Moroccan women standing next to me fainted. They wore cotton, not silk, headscarves, which marked them as working class. The king's holy blessings, or *baraka*, as another member of the crowd explained, had caused them to swoon with joy.

Nearly ten years after witnessing the king's arrival in Fez, I now realize that my interest in exploring the roots of Moroccan conservatism began on that October day. Today, Morocco remains a poor nation, like other countries in Africa and the Middle East, but, and in contrast to its counterparts in the Arab-Islamic world, its government has proved exceptionally stable. By tracing the consumption of flour and meat, I have tried to provide what the anthropologist Clifford Geertz might term a "thick description" of the social history and political economy of Morocco, one that explains why most Moroccans acquiesce to a paternalistic political system premised on divine kingship.[1]

The work of millers and butchers in Fez between 1878 and 1937 helps identify factors that contribute to Morocco's stability. Flour production forged highly personal social institutions in this semiarid land. It was—and still is—a process requiring people with different levels of wealth or rank in the urban hierarchy to work together in order to provide staples in urban markets, a shared goal often enunciated in terms of Islamic charity. Meat, especially when the head of an elite household performed the ritual sacrifice, represented an expression of political authority when distributed to subordinate clients. Although based on the traditions of the Prophet Mohamed, meat played more than a religious role in this society, for, as a taxable commodity, its consumption ensured the care of the poor during periods of environmental crisis.

The late nineteenth and early twentieth centuries were a critical moment in the political and economic development of Morocco, and this study shows the importance of provisioning policies in Morocco's semiarid lands. Yet, the ideas outlined below help to explain the present-day choices of Moroccans and of the Alaouite rulers who have led them for nearly 350 years.

*Ensuring food security is a core concern of ordinary Moroccans, thereby shaping the policies of Alaouite rulers intent on prolonging their own reign and of perpetuating their dynasty.* In the precolonial era, Moroccan sultans ensured the urban food supply, even if it meant incurring debts to European countries. When the French set up the protectorate, its officials realized that they too must guarantee access to food in Morocco's densely populated cities. It was only when a drought hit Morocco during a global recession that protectorate officials, ultimately linked to continental France and its citizens, could no longer provide for the working majority. This failure was a catalyst for the nationalist movement. The elite leaders of the movement, though making claims in regard to demanding political rights, actually courted popular support by ensuring the provisioning of their impoverished social inferiors.

Concerns for food security still shape relations between state and society in Morocco. The last major drought occurred between 1981 and 1984, during the reign of Hassan II, great-grandson of Moulay Hassan. At the drought's start, the International Monetary Fund convinced the government to eliminate food subsidies, with an anticipated 40 percent increase to the cost of wheat flour. Anticipating a rise in the price of staple foods, workers in Casablanca took to the streets. The army cracked down on these "bread riots," leaving 637 people dead, and this incident offers an undeniable example of state violence.[2] In the aftermath of the riot, however, the makhzan, in its present-day form, once again instituted food subsidies, thereby reinstating a historical social contract by which the government exchanged cheap food for political quiescence.[3]

*Modernity, as measured by technological and commercial innovation, takes many forms, and not just that of full-scale industrialization as experienced in the West.* Regular cycles of environmental crises made manual technology operated by craftsmen more adaptable than machinery imported from Europe. Moroccan leaders and the workers supporting them shunned industrial facilities that mass-produced food, whether flour or meat.

Nevertheless, Moroccans did engage in both technological and commercial innovation at the work site of millers and butchers. During the drought of the 1930s, the mechanized moulin du quartier began to compete with Fez's water mills, although its owners maintained the principles of the water mill's small-scale commercial venture. In like manner, butchers transformed their commercial practices, with chevillards beginning to wholesale meat even as they rejected an industrial slaughterhouse in the 1930s. In both instances, Moroccans adopted principles associated with Western development only to the extent that they could improve the provisioning of local markets, stopping short of costly investments for which profits depended on markets secured beyond the urban limits.

Today, some factories in Morocco do mass-produce flour for a national market, but these industrialized facilities have not replaced the small-scale ventures of the moulin du quartier. By 1963, the moulin du quartier had largely displaced traditional technology, with only twenty-six water mills still in operation.[4] The makhzan offered the Moroccans running these water mills the funds to create industrialized cooperatives, thereafter diverting water from Fez's subterranean canals. Still, the government issued permits to the operators of these defunct water mills so that they could set up small-scale machines at their former workplace, custom grinding wheat for local consumers.

Some millers hedged their bets. Hadj Mohamed Filalli "al-Terras," for example, joined with the millers Abderrahman Hasnaoui and Abdelwahed Ouali in founding the industrial Moulins Najah, but he made sure that his son set up a moulin du quartier at the site of his former water mill.[5] Fez's residents, including rich Moroccans, still frequent these moulins du quartier. Zaki Berrada, a wealthy landlord and head librarian at Fez's Collège Moulay Idriss, still has flour custom ground at a moulin du quartier, especially, he notes, when winter rains ensure successful wheat crops.[6] In fact, at least 50 percent of Moroccans throughout the kingdom do not purchase factory-produced flour, frequenting instead small-scale commercial ventures serving a local clientele.[7]

The organization of the butcher's trade also reflects patterns of the precolonial past, for these workers remain independent artisans selling a consumable luxury. Some octogenarian butchers like Abdellatif Bouayad look back with nostalgia on French policies, leading his colleagues at Fez's municipal slaughterhouse to teasingly refer to him as a *himayya*, or protégé.[8] His nostalgia is based on the tried-and-true formula that a price increase in meat leads to a decreased volume in sales for the butcher. To increase their volume of sales, some butchers still engage in strategies bordering on civil disobedience. Some butchers, like Hadj Mohamed Sharqi "al-Sabaʿ," who trained at Bayn al-Madun in the 1930s, have set up a gurna outside of Fez's city limits, where municipal authorities cannot collect taxes or oversee the quality of their meat.[9]

Since Islamic law permits the slaughter of animals at home, these butchers often compete with private residents who slaughter animals themselves. Some consumers, like the father of a friend raised in Casablanca, began to engage in the practice of *luzia* when the government raised meat taxes in Casablanca. In this way, several households would purchase a sheep, privately sacrifice it, and then share its meat. As another example, the head of Fez's chevillards began to engage in luzia when the government raised meat taxes in Casablanca. The head of Fez's chevillards notes that he caught one man slaughtering mules at home, afterward selling the meat as hamburger.[10] Meat remains a consumable luxury, and so a powerful reminder of sociopolitical authority. On ʿId al-Kabir, most Moroccan households turn to the local station broadcasting the sacrifice performed by Mohamed VI in the name of his people.

*Most important, this book shows the logic of centralized political control and a conservative state ideology as a rational response to economic and environmental conditions.* In the precolonial and colonial era, networks of patronage underpinned the political life of the kingdom. In the nineteenth century, undercapitalized workers and the makhzan were two conservative groups that forged a tacit alliance against modernizing notables of the mercantile elite. The French perpetuated this social contract between workers and the state, spending a great deal of money funding social welfare programs until the drought and global depression of the 1930s bankrupted the protectorate as well as metropolitan France. Within this period of time, there were moments of revolt and of quiescence, which, despite frequent adoption of Islamic rhetoric, make sense in retrospect when superimposed with a chronology of rainfall and subsequent harvests.

In no instance is this more true than in the 1930s, when the religious scholar Allal al-Fassi headed a nationalist movement premised on the perpetuation of the Alaouite monarchy and the paternalistic networks that had long ensured the care of the poor. Elite leaders of this nationalist movement sometimes established machines to produce local goods, thereby contradicting the interests of some artisans, but their political organization publicly advocated increased responsibility for the care of their social inferiors. After independence, Allal al-Fassi became a minister in the government, and the king continued to rule through patron-client networks, playing interest groups off each other.[11]

Whether for humanitarian reasons or for a self-centered desire to hold on to power, royal beneficence toward the masses has remained a key to Alaouite success. As a social and political outlook refined in a semiarid land, Moroccan conservatism holds the promise of food provisioning to each urban household, no matter their income level. This shared philosophy helps account for my friend Adil's enthusiastic reception of the king in October 1999, who, exactly like the tailor Moulay Ahmed in 1937 described in chapter 7, handed his ruler a letter asking for assistance. As agents of urban food supply, millers and butchers played an important role in implementing royal policies aimed at caring for the sultan's subjects, who purchased food from their shops.

Popular concerns for local food supply shaped the modern political institutions of the kingdom. This study of "politics from below" ultimately advocates a reconsideration of the historical forces shaping other places in the Arab-Islamic world. These countries share the same environmental conditions of Morocco, which, according to the logic presented in this book, suggests that the political events of these places may well have been shaped by the central government's ability—or, as more often the case, its lack thereof—to provide food to its citizens and subjects.

# Glossary

General Terms

**amin**: The term used by colonial administrators to identify the head of a group of workers, which they called a corporation. The amin differed from the precolonial arif because the French gave him and his corporation a legal status. Under the French, the amin was responsible not only for negotiating the price of finished products but also for negotiating the terms of loans that a corporation's members were obligated to pay back.

**arif**: A master craftsman who, by virtue of the respect of his peers, represented the milling trade vis-à-vis the makhzan in the late nineteenth and early twentieth centuries. The French would change the term to *amin*.

**basha**: The royal appointee who managed a city in both the precolonial and colonial eras. In the latter period, his French counterpart was the chief of the municipality. His duties included the implementation of legislation, oversight of tax collection, and administration of justice.

**dahir**: A decree issued by the sultan.

**hadiyya**: An obligatory gift to the sultan that provided tangible evidence of loyalty. Such a gift was given to the sultan at a special ceremony after the performance of a sacrifice for ʿId al-Kabir.

**hubus** (pl. **ahbas**): A religious endowment with a charitable purpose. It is deemed *waqf* (pl. *awqaf*) in Modern Standard Arabic. Hubus was a legal institution by which rich Muslims bequeathed income-generating properties in perpetuity in order to preserve Islamic culture. A benefactor might, for example, specify that revenues from his bequest be used to pay a prayer leader. Or, he might stipulate that income from the property be used to purchase food for the poor.

**ʿId al-Fitr**: The holiday marking the end of Ramadan, a holy month of fasting in the Islamic lunar calendar. In Morocco, it is often referred to as ʿId al-Saghir.

**'Id al-Kabir**: The Moroccan designation for 'Id al-Adha, or the Feast of the Great Sacrifice. It falls on the tenth day of Dhu'l-Hijja, which is the twelfth month in the Islamic lunar calendar. On this day, the sultan of Morocco—now king—sacrifices a ram on behalf of his subjects, thereby asserting his political legitimacy.

**imam**: Muslim prayer leader. The sultan adopted this term for himself as a title that reflected his role as imam of his community of subjects, both Muslim and Jewish. As imam, the sultan had not only secular authority over his subjects but also a moral obligation to serve them.

**khalifa**: The royal appointee who represented the sultan in a city or region, thereby outranking the basha and muhtasib.

**majlis**: An assembly. The French adopted this term as a designation for the consultative bodies of urban notables in Moroccan cities. In Fez, the eight men serving on the majlis were elected by their peers, but the French appointed members of the majlis in all other cities.

**maks**: A tax collected on goods at the gates of the city. Since it affected the price of food, unrest threatened after an increase in its rate. Such was the case in Fez in 1873, when the Tanner's Revolt broke out at the very start of Moulay Hassan's reign.

**muhtasib**: A royal appointee who oversaw transactions in the marketplaces of a city in the precolonial and colonial eras. He verified weights and measures and regulated the quality of goods. Most importantly, he set the prices of goods—including flour and meat—produced by local workers.

**oued**: Either a river or a tributary of a river.

**sharif** (pl. **shurafa'**): A person claiming descent from the Prophet, which increases his social status. The sultan, himself a putative descendant of the Prophet, provided these people with special privileges, such as the distribution of meat or an exemption from paying taxes.

Sacrifice and Slaughter

**battoir**: Adopted from the French word "abbatoir," a word designating a modern slaughterhouse managed by the state. It was composed of a set of functionally specific buildings.

**chevillard**: A butcher who sells meat wholesale. This category of butchers differed from the small-scale operations of precolonial butchers who both slaughtered animals and retailed their meat.

**guerjouma**: A tax on meat levied by the precolonial makhzan and the

French protectorate. The fee that butchers paid was based on the number of animals slaughtered.

**gurna**: The type of slaughtering facility used primarily in the precolonial era. It was an open space devoid of functionally specific buildings for penning animals or for slaughtering them. This term, however, is still used to describe sites of slaughter used by those who produce and provide meat beyond state control.

**khaliʻa**: A type of dried meat of either camel or cattle that is conserved in fat and spices. The animals would be slaughtered in the summer, when at the peak of good health, and their meat hung to dry on a house's roof. This food is a culinary delicacy that embodies status.

**makruh**: A judicial term in Islamic law that indicates a state that falls between licit and illicit. If, for example, a woman sacrifices an animal, many scholars would term this *makruh*, for men should be the ones to perform this sacrifice. Scholars would also term the eating of kosher meat sacrificed by Jews as *makruh*.

**mashwi**: Sheep roasted on a spit, which is a high-status delicacy served to large groups of people.

**musalla**: A "place of prayer." It is a large tract of land outside a city or village, where community prayers for ʻId al-Adha are held. During the public celebration of this holiday, the sultan sacrificed a sheep on behalf of his subjects in the musalla. Fez has two musallas, the royal musalla and the *musulla du pacha*.

## The Production and Sale of Flour

**farina**: A finely ground flour of soft wheat. The French introduced it during the protectorate. Until that time, Moroccans exclusively ground hard wheat.

**khalis**: The type of flour desired by most consumers in Fez, including the sultan. It consisted of two parts of finely ground zrif and one part quwayshi.

**maʻallam**: A master miller. Most maʻallams in Fez operated a single mill. They oversaw the work of at least two journeymen and two apprentices.

**makina**: The term for a mechanized mill. Such mills were introduced to Morocco in 1862 by Sultan Sidi Mohamed, who installed one in Tangier. It was powered by charcoal, steam, petroleum, or electricity. The engine was simply harnessed to the equipment of an extant water mill.

**moulin du quartier**: Installed in the medina of Fez in the 1930s, these grinding facilities mechanized the small-scale commercial operation of the water mill. At that time, they had one-tenth the capacity of factories producing flour, but they could grind ten times more than water mills. By 1935, there were fifteen of these in the medina of Fez.

**mudd**: A unit of measure for flour. In Fez, it was equivalent to approximately forty kilograms or sixty-four liters. The average watermill in Fez—when endowed with a single waterwheel—ground fifteen mudds of flour each day.

**quwayshi**: The coarsely ground flour produced by a water mill after a turn through the grinding stones. The makhzan often distributed it to the poor.

**rahaba**: A market designated exclusively for the sale of wheat and other cereal grains. Fez had four of these.

**rha**: The term used in Morocco to designate a water mill. Water mills consisted of a horizontal waterwheel with twenty-six flat planks of wood. A wooden pole ran up from the subterranean waterwheel and turned the grinding stones. The average water mill in Fez produced 310 kilograms of flour every day, and it often operated day and night.

**tahaniyyin**: The collective designation for millers who custom ground flour for clients. Some families—the rich ones—purchased wheat in bulk and then ordered it custom ground from these millers as needed by their household.

**tarrahiyyin**: The collective designation for commercial millers. After buying and grinding wheat, they sold flour at shops. Thus, they served workers and the poor, who could not afford to buy wheat and have it custom ground.

**zrif**: This term refers to a very finely ground flour.

Legal Terms Designating the Possession of a Water Mill

**asl**: A judicial term that indicates the possession of a mill's structure, which includes the ceiling, the walls, the supporting columns, and the wooden water canals.

**galsa**: A judicial term—pronounced 'jalsa' in Modern Standard Arabic—that indicated the possession of a mill's site. This consisted of the leveled earth (*taswiyya al-ard*) and a whitewashed floor (referred to as either *dus* or *tajsis*).

**i'qamat al-mal'ab**: A judicial term that indicated the possession of a water mill's tools, including sieves, mats, baskets, a pulley for lifting millstones, chisels, a scale and weights, chairs, brooms (*shtaba, shtatib*), and lamps.

**i'qamat min al-zayri ila al-wadi**: A judicial term that indicates the possession of a mill's equipment, which included the hopper, millstones, waterwheels, and any accoutrements attached to them, such as the pole (*'anq*) running from the waterwheel to the millstones.

**miftah**: A judicial term that indicates the possession of a mill's use. In some documents, notaries also referred to this as the *ghibta* or the *zina*. The only physical possession associated with a mill's use was the door and its key, for which the legal term is *bab bi-farkhatiha*.

The Equipment and Tools of a Watermill

**'anq**: The pole running from the bottom of a mill's subterranean cavity, through the horizontal waterwheel, and then to the top millstone. As the waterwheel forced this pole to turn, it, in turn, made turn the top millstone.

**brinqa**: The wooden pulley used by millers when they needed to lift the millstones in order to either replace them or, if worn but still usable, to dress them.

**busiyyar**: A sieve with very large holes, used to separate pebbles from wheat. It was also called a *srnd*.

**duwwar**: The water wheel, which had twenty-six planks of wood sticking out of it. It was powered by a flume constructed at a downward slope. A pole led from it to the top grinding stone, which then turned.

**guwwaz**: A sieve used to separate fine flour from coarse flour, which was then ground a second time. It was one of many types of sieves used by mill workers. The other sieves found were called the *siyyul, tathir, ragig* (*raqiq* in Modern Standard Arabic), *zarif*, and *takhmis*.

**hajr**: This term denotes the millstones that turned, thereby grinding the wheat. In Fez, a miller received his grinding stones from a quarry Batit, found in the region of Meknes, and so millers referred to these millstones as *hajr batit*. Workers at this quarry shaped the stones and put a hole in their center. They would then transport them to Fez by mule. At Fez's gates, local porters took them off the mule. The porters put a pole in the stone's middle hole and rolled them through the streets until reaching the watermill for which they were intended. Millstones would last at least twenty years before needing to be replaced.

**manqash**: An iron chisel with a flat head used to dress the millstones in order to improve the grinding.

**masrah**: The lock gate, which, always located upstream from a water mill, consisted of a plank of wood (*luwwh*).

**mijam**: A plank of wood used by millers to open and close the lock gate, thereby allowing them to control the flow of water to their mill. It is also referred to as *raqad*.

**mizab**: The flume that directed water from a principal water canal to the subterranean cavity that housed the waterwheel. It was constructed of wood.

**mnqar**: A long iron chisel with a bent and pointed head used to dress millstones in order to improve the grinding, thus lengthening the life of the millstones.

**qadum**: A short iron chisel with a bent head used to dress the millstones in order to improve the grinding.

**sajan**: The subterranean cavity, constructed directly below the grinding stones, that housed the waterwheels.

**sana**: A hook used to clean the water canals of weeds or garbage blocking the flow of water to a mill.

**shaduq**: The rounded wooden frame of a sieve. In Fez, the wood was made round by placing it in a water source near the Moulay Idriss mausoleum for one year. This method was also used to bend the wood needed for the arches in ceilings or window frames. In Modern Standard Arabic, this rounded wooden arch was called *qus* (pl. *aquwwas*).

**tamag**: A pair of leather slippers (*blaghi*) that millers kept at their work site in case they needed to descend into the cold subterranean cavity in order to repair the equipment of the watermill located there.

**tararib**: Baskets of esparto grass (*halfa'*), also called *qafaf* by Fez's millers. Mill workers used them to clean the wheat in the pool outside the mill. They would also put baskets of wheat on their head in order to be able to reach the top of the hopper. These baskets held the clean wheat poured into the hopper, which descended to the millstones.

**zayr**: The square hopper, shaped like a funnel, that millers attached to the ceiling with four cords.

**zrraf**: The opening of the flume, where water poured into the subterranean cavity housing the waterwheel.

# Notes

**Abbreviations**

| | |
|---|---|
| ADN | Centre des Archives Diplomatiques (Nantes, France) |
| AMC | Archives of the Ministry of Culture (Rabat, Morocco) |
| AMF | Archives of the Municipality of Fez (Fez, Morocco) |
| BGA | Bibliothèque Générale et Archives (Rabat, Morocco) |
| BR | Bibliothèque Royale (Rabat, Morocco) |
| CAC | Centre des Archives Contemporaines (Fontainebleau, France) |
| CD | Cabinet Diplomatique |
| CDRG | Cabinet du Délégué à la Résidence Générale |
| CFCC | Bibliothèque Centrale de l'Administration de la Conservation Foncière du Cadastre et de la Cartographie (Rabat, Morocco) |
| CHEAM | Centre des Hautes Études d'Administration Marocaine |
| DACH | Direction des Affaires Chérifiennes |
| DAI | Direction des Affaires Indigènes |
| DAR | Direction des Archives Royales (Rabat, Morocco) |
| DI | Direction de l'Intérieur |
| HS | Al-Hizana al-Subihiyya (Salé, Morocco) |
| MO | Musée des Oudaia (Rabat, Morocco) |
| MAM | Musée des Arts et Métiers (Paris, France) |
| OCF | Office de la Conservation Foncière (Fez, Morocco) |
| ONICL | Office National Interprofessionnel des Céréales et des Légumineuses (Rabat, Morocco) |
| PJ | Palais de Justice (Salé, Morocco) |

**Introduction**

1. Lewis, *What Went Wrong?*
2. Binder, *Islamic Liberalism*. See also Zubaida, *Islam*; Hafez, *Why Muslims Rebel*.
3. Roy, *Politics of Chaos*, 158–159.
4. Eickelman and Piscatori, *Muslim Politics*.
5. Wittfogel, *Oriental Despotism*.
6. Worster, *Rivers of Empire*, 7.
7. Phillips, *This Land*.
8. Imber, *Ottoman Empire*. See also Quataert, *Ottoman Empire*.

9. Murphey, "Provisioning Istanbul."
10. Singer, *Constructing Ottoman Beneficence*.
11. Cohen, *Economic Life*.
12. Murphey, "Provisioning Istanbul," 246.
13. Scott, *Seeing like a State*.
14. Berman and Lonsdale, *Unhappy Valley*.
15. Khouri-Dagher, "The State," 110.
16. Singerman, *Avenues of Participation*.
17. Toth, "Letter from Algiers."
18. Holden, "Mauritanians Want Food."
19. Hoisington, *Lyautey*. See also Rivet, *Lyautey*.
20. Nordman, "Les expéditions de Moulay Hassan."
21. Michel, *Une économie de subsistances*.
22. Brown, *People of Salé*. See also Burke, *Prelude to Protectorate*.
23. Hammoudi, *Master and Disciple*. For another analysis of the religious underpinnings of sultanic authority, see Munson, *Religion and Power*. See also Cornell, *Realm of the Saint*; Tozy, *Monarchie*; Bennison, *Jihad*.

## Chapter 1. The Political Economy of Moroccan Hunger

1. Burke, *Prelude to Protectorate*, 23.
2. Miège, *Le Maroc*, 3:393.
3. Trotter, *Our Mission*, 75.
4. Miège, *Le Maroc*, 3:393.
5. Trotter, *Our Mission*, 165.
6. Al-Wazzani al-Imrani, *Al-Nawazil al-jadidah*.
7. Le Tourneau, *Fès*, 153–159.
8. Parker, *Islamic Monuments*, 115. For a detailed account of precolonial Fez, see Le Tourneau, *Fès*.
9. Le Tourneau, *Fès*, 374–376.
10. Al-Hajwi, *Voyage d'Europe*, 106.
11. Le Tourneau, *Fès*, 154.
12. See Massignon's analysis of Moroccan trades in "Enquête," 4.
13. Ricard, "Chronique de Fès: L'évolution," 157–158; see also Revault et al., *Palais et demeures*, vol. 3, *Époque alawite*.
14. Odinot, *Le monde marocain*, 151–154.
15. Chevrillon, *Un crépuscule d'Islam*, 118–122.
16. Michel, *Une économie de subsistances*, 2:543.
17. Le Tourneau, *Fès*, 155.
18. Bertagnin et al., "Inscribing Minority Space," 313. For the Moroccan mellah, see Gottreich, *Mellah of Marrakesh*.
19. Sémach, "Une chronique juive," 87–91.
20. Le Tourneau, *Fès*, 104.
21. Great Britain, *Correspondence*; see also France, *Documents diplomatiques*.
22. Rosenberger, *Société, pouvoir et alimentation*.

23. Al-Nasiri, "Kitab al-istiqsa'," 143.
24. Sémach, "Une chronique juive," 93.
25. Miège, *Le Maroc*, 2:39.
26. Michel, *Une économie de subsistances*, 2:531.
27. Miège, *Le Maroc*, 2:35.
28. Ibid., 2:41.
29. Ibid., 3:426.
30. Michel, *Une économie de subsistances*, 2:533–535.
31. Miège, *Le Maroc*, 4:406.
32. D'Anfreville, "Les Marocains," 155–156.
33. Miège, *Le Maroc*, 4:406.
34. Gouvion and Gouvion, *Kitab Aâyane*, 1:271–274.
35. Pennell, *Morocco since 1830*, 92–93.
36. Ibid., 76.
37. Miège, *Le Maroc*, 3:425.
38. Ibid., 3:412–418.
39. Michel, *Une économie de subsistances*, 2:534.
40. Miège, *Le Maroc*, 3:32.
41. Ibid., 3:450.
42. Ibid., 3:451.
43. ADN, Mémoires de stage des contrôleurs, no. 87, J. Grapinet, "Études sur les relations sociales et économiques entre fassis et gens du bled." See also Grapinet, "La colonisation citadine," 181–182; Michel, *Une économie de subsistances*, 2:493–497.
44. The Moqris provided two biographers with information on their family in the 1920s. For an account by French authors, see Gouvion and Gouvion, *Kitab Aâyane*, 1:250–259. For an account by a resident of Fez, see al-Kittani, *Biyutat ahl fas*.
45. Revault et al., *Époque alawite*, 3:121–146.
46. Chevrillon, *Un crépuscule d'Islam*, 165–172.
47. ADN, Tanger, série A, Fez, 829, Situation générale à Fès, 29 March 1906.
48. Issawi, *Economic History*, 100.
49. Miège, *Le Maroc*, 3:385.
50. Ibid., 3:389.
51. Iliffe, *African Poor*.
52. René-LeClerc, "Troisième partie," 339.
53. Ibid., 343.
54. Miège, *Le Maroc*, 3:438.
55. El Mansour, "Sanctuary," 49–73.
56. Al-Nasiri, "Kitab al-istiqsa'," 279.
57. Pennell, *Morocco since 1830*, 96.
58. Miège, *Le Maroc*, 3:438.
59. Burke, *Prelude to Protectorate*, 56–57.
60. For an eyewitness account of this incident, see DAR, Mohamed ben Abdallah al-Boukili to Sidi Abdelkerim ben Sliman, 3 Qa'dah 1321 (21 January 1904). For an analysis based on other accounts, see Pascon, *Le Haouz de Marrakesh*, 435–437.

61. Pennell, *Morocco since 1830*, 128.
62. René-LeClerc, "Deuxième partie," 321.
63. ADN, Tanger, série A, Fez, 829, Situation générale à Fès, 29 March 1906.
64. Gaillard, "Commerce de Fès," 330.
65. Marchand, "La situation commerciale à Fez," 421.
66. ADN, Tanger, série A, Fez, 829, Situation générale à Fès, 29 March 1906.
67. Ben Cheneb, *Proverbes arabes*, 1:146.
68. Pennell, *Morocco since 1830*, 12.
69. Al-Nasiri, "Kitab al-istiqsa'," 133.
70. René-LeClerc, "Deuxième partie," 309.
71. DAR, al-Arbi Ould Ba Mohamed to Moulay Hassan, 30 Qa'dah 1299 (13 October 1882).
72. Trotter, *Our Mission*, 113.
73. For rural taxes and the coexistence of barter and money, see Michel, *Une économie de subsistances*, 2:413–419.
74. Ibid., 2:568.
75. Pennell, *Morocco since 1830*, 42.
76. Le Tourneau, *Fès*, 198–199.
77. DAR, Abdesselam ben Mohamed al-Moqri to Ahmed ben Moussa, 5 Safar 1315 (6 July 1897).
78. Michel, *Une économie de subsistances*, 2:572.
79. Burke, *Prelude to Protectorate*, 57.
80. Ibid., 90–91.
81. BR, 12453/4, Abou al-Abbas Ahmed ben Said, "al-Taysir fi ahkam al-tas'air," 11 Jumada I 1316 (27 September 1898), folio 53.
82. Ibid.
83. DAR, Mohamed Chami to Moulay Abdelaziz, 5 Hijja 1311 (9 June 1894).
84. René-LeClerc, "Deuxième partie," 321.
85. René-LeClerc, "Troisième partie," 345.
86. BR, 12453/4, Abou al-Abbas Ahmed ben Said, "al-Taysir fi ahkam al-tas'air," 11 Jumada I 1316 (27 September 1898), folio 53.
87. Michel, *Une économie de subsistances*, 2:491.
88. Amahan and Cambazard-Amahan, *Arrêts sur sites*, 107.
89. Michel, *Une économie de subsistances*, 2:626.
90. Ibid., 2:528.
91. Ibid., 2:626.
92. DAR, Moulay Hassan to Hadj Mehdi Bennani, 16 Hijja 1299 (29 October 1882).
93. Michel, *Une économie de subsistances*, 2:565.
94. ADN, Tanger, série A, Fez, 829, Situation générale à Fès, 29 March 1906.
95. DAR, Moulay Hassan to Taib ben Hima, 12 Sha'ban 1300 (18 June 1883).
96. DAR, Moulay Hassan to Hadj Mehdi Bennani, 25 Rabi I 1296 (19 March 1879).
97. ADN, Tanger, série A, Fez, 829, Situation générale à Fès, 29 March 1906. See also Le Tourneau, *Fès*, 258; Michel, *Une économie de subsistances*, 2:626.
98. Burke, *Prelude to Protectorate*, 17.

99. Sémach, "Une chronique juive," 87–91.
100. Ibid., 93.
101. Ibid., 88.
102. Larhmaid, "Collecting Jizya."
103. *Times of Morocco*, no. 88, 20 August 1887.
104. Luccioni, *Les fondations*, 128.
105. BGA, 25 register 137, *Hawalat ahbas al-maristan bi-fas*, 271; DAR, royal decree, 15 Jumada II 1304 (11 March 1887).
106. BGA, 157 register 45, *Hawalat al-jadid al-ahbas*.
107. Pennell, *Morocco since 1830*, 94.
108. Ben Cheneb, *Proverbes arabes*, 1:68.
109. Al-Kittani, *Biyutat ahl fas*, 1:234–235.
110. BGA, 180 register 62, *Hawalat ahbas al-maristan bi-fas*, 256; see also BGA, 137 register 25, *Hawalat ahbas al-maristan bi-fas*, 257.
111. The bequest also legated funds for feeding prisoners. For prisons in Fez, see Le Tourneau, *Fès*, 213, 255–256.
112. Ibid., 488–489.
113. BGA, 178 register 60, *Ahbas al-hurm al-idrissi bi-fas*, 122.
114. Le Tourneau, *Fès*, 489.
115. Ibn Zaydan, *Itahaf 'alam al-nas*, 5:290.
116. Le Tourneau, *Fès*, 462–465.
117. BGA, 113 register 22, *Hawalat ahbas al-qarawiyyin fas*, 257.
118. Al-Kittani, *Salwat al-anfas*, 1:373.
119. Martin, "Description de la ville," 440–441.
120. René-LeClerc, "Troisième partie," 346.
121. Le Tourneau, *Fès*, 613.
122. Al-Kittani, *Salwat al-anfas*, 1:290.
123. Ibid., 1:227.
124. Ibid., 1:148–149.
125. Michel, *Une économie de subsistances*, 2:622.
126. For an account written by a member of this family, see al-Kittani, *Tarjamat shaykh mohamed*. See also al-Kittani, *Shurafa' al-kattaniyyun*.
127. Al-Kittani, *Biyutat ahl fas*, 2:295–296.
128. Pennell, *Morocco since 1830*, 131.
129. Burke, *Prelude to Protectorate*, 38.
130. Ibid., 134–135.

## Chapter 2. Industrialism and Participatory Politics at the Water Mill

1. René-LeClerc, "Troisième partie," 349–350.
2. Michel, *Une économie de subsistances*, 508. For a later reference to it, see DAR, Mohamed ben al-M'feddel Benjelloun and Boubaker Danih to Abou Abdallah Sidi Mohamed ben Sidi al-Arbi, 30 Ramadan 1303 (2 July 1886). For other steam mills in Tangier, see Miège, *Le Maroc*, 4:337–338.
3. For mills in Paris, see Fierro, *Histoire*. For their preservation, see Sellier, "Les moulins," 5–23.

4. ADN, DAI, 320, Traduction du rapport du medjless el Baladi au sujet du projet d'arrêté du directeur des travaux publics portant la règlementation des eaux du bassin de l'Oued Fès et de leur répartition, 10 December 1929, 26. This file also contains a copy of the original report in Arabic.

5. Ibid., 30.

6. Le Tourneau, *Fès*, 223.

7. For the Norse-type direct-drive mill, see Storck and Teague, *Flour for Man's Bread*, 98. For the Moroccan water mill, see Joly, "L'industrie à Tétouan," 216–219. The vocabulary for milling in Fez differed from other cities, but a mill's equipment was identical. I would like to thank Mohamed Alami for reviewing this article's diagram with me.

8. On 21 November 2000, Aziz Mezian of ADER-Fez introduced me to four buildings that had once been mills, giving me an initial sense of the foundation's layout in relation to its water canals. Mohamed Alami now sells flour from the mill where he used to work. He has kept the core of a waterwheel as well as its grinding stones, which he showed me on 12 June 2001. Perigny provides a description of mills in *Au Maroc*, 137. A schoolteacher in Fez also describes the physical organization of a mill in Mammeri, "L'Oued-Fez," 196–197.

9. Michaux-Bellaire, "Description," 302.

10. Michel, *Une économie de subsistances*, 2:506.

11. BGA, 180 register 62, *Hawalat ahbas al-maristan bi-fas*, 110–114.

12. Ibid., 265.

13. BGA, H6, Moulin Derb el Bouacq, Muraqib of Fez to the Ministry of Religious Endowments in Rabat, letter received on 23 March 1915.

14. BGA, H6, Moulin Derb el Bouacq, Ahmed Tazi to al-Said al-Hadj Ahmed al-Jay, 1 Rajab 1333 (15 May 1915).

15. BGA, 180 register 62, *Hawalat ahbas al-maristan bi-fas*, 216–218.

16. Al-Kittani, *Biyutat ahl fas*, 2:354.

17. BGA, 180 register 62, *Hawalat ahbas al-maristan bi-fas*, 110–114.

18. DAR, Abdallah ben Ahmed to Sidi Mokhtar, 6 Safar 1295 (9 February 1878).

19. DAR, Moussa ben Ahmed to Sidi Abdallah ben Ahmed, 24 Sha'ban 1295 (23 August 1878); DAR, Mohamed Barghash to Moussa ben Ahmed, 26 Sha'ban 1295 (25 August 1878).

20. DAR, Abdallah ben Ahmed to Sidi Mokhtar, 23 Safar 1296 (16 February 1879).

21. BGA, *dal* 3410, *Majmu'a daha'ir 'alawiyya hassaniyya*, no. 219, Moulay Hassan to Moulay Abdallah Ben Ibrahim al-Boukili, 7 Shawwal 1306 (6 June 1889).

22. Michel, *Une économie de subsistances*, 2:638–640.

23. BGA, Hab. Cont. 40, Droits de Jouissance, Salvatore Gallos, Verification of mill's history, muraqib of Fez, 16 Ramadan 1336 (25 June 1918).

24. For precolonial protection, see Kenbib, *Les protégés*.

25. DAR, Mohamed Chami to Moulay Hassan, 13 Ramadan 1311 (20 March 1894).

26. ADN, CD, 508, Conseiller du Gouvernement Chérifien to Chef du Cabinet Diplomatique, 30 April 1919.

27. ADN, CD, 506, Conseiller du Gouvernement Chérifien to Secrétaire Général Adjoint du Protectorat Chef du Cabinet Diplomatique, 20 March 1920.

28. Michel, *Une économie de subsistances*, 616–617.

29. Miège, *Le Maroc*, 2:339.

30. John Drummond-Hay, British Consul in Tangier, to al-Said al-'Abas Imqashad, 5 December 1882, in Ben Srhir, *al-Maghrib*, 362–363.

31. Michel, *Une économie de subsistances*, 2:506.

32. DAR, Moussa ben Ahmed to Sidi Abdallah ben Ahmed, 2 Ramadan 1295 (30 August 1878).

33. Michel, *Une économie de subsistances*, 2:508. For an early reference to the steam mill by Moroccan administrators, see BGA, *dal* 3410, *Majmu'a daha'ir 'alawiyya hassaniyya*, no. 69, Moulay Hassan to Moulay Abdallah Ben Ibrahim al-Boukili, 12 Ramadan 1300 (17 July 1883).

34. Michel, *Une économie de subsistances*, 2:506.

35. DAR, al-M'feddel ben Idriss al-Serraj to Ahmed ben Moussa, 11 Jumada II 1316 (27 October 1898).

36. Issawi, *Economic History*, 101.

37. DAR, Abderrahmane Lebrisse to Moulay Hassan, 29 Muharram 1305 (17 October 1887). Moroccans referred to a water mill by the legal term *iqama* or as a *rha*, which refers to the equipment of the mill, specifically the millstones.

38. DAR, Moulay Hassan to Mohamed ben al-Arbi al-Torres, 24 Rabi II 1308 (7 December 1890). *Tahuna* is now a standard designation, but Moroccans then referred to water and horse mills as *rha*.

39. Macnab, *Ride in Morocco*, 219.

40. Miège, *Le Maroc*, 4:402.

41. Macnab, *Ride in Morocco*, 218.

42. Pobegun, "Notes sur Mogador," 60.

43. Mougin, "Oujda," 257.

44. DAR, unidentified official to Mohamed ben al-Arbi al-Torres, 13 Safar 1315 (14 July 1897).

45. Mougin, "Oujda," 258.

46. Miège, *Le Maroc*, 3:385.

47. DAR, Moulay Hassan to Mohamed Bargash, 26 Rabi I 1295 (30 March 1878).

48. *Times of Morocco*, no. 59, 25 December 1886. See also *Times of Morocco*, no. 60, 31 December 1886.

49. DAR, Mohamed ben Abdelkebir Tazi and Mohamed Raghouh to Moulay Hassan, 29 Sha'ban 1305 (11 May 1888).

50. DAR, Abdelkarim ben Sliman to Count Koutrad de Beauyasrit, 11 Jumada I 1322 (25 June 1904).

51. Miège, *Le Maroc*, 4:402.

52. DAR, Mohamed ben al-Arbi al-Torres to Moulay Hassan, 13 Shawwal 1305 (23 June 1888).

53. *Times of Morocco*, no. 144, 11 August 1888.

54. *Times of Morocco*, no. 187, 8 June 1889.

55. Miège, *Le Maroc*, 4:337.

56. DAR, Moulay Hassan to Hadj Mohamed ben al-Arbi al-Torres, 9 Sha'ban 1307 (31 March 1890).

57. BGA, *dal* 3410, *Majmu'a daha'ir 'alawiyya hassaniyya*, no. 318, Moulay Hassan to Moulay Abdallah Ben Ibrahim al-Boukili, Rabi I 1301 (January 1884).

58. DAR, Moulay Abdelhafid to Mohamed al-Guebbas, Minister of War, 3 Safar 1327 (24 February 1909).

59. *Times of Morocco*, no. 59, 25 December 1886.

60. *Times of Morocco*, no. 80, 19 May 1887.

61. For Ksar al-Kabir, see *Times of Morocco*, no. 217, 4 January 1890. See also DAR, Moulay Hassan to Mohamed ben al-Arbi al-Torres, 9 Sha'ban 1307 (31 March 1890).

62. Michel, *Une économie de subsistances*, 2:506.

63. *Times of Morocco*, no. 59, 25 December 1886.

64. For three notarized documents addressing the incident, see DAR, notarized testimony describing the attack on a mechanized mill in the mellah of Fez, 9 Sha'ban 1315 (3 January 1898). The status of the Moroccan partners is suggested in information provided by the British legation in Archives de la Bibliothèque Générale de Tetouan, dossier 44, doc. 83, a British diplomat to Mohamed Torres, 18 Shawwal 1315 (11 March 1898). I would like to thank Khalid ben Srhir for drawing my attention to this document. For the arrest of workers, see DAR, Abdelmajid ibn Chaqroun to Said Hadj Mohamed Torres, 26 Sha'ban 1315 (20 January 1898).

65. For a description of precolonial milling, see Michaux-Bellaire, "Description," 317. Mohamed Alami, interview by author, 12 June 2001.

66. For a firsthand account of nighttime milling, see Chevrillon, *Un crépuscule d'Islam*, 236.

67. Mohamed Alami, interview by author, 12 June 2002.

68. Boujima Mernissi, interview by author, 11 July 2001.

69. Mohamed Alami, interview by author, 12 June 2002.

70. Muhammed ben Ja'far ben Idris al-Kittani, *Salwat al-anfas*, 2:19.

71. Kaplan, *Provisioning Paris*, 325–326.

72. Hadj Abdelwahed Ouali, interview by author, 22 March 2001.

73. All of the millers whom I interviewed identified these two saints as belonging to custom or commercial millers. Louis Massignon addresses Sidi Hamamoush in his discussion of the corporation in *Revue du Monde Musulman* 58 (1924): 147.

74. Hadj Mohamed Filalli "Terras," interview by author, 9 June 2001.

75. Hadj Abdelwahed Ouali, interview by author, 22 March 2001.

76. Michel, *Une économie de subsistances*, 2:506.

77. Joly, "L'industrie à Tétouan," 220.

78. DAR, Moulay Hassan to Hadj Mehdi Bennani, 4 Qa'dah 1299 (17 September 1882).

79. DAR, al-Arbi Ould Ba Mohamed to Moulay Hassan, 30 Qa'dah 1299 (13 October 1882).

80. DAR, unidentified official to Moulay Hassan, 22 Rajab 1300 (29 May 1883).

81. DAR, Moulay Hassan to Moulay Ismael, 14 Sha'ban 1300 (20 June 1883).

82. Ibn Zaydan, *Itahaf 'alam al-nas*, 235–239.

83. Moulay Hassan, "Moujeb," 229–241. Unless otherwise noted, it is this document that supplies information pertaining to this committee and its findings.

84. Al-Kittani, *Biyutat ahl fas*, 1:133–136.
85. DAR, al-M'feddel ben Idriss al-Serraj to Ba Ahmed, Grand Vizir, 1 Rajab 1315 (26 November 1897).
86. BGA, Hab. Cont. 40, Verification of Mill's History, muraqib in Fez, 8 Qaʿdah 1337 (5 August 1919).
87. *Times of Morocco*, no. 89, 21 July 1887.
88. Haroun, "Consultation juridique," 14.
89. Michel, *Une économie de subsistances*, 640.
90. DAR, Mohamed Chami to Moulay Abdelaziz, 5 Hijja 1311 (9 June 1894).
91. DAR, al-M'feddel ben Idriss al-Serraj to Ba Ahmed, Grand Vizir, 1 Rajab 1315 (26 November 1897).
92. Mohamed Alami, interview by author, 12 June 2002.
93. Perigny, *Au Maroc*, 136.
94. Hadj Abdelwahed Ouali, interview by author, 22 March 2001.
95. DAR, Abdelmajid Ibn Cheqroun to Qaid Idriss ben al-Alami, 5 Rabi II 1315 (3 September 1897).
96. Michel, *Une économie de subsistances*, 643.
97. DAR, Abdelmajid Ibn Chaqroun to Qaid Idriss ben al-Alami, 5 Rabi II 1315 (3 September 1897).
98. Ibid., 6 Jumada I 1316 (22 September 1898).
99. Pennell, *Morocco since 1830*, 62–63.
100. Unidentified official to the Ministre plénipotentiaire du Gouvernement français, 1 Muharram 1292 (7 February 1875), cited in Fumey, *Choix de correspondance marocains*, 21–23.
101. DAR, anonymous official to Moulay Hassan, 6 Jumada II 1303 (12 March 1886).
102. BGA, *dal* 3410, *Majmuʿa dahaʾir ʿalawiyya hassaniyya*, no. 318, Moulay Hassan to Moulay Abdallah Ben Ibrahim al-Boukili, Rabi I 1301 (January 1884).
103. Ibid., no. 69, Moulay Hassan to Moulay Abdallah ben Ibrahim al-Boukili, 12 Ramadan 1300 (17 July 1883).
104. Michel, *Une économie de subsistances*, 625.
105. Pennell, *Morocco since 1830*, 77.
106. *Times of Morocco*, 24 January 1891.
107. Pennell, *Morocco since 1830*, 63.
108. Ibid., 77.
109. Ben Srhir, *Al-Maghrib*, 362–363.
110. *Times of Morocco*, no. 145, 18 August 1888.
111. DAR, Hadj Ahmed ben Ali to Mohamed ben al-Arbi al-Torres, 23 Rabi II 1312 (24 October 1894).
112. DAR, Mohamed ben al-M'feddel Benjelloun and Boubaker Danih to Abou Abdallah Sidi Mohamed ben Sidi al-Arbi, 30 Ramadan 1303 (2 July 1886). See also *Times of Morocco*, no. 162, 1888.
113. BGA, *dal* 3410, *Majmuʿa dahaʾir ʿalawiyya hassaniyya*, no. 287, Moulay Hassan to Umanaʾ of Royal Offices in Marrakesh, 10 Shaʿban 1304 (4 May 1887).
114. BGA, *dal* 3410, *Majmuʿa dahaʾir ʿalawiyya hassaniyya*, no. 269, Moulay Hassan to Umanaʾ of Royal Offices in Marrakesh, 18 Jumada I 1305 (1 February 1888).

115. BGA, *dal* 3410, *Majmu'a daha'ir 'alawiyya hassaniyya*, no. 18, Moulay Hassan to Moulay Abdallah Ben Ibrahim al-Boukili, 18 Jumada 1305 (1 February 1888); DAR, Mohamed al-Mehdi Bennani to Moulay Hassan, 6 Ramadan 1303 (8 June 1886); DAR, Moulay Hassan to al-Mehdi Bennani, 26 Shawwal 1303 (28 July 1886).

116. DAR, al-M'feddel ben Idriss al-Serraj to Ba Ahmed, 1 Jumada II 1316 (17 October 1898).

117. Michel, *Une économie de subsistances*, 543.

118. ADN, Tanger, série A, 828, Henri Gaillard, Consul de France, to Monsieur Regnault, Ministre de France au Maroc, 9 January 1907.

119. Veyre, *Au Maroc*.

120. Hoisington, *Lyautey*, 140–147.

121. Rainero, "Creation," 177–196. For problems with its construction, see DAR, Missione Militaire Italiana to al-M'feddel ben Mohamed Gharnit, 13 Jumada I 1308 (22 December 1890).

122. BGA, Hab. Cont. 58 (2), Action des Habous cf. M. Campini, Détenteur de la Mosquée Moulay Omar, 1919–1924.

123. BGA, 1652, Propriétés proposées à l'échange, 4 June 1924; AMC, unclassified, Rougemont to Maurice Tranchant de Lunel, 2 April 1918.

124. ADN, CD, 517, Giuseppe Campini to Hubert Lyautey, 10 May 1916.

125. BGA, 1652, Mémoire de Campini, 6 February 1923.

126. René-LeClerc, "Troisième partie," 336.

127. Gordon, "Industrialization and Republican Politics," 117–138.

## Chapter 3. Commerce and Class Tensions at the Butcher Shop

1. Aubin, *Le Maroc*, 136–145.

2. Montanari, *Culture of Food*, 154–156; see also Horowitz et al., "Meat for the Multitudes."

3. Moreau, *L'abbatoir moderne*; see also Loverdo, *Construction*.

4. Aubin, *Le Maroc*, 137.

5. Le Tourneau, *Fès*, 594.

6. Ibid., 313.

7. Westermarck, *Ritual and Belief*, 2:120.

8. Le Tourneau, *Fès*, 256.

9. BR, 7/11333, Mohamed ben Mohamed Abd al-Qadir Bennani, *'Aqd al-lali wa al-durar fi jawaz t'adud salat al-'id 'ala al-qul al-m'atabar*, folio 92. The text suggests that Bennani wrote this document between 1889 and 1912.

10. I visited the royal musalla of Fez in June 2002.

11. For the al-Fassi family, see al-Kittani, *Biyutat ahl fas*, 83–85. See also Gouvion and Gouvion, *Kitab Aâyane*, 2:761–767.

12. DAR, Mohamed ben al-Ma'ti to Mohamed ben Mohamed Gharnit, Grand Vizir, Hijja 1321 (February/March 1904); DAR, Qaid Abdeselam ben Ali al-Sahim to Mohamed ben Mohamed Gharnit, 6 Hijja 1321 (23 February 1904).

13. Aubin, *Le Maroc*, 141.

14. Less than a year before Aubin watched the sultan's sacrifice, angry crowds killed a

British missionary when he entered the mausoleum of Moulay Idriss. See Mohamed El Mansour, "Sanctuary," 68.

15. Combs-Schilling, *Sacred Performances*.
16. Arnaud, *Au temps des mehallas*, 75–90.
17. DAR, 9 Hijja 1311 (13 June 1894).
18. Burke, *Prelude to Protectorate*, 64.
19. Aubin, *Le Maroc*, 141.
20. Burke, *Prelude to Protectorate*, 114–117. Burke emphasizes the Islamic roots of precolonial protest, but he does not highlight the significance of the transfer of power during the celebration of 'Id. He researched this study before Morocco opened its precolonial archives, so it is possible that his reliance on European documents, which were dated according to the Gregorian calendar, obscured this pattern.
21. ADN, Tanger, série A, 830, Gérant du Consulat de France à Fez to Robert de Billy, Chargé d'Affaires de France au Maroc, 8 December 1911.
22. Ibn Zaydan, *Itahaf 'alam al-nas*, 283.
23. Bonsal, *Morocco as It Is*, 88–109.
24. Westermarck, *Ritual and Belief*, 2:145–146.
25. ADN, Tanger, série A, 831, Gérant du Consulat de France à Fez to Robert de Billy, Chargé d'Affaires de France au Maroc, 17 December 1910.
26. Westermarck, *Ritual and Belief*, 2:113.
27. Burke, *Prelude to Protectorate*, 190.
28. Haji, *Musu'aa a'alam tasnif*, 8:2941–2942.
29. HS, 2/156, Ahmed ben Mohamed Ibn al-Khayat al-Zakari al-Houseini, Risala fi dabh al-adhiyya bi-fas b'ad dabh imam al-sala qabl dabh al-sultan. Though not dated, the text suggests that it appeared between 1908 and 1912.
30. BR, 7/11333, Mohamed ben Mohamed Abd al-Qadir Bennani, *'Aqd al-lali wa al-durar fi jawaz t'adud salat al-'id 'ala al-qul al-m'atabar*.
31. René-LeClerc, "Troisième partie," 347.
32. Driss Rabani, interview by author, 12 July 2002.
33. Sefrioui, *La boîte à merveilles*, 1063.
34. PJ, *alif-qaf*, 13/16, Rapport du Commissaire du Gouvernement Chérifien, 19 January 1928.
35. Michaux-Bellaire, "Description," 303.
36. Burke, *Prelude to Protectorate*, 71–74.
37. Le Tourneau, *Fès*, 165.
38. Burke, *Prelude to Protectorate*, 94.
39. ADN, DACH, 89, Commandant de la Région de Fez to Résident Général, 10 July 1913.
40. *Gurna* probably originates from the term *jiran*, signifying a camel's neck. Camels were a regular part of the Muslim diet in Morocco until the mid-twentieth century. For a discussion of *jiran* based on the text of Ibn Mandhour, who, in the late thirteenth and early fourteenth centuries, 'fathered' the Arabic dictionary, see Hyat and Moura'shli, *Lisan*, 1:447–448. In the nineteenth century, most notaries in Fez substituted the term *gurna* for the classical term *magzara* when referring to designated sites of slaughter.

41. There was at least one exception to this model. In Meknes, butchers set up a gurna in a mosque after its fountain stopped providing water. Butchers used half of it for slaughter and the other half for holding livestock. This gurna did not stop operating until the French established the protectorate. See Ibn Zaydan, *Itahaf 'alam al-nas*, 1:221.

42. My description of Sidi Bou Nafa's gurna is based on a visit to the site in July 2001. It is now an airy family compound, with two small houses surrounded by a paved yard. The high walls block out noise from the streets, and the yard allows for the enjoyment of air and sunlight.

43. BGA, 136 register 24, *Hawalat ahbas fas al-'ulia*, 3. See also BGA, 161 register 45, *Hawalat ahbas fas al-'ulia*, 4.

44. Casinière, *Les municipalités marocaines*.

45. Gaillard, *Une ville de l'Islam*, 171.

46. Appel, *Concise Code*, 231–258.

47. René-LeClerc, "Deuxième partie," 317.

48. For an imam in Essaouira, see Amara Ibn Saddeq, 'Amal of Essaouira, to Mohamed Bargach, 10 Sha'ban 1293 (1 August 1876), quoted in *El Ouataiq: Recueils périodiques publiés par la Direction des Archives Royales*, no. 5 (Rabat: Imprimerie Royal, 1981), 99–100. For mention of an imam in Tangier, see Dehors, "Commerce," 353.

49. BGA, A1074, Note pour les Services Municipaux, 4 January 1914.

50. Chevrillon, *Un crépuscule d'Islam*, 231.

51. BGA, A753, Arrêté municipal, 5 February 1914.

52. Amicis, *Morocco*, 277.

53. René-LeClerc, "Deuxième partie," 309.

54. Maclagan, "Food and Gender," 159–172.

55. Michaux-Bellaire, "Description," 322.

56. BR, 12453/4, Abou al-Abbas Ahmed ben Said, *al-Taysir fi ahkam al-tas'air*, 11 Jumada I 1316 (27 September 1898), folio 55.

57. BR, *Bayan malzumat al-lahm wa ghayrih li al-dar al-'ulia bi-allah*, register 452.

58. BR, 12453/4, Abou al-Abbas Ahmed ben Said, *al-Taysir fi ahkam al-tas'air*, 11 Jumada I 1316 (27 September 1898), folio 55.

59. René-LeClerc, "Deuxième partie," 347.

60. Amnon Cohen analyzes the muhtasib and butchers in Ottoman Jerusalem in the chapter "Butchers and Meat Consumption," in *Economic Life in Ottoman Jerusalem*, 11–60.

61. BR, 12453/4, Abou al-Abbas Ahmed ben Said, *al-Taysir fi ahkam al-tas'air*, 11 Jumada I 1316 (27 September 1898), folio 52.

62. BR, dossier 570, Moulay al-Hadj al-Alaoui to M'feddel Gharnit, 14 Rajab 1319 (27 October 1901).

63. Ben Cheneb, *Proverbes populaires*, 1:177–178.

64. BR, 12453/4, Abou al-Abbas Ahmed ben Said, *al-Taysir fi ahkam al-tas'air*, 11 Jumada I 1316 (27 September 1898), folio 57.

65. Ibid., folio 57.

66. Ibid., folio 53.

67. Léon l'Africain, *Description de l'Afrique*, trans. Epaulard (16th c.; reprint, Paris:

n.p., 1956): 208, quoted in Abderrahim Benhadda and Laila Benkirane, "Nourritures," in Mezzine, *Fès médiévale*, 158.

68. Ben Cheneb, *Proverbes populaires*, 1:52.

69. Mohamed ben al-Hassan al-Hajoui left a record providing a window into daily life in Fez. For a description of butcher shops dating to 24 Rabi II 1328 (5 May 1910), see BGA, H128, *Qanash bi-hi taqaiyyid ʿalmiyya wa-tarikhiyya*, 51.

70. Miège, *Le Maroc*, 3:383.

71. Ibid., 3:403.

72. Trotter, *Our Mission*, 78–79.

73. Michel, *Une économie de subsistances*, 531.

74. DAR, Mohamed ben al-ʿArbi to Fiqh Said Abdallah ben Ahmed, 29 Jumada I 1297 (9 May 1880).

75. DAR, Ben Hayim ben Abou to Ahmed ben Moussa, 16 Qaʿadah 1316 (28 March 1899).

76. *Times of Morocco*, no. 201, 14 September 1889.

77. For a detailed treatise on slaughter and sacrifice within the canon of Malekite jurisprudence, see Ibn Jizzy, *al-Qawannin*, 156–166. For a modern handbook of Islamic law, see al-Djazairi, *Le precepte du Musulman*, 385–391.

78. Ibn Jizzy, *Al-Qawannin*, 157.

79. Ben Cheneb, *Proverbes arabes*, 1:89–90.

80. Driss Rabani, interview by author, 13 June 2002.

81. Zaki Berrada, conversation with author, 1 July 2001.

82. Driss Rabani, interview by author, 13 June 2002.

83. Ibid., 2 June 2001.

84. Al-Ouazzani, *Ayam fas al-jamila*, 2:210.

85. Ibn Zaydan, *Ithaf ʿalam al-nas*, 2:137.

86. DAR, Moulay Ahmed ben Abdeselam ben Abdallah ben Suleiman to Mohamed al-M'feddel Gharnit, 23 Jumada I 1324 (15 July 1906).

87. René-Leclerc, "Troisième partie," 317.

88. Driss Rabani, interview by author, 2 June 2001.

89. Aicha Hariri, conversation with author, September 2001.

90. Driss Rabani, interview by author, 13 June 2002.

91. Ibid., 2 June 2001.

92. DAR, Mohamed Chami to Moulay Hassan, 8 Safar 1309 (23 September 1890).

93. Ibn Zaydan, *Ithaf ʿalam al-nas*, 2:529.

94. BR, Palace Affairs, dossier 14/II, Mohamed ben Driss to Bou Salham ben Ali, 10 Jumada II 1261 (16 June 1845). See also BR, Palace Affairs, dossier 15/II, Mohamed ben Driss to Bou Salham ben Ali, 19 Jumada II 1262 (13 June 1846).

95. BR, dossier 220, Mohamed Chami to Aba Alabasse Sidi Ahmed ben Sidi Mousa, 25 Rabi II 1314 (3 October 1896).

96. DAR, Sidi Mehdi ben al-Arbi, 24 Shaʿban 1319 (12 June 1901).

97. Michel, *Une économie de subsistances*, 1:573–578.

98. Weisgerber, *Le Maroc*, 29. For legitimate signs of life that permit a sacrifice, see Ibn Jizzy, *al-Qawannin*, 158.

99. In *Embarrassment of Riches*, Simon Schama attributes the seventeenth-century success of the Dutch navy to its diet of 4,800 calories a day.

100. DAR, Ahmed ben Moussa to Sidi Abdallah ben Ahmed, 9 Muharram 1297 (23 December 1879).

101. DAR, Ahmed ben Moussa ben Hamed to the *umana'* of royal expenses in Marrakesh, 21 Hijja 1300 (23 October 1883).

102. DAR, Moulay Abdelhafid to Umana' of Dar Adiyal, 1 Qa'dah 1328 (4 November 1910).

103. BR, dossier 605, Mohamed M'feddel Ben Mohamed Gharnit to Muhtasib of Fez, 1 May 1904.

104. Al-Lahya, *Al-Hayat al-iqtisadiyya*, 247.

105. Ibn Jizzy, *Al-Qawannin*, 163.

106. Dehors, "Commerce," 355.

107. Moulay Hassan to Caid Bouchta al-Baghdadi, 9 Qa'dah 1305 (18 July 1888), quoted in Touzani, *al-Umana'*, 347.

108. BR, 12453/4, Abou al-Abbas Ahmed ben Said, *al-Taysir fi ahkam al-tas'air*, 11 Jumada I 1316 (27 September 1898), folio 57.

109. DAR, Abdallah ben Ibrahim al-Boukili to Moulay Hassan, 17 Muharram 1297 (31 December 1879); DAR, Moulay Hassan to Moulay Abdallah ben Ibrahim al-Boukili, 7 Safar 1297 (20 January 1880).

110. DAR, Moulay Abdallah Boukili to Moulay Hassan, 23 Rabi I 1298 (23 February 1881).

111. DAR, Moulay Hassan to Moulay Abdallah Boukili, 18 Jumada 1298 (18 April 1881).

112. DAR, Moulay Hassan to Hadj al-Mehdi Bennani, 13 Rabi II 1296 (6 April 1879).

113. Michel, *Une économie de subsistances*, 2:634.

114. DAR, Bouchta ben al-Baghdadi to Moulay Hassan, 25 Shawwal 1307 (14 June 1890).

115. Barret, *Work*.

116. Miège, *Le Maroc*, 3:403.

117. *Times of Morocco*, 13 July 1889.

118. DAR, Representative of German Affairs to al-Hadj Mohamed ben al-Arbi al-Torres, 14 April 1887 (10 Ramadan 1303).

119. DAR, Moulay Abdelaziz to al-Hadj Radi al-Tahar al-Herraq, 26 Jumada II 1320 (30 September 1903).

120. DAR, dossier Amara, Amara Ibn Saddeq to Mohamed Bargach, 2 Jumada I 1296 (24 May 1879); see also DAR, Moulay Abdelaziz to al-Hadj Radi al-Tahar al-Herraq, 26 Jumada II 1320 (30 September 1903).

121. Miège, *Le Maroc*, 3:385–388.

122. Amara Ibn Saddeq to Mohamed Bargach, 10 Sha'ban 1293 (1 August 1876), quoted in *El Ouataiq: Recueils périodiques publiés par la Direction des Archives Royales*, no. 5 (Rabat: Imprimerie Royal, 1981), 99–100; DAR, Moulay Hassan to Mohamed Bargash, 30 Jumada I 1295 (1 June 1878).

123. DAR, Dossier Amara, Amara Ibn Saddeq to Mohamed Bargach, 2 Jumada II 1296 (24 May 1879).

124. DAR, Mohamed ben al-Arbi al-Torres to Hamou ben al-Gilani, 27 Jumada II 1312 (26 December 1894).

125. Miège, *Le Maroc*, 3:385–388.

126. DAR, Moussa ben Ahmed to Sidi Abdallah ben Ahmed, 24 Shaʻban 1295 (23 August 1878).

127. DAR, Mohamed Bargash to Moussa Ibn Ahmed, 26 Shaʻban 1295 (25 August 1878).

128. DAR, Moulay Hassan to Hadj Mehdi Bennani, 4 Qaʻdah 1299 (17 September 1882).

129. DAR, Moqri to undesignated official, 16 Rajab 1303 (18 April 1886).

130. BGA, 136, register 24, *Hawalat ahbas fas al-ʻulia*, 3. For a copy of the same document, see also BGA, 161, register 45, *Hawalat ahbas fas al-ʻulia*, 4.

131. DAR, Mohamed Chami to Fiqh Abou Abdallah Sidi al-Senaji, Minister, 14 Ramadan 1306 (14 May 1889).

132. DAR, Portuguese diplomat (illegible signature) to Mohamed Torres, 9 Safar 1307 (5 October 1889).

## Chapter 4. The Economic and Political Order of Colonial Morocco

1. For unrest in Fez, see Rivet, *Lyautey*, 1:125–132; see also Pennell, *Morocco since 1830*, 155–156; Burke, *Prelude to Protectorate*, 180–187.

2. Selous, *Appointment to Fez*, 123.

3. BGA, H128, Mohamed ben al-Hassan al-Hajoui, *Qanash bi-hi taqaiyyid ʻalamiyya wa-tarikhiyya*, 25 Rabi II (13 April 1912), 73.

4. Selous, *Appointment to Fez*, 144–145; Mercier, "Souvenirs des massacres," 14.

5. Selous, *Appointment to Fez*, 145.

6. Mercier, "Souvenirs des massacres," 14.

7. For the policy of association, see Pennell, *Morocco since 1830*, 158–160. See also Rivet, *Lyautey*, 1:165–175; Hoisington, *Lyautey*, 41–53.

8. Pennell, *Morocco since 1830*, 161; see also Rivet, *Lyautey*, 1:166–175.

9. In February 1914, the sum of 131 francs was equivalent to 132 PH. I use a 1:1 ratio until the devaluation of the franc after World War I.

10. Gaillard, "La réorganisation," 158. The French budgeted 3,550,000 PH for the maintenance of the palace, which provided for an honor guard of 400 men, 360 members of the sultan's family in Fez and Marrakesh, and 400 servants.

11. Gouvion and Gouvion, *Kitab Aâyane*, 280–281.

12. Luccioni, *Les fondations pieuses*, 128. Luccioni began to work for the French Service du Contrôle des Habous in 1927.

13. Milliot, *Démembrements du habous*.

14. For an inventory of correspondence between Djai and local administrators, see Mabrouk, *Les habous au Maroc*.

15. Luccioni, "Les habous," 373.

16. BGA, Hab. Cont. 60, Chef des Services Municipaux to Délégué à la Résidence Générale, 5 June 1920.

17. Luccioni, "Les biens habous," 385.

18. Ibid., 384.

19. Rivet, *Lyautey*, 2:143.
20. Luccioni, "Les biens habous," 384.
21. For al-Hajoui's biography, see ADN, DACH, 120. See also Gouvion and Gouvion, *Kitab Aâyane*, 263–270. For al-Hajoui's call for "moderate liberal reformism," see Laroui, *Esquisses historiques*, 115–121.
22. Rivet, *Lyautey*, 1:177.
23. For al-Moqri's bid for power, see Rivet, *Lyautey*, 1:176–178. Al-Moqri's political career did not have a happy ending. He supported the forced exile of Mohamed V, who confiscated his property after regaining the throne in 1955.
24. See Casinière, *Les municipalités marocaines*; see also Decroux, *La vie municipale*. For a secondary account, see Yakhlef, *Municipalité de Fez*.
25. "Dahir du 8 Avril 1917 sur l'organisation municipale," *Bulletin Officiel du Protectorat de la République Française du Maroc* 236 (1917): 486–489.
26. Decroux, *La vie municipale*, 53.
27. For a biography by the nephew of the basha, see Baghdadi and Baghdadi, *Le pacha-soldat*.
28. ADN, DACH, 90, Chef du Service des Domaines to Directeur des Affaires Chérifiennes, 22 November 1917.
29. ADN, DACH, 100, Commissaire du Gouvernement auprès du Tribunal du Pacha-Contrôleur des Juridiction Chérifiennes et des Habous to Conseiller du Gouvernement Chérifien-Directeur Général des Affaires Chérifiennes, 28 November 1928.
30. Weisgerber, "Trois marocains," 292–296.
31. Casinière, *Les municipalités marocaines*, 14.
32. Decroux, *La vie municipale*, 47.
33. Weisgerber, "Trois marocains," 292–296.
34. ADN, DACH, 119, Général Gouraud to Hubert Lyautey, 17 October 1912.
35. Ricard, "Chronique de Fès: L'évolution de l'architecture," 157.
36. Decroux, *La vie municipale*, 50.
37. ADN, DACH, 121, Commissaire du Gouvernement auprès du Tribunal du Pacha to Conseiller du Gouvernement Chérifien, 23 April 1929.
38. Le Tourneau, *Fès*, 293–294 n 2.
39. ADN, DACH, 121, Conseiller du Gouvernement Chérifien to Secrétaire Général du Protectorat, 16 April 1934.
40. ADN, DACH, 121, Directeur des Affaires Politiques to Conseiller du Gouvernement Chérifien, 26 January 1938.
41. Drocourt, *Maroc*, 48–61.
42. Yakhlef, *La municipalité de Fez*, tableau 8.
43. Vattier, "La municipalité de Fez," 385; see also Rivet, *Lyautey*, 2:158.
44. Haour, "Participation marocaine," 19.
45. Terrier, "Impressions du Maroc," 256.
46. Unless noted, see Yakhlef, *La municipalité de Fez*, tableau 8.
47. Abdelkabir ben Hachim al-Kittani, *Biyutat ahl fas*, 1:293.
48. Selous, *Appointment to Fez*, 132.
49. Lucas, *Fès*, 21. In 1926, the French expressed concern that their effort to count

urban residents had been faulty, so these numbers are based on the censuses of 1931 and 1936.

50. Rivet, *Lyautey*, 2:191.
51. Ibid., 2:191.
52. MO, Fonds Ricard, no. 500, Jean Baldoui, La protection des industries d'art au Maroc, 1935.
53. BGA, A1465, Rapport mensuel, January 1914.
54. Ibid., April 1914.
55. BGA, A1465, Rapport mensuel, November 1913; see also BGA, A1465, Rapport mensuel, February 1914.
56. BGA, A1465, Rapport mensuel, February 1914.
57. Ibid., March 1914.
58. Ibid., May 1915.
59. BGA, A1765, Budget ordinaire, 1915–1916.
60. Gaillard, "La réorganisation," 167.
61. BGA, A1465, Rapport mensuel, January 1915.
62. For a census of workers, see René-LeClerc, "Troisième partie," 337–350. For unemployment rates in 1915, see BGA, A1465, Rapport mensuel, December 1915.
63. BGA, A1465, Rapport mensuel, December 1915.
64. Ibid., January 1915.
65. AMC, unclassified, curriculum vitae of M. Prosper Ricard, n.d. (1933).
66. BGA, A1465, Rapport mensuel, April 1915.
67. Ricard, "Les métiers," 205.
68. MO, Fonds Ricard, no. 522, L'artisanat marocain, 24 February 1928.
69. Ricard, "Les métiers," 205.
70. BGA, A1465, Rapport mensuel, April 1915.
71. Gallotti, "Les métiers d'art," 14.
72. BGA, A1465, Rapport mensuel, December 1917.
73. Ricard, "Chronique de Fès: Les industries," 332.
74. Bel, "Potiers," 79–82.
75. BGA, A1465, Rapport mensuel, May 1918. See also BGA, A1465, Rapport mensuel, June 1918; BGA, A1465, Rapport mensuel, August 1918.
76. Bel, "Potiers," 80.
77. BGA, A1465, Rapport mensuel, July 1917.
78. Ricard, "Arts indigènes et musées," 213.
79. BGA, A1465, Rapport mensuel, March 1920.
80. Ricard, "L'artisan de Fez," 276.
81. Ricard, "Arts indigènes et musées," 214.
82. For an inventory of lithographic texts published in Fez, see Fawzi, *al-Matbuat al-'ajariyah*.
83. Ricard, "La reliure," 19.
84. Ibid., 19.
85. Ricard, *Art de la relieur*.
86. For Ricard's interest in the bookbinder's trade, see Ricard, "La rénovation," 62–66. See also Ricard, *La renaissance*; Ricard, "Le vieux relieur," 224.

87. Ricard, "La reliure," 19.
88. BGA, A1465, Rapport mensuel, December 1915.
89. Al-Kittani, *Biyutat ahl fas*, 1:371–373.
90. Ricard, "La reliure," 19.
91. Al-Kittani, *Biyutat ahl fas*, 1:371–373.
92. Ricard, "La reliure," 19.
93. Ricard, *Le Maroc*, 290.
94. Al-Kittani, *Biyutat ahl fas*, 1:371–373.
95. BGA, Personnel files of the Department of Fine Arts and Historic Monuments, unclassified, Prosper Ricard, Inspecteur des Arts Industriels de Fès-Meknes, to Directeur des Services des Beaux-Arts, 18 March 1916.
96. BGA, A1465, Rapport mensuel, July 1917.
97. Ricard, "La reliure," 18.
98. Ibid., 20.
99. AMC, unclassified, curriculum vitae de M. Prosper Ricard, n.d. (1933).
100. BGA, A1465, Rapport mensuel, July 1917.
101. Ricard, "La reliure," 20.
102. BGA, A1465, Rapport mensuel, January 1919.
103. Ibid., December 1917.
104. Ibid., April 1918.
105. Rivet, *Lyautey*, 2:194.
106. In May 1923, Louis Massignon published a census of trades in Fez by the muhtasib in a special edition of *Revue du Monde Musulman* 58 (1294): 4.
107. BGA, A1465, Rapport mensuel, December 1917.
108. Ibid., June 1918.
109. BGA, A521, Chef des Services Municipaux to Directeur des Affaires Civiles, 29 January 1919.
110. BGA, A521, Décision, Directeur des Affaires Civiles, 16 February 1920.
111. MO, Fonds Ricard, no. 150, "Un type d'artisan marocain: Ahmed Bennani, menuisier-sculpteur," n.d. [1945]. Unless otherwise noted, information on Bennani comes from this transcript of a show on Radio-Maroc.
112. Al-Kittani, *Biyutat ahl fas*, 1:172.
113. Koechlin, "Les industries d'art indigène," 18.
114. BGA, A1465, Rapport mensuel, December 1915.
115. BGA, A1702, Procès verbal, French Municipal Commission, 17 May 1919.
116. BGA, A1465, Rapport mensuel, November 1919.
117. Ricard, *Le Maroc*, 287.
118. BGA, A833, Rapport mensuel, September 1920.
119. In Arabic, see Benjelloun, *Fi al-tufula*, 195–196. In French, see Benjelloun, *Enfance*, 213–214.
120. Benjelloun, *Fi al-tufula*, 202. In French, see Benjelloun, *Enfance*, 219.
121. ADN, DACH, 73, Note sommaire au sujet de l'organisation corporative, n.d. (1919–1920).
122. ADN, DACH, 73, Mohamed al-Moqri to al-'Umal al- madun, 9 Ramadan 1337 (8 June 1919).

123. Associations of European workers could not be termed trade unions per se, since colonial officials banned such associations, even for Frenchmen, until 1936.

124. ADN, DACH, 73, Mohamed al-Moqri to al-'Umal al-madun, 9 Ramadan 1337 (8 June 1919).

125. ADN, DACH, 73, Mohamed ben Bouchta al-Baghdadi to Mohamed al-Moqri, 15 Qa'dah 1337 (12 August 1919).

126. Al-Hajwi, *Voyage d'Europe*, 157–159.

127. Ricard was proposing a radical innovation. To date, I have not come across the term *hanati* in precolonial correspondence. Royal officials in the nineteenth century identified a worker as an individual practicing a specific trade (*hirfa*), not by his adherence to a corporate group (*hanati*). The sultan, however, did acknowledge an arif as a specialist representing the interests of workers in his trade. According to Ibn Mandhour, the term *hinta* refers to the specific occupation of a person selling grain. See Hyat and Moura'shli, *Lisan al-'arab* 1:737. Referring to colonial documents, Mohamed Bousselam describes the corporate significance of this term in "al-Hanta," 3622–3623.

128. For Ricard's vision of a corporation, see MO, Fonds Ricard, no. 49, Les corporations d'arts et métiers indigènes, Institute des Hautes Études, 1937–1937. See also MO, Fonds Ricard, no. 522, Corporation marocaines: Observations à Fès, réorganisation à Salé, December 1936.

129. MO, Fonds Ricard, no. 522, L'artisanat marocain, 24 February 1928.

130. MO, Fonds Ricard, no. 500, Jean Baldoui, La protection des industries d'art au Maroc, 1935. Baldoui began his colonial career in 1922 as an inspector of indigenous arts and industries in Fez. In 1935, he replaced Ricard as director of the Department of Indigenous Arts and Industries.

131. Du Gast, *Le statut ouvrier au Maroc*, 198.

132. De Sauvigny, *Histoire de France*, 412.

133. Rivet, *Lyautey*, 2:243–5.

134. ADN, DACH, 73, Projet de dahir reconnaissant aux corporations indigènes la capacité civile, 20 October 1920.

135. ADN, DACH, 73, Chef du Service du Commerce et de l'Industrie to Secrétaire Général du Protectorat, 12 November 1920.

136. ADN, DACH, 73, Conseiller du Gouvernement Chérifien to Secrétaire Général du Protectorat, 26 November 1920.

137. ADN, DACH, 73, note personnelle de M. de la Nézière, 1 February 1921.

138. For colonial architecture and urbanism in North Africa, see Wright, *Politics of Design*. See also Béguin, *Arabisances*; Abu-Lughod, *Rabat*; Celik, *Urban Forms*; Prochaska, *Making Algeria French*; Rabinow, *French Modern*; Taylor, "Planned Discontinuity," 52–66.

139. Ricard, "Métiers manuels," 205.

140. BGA, A1465, Rapport mensuel, September 1915.

141. ADN, DACH, 73, Directeur Général des Travaux Publics to l'Ingénieur Municipal, 1 October 1915.

142. For preservation, see Abu-Lughod, "Moroccan Cities."

143. Drocourt, *Maroc*, 12–18.

144. Ibid., 41–46.

145. AMC, unclassified, Léon Dumas to Maurice Tranchant de Lunel, Chef du Service des Beaux Arts, 28 October 1915.

146. Tranchant de Lunel, *Au pays du paradoxe*, 198–199.

147. AMC, unclassified, Léon Dumas to Chef du Services des Beaux-Arts, 25 April 1917.

148. Koechlin, "Les industries d'art indigène," 61.

149. Saladin, "La main-d'oeuvre indigène," 66.

150. BGA, unclassified, accounting ledger for Madrasa al-Saharidj, 1922.

151. Ricard, "Chronique de Fès: L'évolution," 158.

152. Tranchant de Lunel, *Au pays du paradoxe*, 145–146.

153. Ricard, "Les arts et industries indigenes."

154. Ricard, "Incendie des souks de Fès," 21.

155. Drocourt, *Maroc*, 72–75.

156. Ibid., 72.

157. Louis Massignon published Driss Moqri's inventory of trades in the *Revue du Monde Musulman* 58 (1924): 3–13.

158. Al-Kittani, *Biyutat ahl fas*, 1:180–181.

159. AMC, unclassified, Boris Maslow to Chef des Services Municipaux, 27 August 1921.

160. Al-Kittani, *Biyutat ahl fas*, 1:199.

161. For information relating to this property's development, see OCF, 488KF, T. Bouayad no. 1.

162. AMC, unclassified, Edmund Pauty to Secrétaire Général du Protectorat, 9 October 1925. See also AMC, unclassified, Taieb ben M'feddel Bouayad to Edmund Pauty, 10 January 1925.

163. For real estate in the medina of Fez, see Ameur, *Fès*.

164. OCF, 8583F, Hammam el Mernissi, requisition no. 4176, 29 October 1943.

165. AMC, unclassified, Prosper Ricard to Joseph Vattier, 5 August 1926.

166. Unless otherwise noted, see Gouvion and Gouvion, *Kitab Aâyane*, 2:793–795.

167. Abdelaziz Mernissi, interview by author, 10 July 2002.

168. OCF, 197KF, Dar Hjaoua, requistion no. 83 K.

169. Hoisington, *Lyautey*, 160–161.

170. AMC, unclassified, Boris Maslow to unidentified official, 2 May 1922.

171. AMC, unclassified, Jules Borély to Chef des Services Municipaux, 19 August 1927.

172. AMC, unclassified, Maison el Mernissi, 22 April 1928.

173. AMC, unclassified, Jules Borély to Commandant de la Région Fez, 11 June 1928.

174. This war is analyzed further in chapters 5 and 6.

175. BGA, A415, Cahiers d'observations annexes au projet du Budget additionnel de l'exercise, 1927.

176. BGA, A1553, Rapport mensuel, March 1927.

177. BGA, A692, Rapport mensuel, January 1927.

178. BGA, A692, Rapport mensuel, February 1927; see also BGA, A692, Rapport mensuel, March 1927.

179. BGA, A719, Cahier des charges speciales imposées pour l'amenagement d'un asile de nuit à Bab Segma, 1927.

180. AMC, unclassified, Inspecteur Regional des Beaux Arts et Monuments Historiques to Chef de Service des Beaux Arts et Monuments Historiques, 7 July 1925.

181. AMC, unclassified, Boris Maslow to unidentified official in Service des Beaux Arts et Monuments Historiques, 2 May 1928.

182. AMC, unclassified, Leonetti to unidentified official, n.d. (1928).

183. Service des Beaux Arts et Monuments Historiques, *Historique*, 286.

184. Mercier, "Souvenirs des massacres," 14.

## Chapter 5. The Colonial Preservation of the Miller's Trade

1. Le Tourneau, *Fès*, 223.

2. I would like to thank Dr. Attilio Petruccioli for providing a copy of this map.

3. Gouraud, *Au Maroc*, 32.

4. Ricard, *Le Maroc*, 281.

5. Leo Africanus, cited in *l'Industrie en marche: Bilan de six années d'activité, 1977–1983* (Fez: Chamber of Commerce and Industry, 1983), 18. This leaflet can be consulted at ONICL.

6. MO, Fonds Ricard, no. 521, *Corporations marocaines*. I do not have a definitive tally of Fez's mills. Perigny counts 220 in *Au Maroc*, 135. As head of Fez's Economic Bureau, Vattier counted 290 in "Fès, cité marchand," 52–55. Louis Massignon counted 320 mills using 567 grinding stones in "Enquête," 39.

7. Ricard, "La main d'oeuvre marocaine," 27.

8. Stewart, *Economy of Morocco*, 128.

9. BGA, H6, Moulin Derb el Bouacq, Muraqib of Fez to Minister of Religious Endowments, no. 516, 7 Jumada I 1333 (23 March 1915).

10. BGA, H6, Ahmed Tazi to Ahmed al-Djai, no. 304, 15 Muharram 1333 (2 December 1914).

11. BGA, H6, Ahmed Tazi to Ahmed al-Djai, no. 571, 3 Rajab 1333 (15 May 1915).

12. Si Mohamed Alami, interview by author, 24 June 2002.

13. BGA, H6, Moulin Eddiban, Ministry of Religious Endowments to Muraqib fas, no. 4741, 20 Jumada I 1334 (25 March 1916).

14. Pennell, *Morocco since 1830*, 161, 208.

15. ADN, Direction des Affaires Chérifiennes (DACH), 89.

16. Ricard, *Guide de Fès*, 5. By 1920, the European population of Fez had grown to 1,500 people. See BGA, A1702, Procès-verbal, French Municipal Commission, 12 February 1920. See also Ricard, *Le Maroc*, 278.

17. BGA, A1465, Rapport mensuel, July 1917.

18. Ibid., August 1917.

19. Ibid., October 1917.

20. Ibid.

21. BGA, Hab. Cont. 58 (2), Ahmed Tazi to Ahmed al-Djai, no. 2500, 25 Safar 1337 (30 November 1918).

22. AMC, unclassified, Général Gouraud to Directeur Général des Travaux Publics, 29 January 1914. For Campini's assertion that he could supply electricity more cheaply,

see AMC, unclassified, Giuseppe Campini to Captain Mellier, Chef des Services Municipaux, 14 December 1914.

23. BGA, Hab. Cont. 40, Droits de Jouissance, Ahmed Tazi to Ahmed al-Djai, no. 2129, 26 Rajab 1336 (7 May 1918).

24. ADN, CD, 517, Giuseppe Campini to Hubert Lyautey, 10 May 1916.

25. Ibid.; ADN, CD, 517, Hubert Lyautey to Charles Sabathier, 29 December 1914.

26. ADN, CD, 517, de Chavigny, Partie du Dossier Campini rendu par M. de Revel, 27 May 1914.

27. ADN, CD, 517, Hubert Lyautey to Charles Sabathier, 20 August 1914.

28. Ibid., 29 December 1914.

29. ADN, CD, 517, Campini to Lyautey, 10 May 1916.

30. ADN, CD, 517, Hubert Lyautey to Charles Sabathier, 20 August 1914.

31. BGA, 1652, Mémoire, March 1924.

32. BGA, 1652, Umberto Campini, Mémoire, n.d. [1925].

33. BGA, 1652, Général Maurial, Commandant de la Région de Fez, to Commissaire Résident Général, 15 December 1921.

34. ADN, CD, 517, Hubert Lyautey to Machwitz, a lawyer in Casablanca, 3 May 1917.

35. BGA, A1465, Rapport mensuel, August 1918.

36. Ibid., November 1918.

37. Ibid., December 1918.

38. BGA, A975, General Dursoy, Directeur de l'Intendance du Maroc, to Directeur des Affaires Civiles, 5 July 1919.

39. BGA, A970, Gacquière to Directeur des Affaires Civiles, 4 December 1919.

40. BGA, A1465, Rapport mensuel, August 1920.

41. Ibid., August 1920.

42. Ibid., December 1918.

43. Ibid., April 1919.

44. BGA, A970, Gacquière to Directeur des Affaires Civiles, 4 December 1919.

45. BGA, A1465, Rapport mensuel, July 1919.

46. Ibid., December 1919.

47. Rivet, *Lyautey*, 2:8.

48. BGA, A975, unidentified official to Directeur de l'Intendance, 20 April 1918.

49. ADN, CD, 517, Giuseppe Campini to Hubert Lyautey, 10 May 1916.

50. BGA, A975, Commandant de la Région de Fez to Alfred de Tarde, Directeur des Affaires Civiles, 21 June 1919.

51. BGA, A975, Intendant Général Durosoy to Alfred de Tarde, Directeur des Affaires Civiles, 22 July 1919.

52. BGA, A1465, Rapport mensuel, October 1919.

53. BGA, A833, Rapport mensuel, February 1920.

54. BGA, A975, Alfred de Tarde to Délégué à la Résidence Générale, 24 June 1919.

55. BGA, A1465, Rapport mensuel, June 1919.

56. BGA, A975, Arrêté municipal, 6 September 1919.

57. BGA, A965, Lafarge, Directeur des Affaires Civiles, to Directeur du Service des Renseignements, 20 November 1920.

58. BGA, A1465, Rapport mensuel, November 1919.
59. ADN, DAI, 60, "al-'Alam bi al-sil'a," *Akhbar talagrafiyya*, 10 April 1916, 4.
60. BGA, A970, Extrait du rapport mensuel, December 1919.
61. BGA, A833, Rapport mensuel, February 1920.
62. Ibid., January 1920.
63. BGA, A970, Chef des Services Municipaux to Alfred de Tarde, 20 May 1920.
64. BGA, A975, Extrait du rapport mensuel, December 1919.
65. BGA, A1702, Procès-verbal, French Municipal Commission, 12 February 1920.
66. Ibid., 10 March 1920.
67. BGA, H17, Muraqib ahbas fas to Ministry of Religious Endowments, no. 3282, 11 Jumada I 1338 (1 February 1920).
68. BGA, A950, P.L., "Bulletin," *Vigie Marocaine*, 6–7 July 1920.
69. Perigny, *Au Maroc*, 137.
70. BGA, A965, Chef des Services Municipaux to Inspecteur des Municipalités, 24 August 1920.
71. BGA, A965, Lafarge to Directeur du Service des Renseignements, 20 November 1920.
72. BGA, A965, Watin to Directeur des Affaires Civiles, 22 February 1921.
73. BGA, A833, Rapport mensuel, March 1921.
74. Ibid., January 1921.
75. BGA, A965, Directeur des Affaires Civiles to Chef des Services Municipaux, April 1921.
76. BGA, A964, Note pour Directeur des Affaires Civiles, 21 June 1921.
77. BGA, A965, Watin to Directeur des Affaires Civiles, 22 February 1921.
78. Yakhlef, *La Municipalité de Fez*, tableau 8.
79. BGA, A965, Procès-verbal du medjless musulman, 29 March 1921.
80. BGA, A965, Directeur des Affaires Civiles to Chef des Services Municipaux, April 1921.
81. Mohamed Filalli "Terras," interview by author, 9 June 2001.
82. BGA, A965, Procès-verbal, réunion, Bureau du Ravitaillement, 10 April 1921.
83. BGA, A1713, Procès-verbal, Medjless musulman, 27 May 1921.
84. BGA, A965, Note pour le Directeur des Affaires Civiles, 2 June 1921.
85. BGA, A965, telegramme, n.d.
86. BGA, A965, telegramme, 7 June 1921.
87. BGA, A965, Procès-verbal, réunion, Bureau du Ravitaillement, 10 April 1921.
88. BGA, A965, Rapport mensuel, June 1921.
89. BGA, A965, Procès-verbal, Medjless musulman, 14 June 1921.
90. BGA, A965, Rapport mensuel, June 1921.
91. BGA, A965, Note pour Directeur des Affaires Civiles, 9 July 1921. See also BGA, 1652, Watin to Agent Comptable du Ravitaillement, Direction Générale des Finances, 30 July 1921.
92. BGA, A965, Directeur des Affaires Indigènes et du Service des Renseignements du Maroc to Directeur des Affaires Civiles, 30 July 1921.
93. BGA, 1652, Giuseppe Campini to Chef des Services Municipaux, 30 July 1921.

94. BGA, 1652, Service de l'Administration Municipale to Secrétaire Générale du Protectorat, 7 July 1921.
95. BGA, 1652, Services Municipaux, Stock municipal de blé constitué à la Minoterie Campini, 30 July 1921.
96. Ibid.
97. BGA, 1652, Watin to Directeur des Affaires Civiles, 27 June 1921.
98. BGA, A949, Watin to Directeur des Affaires Civiles, 22 September 1921.
99. BGA, A832, Rapport mensuel, November 1923.
100. Stewart, *Economy of Morocco*, 88, 128.
101. Perigny, *Au Maroc*, 138.
102. Ibid.
103. Ibid.
104. Ibid.
105. Massignon, "Enquête," 39.
106. BGA, 1652, Umberto Campini, Mémoire, 6 February 1923.
107. Massignon, "Enquête," 39.
108. Ibid., 38.
109. Al-Kittani, *Biyutat ahl fas*, 1:197–198.
110. Abdelwahed Ouali, interview by author, 22 March 2001.
111. Ibid., 11 June 2002.
112. Si Mohamed Alami, interview by author, 22 March 2001.
113. Massignon, "Enquête," 52.
114. Hadj Mohamed Filalli "Terras," interview by author, 9 June 2001.
115. BGA, A832, Rapport mensuel, November 1923.
116. Ibid., February 1924.
117. Ibid., May 1923. See also BGA, A832, Rapport mensuel, June 1923.
118. BGA, A832, Rapport mensuel, December 1923. See also BGA, A832, Rapport mensuel, January 1924.
119. PJ, *alif-qaf*, 43/45, Fez, Lahcen ben Ahmed Sanhadji, 1923.
120. PJ, *alif-qaf*, 96/100, Fez, El Hadi ben Mohamed Slaoui, 1925.
121. BGA, 1652, Umberto Campini, Mémoire, n.d. [1925].
122. Ibid.
123. Ibid.
124. BGA, 1652, "La minoterie Campini brule à Fez," *La Vigie Marocaine*.
125. BGA, 1652, Chef des Services Municipaux, to Secrétaire Général du Protectorat, 28 September 1925.
126. Ibid.
127. BGA, A962, Blondelle, Chef de l'Office Économique, to Chef du Service du Commerce et de l'Industrie, 29 July 1926.
128. BGA, A978, Chef des Services Municipaux, État presentant les besoins des indigènes en blé dur et orge jusqu'à la soudure, 1926.
129. BGA, A962, Blondelle to Chef du Service du Commerce et de l'Industrie, 29 July 1926.
130. BGA, A978, Chef des Services Municipaux, État presentant les besoins des indigènes en blé dur et orge jusqu'à la soudure, 1926.

131. Odinot, *Le monde marocain*, 187.

132. Louis Massignon identified milling as one of Fez's most important trades, but he also insisted that "the indigenous millers suffer... the effects of an ensemble of unfavorable conditions since the arrival of Europeans." See Massignon, "Enquête," 180.

133. Stewart, *Economy of Morocco*, 128.

134. Office National Interprofessionnel des Céréales et des Légumineuses, *La meunerie*.

## Chapter 6. Fiscal Politics at the Municipal Slaughterhouse

1. J. Desparmet, "Les reactions nationalitaires en Algérie jugée par les indigènes," *Bulletin de la Société de Géographie d'Algérie et de l'Afrique du Nord*, 15 (1910): 177, quoted in Lazreg, *Eloquence of Silence*, 52–53.

2. Gouvion and Gouvion, *Kitab Aâyane*, 267.

3. Al-Hajwi, *Voyage d'Europe*, 124.

4. Telegram from Hubert Lyautey dated 23 November 1912, quoted in Rivet, *Lyautey*, 1:174.

5. ADN, DACH, 149, note no. 1 au sujet de la 'hedia' de l'aid el kebir, 17 November 1913.

6. ADN, DACH, 149, Hubert Lyautey to Colonels Commandants of Fez, Meknes, Rabat, Chaouia, Tadla Zaian, Marrakesh, 20 December 1914.

7. ADN, DACH, 149, Hubert Lyautey, memo, 31 October 1914.

8. Ibid.

9. ADN, DACH, 149, Hubert Lyautey to Colonels Commandants of Fez, Meknes, Rabat, Chaouia, Tadla Zaian, Marrakesh, 20 December 1914.

10. ADN, DACH, 149, Hubert Lyautey, memo, 31 October 1914.

11. ADN, DACH, 149, Circulaire résidentielle, n.d. (1915).

12. ADN, DACH, 149, note no. 1 au sujet de la 'hedia' de l'aid el kebir, 17 November 1913.

13. ADN, Direction de l'Intérieur (DI), 205, Note fixant le programme des cérémonies de l'Aid el Kebir, 13 August 1921. See also ADN, DACH, 150, Note fixant le programme des cérémonies de l'Aid el Kebir, 31 July 1922.

14. BGA, A1465, Rapport mensuel, September 1913.

15. ADN, DAI, 60, "al-'Id al-adha," *Akhbar talagrafiyya* (Fez), 22 October 1915.

16. ADN, DAI, 203, Secrétaire Général du Gouvernement Chérifien to Directeur du Service des Renseignements, 27 November 1915.

17. Al-Kittani, *Biyutat ahl fas*, 2:84.

18. ADN, DAI, 60, "al-'Id al-adha," *Akhbar talagrafiyya* (Fez), 22 October 1915.

19. Pennell, *Morocco since 1830*, 127–139.

20. Forbes, *El Raisuni*, 153.

21. Pennell, *Morocco since 1830*, 171.

22. Forbes, *El Raisuni*, 194.

23. Ibid., 68–75.

24. ADN, DAI, 203, Agence de France-Tanger to Résident Général, 5 October 1916.

25. Ibid., 7 October 1916.

26. ADN, DAI, 203, L'Aid Kebir, 1916.
27. ADN, DAI, 203, Discours de Lyautey, Aid-al-Kebir, 1917.
28. ADN, DAI, 205, Aid-al-Kebir à Rabat, 1919.
29. Pennell, *Morocco since 1830*, 181.
30. Ibid., 190.
31. ADN, DACH, 150, Commandant de la Région de Taza to Ministre Plénipotentiaire, 12 July 1923; ADN, DAI, 205, Commandant de la Région de Taza to Ministre Plénipotentiaire Délégué, 20 July 1923.
32. Ibid.
33. Pennell, *Morocco since 1830*, 190.
34. Ibid., 192.
35. Gershovich, *French Military Rule*, 163 n. 14.
36. Ibid., 163 n. 15.
37. Pennell, *Country*, 189.
38. ADN, DACH, 150, Hubert Lyautey to Délégué à la Résidence Générale, télégramme officiel, 21 June 1925.
39. Vernon, *Sands, Palms and Minarets*, 169–173.
40. Casinière, *Les municipalités*, 159.
41. BGA, A1074, Compte rendu d'une commission technique, 13 August 1915.
42. ADN, DAI, 321 bis, Général de Division Henrys, Commandant Général du Nord, to Résident Général, 29 August 1915.
43. "Dahir du 25 août 1914 portant règlement des établissements insalubres, incommodes ou dangereux"; see Dr. Eyraud, Chef de Service-Directeur Général de l'Agriculture (Rabat: Imprimerie Officielle, 1935), 117–118.
44. BGA, A1074, Compte rendu d'une commission technique, 13 August 1915.
45. "Dahir du 8 Avril 1917 sur l'organisation municipale," *Bulletin officiel du Protectorat de la République Française du Maroc* 236 (1917): 486–489.
46. BGA, A1074, Colonel Commandant de la Région de Fès to Résident Général, 23 May 1915.
47. Ibid., 18 May 1915.
48. BGA, A1465, Rapport mensuel, April 1914.
49. Ibid., July 1915.
50. BGA, A1074, Compte rendu d'une commission technique, 13 August 1915.
51. BGA, A1765, Chef des Services Municipaux to Résident Générale, 29 March 1916.
52. Moreau, *L'abbatoir moderne*.
53. BGA, A1465, Rapport mensuel, April 1918.
54. Hadj Mohamed Sharqi "al-Saba'," interview by author, 19 July 2001. See also BGA, A1074, Concours, 1 March 1936.
55. BGA, A1465, Rapport mensuel, May 1914.
56. BGA, A1074, Président du Tribunal Rabbinique de Fez to Commissaire du Gouvernement Contrôleur des Juridictions Chérifiennes et des Habous, 18 August 1924.
57. I visited this site in July 2001 and June 2002. Now closed for about sixty years, the slaughterhouse remains intact.

58. BGA, A832, Rapport mensuel, March 1923.
59. Hadj Mohamed Sharqi "al-Saba'," interview by author, 17 July 2001. He worked at Bayn al-Madun in 1936.
60. BGA, A1764, Budget, Exercice 1er Mai 1917–31 Decembre 1917.
61. BGA, A415, Budget de 1927, Cahiers d'observations.
62. BGA, A1465, Rapport mensuel, January 1919.
63. Colombain, "Les coopératives indigènes," 201.
64. BGA, A692, Rapport mensuel, June 1927.
65. BGA, A1074, Président du Tribunal Rabbinique de Fez to Commissaire du Gouvernement Contrôleur des Juridictions Chérifiennes et des Habous, 18 August 1924.
66. BGA, A1074, Conseiller du Gouvernement Chérifien to Directeur des Affaires Chérifiennnes, 24 September 1924.
67. BGA, A80, Budget primitif de l'exercice de 1937.
68. BGA, A1767, Décision d'arbitrage de l'ingenieur des ponts et chaussées, 14 February 1918.
69. Loverdo, *Construction*, 1:114.
70. BGA, A1767, Chef des Services Municipaux to Résident Générale, 1 February 1918.
71. Ricard, *Le Maroc*, 284–285.
72. Ibid., 290.
73. Hamid Aouad, interview by author, 12 June 2002.
74. Gilalli Fakhir "l-Battoir," interview by author, 12 July 2001.
75. Malika Khandagui, conversation with author, September 2001. A native of Fez, she taught Moroccan dialect for the American Institute of Maghrib Studies.
76. Hoisington, *Lyautey*, 140–147.
77. For a description of the slaughterhouse in Casablanca, see Casinière, *Municipalités marocaines*, 160–163. For documents relating to Tazi's investment, see ADN, DAI, 321 bis, Chef des Services Municipaux-Casablanca to Résident Général, 18 November 1917. See also ADN, DAI, 321 bis, Commandant de la Région de Casablanca to Résident Général, 12 December 1917, 25 February 1918
78. BGA, A753, Arrêté municipal, 28 October 1912.
79. BGA, BGA, A1439, Minutes of Jewish Municipal Commission, December 1936.
80. Ricard, *Guide de Fès*, 5.
81. Ricard, *Le Maroc*, 278.
82. Lucas, *Fès dans le Maroc moderne*, 21.
83. Hamid Aouad, interview by author, 12 June 2002. According to Hamid, the al-Qadmiri family was a butchering "dynasty." Mohamed's brothers Abderrahman and M'hammed also worked in the trade. His paternal uncle, Allal, a butcher, would later act as imam at the municipal slaughterhouse.
84. BGA, A753, Arrêté municipal, 5 February 1914.
85. BGA, A1465, Rapport mensuel, May 1914.
86. ADN, DACH, 101, Chef des Service Municipaux to Secrétaire Général du Gouvernement Chérifien, 28 October 1916.
87. BGA, A1465, Rapport mensuel, October 1919.

88. BGA, A1764, Chef des Services Municipaux to Résident Général, 10 February 1917.

89. In 1923, Louis Massignon published a census of trades in a special edition of *Revue du Monde Musulman* 58 (1294): 9.

90. BGA, A1765, Budget ordinaire, 1915–1916.

91. BGA, A1766, Budget 1 Mai 1916 à 30 Avril 1917.

92. BGA, A1465, Rapport mensuel, April 1918.

93. BGA, A833, Rapport mensuel, January 1922.

94. Ibid., February 1922.

95. BGA, A753, Arrêté municipal organisant la perception de la 'guerjouma,' 28 October 1912.

96. BGA, A1465, Rapport mensuel, May 1915.

97. BGA, A753, Colonel Simon to Résident Général, 18 May 1915.

98. BGA, A1074, Colonel Commandant de la Région de Fès to Résident Général, 18 May 1915.

99. BGA, A1104, Procès-verbal, Muslim medjless, 4 May 1918.

100. BGA, A753, Colonel Simon to Résident Général, 18 May 1915.

101. BGA, A1465, Rapport mensuel, June 1915.

102. Ibid., July 1915.

103. BGA, A1104, Arrêté municipal, 5 May 1918.

104. BGA, A1104, Procès-verbal, Medjless musulman, 4 May 1918.

105. BGA, A1104, Captain Gaquiere, Chef des Services Municipaux, to Hubert Lyautey, Résident Général, 20 May 1918.

106. Ibid.

107. BGA, A1104, Hubert Lyautey to Chef des Services Municipaux, 6 July 1918.

108. BGA, A1104, Hubert Lyautey to Captain Gaquiere, Chef des Services Municipaux, 8 September 1918.

109. BGA, A1465, Rapport mensuel, April 1918.

110. Ibid., August 1919.

111. BGA, A833, Rapport mensuel, April 1922.

112. Ibid.

113. Lucas, *Fès*, 62.

114. BGA, H17, Muraqib of Fez to Ministry of Religious Endowments, 23 Shawwal 1339 (30 June 1921).

115. PJ, Cherifian Court of Appeals, *alif-qaf*, 96–100.

116. BGA, A1702, Procès verbal, French Municipal Commission, 4 December 1923.

117. BGA, A833, Rapport mensuel, January 1920.

118. BGA, A1702, Procès verbal, French Municipal Commission, 20 January 1922.

119. Ibid., 16 February 1924.

120. Ibid., 25 January 1925.

121. BGA, A753, Arrêté municipal, 28 October 1912.

122. Ibid., 1 October 1914.

123. BGA, A753, Commandant de la Région de Fès to Secrétariat Général du Gouvernement Chérifien, 1 October 1914.

124. BGA, A753, Arrêté municipal no. 26, 21 October 1914.

125. BGA, A1465, Rapport mensuel, February 1914.

126. ADN, DACH, 136, Report on the sultan's chamberlain Thami Ababou, 28 September 1927.

127. BGA, A753, Arrêté municipal, no. 196, 14 April 1924.

128. ADN, DACH, 150, Note pour le Secrétariat Général du Protectorat, 10 August 1921.

129. ADN, DACH, 150, Note pour Monsieur le Ministre Plénipotentiaire, 25 July 1922. For other copies of the annual decree, see also ADN, DACH, 150, Secrétaire Général du Protectorat to Conseiller du Gouvernement Chérifien, 24 June 1924 and ADN, DAI, 321, Projet de Dahir, 14 Juillet 1917.

130. Borély, *Mon plaisir au Maroc*, 123–124.

131. BGA, A753, Commandant de la Région de Fès to Secrétariat Général du Gouvernement Chérifien, 1 October 1914.

132. BGA, A753, Arrêté municipal, no. 26, 21 October 1914.

133. BGA, A692, Rapport mensuel, July 1922.

134. ADN, DACH, 137, Chef des Services Municipaux de Rabat to Conseiller du Gouvernement Chérifien, 22 September 1922.

135. BGA, A753, Chef des Services Municipaux to Henri de la Casinière, Directeur des Services Municipaux, 19 March 1924.

136. BGA, A753, Arrêté municipal permanent, 29 April 1925.

137. BGA, A692, Rapport mensuel, July 1927.

138. Hoisington, *Casablanca Connection*, 21.

139. BGA, A1713, Procès-verbal, Muslim Municipal Commission, 7 February 1925.

140. Ibid., 29 May 1926.

141. Hamid Aouad, interview by author, 12 June 2002.

142. Hadj Alami, interview by author, 22 March 2001.

143. ADN, DAI, 60, "Samsara biʻa al-lahm li al-junud," *Akhbar talagrafiyya*, 25 February 1916, no. 589, 4.

144. Lucas, *Fès*, 17.

145. PJ, *alif-qaf*, 13/16, Procès-verbal d'information, Moïse Lévy, 14 December 1926. Moïse Lévy was a livestock merchant who did business with both the Tazis and the Slaouis.

146. Gilalli Fakhir "l-Battoir," interview by author, 12 July 2001.

147. Le Tourneau and Paye, "La corporation," 201–202.

148. In 2001, Si Mohamed Najib al-Ouali was president of Fez's *chevillards*. I would like to thank him for speaking to me about this trade's development as well as for putting me in contact with butchers who learned the trade from their father.

149. Gilalli Fakhir "l-Battoir," interview by author, 12 July 2001.

150. PJ, *alif-qaf*, 13/16, Procès-verbal d'information, Mohamed al-Tazi, 2 June 1926.

151. BGA, A1465, Rapport mensuel, May 1919.

152. Ibid.

153. OCF, Tazi-Mernissi, 175KF, requisition no. 81K, 26 February 1924.

154. OCF, Tazi-Mernissi, 175KF, Procès-verbal de saisie-exécution immobilière, 10 January 1938.

155. OCF, Le Saladje, 452F, Vente par adjudication aux enchères publiques, 5 September 1922.

156. OCF, Le Saladje, 452F, Extrait des minutes du Secretariat Greffe du Tribunal de Première Instance de Rabat, 11 January 1927.

157. Gershovich, *French Military Rule*, 13, 129.

158. PJ, *alif-qaf*, 13/16, Rapport du Commissaire du Gouvernement Chérifien, 19 January 1928.

159. OCF, Fonduk Louise II, 247KF, records of purchase recorded 21 October 1926.

160. Dossiers at Fez's Office of Land Titles include paperwork on loans taken against a property.

161. OCF, Fonduk Louise II, 247KF, certification of sale, 25 June 1928.

162. OCF, Dar Slaoui, 2485F, requisition no. 487, 14 August 1931.

163. Sijelmassi, *Fès*, 124, 134–135, 144–145.

164. BGA, A1713, Procès-verbal, Muslim Municipal Commission, 2 August 1924.

165. BGA, A1713, Noms des notables indigènes des différents quartiers de la ville de Fez-al-Bali.

166. Yakhlef, *Municipalité de Fès*, table 8.

### Chapter 7. Struggles for Scarce Resources in the 1930s

1. ADN, DAI, Ministre Plénipotentiaire délégué à la Résidence Générale to Ministre des Affaires Etrangères, 6 September 1930.

2. Pennell, *Morocco since 1830*, 212.

3. ADN, DAI, 320, Exposé sur la question des eaux de Fès, 17 May 1930.

4. ADN, DAI, 320, Traduction du rapport du Medjless el Baladi au sujet du projet d'arrêté du Directeur des Travaux Publics portant réglementation des eaux du bassin de l'Oued Fès et de leur repartition, 10 December 1929.

5. ADN, DAI, 320, Réglement d'eau de l'Oued Fès: Rapport de l'ingénieur, 6 February 1930.

6. ADN, DAI, 320, Ingénieur des ponts et chaussées to Chef des Services Municipaux, 11 February 1930.

7. ADN, DAI, 320, Chef des Services Municipaux to Secrétaire Général du Protectorat, 19 February 1930.

8. ADN, DAI, 320, Directeur Général du Cabinet Militaire et des Affaires Indigènes to Chef du Cabinet Civil, 15 April 1930.

9. ADN, DAI, 320, Réglementation des eaux du bassin de l'Oued Fès et de leur repartition dans la ville de Fès, n.d. (18 April 1930).

10. ADN, DAI, 320, Général Commandant de la Région et Division de Fès to Résident Général, 13 May 1930.

11. ADN, DAI, 320, Taieb al-Moqri to Chef des Services Municipaux, 13 May 1930.

12. ADN, DAI, 320, Direction des Affaires Indigènes, Note sur la question des eaux à Fès, 3 June 1930.

13. Al-Kittani, *Biyutat ahl fas*, 199.

14. ADN, DAI, 320, Note sur les usagers de l'Oued Fès, 24 May 1930.

15. M. Ouazzani, *Mudhkira hyat*, 184.

16. ADN, DAI, 320, Direction des Services de Sécurité du Maroc, Note de renseignements, n.d. (May 1930).
17. ADN, DAI, 320, *Muaradhat ahl fas ala ma' wadi fas*, 10 May 1930.
18. ADN, DAI, 320, Petition to Office of Land Titles, 11 May 1930, 11 May 1930.
19. ADN, DAI, 320, Direction des Services de Sécurité du Maroc, Note de renseignements, 21 May 1930.
20. Lucas, *Fès*, 21.
21. ADN, DAI, 320, Direction des Services de Sécurité du Maroc, Note de renseignements, 12 May 1930.
22. ADN, DAI, 320, Général Commandant de la Région de Fès to Directeur Général des Affaires Indigènes et du Cabinet Militaire, 12 May 1930.
23. ADN, DAI, 320, Commissaire Chef de la Sûreté Régionale to Chef du Service de la Police Générale, 14 May 1930.
24. ADN, DAI, 320, Note sur les usagers de l'Oued Fès, 24 May 1930.
25. ADN, DAI, 320, Maxime de Roquemaure to Voizard, Chef du Cabinet Civil du Résident Général, 14 May 1930.
26. ADN, DAI, 320, Direction des Services de Sécurité du Maroc, Note de renseignements, 21 May 1930.
27. ADN, DAI, 320, Un groupe de Mécontents de la politique Française au Maroc to Président de la République Française, 30 May 1930.
28. ADN, DAI, 320, Chevreux, Note de renseignements, 3 June 1930.
29. ADN, DAI, 320, Menées espagnoles-a/s manifestation O. Fez, 3 June 1930.
30. ADN, DAI, 320, Note au sujet de la question des eaux de l'Oued Fez, 18 June 1930.
31. ADN, DAI, 320, Ministre des Affaires Etrangères to Résident Général, 13 June 1930.
32. ADN, DAI, 320, Note au sujet de la répartition des eaux de l'Oued Fez, 10 June 1930.
33. M. Ouazzani, *Mudhkira hyat*, 3:184.
34. Al-Fassi, *Independence Movements*, 117.
35. Hoisington, *Casablanca Connection*, 34.
36. Pennell, *Morocco since 1830*, 219.
37. CAC, CHEAM, no. 104, "Les corporations au Maroc," 2 March 1937, 15.
38. Pennell, *Morocco since 1830*, 222–223.
39. Ibid., 211.
40. Ibid., 222.
41. Ibid., 224.
42. Hoisington, *Casablanca Connection*, 79.
43. Ibid., 85.
44. CAC, CHEAM, no. 104, "Les corporations au Maroc," 2 March 1937, 15.
45. BGA, A675, Arrêté municipal permanent, no. 104, 28 September 1931.
46. BGA, A1713, Procès-verbal, Medjless, 28 September 1931.
47. BGA, A1336, Procès-verbal, Commission Municipal Mixte, 17 March 1936.
48. *La Dépêche de Fès*, 19 November 1933.

49. Lucas, *Fès*, 21.

50. Baron and Mathieu, "Quelques budgets," 215.

51. Pennell, *Morocco since 1830*, 240.

52. "Mercuriale des produits indigènes de première nécessité," *La Bougie de Fès*, 18 July 1937.

53. MO, Fonds Ricard, no. 521, Corporations marocaines: Observations à Fès, réorganisation à Salé, December 1936.

54. Pennell, *Morocco since 1830*, 240.

55. For the lot of shoemakers and tanners in the 1930s, see Ricard, "La situation," 174. See also Guyot et al., "Résultats," 126–142. See also Guyot et al., "L'Industrie," 219–226; Guyot et al., "La corporation," 167–240; Guyot et al., "Les cordonniers," 9–54.

56. OCF, 6918F, Rahmet Allah, contract between Mernissi and Compagnie Algérienne, 13 December 1935. See also OCF, 770F, Mitoyenneté Mernissi, itemization of properties and loans, n.d. (3 April 1934). The Duplicate de Titre Foncer in this dossier records Mernissi's payment of the entire debt between 1937 and 1940.

57. Abdelaziz Mernissi, interview by author, 10 July 2002.

58. Lucas, *Fès*, 59.

59. AMC, unclassified, Boris Maslow, Inspector of Fine Arts to Jules Borély, 30 June 1933.

60. AMC, unclassified, Boris Maslow to Jules Borély, 22 June 1933.

61. AMC, unclassified, Inspector of Fine Arts and Historic Monuments to Jules Borély, 16 August 1933.

62. BGA, A1336, Procès-verbal, Commission Municipal Mixte, 17 March 1936.

63. MO, Fonds Ricard, no. 781, Chef de la Région de Rabat to Directeur des Affaires Politiques, 15 September 1936.

64. Hoisington, *Casablanca Connection*, 79.

65. Ibid., 75.

66. Ibid., 80.

67. Pennell, *Morocco since 1830*, 277.

68. Al-Fassi, *Independence Movements*, 173.

69. ADN, DI, 367, Note sur la situation politique à Fès, 28 October 1936.

70. ADN, DI, 367, Bulletin de renseignements, 19 November 1936.

71. ADN, DI, 367, Commissaire du Gouvernement auprès du Tribunal du Pacha to Général Chef de la Region, 20 November 1936.

72. ADN, DI, 367, Note de la région, 24 November 1936.

73. Hoisington, *Casablanca Connection*, 52.

74. Pennell, *Morocco since 1830*, 243.

75. ADN, DI, 344, Rapport trimestriel de la région de Fès, 1937.

76. *La Dépêche de Fès*, 16 January 1937.

77. ADN, DI, 344, Rapport trimestriel de la région de Fès, 1937.

78. Yakhlef, *Municipalité de Fez*. See also ADN, DI, 344, Rapport trimestriel de la région de Fès, 1937.

79. ADN, DI, 368, Déclarations du nommé ben M'feddel Zakour mis en état d'arrestation le 1èr Novembre 1937.

80. Pennell, *Morocco since 1830*, 244.
81. ADN, DI, 368, Résident Général, Rapport no. 2123, 5 November 1937.
82. CAC, CHEAM, no. 26, Roger Le Tourneau, "Les corporations au Maroc," 7 June 1938.
83. BGA, A1439, Procès-verbal, Medjless musulman, 21 September 1937.
84. CAC, CHEAM, no. 26, Roger Le Tourneau, "Les corporations au Maroc," 7 June 1938.
85. Hoisington, *Casablanca Connection*, 100–101.
86. Ibid., 95.
87. BGA, A1439, Procès-verbal, Medjless, 21 September 1937.
88. CAC, CHEAM, no. 26, Roger Le Tourneau, "Les corporations au Maroc," 7 June 1938.
89. ADN, DI, 368, Note, 8 February 1937.
90. Al-Fassi, *Independence Movements*, 126.
91. BGA, A612, Procès-verbal, Medjless, 12 September 1935.
92. M. Ouazzani, *Mudhkira hyat*, 4:119.
93. BGA, A1336, Procès-verbal, Medjless, 10 August 1936.
94. "Les bénéfices des minotiers et des boulangers," *La Dépêche de Fès*, 5 August 1933.
95. ONICL, unclassified, Secteur de la minoterie industrielle, comparaison entre les écrasements et la capacité d'écrasements installés, n.d. (1982).
96. ONICL, unclassified, La minoterie artisanale: Problème soulevé par la transformation des minoteries artisanales en minoteries semi-industrielles et en minoteries industrielles, n.d. (1954).
97. MO, Fonds Ricard, no. 521, Corporations marocaines: Observations à Fès, réorganisation à Salé, December 1936.
98. Abderrahman Lahbabi, interview by author, 6 June 2001.
99. ONICL, unclassified, list of Moroccan mills from computerized database, summer 2001.
100. ONICL, unclassified, La minoterie artisanale: Problème soulevé par la transformation des minoteries artisanales en minoteries semi-industrielles et en minoteries industrielles, n.d. (1954).
101. Al-Fassi, *Independence Movements*, 140.
102. Abderrahman Lahbabi, interview by author, 6 June 2001.
103. Larbi ben al-Ghali Laraichi, interview by author, 8 June 2001.
104. ONICL, unclassified, Recensement des moulins mécaniques non adherents à l'APM, n.d.
105. AMC, unclassified, Henri Terrasse to M. Souchon, 2 March 1936.
106. ONICL, unclassified, E. Lotte, Note pour Monsieur le Directeur de l'Agriculture et des Forêts, 20 August 1954.
107. ONICL, unclassified, list of Moroccan mills from ONICL database, summer 2001.
108. Hadj Mohamed Filalli "Terras," interview by author, 9 June 2001.
109. AMC, unclassified, Si Mohamed Belhassan Elmghari to Chef des Beaux-Arts et

Monuments Historiques, n.d.; AMC, unclassified, Si Mohamed Belhassan Elmghari to Chef des Beaux-Arts et Monuments Historiques, 30 April 1930.

110. BGA, A1749, Procès-verbal, Commission israélite, 6 July 1936.

111. AMC, unclassified, official with Fine Arts Department to Directeur des Affaires Politiques, August 1936.

112. Lucas, "Importance et mouvement," 162.

113. AMC, unclassified, map.

114. MO, Fonds Ricard, no. 521, Corporations marocaines: Observations à Fès, réorganisation à Salé, December 1936.

115. Abdelwahed Ouali, interview by author, 22 March 2001.

116. ONICL, unclassified, La minoterie artisanale: Problème soulevé par la transformation des minoteries artisanales en minoteries semi-industrielles et en minoteries industrielles, n.d. (1954).

117. Ibid.

118. Nuret, *Étude*. See also ONICL, *La meneurie*.

119. ADN, DI, 547, Fava Verda, Commissariat Divisionnnaire, Note de renseignement, 25 August 1937.

120. BGA, A1713, Procès-verbal, Medjless musulman, 13 August 1930.

121. M.G.D., "Autour de la viande cachir," *La Dépêche de Fès*, 22 July 1933.

122. ADN, DI, 627, unsigned letter to Chef des Services Municipaux, 18 July 1933.

123. BGA, A761, Procès-verbal, Medjless israélite, 23 June 1933.

124. ADN, DI, 627, unsigned letter to Chef des Services Municipaux, 18 July 1933.

125. ADN, DI, 627, Corporation des orfèvres-tailleurs- menuisiers-savetiers-ferblantiers-et diverses petits artisans de Fès-Mellah to Chef des Services Municipaux, 3 July 1933.

126. BGA, A761, Procès-verbal, Medjless israélite, 23 June 1933.

127. ADN, DI, 627, Général Commandant de la Région de Fès to Secrétaire Général du Protectorat-Administration Municipale, 2 August 1933.

128. Ibid.

129. Ibid.

130. BGA, A1336, Procès-verbal, Medjless israélite, 23 December 1936.

131. ADN, DI, 627, Chef du Service du Contrôle Civil to Secrétaire Général du Protectorat, 14 October 1933.

132. ADN, DI, 627, Note au sujet de la surtaxe d'abatage perçue au profit des oeuvres de bienfaisance musulmanes, 11 February 1936.

133. Ibid.

134. ADN, DI, 627, Secrétaire Général du Protectorat to Chef des Services Municipaux, 2 August 1935.

135. ADN, DI, 627, Note au sujet de la surtaxe d'abatage perçue au profit des oeuvres de bienfaisance musulmanes, 11 February 1936.

136. Baron and Mathieu, "Quelques budgets," 208–215.

137. Lucas and Bahnini, "Budgets citadins."

138. MO, Fonds Ricard, no. 521, Corporations marocaines: Observations à Fès, réorganisation à Salé, December 1936.

139. BGA, A80, Procès-verbal, French Municipal Commission, 31 August 1937.

140. BGA, A1074, "Construction des grands abattoirs modernes: Exposé de M. Lemaire," 18 June 1932, published in an unidentified newspaper.

141. BGA, A1074, Concours en vue de l'établissement du projet de construction d'un abattoir et d'un marché aux bestiaux, 1 March 1936.

142. Ibid.

143. "Bestieu, President of the Chamber of Commerce and Industry," in *Fès et Sa Région*, a publication in magazine format, which, printed in 1935, can be consulted at the library La Source in Rabat.

144. BGA, A1074, Paul Sollier of the Chambre Syndicale Française to Chef des Services Municipaux, 9 May 1933.

145. BGA, A1074, Rapport de Monsieur Thomay sur: L'étude des moyens pour parvenir à la création d'abattoirs modernes à Fès, 30 June 1932. For the transcript of the report, see also *La Dépêche de Fès*, 8 July 1932, 3.

146. BGA, A1074, Chef des Services Municipaux to Secrétaire Général du Protectorat, Direction de l'Administration Municipale, 11 July 1932. For the Chef des Services Municipaux's desire to bring companies from Tangiers, Casablanca, or Paris to build a modern slaughterhouse, see BGA, A1074, Extrait de procès-verbal de la Commission Française, 14 June 1932. See also BGA, A1074, Paul Sollier of the Chambre Syndicale Française to Chef des Services Municipaux, 9 May 1933.

147. BGA, A1074, Procès-verbal, Medjless musulman, 2 July 1932.

148. Grapinet, "Colonisation citadine," 181–182.

149. BGA, A1713, Résultat des élections au Mejless el Medina, n.d. (1912).

150. BGA, Rapport mensuel, 1930s.

151. Benjelloun, *Enfance*, 192–193.

152. Ibid., 200–203.

153. Ibid., 279.

154. BGA, A1713, Procès-verbal, Medjless, 28 September 1931.

155. ADN, DI, 367, Note politique pour la Direction des Affaires Indigènes, 6 November 1936.

156. BGA, A1336, Procès-verbal, Medjless musulman, 1 February 1936.

157. Ibid., 17 March 1936.

158. BGA, A1074, Extrait du procès-verbal du medjless el Baladi, 30 November 1935.

159. BGA, A1074, Secrétariat Général du Protectorat to Directeur du Service de l'Administration Municipale, 24 October 1935.

160. BGA, A1074, Procès-verbal, Medjless musulman, 30 November 1935.

161. BGA, A1074, Commissaire Résident Général to Président de la Chambre de Commerce et d'Industrie de Fès, n.d. (spring 1937).

## Chapter 8. Famine and the Emergence of Popular Nationalism

1. ADN, DI, 371, Fava Verde, Note de renseignements, 9 April 1937.

2. Gaudio, *Allal el Fassi*. See also el Alami, *Allal el Fassi*. Unless otherwise noted, these books have provided information on the nationalist movement.

3. Al-Fassi, *Independence Movements*, 132–133.

4. El Alami, *Allal el Fassi*, 55.
5. Pennell, *Morocco since 1830*, 228.
6. Ibid., 230–231.
7. ADN, DACH, 300, Ponsot, Commissaire Résident Général, to Ministre des Affaires Etrangères, 6 November 1934.
8. ADN, DACH, 300, Résident Général to Ministre des Affaires Etrangères, n.d.
9. ADN, CD, 318, Contrôleur des Autorités Chérifiennes de la Zone de Tanger to Commissaire Résident Général, 19 November 1934.
10. ADN, CD, 318, Directeur des Affaires Indigènes to Ministre Plénipotentiaire, 21 June 1934.
11. Pennell, *Morocco since 1830*, 231.
12. Al-Fassi, *Independence Movements*, 112.
13. See Massignon, "Enquête," 140.
14. Pennell, *Morocco since 1830*, 96.
15. ADN, DI, 366, Mohamed Lyazide and Ahmed Cherkaoui, Note sur la répression d'actes barbares émanant de certaines confréries au Maroc, 4 May 1936.
16. ADN, DI, 344, Fava Verde, Commissaire Divisionnaire, Note de renseignements, 24 October 1937.
17. *La Dépêche de Fès*, 4 November 1933.
18. AMC, unclassified, Chef des Services Municipaux to Inspecteur Régional des Beaux-Arts, 8 April 1932.
19. BGA, A761, Procès-verbal, Medjless, 27 December 1933.
20. ADN, CD, 627, Contrôleur Civil, Chef de la Région, to Résident Général, 22 March 1934.
21. BGA, A612, Procès-verbal, Medjless, 13 March 1935.
22. ADN, DI, 758, Secrétaire Général du Protectorat to Directeur des Affaires Indigènes, 3 March 1936.
23. ADN, DI, 344, Santini, Commissaire Divisionnaire, Note de renseignements, 6 February 1937.
24. ADN, DI, 344, Fava Verde, Commissaire Divisionnaire, Note de renseignements, 13 February 1937.
25. ADN, DI, 371, Bulletin de renseignements, 5 February 1937.
26. ADN, DI, 371, Commissaire-Chef de la Sûreté Régionale to Sous-Directeur Chef du Service de la Sécurité, 20 February 1937.
27. Pennell, *Morocco since 1830*, 246.
28. ADN, DI, 371, 26 February 1937.
29. ADN, DI, 368, Note de renseignements de Petitjean, 27 March 1937.
30. Pennell, *Morocco since 1830*, 246.
31. ADN, DI, 371, Fava Verde, Note de renseignements, 8 April 1937.
32. Ibid., 9 April 1937.
33. Hoisington, *Casablanca Connection*, 58.
34. Hadj Alami, interview by author, 22 March 2001.
35. Boutaleb, "Idriss Slaoui."

36. BGA, A1074, "Construction des grands abattoirs modernes: Exposé de M. Lemaire," 18 June 1932, published in an unidentified newspaper.
37. M. Ouazzani, *Mudhkira hyat*, 4:258–260.
38. ADN, DI, 344, Fava Verde, Commissaire Divisionnaire, to Sous-Directeur Chef du Service de la Police Générale, 4 August 1937.
39. Al-Fassi, *Independence Movements*, 175.
40. Ibid., 175.
41. ADN, DI, 627, 12 April 1934.
42. Guyot et al., "Résultats d'une enquête," 137–141.
43. ADN, DI, 547, Général de Division Blanc-Chef de la Région de Fès to Directeur des Affaires Politiques, 31 August 1937.
44. ADN, DI, 344, Fava Verde, Note de renseignement, 30 August 1937.
45. M. Ouazzani, *Combat d'un nationaliste*, 2:262–264.
46. Hoisington, *Casablanca Connection*, 61–65.
47. For water distribution in Meknes, see ADN, DAI, 320. For the protest in September 1937, see ADN, CDRG, 212.
48. Pennell, *Morocco since 1830*, 247.
49. ADN, CDRG, 212, Direction des Affaires Politiques, Note de renseignements, 6 September 1937.
50. ADN, CDRG, 212, Délégué à la Résidence Général, telegram, 4 September 1937.
51. Hoisington, *Casablanca Connection*, 65.
52. ADN, CDRG, 212, Fava Verde, Commissaire Divisionnaire, Renseignements, 5 September 1937.
53. ADN, CDRG, 212, Délégué à la Résidence Général, telegram, 4 September 1937.
54. ADN, DI, 371, Palmade, Commissaire Divisionnaire, Note de renseignements, 14 October 1937.
55. ADN, DI, 371, Fava Verde, Commissaire Divisionnaire, Note de renseignements, Politique indigène, 18 October 1937.
56. Pennell, *Morocco since 1830*, 247.
57. ADN, DI, 344, Fava Verde, Eloignement des leaders nationalistes, 26 October 1937.
58. Ibid.
59. Hoisington, *Casablanca Connection*, 69.
60. ADN, DI, 344, Fava Verde, Eloignement des leaders nationalistes, 26 October 1937.
61. Ibid.
62. CAC, CHEAM, Roger Le Tourneau, "Les émeutes de Fès," no. 25, 1938.
63. ADN, DI, 371, Fava Verde, Notes de renseignements, Agitation nationaliste, 27 October 1937.
64. Hoisington, *Casablanca Connection*, 69.
65. ADN, DI, 371, Direction des Affaires Politiques, Note de renseignements, Politique indigène, 27 October 1937.
66. Ibid.

67. ADN, DI, 371, Fava Verde, Notes de renseignements, Agitation nationaliste, 27 October 1937.

68. ADN, DI, 371, Direction des Affaires Politiques, Note de renseignements, Politique indigène, 27 October 1937.

69. ADN, DI, 371, Fava Verde, Notes de renseignements, Agitation nationaliste, 27 October 1937.

70. Ibid.

71. Hoisington, *Casablanca Connection*, 69.

72. ADN, DI, 371, Fava Verde, Notes de renseignements, Agitation nationaliste, 27 October 1937.

73. Ibid.

74. Hoisington, *Casablanca Connection*, 71–72.

75. AMC, unclassified, Henri Terrasse to Inspector of Beaux-Arts, 22 November 1937.

## Conclusion

1. Geertz, "Thick Description."

2. Slyomovics, *Performance*, 101–131.

3. Payne, "Food Deficits and Political Legitimacy," 153–172. Payne notes that the "prevalence of cheap food policies is related to the requisites of political stability" and condemns this food deficit as evidence of "political limitations." She anticipated regime change in Morocco, but, in fact, twenty years after this prediction, the monarchy remains strong, underscoring my assertion that food subsidies build upon the historic expectations of workers.

4. ONICL, M. Gharbi, Compte rendu de la mission effectuée à Fès-minoterie artisanale, 30 November 1963.

5. Hadj Mohamed Filalli "Terras," interview by author, 9 June 2001.

6. Zaki Berrada, conversation with author, 1 July 2001.

7. Belghazi and El Mir, *La minoterie artisanale*.

8. Abdellatif Bouayad, interview by author, 5 July 2001.

9. Hadj Mohamed Sharqi "al-Saba'," interview by author, 19 July 2001.

10. Si Mohamed Najib al-Ouali, interview by author, 14 June 2001.

11. Waterbury, *Commander of the Faithful*.

# Bibliography

## Archives

Bibliothèque Centrale de l'Administration de la Conservation Foncière du Cadastre et de la Cartographie, Rabat, Morocco.
Bibliothèque Générale et Archives, Rabat, Morocco.
Bibliothèque Royale, Rabat, Morocco.
Centre des Archives Contemporaines, Fontainebleau, France.
Centre des Archives Diplomatiques de Nantes, Nantes, France.
Direction des Archives Royales, Rabat, Morocco.
Al-Hizana al-Subihiyya, Salé, Morocco.
Ministry of Culture, Rabat, Morocco.
Municipality of Fez, Fez, Morocco.
Musée des Oudaia, Rabat, Morocco.
Office de la Conservation Foncière, Fez, Morocco.
Office National Interprofessionnel des Céréales et des Légumineuses, Rabat, Morocco.
Palais de Justice, Salé, Morocco.

## Primary Sources

Amicis, Edmondo de. *Morocco: Its People and Places*. Translated by C. Rollin-Tilton. 1882. Reprint, London: A. Wheaton, 1985.
Arnaud, Louis. *Au temps des mehallas: Ou le Maroc de 1860 à 1912*. Casablanca: Éditions Atlantides, 1952.
Aubin, Eugène [M. Descos]. *Le Maroc d'aujourd'hui*. 1904. Reprint, Paris: Librairie Armand Colin, 1913.
Azan, Paul. *L'expédition de Fez*. Paris: Berger-Levrault, 1924.
Baghdadi, Bouchta, and Zora Baghdadi. With Christian Richard. *Le pacha-soldat: Vie du Pacha Si Mohammed El Baghdadi*. Paris: Larose Éditeurs, 1936.
Baron, R., and J. Mathieu. "Quelques budgets de travailleurs indigènes." *Bulletin Économique du Maroc* 4, no. 7 (1937): 215.
Bel, Alfred. "Potiers et faïenciers de Fez." *France-Maroc* (15 March 1919): 79–82.
Ben Cheneb, Mohammed. *Proverbes arabes de l'Algérie et du Maghreb*. 2 vols. Paris: Ernest Leroux, 1905.
Benjelloun, Abdelmajid. *Enfance entre deux rives*. Translated by Francis Gouin. Casablanca: Wallada, n.d.

———. *Fi al-tufula*. N.d. Reprint, Casablanca: Dar Nashar al-Maʿrifa, 2001.

Bennani-Smirès, Latifa. *La cuisine marocaine*. Casablanca: Societé d'Édition et de Diffusion al Madariss, 2000.

Ben Srhir, Khalid, ed. *Al-Maghrib fi al-arshif al-biritani: Murasalat John Drummond-Hay maʿa al-makhzan, 1846–1886*. Casablanca: Al-Sharikah al-Maghribiyya lil-Nashr, 1992.

Bonsal, Stephen. *Morocco As It Is: With an Account of Sir Charles Euan Smith's Recent Mission to Fez*. New York: Harper and Brothers, 1893.

Borély, Jules. *Mon plaisir au Maroc*. Paris: Imprimerie Delpuech, 1927.

Casinière, Henri de la. *Les municipalités marocaines: Leur développement, leur législation*. Casablanca: Imprimerie Marocaine, 1924.

Chevrillon, André. *Un crépuscule d'Islam: Au Maroc en 1905*. 1906. Reprint, Casablanca: Éditions EDDIF, 1999.

Colombain, M. "Les coopératives indigènes au Maroc." *Bulletin Économique du Maroc* 14, no. 17 (1937): 201.

d'Anfreville, L. "Les Marocains en Afrique Occidentale." *Renseignements Coloniaux et Documents* no. 3, supplement to *Bulletin du Comité de l'Afrique Française* no. 3 (March 1905): 155–56.

Decroux, Paul. *La vie municipale au Maroc*. Lyons: Bosc Frères, 1932.

Dehors, Gabriel. "Le commerce de la viande à Tanger." *Renseignements Coloniaux et Documents* no. 9, supplement to *Bulletin du Comité de l'Afrique Française* no. 9 (September 1905): 353.

Drocourt, Daniel, ed. *Maroc, medina de Fès: Histoire et législation avec recueil de textes et avis divers concernant la protection de la medina de Fès*. Marseilles: Organisation des Nations Unies pour l'Éducation, la Science et la Culture, 1992.

Elsner, Eleanor. *The Magic of Morocco*. New York: Dodd, Mead, 1928.

Fassi, Allal al-. *The Independence Movements in Arab North Africa*. Translated by Hazem Zaki Nuseibeh. Washington, D.C.: American Council of Learned Societies, 1954.

Forbes, Rosita. *El Raisuni, the Sultan of the Mountains*. London: Thornton Butterworth, 1924.

France. *Documents diplomatiques: Question de la protection diplomatique et consulaire au Maroc*. Paris: Imprimerie Nationale, 1880.

Fumey, Eugene, ed. *Choix de correspondance marocains*. Paris: Maisonneuve, 1903.

Gaillard, Henri. "Le commerce de Fès en 1902." *Bulletin du Comité de l'Afrique Française* no. 12 (December 1904): 330–31.

———. "La réorganisation du gouvernement marocain." *Renseignements Coloniaux et Documents* no. 6, supplement to *Bulletin du Comité de l'Afrique Française* 26, no. 6 (June 1916): 158.

———. *Une ville de l'Islam: Fès*. Paris: J. André, 1903.

Gallotti, Jean. "Les métiers d'art au Maroc." *France-Maroc* (15 May 1917): 8–19.

Ganoun, Abdellah. *Mudhkira ghayr shakhsiyya*. Tangier: Matbaʿat Altoubris, 2000.

Gast, Camille du. *Le statut ouvrier au Maroc: Rapport addressé au Ministre du Travail*. Paris: Imprimerie Nationale, 1921.

Ghallab, Abdelkrim. *Tarikh al-harka al-wataniyya bi al-maghreb.* 2 vols. Casablanca: Matba'at al-Najah al-Jadida, 2000.

Gouraud, Henri. *Au Maroc: Souvenirs d'un Africain, 1911–1914.* Paris: Librairie Plon, 1949.

Gouvion, Edmond, and Marthe Gouvion. *Kitab Aâyane El Maghrib al-Aqça: Esquisse générale des Moghrebs de la genèse à nos jours et le livre des grands du Maroc.* 2 vols. 1939. Reprint, Casablanca: Frontispice, 2001.

Grapinet, J. "La colonisation citadine aux environs de Fès." *Bulletin Économique du Maroc* 1, no. 3 (January 1934): 181–82.

Great Britain. *Correspondence Relative to the Conference Held at Madrid in 1880.* London: Government Printer, 1880.

Guineaudeau, Z. *Fès vue par sa cuisine.* Rabat: Imprimeries Françaises et Marocaines, 1957.

Guyot, R., Roger Le Tourneau, and Lucien Paye. "Les cordonniers de Fès." *Hespéris* 23 (1936): 9–54.

———. "La corporation des tanneurs et l'industrie de la tannerie à Fès." *Hespéris* 21 (1935): 167–240.

———. "L'industrie de la tannerie à Fès." *Bulletin Économique du Maroc* no. 9 (1935): 219–26.

———. "Résultats d'une enquête du cuir à Fès (1935)." *Revue Africaine* 79 (1936): 126–42a.

Hajwi, Muhammad Ibn Al Hassan al-. *Voyage d'Europe: Le périple d'un réformiste.* Translated by Alain Roussillon and Abdellah Saâf. Casablanca: Afrique Orient, 2001.

Haroun, Ali ben. "Consultation juridique sur le régime des eaux." Translated by G. Ammar. *Revue Marocaine de Législation, Doctrine, Jurisprudence Chérifiennes* no. 6–7 (1936): 14.

Harris, Lawrence. *With Mulai Hafid at Fez: Behind the Scenes in Morocco.* London: Smith, Elder, 1909.

Hyat, Youssef, and Nadim Moura'shli. *Lisan al-'arab.* Beirut: Dar Lisan al-Arabi, n.d.

Ibn Zaydan, Moulay Abderrahman. *Itahaf 'alam al-nas bi-jamal akhbar hadirat maknas.* 5 vols. 1931. Reprint, Casablanca: Imprimerie Idéale, 1990.

Joly, André. "L'industrie à Tétouan, 4ème partie." *Archives marocaines* 18 (1912): 216–19.

Kittani, Abdelkabir ben Hachim al-. *Zahri al-ass fi biyutat ahl Fas.* Followed by Mohammed ben Abdelkabir ben Hachi al-Kittani, *Tuhfat al-akyass wa mufakahat al-julass.* Edited by Ali ben al-Montassir al-Kittani. 2 vols. Casablanca: Matba'at al-Najah al-Jadida, 2002.

Kittani, Ali ben al-Montassir al-. *Shurafa' al-kattaniyyun fi al-madhi wa al-hadir.* N.p.: Jamayatt Achurafa al-Kittaniyyin, 1999.

Kittani, Mohamed al-Baqir al-. *Tarjamat Shaykh Mohamed al-Kittani achahid.* N.p.: Matba'at al-Fajir, 1962.

Kittani, Mohamed ben Ja'far ben Idris al-. *Salwat al-anfas wa-muhadathat al-akyas bi-man adbir min al-'ulama wa- sulaha bi-fas.* 2 vols. Fez: Royal Lithograph, 1314/1896–97.

Koechlin, Raymond. "Les industries d'art indigènes." *France-Maroc* (15 January 1917): 18.

Le Tourneau, Roger, and Lucien Paye. "La corporation des tanneurs et l'industrie de la tannerie à Fès." *Hespéris* 21 (1935): 201–202.

———. "La répartition de l'eau dans la médina de Fès." In *Mélanges offerts à William Marçais*, edited by l'Institut d'Études Islamiques de l'Université de Paris, 191–204. Paris: G.-P. Maisonneuve, 1950.

Loverdo, J. de. *Construction et agencement des abattoirs.* Vol. 1, *Les abattoirs publics.* Paris: Dunod et Pinat, 1906.

Lucas, Georges. *Fès dans le Maroc moderne.* Paris: Librairie du Recueil Sirey, 1937.

———. "Importance et mouvement de la population à Fès et dans sa région." *Bulletin Économique du Maroc* 2, no. 8 (April 1935): 162.

Lucas, George, and Ahmed Bahnini. "Budgets citadins à Fès." *Bulletin Économique du Maroc* 5, no. 19 (January 1938): 26–30.

Luccioni, Joseph. "Les biens habous au Maroc." *Bulletin Économique du Maroc* no. 5 (1934): 385.

———. *Les fondations pieuses "habous" au Maroc depuis les origines jusqu'à 1956.* Rabat: Imprimerie Royale, 1982.

———. "Les habous dans l'économie marocaine." In *4ème Congrès de la Fédération des Sociétés Savantes de l'Afrique du Nord.* Algiers: La Société Historique Algérienne, 1938.

Macnab, Frances [Agnes Fraser]. *A Ride in Morocco among Believers and Traders.* London: E. Arnold, 1902.

Mammeri. "L'oued-Fez." *France-Maroc* no. 7 (15 July 1919): 196–97.

Marchand, G. "La situation commerciale à Fez." *Bulletin du Comité de l'Afrique Française* no. 12 (December 1906): 421–22.

Martin, L. "Description de la ville de Fès, quartier du Keddan." *Revue du Monde Musulman* 9, no. 11 (November 1909): 433–43.

Maslow, Boris. *Les mosquées de Fès et du nord du Maroc.* Paris: Les Éditions d'Art, 1937.

Massignon, Louis. "Enquête sur les corporations musulmanes d'artisans et de commerçants au Maroc." *Revue du Monde Musulman* 58 (1924).

Mazières, Marc de. *Promenades à Fès.* Casablanca: Édition du Moghreb, 1934.

Meakin, Budgett. *The Moors: A Comprehensive Description.* London: Swan Sonnenschein, 1902.

Mercier, L. "Souvenirs des massacres de Fez, Avril 1912." *France-Maroc* (April 1917): 14.

Michaux-Bellaire, E. "Description de la ville de Fès." *Archives Marocaines* 11, no. 2 (1907): 252–330.

Milliot, Louis. *Démembrements du habous.* Paris: Librairie Leroux, 1918.

Moreau, A. *L'abbatoir moderne: Construction, installation, administration.* Paris: Asselin et Houzeau, 1916.

Mougin, Capitaine. "Oujda: Historique, organisation, commerce." *Renseignements Coloniaux et Documents* no. 8, supplement to *Bulletin du Comité de l'Afrique Française* no. 8 (August 1906): 257.

Moulay Hassan. "Moujeb de l'an 1301/1884, dit 'Moujeb al Soueïri.'" Translated by Jean Raymond. *Revue du Monde Musulman* 58 (1924): 229–41.

Mouline, Said. *Repères de la mémoire, Fès.* Rabat: Ministère de l'Habitat, 1993.

Musée Albert Khan. *Maroc: Mémoire d'avenir, 1912–1926 . . . 1999.* Boulogne-Billancourt: Musée Albert Khan, 1999.

Nasiri, Ahmad ben Khalid al-. "Kitab al-istiqsa' li-akhar duwal al-maghrib al-aqsa." Translated by Eugene Fumey. *Archives Marocaines* 10 (1907): 277–83.

Nuret, H. *Étude sur la meunerie marocaine.* Rabat: Office National Interprofessionnel des Céréales et des Légumineuses, 1951.

Odinot, Paul. *Le monde marocain.* Paris: Marcel Riviere, 1926.

Office National Interprofessionnel des Céréales et des Légumineuses. *La meunerie.* Rabat: Office National Interprofessionnel des Céréales et des Légumineuses, 1974.

Ouazzani, Abdelali al-. *Ayam fas al-jamila.* 2 vols. Fez: Maktab Sh'abiyya, 2000.

Ouazzani, Mohamed Hassan. *Mudhkira hyat wa-jihad.* 4 vols. Beirut: Dar al-Gharb al-Islami, n.d.

Perigny, Maurice de. *Au Maroc: Fez, capitale du Nord.* Paris: Roger, 1917.

Pobegun, M. E. "Notes sur Mogador." *Renseignements Coloniaux et Documents* no. 2 bis, supplément to *Bulletin du Comité de l'Afrique Française* no. 2 (February 1906): 60.

René-LeClerc, Charles. "Le commerce et l'industrie à Fès." *Renseignements Coloniaux et Documents* no. 7, supplement to *Bulletin du Comité de l'Afrique Française* no. 7 (July 1905): 229–53.

———. "Le commerce et l'industrie à Fès, deuxième partie." *Renseignements Coloniaux et Documents* no. 8, supplement to *Bulletin du Comité de l'Afrique Française* no. 8 (August 1905): 295–321.

———. "Le commerce et l'industrie à Fès, troisième partie." *Renseignements Coloniaux et Documents* no. 9, supplement to *Bulletin du Comité de l'Afrique Française* no. 9 (September 1905): 337–50.

Ricard, Prosper. "L'aide à l'artisanat indigène en Afrique du Nord Française." *Bulletin Économique du Maroc* no. 10 (1935): 277–80

———. *Art de la relieur et de la dorure.* Fez: Imprimerie Municipale, 1920.

———. "L'artisan de Fez." *France-Maroc* (15 September 1918): 273–77.

———. "L'artisanat indigène en Afrique du Nord." *Bulletin Économique du Maroc* no. 8 (1935): 131–32.

———. *L'artisanat indigène en Afrique du Nord: Rapport déposé par M. Prosper Ricard.* Rabat: École du Livre, 1935.

———. "Arts indigènes et musées." In *La renaissance du Maroc: Dix ans de Protectorat*, 211–15. Rabat: Résidence Générale de la République Française, 1923.

———. "Arts ruraux et arts citadins dans l'Afrique du Nord." *France-Maroc* (15 May 1917): 20–27.

———. "Les beaux-arts: À propos d'un manuscript enluminé." *France-Maroc* (15 February 1918): 62–63.

———. "Chronique de Fès: Une belle oeuvre." *France-Maroc* (15 May 1920): 119–20.

———. "Chronique de Fès: L'évolution de l'architecture et de la décoration." *France-Maroc* (15 June 1920): 157–58.

———. "Chronique de Fès: Les industries de la céramique." *France-Maroc* (15 November 1919): 331–33.

---. "Chronique de Fès: Le moussem de Moulay Idriss." *France-Maroc* (15 August 1920): 179–80.
---. "La grande mosquée cathédrale El-Qaraouiyîne." *France-Maroc* (15 March 1918): 79–85.
---. *Guide de Fès*. Fez: Imprimerie Municipale, 1916.
---. "Incendie des souks de Fès." *Bulletin de la Société de Géographie du Maroc* no. 6–7 (December 1918): 21.
---. "L'industrie indigène au Maroc." *Bulletin Économique du Maroc* no. 6 (1934): 423–27.
---. "Une lignée d'artisans: Les Ben Chérif de Fès." *Hespéris* 37 (1950): 11–19.
---. "La main d'oeuvre marocaine et le role économique du Maroc après la guerre." *France-Maroc* (15 January 1918): 27–28.
---. "Un mariage fasi." *France-Maroc* (15 January 1920): 21–22.
---. *Le Maroc (Les guides bleus)*. 3rd ed. Paris: Librairie Hachette, 1925.
---. "Les métiers manuels à Fès." *Hespéris* 4 (1924): 205–24.
---. "Méthodes de l'artisanat indigène rénové." *Bulletin Économique du Maroc* no. 11 (1936): 43–44.
---. "Les origines antiques de Fez." *France-Maroc* (15 December 1918): 362–63.
---. "Pour une rénovation méthodique de l'artisanat marocain." *Bulletin Économique du Maroc* no. 16 (1937): 99–103.
---. "La reliure d'art à Fez." *France-Maroc* (15 January 1919): 18–20.
---. *La renaissance de la reliure d'art à Fès*. Paris: Jouve, 1925.
---. "La rénovation de l'art de la reliure à Fès." *Bulletin de l'Enseignement Public au Maroc* 39 (March 1922): 62–66.
---. "Le réveil des corporations marocaines." *Bulletin Économique du Maroc* no. 16 (1937): 101–102.
---. "La situation des industries indigènes du cuir." *Bulletin Économique du Maroc* no. 3 (1933): 174.
---. "Le souq El-Morqtân et les broderies de Fez." *France- Maroc* (1917): 29–32.
---. "Le vieux relieur." *France-Maroc* (August 1922): 224–25.
Saladin, Henri. "La main-d'oeuvre indigène." *France-Maroc* (15 February 1918): 64–66.
Sefrioui, Ahmed. *La boîte à merveilles*. 1954. Reprint, Paris: Omnibus, 1996.
Sellier, Charles. "Les moulins à vent du vieux Paris." *Bulletin de la Société des Amis des Monuments Parisiens* 7 (1893): 5–23.
Selous, G. H. *Appointment to Fez*. London: Richards Press, 1956.
Sémach, Y. D. "Une chronique juive de Fès: Le 'Yahas Fès' de Ribbi Abner Hassarfaty." *Hespéris* 19 (1934): 79–94.
Service des Beaux Arts et Monuments Historiques. *Historique de la Direction Générale de l'Instruction Publique, des Beaux Arts, et des Antiquités, 1912–1930*. Rabat: The Protectorate, 1931.
Terrier, Auguste. "Impressions du Maroc." *Bulletin du Comité de l'Afrique Française* 22, no. 7 (July 1913): 256.
Tranchant de Lunel, Maurice. *Au pays du paradoxe*. Paris: Bibliothèque Charpentier, 1924.

Trotter, Philip Durham. *Our Mission to the Court of Morocco in 1880, under Sir John Drummond Hay*. Edinburgh: D. Douglass, 1881.
Vattier, Jos. "Fès, cité marchand." *France-Maroc* (February 1920): 52–55.
———. "La Municipalité de Fez." *Renseignements Coloniaux et Documents* 33, no. 12, supplement to *Bulletin du Comité de l'Afrique Française* no. 12 (December 1924): 385.
Vernon, Madeleine. *Sands, Palms and Minarets*. London: Geoffrey Bles, 1927.
Veyre, Gabriel. *Au Maroc: Dans l'intimité du sultan*. Paris: Librairie Universelle, 1905.
Wazzani al-Imrani, Muhammad al-Mahdi ibn Muhammad al-. *Al-Nawazil al-jadidah al-kubra fima li-ahl fas wa-ghayrihim min al-badw wa-al-qura al-musammah bi-al-m'iyar al-jadid al-jam'a al-maghrib 'an fatawa al-muta'khariin min 'ulama al-maghrib*. Early twentieth century. Reprint, Rabat: Wizarat al-Awqaf, 1996.
Weisgerber, Félix. *Le Maroc il y a 30 ans*. Casablanca: Imprimeries réunies de *La Vigie Marocaine* et du *Petit Marocain*, 1928.
———. "Trois marocains de l'ancien régime." *Bulletin du Comité de l'Afrique Française* no. 5 (May 1934): 292–96.
Westermarck, Edward Alexander. *Ritual and Belief in Morocco*. 2 vols. 1926. Reprint, New York: University Books, 1968.

## Secondary Sources

Abu-Lughod, Janet. "Moroccan Cities: Apartheid and the Serendipity of Conservation." In *African Themes: Northwestern University Studies in Honor of Gwendolen M. Carter*, edited by Ibrahim Abu-Lughod, 77–111. Evanston, Ill.: Northwestern University Press, 1975.
———. *Rabat: Urban Apartheid in Morocco*. Princeton, N.J.: Princeton University Press, 1980.
Abun-Nasr, Jamil M. *A History of the Maghrib in the Islamic Period*. Cambridge: Cambridge University Press, 1987.
Alami, Mohamed el. *Allal el Fassi: Patriarche du nationalisme marocain*. Casablanca: Dar el Kitab, 1972.
Alsayyad, Nezzar. *Forms of Dominance: On the Architecture and Urbanism of the Colonial Enterprise*. Brookfield: Avebury, 1992.
Amahan, Ali, and Catherine Cambazard-Amahan. *Arrêts sur sites: Le patrimoine culturel marocain*. Casablanca: Éditions Le Fennec, 1999.
Ameur, Mohamed. *Fès . . . Ou l'obsession foncière*. Tours: CNRS Urbama, 1993.
Amster, Ellen. "The Many Deaths of Dr. Emile Mauchamp: Medicine, Technology, and Popular Politics in Pre-Protectorate Morocco, 1877–1912." *International Journal of Middle East Studies* 36, no. 3 (August 2004): 409–28.
Appel, Gersion. *The Concise Code of Jewish Law*. New York: Yeshiva University Press, 1977.
Arnaud, Louis. *Au temps des mehallas ou le Maroc de 1860 à 1912*. Casablanca: Éditions Atlantides, 1952.
Barret, James R. *Work and Community in the Jungle: Chicago's Packinghouse Workers, 1894–1922*. Urbana: University of Illinois Press, 1987.

Béguin, François. *Arabisances: Décor architectural et tracé urbain en Afrique du Nord, 1830–1950.* Paris: Dunod, 1983.

Belghazi, Saad, and Mhamed El Mir. *La minoterie artisanale.* Rabat: Office National Interprofessionnel des Céréales et des Légumineuses, 1990.

Bennison, Amira. *Jihad and Its Interpretations in Pre-Colonial Morocco: State-Society Relations during the French Conquest of Algeria.* New York: Routledge, 2002.

Berman, Bruce, and John Lonsdale. *Unhappy Valley: Conflict in Kenya and Africa.* London: J. Currey, 1992.

Bertagnin, Mauro, Susan Gilson Miller, and Attilio Petruccioli. "Inscribing Minority Space in the Islamic City: The Jewish Quarter of Fez (1438–1912)." *Journal of the Society of Architectural Historians* 60, no. 3 (September 2001): 310–27.

Binder, Leonard. *Islamic Liberalism: A Critique of Development Ideologies.* Chicago: University of Chicago Press, 1988.

Bonte, Pierre, Anne-Marie Brisebarre, and Altan Gokalp, eds. *Sacrifices en Islam: Espaces et temps d'un rituel.* Paris: CNRS, 1999.

Bourillon, Florence. *Les villes en France au XIXe siècle.* Paris: Éditions Ophrys, 1995.

Bourqia, Rahma, and Susan Gilson Miller, eds. *In the Shadow of the Sultan: Culture, Power and Politics in Morocco.* Cambridge, Mass.: Harvard Center for Middle Eastern Studies, 1999.

Bourkiba, al-Said. *Duwar al-waqf fi al-hyat al-thaqafiyya bi-al-maghrib fi 'ahd al-daula al-'alawiyya.* 2 vols. Rabat: Ministry of Religious Endowments, 1996.

Bousselam, Mohamed. "Al-Hanta." In Hajji, *M'alamat al-maghrib*, 3622–3623.

Boutaleb, Ibrahim. "Idriss Slaoui." In Hajji, *M'alamat al-maghrib*, 5074.

Brisebarre, Anne-Marie, ed. *La fête du mouton: Un sacrifice musulman dans l'espace urbain.* Paris: CNRS, 1998.

Bromley, Simon. *Rethinking Middle East Politics.* Austin: University of Texas Press, 1994.

Brown, Kenneth L. *People of Salé: Tradition and Change in a Moroccan City.* Manchester: Manchester University Press, 1976.

Burke, Edmund, III. *Prelude to Protectorate in Morocco: Precolonial Protest and Resistance, 1860–1912.* Chicago: University of Chicago Press, 1976.

Carls, Kenneth, and James Schmiechen. *The British Market Hall: A Social and Architectural History.* New Haven, Conn.: Yale University Press, 1999.

Celik, Zeynep. *Urban Forms and Colonial Confrontations: Algiers under French Rule.* Berkeley: University of California Press, 1997.

Certeau, Michel de. *The Practice of Everyday Life.* Translated by Steven Rendall. Berkeley: University of California Press, 1984.

Cigar, Norman. "Socio-economic Structures and the Development of an Urban Bourgeoisie in Pre-Colonial Morocco." *Maghreb Review* 6, no. 3–4 (1981): 55–76.

Cohen, Amnon. *Economic Life in Ottoman Jerusalem.* Cambridge: Cambridge University Press, 1989.

Combs-Schilling, M. Elaine. *Sacred Performances: Islam, Sexuality and Sacrifice.* New York: Columbia University Press, 1989.

Cooper, Frederick. *Colonialism in Question: Theory, Knowledge, History*. Berkeley: University of California Press, 2005.
Cornell, Vincent J. *Realm of the Saint: Power and Authority in Moroccan Sufism*. Austin: University of Texas Press, 1998.
De Sauvigny, G. de Berthier. *Histoire de France*. Paris: Flammarion, 1990.
Djazairi, Abou Bakr Djaber al-. *Le précepte du Musulman*. Translated by Mohammed al-Hamoui. 1964. Reprint, Casablanca: Librairie Es-salam Al-Jadida, 2000.
Eickelman, Dale F., and James Piscatori. *Muslim Politics*. Princeton, N.J.: Princeton University Press, 1996.
El Mansour, Mohamed. "The Sanctuary (Hurm) in Precolonial Morocco." In Bourqia and Miller, *In the Shadow of the Sultan*, 49–73.
Fawzi, Abdulrazak. *Al-Matbuat al-'ajariyah fi al-maghrib: Fihris ma'a muqaddimah tarikhiyya*. Rabat: Dar Nashar al-Ma'rifa, 1989.
Fierro, Alfred. *Histoire et dictionnaire des 300 moulins de Paris*. Paris: Parigramme, 1999.
Gallissot, René. *Le patronat européen au Maroc (1931–1942)*. Casablanca: Éditions EDDIF, 1990.
Gaudio, Attilio. *Allal el Fassi: Ou l'histoire de l'Istiqlal*. Paris: Éditions Alain Moreau, 1972.
Geertz, Clifford. "Thick Description: Toward an Interpretive Theory of Culture." In *Contemporary Field Research Perspectives and Formulations*, edited by Robert M. Emerson, 55-75. Prospect Heights, Ill.: Waveland Press, 2001.
Gershovich, Moshe. *French Military Rule in Morocco: Colonialism and Its Consequences*. London: F. Cass, 2000.
Gordon, David C. "Industrialization and Republican Politics: The Bourgeois of Reims and Saint-Étienne under the Second Empire." In *French Cities in the Nineteenth Century*, edited by John M. Merriman, 117–38. New York: Holmes and Meier, 1981.
Gottreich, Emily. *The Mellah of Marrakesh: Jewish and Muslim Space in Morocco's Red City*. Bloomington: Indiana University Press, 2007.
Hafez, M. M. *Why Muslims Rebel: Repression and Resistance in the Islamic World*. Boulder, Colo.: Lynne Rienner, 2003.
Hajji, Muhammad, ed. *M'alamat al-maghrib qamus murattab 'ala huruf al-hija' yuhit bi-al-m'arif al-muta'liqa bi-mukhtalaf al-jawanib al-tarikhiyya wa al-jughrafiyya wa al-bashariyya wa-al-hadariyya li-al-maghrib al-aqsa*. Salé: Imprimerie de Salé, 1989.
Hammoudi, Abdellah. *Master and Disciple: The Cultural Foundations of Moroccan Authoritarianism*. Chicago: University of Chicago Press, 1997.
Hoisington, William A. *The Casablanca Connection: French Colonial Policy, 1936–1943*. Chapel Hill: University of North Carolina Press, 1984.
———. *Lyautey and the French Conquest of Morocco*. New York: St. Martin's Press, 1995.
Holden, Stacy E. "Mauritanians Want Food, Not Democracy." *ISIM Review* 17 (Spring 2006): 33.
Horowitz, Roger, Jeffrey M. Pilcher, and Sydney Watts. "Meat for the Multitudes: Market Culture in Paris, New York City, and Mexico over the Long Nineteenth Century." *American Historical Review* 109, no. 4 (October 2004): 1055–83.

Ibn Jizzy. *Al-Qawannin al-fiqihiyya*. 14th century. Reprint, Casablanca: Dar Maʿrifa, 2000.

Iliffe, John. *The African Poor: A History*. Cambridge: Cambridge University Press, 1987.

Imber, Colin. *The Ottoman Empire, 1300–1650: The Structure of Power*. New York: Palgrave Macmillan, 2004.

Issawi, Charles. *An Economic History of the Middle East and North Africa*. New York: Columbia University Press, 1982.

Kaplan, Steven Laurence. *Provisioning Paris: Merchants and Millers in the Grain and Flour Trade during the Eighteenth Century*. Ithaca, N.Y., and London: Cornell University Press, 1984.

Kebbaj, Abd el Khalek. *L'économie céréalière au Maroc, étude statistique*. N.p.: Office Chérifien Interprofessionnel des Céréales, 1962.

Kenbib, Mohamed. *Les protégés: Contribution à l'histoire contemporaine du Maroc*. Rabat: Faculté des Lettres et des Science Humaines, 1996.

Khouri-Dagher, Nadia. "The State, Urban Households, and Management of Daily Life: Food and Social Order in Cairo." In *Development, Change, and Gender in Cairo: A View from the Household*, edited by Diane Singerman and Homa Hoodfar, 110–33. Bloomington and Indianapolis: Indiana University Press, 1996.

King, Anthony. *Colonial Urban Development: Culture, Social Power and Development*. London: Routledge-Kegan Paul, 1976.

Lahya, M. al-. "Al-Hayat al-iqtisadiyya bi-madinat maknas fi al-qarn al-tasiʿa ʿashara (1850–1912)." Ph.D. diss., Université Mohamed V, 1404/1984.

Larhmaid, Abdellah. "Collecting Jizya: Commerce, Power and Religious Identity in Goulmime, 1859–1894." Paper presented at the conference Islam in Africa: Global, Cultural, and Historical Perspectives, Institute of Global Cultural Studies, Binghamton University, April 2001.

Laroui, Abdallah. *Esquisses historiques*. Casablanca: Afrique Orient, 1992.

Lazreg, Marnia. *The Eloquence of Silence: Algerian Women in Question*. New York: Routledge, 1994.

Lefebvre, Henri. *The Production of Space*. Translated by Donald Nicholson-Smith. Oxford: Blackwell, 1991.

Le Tourneau, Roger. *Fès avant le protectorat*. 1949. Reprint, Rabat: Éditions de la Porte, 1987.

Lewis, Bernard. *What Went Wrong? The Clash between Islam and Modernity in the Middle East*. New York: Perennial, 2003.

Mabrouk, Ez-Zahra. "Les habous au Maroc: Étude du fonds d'archives du Service du Contrôle des Habous sous le protectorat." Ph.D. diss., École des Sciences de l'Information, 1984.

Maclagan, Ianthe. "Food and Gender in a Yemeni Community." In *Culinary Cultures of the Middle East*, edited by Sami Zubaida and Richard Tapper, 159–72. London and New York: I. B. Tauris, 1994.

Mezzine, Mohamed, ed. *Fès médiévale*. Paris: Éditions Autrement, 1992.

Michel, Nicolas. *Une économie de subsistances: Le Maroc précolonial*. 2 vols. Cairo: Institut Français d'Archéologie Orientale, 1997.

Miège, Jean-Louis. *Le Maroc et l'Europe*. 5 vols. Paris: Presses Universitaires de France, 1961.

———. "Note sur l'artisanat marocain en 1870." *Bulletin Économique et Social du Maroc* 17, no. 59 (1953): 91–93.

Montanari, Massimo. *The Culture of Food*. Translated by Carl Ipsen. Cambridge, Mass.: Basil Blackwell, 1994.

Munson, Henry. *Religion and Power in Morocco*. New Haven, Conn.: Yale University Press, 1993.

Murphey, Rhoads. "Provisioning Istanbul: The State and Subsistence in the Early Modern Middle East." *Food and Foodways* 2 (1988): 217–63.

Nordman, Daniel. "Les expéditions de Moulay Hassan, essai statistique." In *Profiles du Maghreb, frontiéres (XVIII–XX siècle)*, 101–126. Rabat: Université Mohammed V, 1996.

Ouazzani, Mohamed Hassan. *Combat d'un nationaliste marocain*. Casablanca: Fondation Mohamed Hassan Ouazzane, 1989.

Parker, Richard. *A Practical Guide to Islamic Monuments in Morocco*. Charlottesville, Va.: Baraka Press, 1981.

Pascon, Paul. *Le Haouz de Marrakech*. Paris: CNRS, 1977.

Payne, Rhys. "Food Deficits and Political Legitimacy: The Case of Morocco." In *Africa's Agrarian Crisis: The Roots of Famine*, edited by Stephen K. Commins, Michael F. Lofchie, and Rhys Payne, 153–72. Boulder, Colo.: Lynne Rienner, 1986.

Pennell, C. R. *A Country with a Government and a Flag: The Rif War in Morocco, 1921–1926*. Wisbech: Middle East and North African Studies Press, 1986.

———. *Morocco since 1830: A History*. New York: New York University Press, 2000.

Phillips, Sarah T. *This Land, This Nation: Conservation, Rural America, and the New Deal*. Cambridge: Cambridge University Press, 2007.

Prochaska, David. *Making Algeria French: Colonialism in Bône, 1870–1920*. Cambridge: Cambridge University Press, 1990.

Quataert, Donald. *The Ottoman Empire, 1700–1922*. Cambridge: Cambridge University Press, 2000.

Rabinow, Paul. *French Modern: Norms and Forms of the Social Environment*. Chicago: University of Chicago Press, 1989.

Rainero, Romain H. "La creation de la fabrique d'armes de Fès, la 'Makina' dans la politique marocaine de l'Italie." *Maroc-Europe* 7 (1994): 177–96.

Revault, Jacques, Ali Amahan, and Lucien Golvin. *Époque alawite (XIXe et XXe siècles)*. Vol. 3 of *Palais et demeures de Fès*. Paris: CNRS, 1992.

Rivet, Daniel. *Lyautey et l'institution du protectorat français au Maroc, 1912–1926*. 2 vols. Paris: L'Harmattan, 1988.

Rosenberger, Bernard. *Société, pouvoir et alimentation: Nourriture et précarité au Maroc précolonial*. Rabat: Alizés, 2001.

Roy, Olivier. *The Politics of Chaos in the Middle East*. Translated by Ros Schwartz. New York: Columbia University Press, 2008.

Said, Edward. *Orientalism*. New York: Vintage Books, 1978.

Salzman, Ariel. "Aspects of the Ottoman Elite's Food Consumption: Looking for 'Staples,'

'Luxuries,' and 'Delicacies' in a Changing Century." In *Consumption Studies and the History of the Ottoman Empire, 1550–1922*, edited by Donald Quataert, 107–200. New York: State University of New York Press, 2000.

Schama, Simon. *The Embarrassment of Riches: An Interpretation of Dutch Culture in the Golden Age*. New York: Vintage Books, 1997.

Schroeter, Daniel. *Merchants of Essaouira: Urban Society and Imperialism in South-Western Morocco, 1844–1886*. Cambridge: Cambridge University Press, 1988.

Scott, James C. *Seeing like a State: How Certain Schemes to Improve the Human Condition Have Failed*. New Haven, Conn.: Yale University Press, 1998.

Sen, Amartya. *Poverty and Famines: An Essay on Entitlement and Deprivation*. Oxford: Oxford University Press, 1981.

Sijelmassi, Mohamed. *Fès: Cité de l'art et du savoir*. Paris: ACR Édition International, 1991.

Singer, Amy. *Constructing Ottoman Beneficence: An Imperial Soup Kitchen in Jerusalem*. Albany: State University of New York Press, 2002.

Singerman, Diane. *Avenues of Participation: Family, Politics and Networks in Urban Quarters of Cairo*. Princeton, N.J.: Princeton University Press, 1995.

Slyomovics, Susan. *The Performance of Human Rights in Morocco*. Philadelphia: University of Pennsylvania Press, 2005.

———, ed. *The Walled Arab City in Literature, Architecture and History: The Living Medina in the Magrhib*. London: Frank Cass, 2001.

Stewart, Charles F. *The Economy of Morocco, 1912–1956*. Cambridge, Mass.: Harvard University Press, 1964.

Storck, John, and Walter Dorwin Teague. *Flour for Man's Bread: A History of Milling*. 1952. Reprint, Minneapolis: University of Minnesota, 2008.

Tavernise, Sabrina. "'Sects' Strife Takes a Toll on Baghdad's Daily Bread." *New York Times*, 21 July 2006.

Taylor, Brian Brace. "Planned Discontinuity: Modern Colonial Cities in Morocco." *Lotus International* 26 (1980): 52–66.

Toth, Anthony. "Letter from Algiers." *MERIP Middle East Report* no. 145 (March-April 1987): 43–44.

Touzani, Naima Harraj. "Al-Umana' bi al-maghrib fi 'ahd as-sultan Mawlay al-Hasan (1290–1311/1873–1894)." Ph.D. diss., Université Mohamed V, 1979.

Tozy, Mohamed. *Monarchie et Islam politique au Maroc*. Paris: Presses de Sciences Po, 1999.

Waterbury, John. *The Commander of the Faithful: The Moroccan Political Elite—a Study in Segmented Politics*. New York: Columbia University Press, 1970.

Wittfogel, Karl. *Oriental Despotism: A Comparative Study of Total Power*. New Haven, Conn.: Yale University Press, 1957.

Worster, Donald. *Rivers of Empire: Water, Aridity, and the Growth of the American West*. Oxford: Oxford University Press, 1985.

Wright, Gwendolyn. *The Politics of Design in French Colonial Urbanism*. Chicago: University of Chicago Press, 1991.

Yakhlef, Mohamed. "La Municipalité de Fez à l'époque du Protectorate, 1912–1956." Ph.D. diss., Université Libre de Bruxelles, 1990.

Zubaida, Sami. *Islam, the People and the State: Essays on Political Ideas and Movements in the Middle East*. New York: Routledge, 1988.

# Index

Ababou, Thami, 121
Abdallah, Abou, 38
Abdelaziz, Moulay (sultan), 6, 24, 27, 31, 33, 36, 42, 49, 57, 63, 68–69, 104, 147, 169, 203; butchers under, 65, 157; water mill construction under, 49–51, 61
Abdelhafid, Moulay (sultan), 6, 28, 39–40, 42, 51, 62–63, 70, 80, 124–25, 144, 147, 157, 199, 201; under French colonialism, 95–96, 200
Abdemalek, Moulay, 69
Abderrahman, Moulay (sultan), 5, 23–25, 97, 147
*L'Action du Peuple*, 205
Afghanistan, 4
Africanus, Leo, 76, 119
*Afrique Française*, 49
Agriculture, state policies for, 3–4; in Egypt, 4; Tennessee Valley Authority and, 4; in U.S., 3–4; for wheat, 30
Ahmed, Moulay, 71, 197–98, 203, 218
*Akhbar talagrafiyya*, 167
Akoulid, Samuel, 86
Alami, Hadj, 167, 203
Alami, Mohamed, 230n8
Alami, Sherif Sidi Mehdi Sidi Hassan, 43
Alaoui, Moulay al-Hadj, 75
Alaouite dynasty, in Morocco, 5–6; The Great Sacrifice and, role in, 67
Algeria, 4
Almohad dynasty, 21
al-Amrani, Sidi al-Ghali, 176
Anoun, Hadj Abdelmalek, 162
Aouad, Hamid, 156–57
al-Arbi, Abou Hamid, 38
Arouifi, Abdelmalek, 38
"Association" policy, in colonial Morocco, 7–8, 94–95

Attar, David, 154–55
Azeroual, Si Mohamed ou Belkacem, 149
Azulay, David, 50

Ba Ahmed, 24, 68
al-Baghdadi, Mohamed ben Bouchta, 70, 97–98, 166, 175
Baraicha, Ahmed ben al-Mekki, 55
Baraicha, Bouaza, 55
Baraicha, Hadj Mohamed ben Qasm, 55
Baraicha, Qasm, 55
Baraicha, al-Said Hadj Balqacem, 44
Basha (city administration manager), 31, 146
Battle of Tetouan, 27
l-battoir (slaughterhouse), 156–57
Bayn al-Madun neighborhood, slaughterhouse construction in, 151–54; butchers in, 152–54
ben Abdeljellil, Omar, 207
ben Abderrahman, Sidi Mohamed (sultan), 5
ben Abdeselam, Moulay Ahmed ben Driss, 197
ben Ahmed, Abdallah, 45
ben Ahmed, Moussa, 48
ben Aich, Driss, 68, 95, 169
ben Aich, Mohamed, 24
ben al-Amine, Hadj Tahar, 100, 170
Benchaqroun, Ahmed, 99
ben Gharbrit, Si Kaddour, 146
ben Hima, Taib, 33
Beni Mguild people, 82
ben Ja'far al-Kittani, Mohamed, 38
Benjedia, Abderrahman, 48
Benjelloun, Abdelmajid, 107–8, 199
Benjelloun, Hadj al-Barnoussi, 39
Benjelloun, Hadj Mohamed, 36, 175
Benjelloun, Mohamed ben Abdelmajid, 194
Benjelloun, Mohamed ben M'Feddel, 169
Benkirane, Azouz, 24

Benkirane, Hadj Abdelaziz, 36
ben Moussa, Hadj Abdesselam ben Sidi, 44–45
Bennani, Ahmed, 106–7, 182
Bennani, Allal ben al-hadj Mohamed, 46
Bennani, Mohamed ben Abdeselam, 38
Bennani, Mohamed ben Mohamed ben Abd al-Qadir, 71
Bennani, Mohamed ben Mohamed ben Hadj Mahdi, 56–57
Bennani, Taieb, 169
ben Nasser, Sidi Ahmed, 177
Bennis, Abderrahman, 114
Bennis, Mohamed ben Mohamed ben al-Arbi, 47
ben Qacem, Sidi, 67
ben Said, Abou al-Abbas Ahmed, 75
ben Samhoun, Ibn Yamin, 51–52
ben Tachfine, Youssef, 119
ben X, Bachir ben Mohamed, 208
ben X, Si Hamed ben Abderrahman, 208–9
ben Youssef, Sidi Mohamed, 197, 199–200
ben Zakour, al-Mekki ben Hadj Madani, 46
Berrada, Zaki, 216
Bookbinding, in colonial Morocco, 104–5
Bouayad, Abdellatif, 216
Bouayad, al-Arbi, 176
Bouayad, Hassan, 176, 179, 201
Bouayad, Taieb ben M'Feddel, 115
Bread, distribution of, 198–205
"Bread riots," 215
Building construction, in Morocco, 111–17; colonial style of, 113–17; "Fassi" style of, 114; in Fez, 113–17; historic preservation of monuments and, 112–13; private, 117
Burke, Edmund, 31, 68
Burnus (cape), 149
Butchers, 7, 65–89; under Moulay Abdelaziz, 65, 157; associations, 154; in Bayn al-Madun neighborhood, 152–54; chevillard, 167–70, 217, 253n148; commercial laws for, 74–75; commercial objectives of, 81–85; European support for, 162; failed industrialization of, 189–96; in Fez, 83; during The Great Sacrifice, 71–75; guerjouma and, 85–88; gurnas and, 73–74, 236n41; hubus funds and, 74; incomes for, 75; Jewish, 77, 82, 157–58; livestock purchases by, 159–60; muhtasib and, 74–75; in October Protests, 208–9; royal, 79–80; sanitation issues for, 86–87; in social hierarchy, 7, 87, 163–66; strikes by, 154–55; in Ville Nouvelle, 162. *See also* Chevillard

Campini, Guisseppe, 62, 123–27, 139; wheat distribution under, 135
Campini, Umberto, 139–40
Canu, René, 156
Casablanca, 48–49; slaughterhouse construction in, 157; water mills in, 48–49
Chami, Mohamed, 46, 56, 58, 87–88, 176
Charity, 33–40; in colonial Morocco, 96, 101; enforced, under sultan rule, 33–34; faith as factor in, 34–40; food as, 101; hubus and, 36; for the poor, 33–34, 37–40; for spinsters, 37–38; by the wealthy, 34–35
Cherabliyyin Mosque, 19–20
Cherkaoui, Ahmed, 201
Chevillard (wholesale butchers), 167–70, 217, 253n148; benefits for, 167–68; profits of, 168; during Rif War, 169
Chevrillon, André, 26
Cholera, in Morocco, 85–86
Cohen, Ammon, 3
Colonial Morocco, 93–118; Abdelhafid during, 95–96, 200; anti-fraud laws in, 99; "Association" policy and, 7–8, 94–95; bookbinding in, 104–5; building construction in, 111–17; charitable endowments during, 96, 101; corporations in, 110–11; devaluation of franc in, 127–28; droughts, 95; electric companies in, 125–26; Fez, 95–100; foreign soldiers in, 93–94; furniture making in, 106–8; importation of wheat into, 129–30, 136; imports into, influence on economy, 102; industrialization in, 123–27; inflation in, 95, 108; local merchants in, 100–106; under Lyautey, 144–51; majlis during, 99–100; the poor in, 101–2; public works in, 102; religious endowments during, 96; religious scholars in, 100–106; Rif War and, 95; riots in, 94; royal family during, 95–96; social mobility of, 106–17; support of local artists in, 103, 105–6; tax exemptions abolished in, 93; tourism in, development of, 107, 115; trade unions in, 108–10, 243n127; wheat shortages in, after WWI, 127–32, 207
Comité du Maroc, 41
Compagnie Marocaine, 72

Corporations: in colonial Morocco, 110–11; revival of, 184
Cotton, as import, 25
Cults, during famines, 38

Dagga, Sharif Sidi Ahmed, 76
Dams, construction of, 54; illegal, 54
Darqawiyya (religious brotherhood), 71
Delphin, Jacinthe, 168
de Lunel, Maurice Tranchant, 112–13
Department of Fine Arts and Historic Monuments, 112–14, 116. *See also* Building construction, in Morocco
Department of Indigenous Arts and Industry, 112, 115
de Tarde, Alfred, 128
Djai, Ahmed, 95–96
al-Draoui, Mohamed ben Abdeselam, 45
al-Draoui, Mohamed ben Idriss, 45
Droughts: colonial Morocco and, 95; guerjouma during, 160–61; meat consumption during, 76; in Morocco, 7, 17, 25; political instability during, 4; violence during, 22; water mills during, 47–52
Drummond-Hay, John, 47–48
du Gast, Camille, 110
Dumas, Léon, 113

Egypt, 4
Electric companies, in colonial Morocco, 125–26; electricity rights in, 174–75
Elmghari, Si Mohamed Belhassan, 188
Essaouira, 26; water mills in, 59
Europe: grain trade with Morocco, 23–24; natural resources in Morocco, access to, 59–60; offal sales to, 84–85; union strikes in, 109; water mills investments, 49–51, 58–59, 123, 134–35

Faith: religious endowments for, 36; separation by, in slaughterhouses, 153; social responsibility and, 34–40
Fakhir, Gilalli, 156–57, 168
Famines: cults during, 38; Great Famine, 7, 23–26; mechanized milling during, 60–61; riots during, 22; socioeconomic definition of, 23–29; urban exodus as response to, 23; violence during, 22. *See also* Great Famine
Farina (finely ground soft flour), 122

al-Fassi, Abdallah ben Abdeselam ben Alli, 67–68
al-Fassi, Allal, 179, 184, 187, 197–200, 207, 217; as political threat, 199. *See also* Nationalist movements, in Morocco
al-Fassi, Si Abdallah, 147
al-Fayda, Hadj Djilalli, 138
el Fekhkhar, Sidi Mimoun, 38
Female livestock, prohibition on slaughter of, 81–83
Fête de Trône, 200
Fez: building construction in, 113–17; clothing of residents in, 20–21; during colonization of Morocco, 95–100; as cultural capital, 18; enforced social responsibility in, 33–40; European population in, 158; famines and, urban exodus from, 23–26; food provisioning in, 34–40; founder of, 19; geography of, 18; government structure development in, 97; gurnas in, 73–74; home construction in, 20; housing shortages in, 116–17; increased emigration to, 181; Jewish population in, 21–22, 35–37; meat industry in, 157–63, 192–96; medina of, 18–22; modernization of, inhibiting factors to, 125; Muslim butchers in, 83; notable citizens in, 95–100; population increase in, 181; potters in, 103; residential neighborhoods in, 20; during Rif War, 139–40; rivers throughout, 18–20; water mills in, 42–47; water rights in, 174–77, 211
Fez al-Bali, in medina, 18–20; design of, 19; population of, 20
Fez al-Jadid, in medina, 18, 21–22; history of, 21; Merenids and, 21; population of, 21
Filalli, Hadj Mohamed, 138, 187, 216
Fish, under Islamic law, 166
Flour, 52–55; distribution of, through nationalist movements, 204; European investment in, 49; farina, 122; grinding fees for, 57; importation limits for, during WWI, 120; khalis, 57–58, 122, 137; ma'allam and, 52–53; milling process for, 52–53; politics and, production levels' role in, 62; pricing for, 56–57; quwayshi, 57, 137; royal distribution of, 29–34; semolina, 141; shortages of, 140–41; during social revolts, 61; storage of, 32–33; water mills and, production by, 49, 52–55; zrif, 57, 137

Food provisioning, 34–40; Middle East policies for, 4
Food shortages, 27–28; political stability and, 262n3; potatoes as alternative during, 30; revolts as result of, 27–28
Forbes, Rosita, 148
France: devaluation of franc, 127–28; Morocco as protectorate of, 6–7; urbanization in, as influence on Morocco, 64. *See also* Colonial Morocco
Frej, Sidi, 164
French League for the Defense of the Rights of Man and Citizen, 188
Furniture making, in colonial Morocco, 106–8

Gaillard, Henri, 146
Gallos, Salvatore, 123
Gallotti, Jean, 103
Geertz, Clifford, 214
Ghalib, Sidi Ali ben Abi, 53
Ghallab, Hadj Hadi, 100
Gharnit, Mohamed Feddoul, 115
al-Glaoui, Thami, 200
Gouraud, Henri, 119
Grain trade, with Europe, 23–24; during Great Famine, 24
Great Britain: commercial treaties with Morocco, 23; investment in water mills by, 58–59; Moroccan emigrants in, 24
Great Famine (1878–1884), 7, 23–26, 45; grain trade as result of, 24; meat consumption during, 76; riots during, 22; social responsibility during, 35–36; speculation of food stocks during, 33; water mill policy during, 44, 56; the wealthy during, 26
The Great Sacrifice, 28, 65–71, 145–51; Alaouite dynasty role in, 67; animals chosen for, 66–67; boycotts of, 202–3; butchers' role in, 71–75; charity during, 67; food during, 65; foreigners during, 70, 234n14; under French rule, 145, 165; hadiyya during, 69; hallal, 66; under Islamic law, 66; musalla during, 70–71; political implications of, 145–51; riots during, 69–70; role of meat in, 144–45; royal transfers of power during, 68–69; slaughter sites for, 71–75; social status and, 71–75; sultans during, 67–68; taxes for, 201–2;

during Youssef rule, 145. *See also* Slaughter, of animals
Grinding fees, for flour, 57
Guebbas, Mohamed, 96–97
Guerjouma (tax on meat), 85–88; during droughts, 160–61; increase of, 160–61
"al-Guezzar" ("The Butcher"). *See* Tazi, Mohamed
*Guide bleu*, 107, 119, 156
Gurnas (sites for slaughter), 73–74, 235n40, 236n41; in Fez, 73–74

Hadiyya (sacrificial ceremony), 69, 145
Al-hadiyya al-wataniyya (nationalist tribute), 200
el Haiani, Mohamed, 181
al-Hajoui, Mohamed ben al-Hassan, 96, 109, 115, 143–44
Hallal (meat permitted for consumption), 66, 144
Hammoudi, Abdellah, 8
Hanati (trade organization), 109
Hardy, George, 110
Hasnaoui, Abderrahman, 216
al-Hassan, Abou Ali, 38
Hassan, Moulay (sultan), 5–6, 24, 26–27, 33–34, 42, 98, 103–4, 123, 145, 195, 197, 201, 215; dam construction under, 54; death of, 68; guerjouma under, 85–88; natural resource conservation under, 59–60; religious endowments under, 36; taxation of food under, 27, 30–31; water mill construction under, 48, 50–51
Himara, Abu, 28, 31, 68–69; revolts under, 28, 61
Hoisington, William, 182, 184
al-Housseini, Moulay Ahmed ben Mohamed Ibn al-Khayat al-Zakar, 71
Hubus (legal act of bequeathing property), 36, 43–44; butchers and, 74; proportion of property under, 96; water mills and, 43–44, 121
Hunger, as political issue, 17–18

Ibn Zaydan, Moulay Abderrahman, 69, 200
'Id al-Kabir. *See* The Great Sacrifice
Idriss, Moulay, 19, 58, 177
Imam (Islamic leader), 6

Indigenous Chamber of Commerce and Agriculture, 175
Industrialization, in Morocco: of butchers, 189–96; for slaughterhouses, 193; of water mills, 123–27
International Monetary Fund, 215
Islam: hubus and, 36; imam in, 6; principles of, 1–2
Islamic law: The Great Sacrifice and, 66; meat v. fish under, 166; private property under, 25; slaughter under, 143–44, 217
Ismail, Moulay, 29, 69

Jewish butchers, 77, 82, 157–58; under muhtasib, 82–83; in slaughterhouses, separation from Muslims, 153
Jews: in Fez, 21–22, 35–37; social responsibility for, in Morocco, 35–36; tithing to sultans, for protection, 35; violence against, during riots, 94

Kasra (round flat bread), 131
Kenya, 4
Khali'a (dried spiced meat), 78–80
Khalifa (sultan's representative), 31, 146
Khalis (mixed flour), 57–58, 122, 137
al-Kharim, Abd, 169
al-Kharim, Mohamed ben Abd, 149–51; defeat of, 151; public support for, 150
al-Kittani, Abdelkabir ben Hachim, 137–38
al-Kittani, Mohamed ben Abdelkabir, 39
al-Kittani, Mohamed ben Ja'far, 38
al-Kittani, Mohamed ben Sidi Abdelaziz, 45
al-Kittani, Taieb ben Moulay Mohamed, 39
Kittaniyya (religious brotherhood), 39–40, 94; elimination of, 201
Kosher meat, taxes on, 158–59, 190

Lahbabi, Hossein, 186–87
Lahlou, Mohamed al-Arbi, 104–5
Larachi, Abdelhamid, 187
Larachi, Abdeselam, 187
Larachi, El-Ghali, 187
Larachi, Mohamed, 187
Larachi, Mohamed Bedaoui, 187
el Laraki, Mehdi, 177
Le Tourneau, Roger, 209
Levy, Moïse, 126, 188

Lewis, Bernard, 1
Livestock: butchers' purchases of, 159–60; female, prohibition on slaughter of, 81–83; male v. female, 81–83
Lyautey, Louis-Hubert, 6, 94–95; colonial Morocco under, 144–51
Lyazide, Mohamed, 201

Ma'allam (flour miller), 52–53
Maclagan, Ianthe, 74
Madrasas, in Fez, 18; historic preservation of, 112–13
*Mahiya* (fruity wine), 21
Majlis (notable citizens), 99–100; taxation of meat by, 160; wheat distribution under control of, 132–35
Makhzan (royal administration), 6, 24
Makina (Italian arms factory), 62
Maks (import tax), 27
Maristan Fund, 43–44
Marrakech, 27; water mills in, 48, 51, 59, 61
Masanou, Hadj Mohamed, 57
Mashwi (sheep roasted on a spit), 77–79; collective purchases for, 79
Maslow, Boris, 114
Massignon, Louis, 249n132
Meat: distribution of, under nationalist movements, 198–205; fish v., under Islamic law, 166; in The Great Sacrifice, 144–45; guerjouma and, 85–88, 160–61; kosher, 158–59; from male v. female livestock, 81–83; price controls for, 81; taxes on, 157–63, 190–91
Meat consumption, 65; as determined by sultans, 76–77; during droughts, 76; during Great Famine, 76; hallal and, 66, 144; legislation for, 163–64; for offal, 84–85; by soldiers, 80; as symbol of wealth, 76–80, 163–66; wholesale trade for, 167
Meat industry, 157–63, 192–96. *See also* Slaughterhouses
Mechanized milling, 47–52, 60–61; during famines, 60–61
Medina (walled center), of Fez, 18–22; al-Bali section of, 18–20; design of, 18–20; al-Jadid section of, 18, 21–22; suq in, 19
Mekki, Hadj, 26
Mekouar, Ahmed, 207
Mekouar, Ahmed ben Tahar, 168–69

Mekouar, Mohamed, 133, 177
Mekouar, Tahar, 177
al-Menehbi, al-Mahdi, 68
Merenid dynasty, 21
Mernissi, Mohamed ben Larbi, 115–16, 168, 176–77, 182, 195
al-Mernissi, Si Mohamed ben Larbi, 168
Mezian, Aziz, 230n8
Middle East: access to natural resources in, 2; food provisioning policies in, 4; geographics of, as factor in food availability, 2; Ottoman Empire in, 2–3
Millerand, Alexandre, 110
Millers, 7, 119–42; commercial, 137; dynastic families of, 53, 138; for flour, 49, 52–53; mechanization and, 47–52, 60–61; prosperity of, 136–42; in social hierarchy, 7, 249n132; subsidies for, 136; Tarrahiyyin, 29; for wheat, 29–31
Ministry of Religious Endowments, 101, 153
al-Missouri, Ahmed ben al-Saghir, 45
al-Missouri, Mohamed ben Abdallah, 45
Mohamed V (sultan). *See* Sidi Mohamed ben Youssef (sultan)
Mohamed VI (sultan), 213
Mohring, M., 126
*Le monde marocain* (Odinot), 141
Monument preservation, of historic sites/buildings, 112–13; of madrasas, 112–13
al-Moqri, Ahmed, 98, 123
al-Moqri, Driss, 98–99, 133, 169, 209
al-Moqri, Mohamed, 26, 31, 36, 96–97, 108–9
al-Moqri, Taieb, 175
"Moroccan Labor and the Economic Role of Morocco after the War" (Ricard), 120
Morocco: Alaouite dynasty in, 5–6; Almohad dynasty in, 21; building construction in, 111–17; colonialism in, 93–118; conservative ideology in, under sultan rule, 6; cotton as import from, 25; disease epidemics in, 85–86; droughts in, 7, 17, 25; emigration to Great Britain, 24; grain trade with Europe, 23–24; Great Britain and, commercial treaties with, 23; Great Famine in, 7; lack of natural resources in, 60; Merenid dynasty in, 21; Muslim/Jewish division in, 35–37; National Action Party in, 202; nationalist movements in, 183–85, 197–210; policy of "association" in, 7–8; political stability of, 5; Portugal and, commercial treaties with, 23; precolonial protest in, 235n20; as protectorate, under French rule, 6–7; Saadian dynasty in, 29; sociopolitical hierarchy in, 214; in Spanish Moroccan War, 27; tea as import from, 25; urbanization in France and, influence on, 64; urban migration within, 27; water mills in, 41–64. *See also* Casablanca; Colonial Morocco; Essaouira; Fez; Industrialization, in Morocco; Marrakech; Morocco, in 1930s; Rabat, water mills in; Tangier

Morocco, in 1930s, 173–96: builders' trade in, 182; electricity rights in, 174–75; employment programs in, 178; environmental crises in, 180; export decrease during, 179–80; government programs in, 180; nationalist movement in, 183–85; natural resources in, control of, 174–79; patronage during, 179–85; the poor in, 179–85, 189; population increase in, 181; revival of corporations in, 184; social unrest in, 178; tanners in, 181; trade unions during, 183–84; water rights in, 174–77; Water Riots in, 205–7; water shortages in, 173
Moulin du Quartier (non-industrial mill), 185–89
Muhtasib (commerce official), 31–33; food pricing under, 32–33; grinding fees under, 57; Jewish butchers under, 82–83; legal authority of, 32; meat sales under, 74–75
Murphey, Rhoads, 3
Musalla, 70–71

Nafissa, Lalla, 72
National Action Party, 202
Nationalist movements, in Morocco, 197–210; for distribution of bread and meat, 198–205; Fête de Trône and, 200; French response to, 210–11; Al-hadiyya al-wataniyya and, 200; National Action Party, 202; in 1930s, 183–85; October Protests under, 207–10; trade unions and, 184–85; Water Riots and, 205–7
Natural resources, access to, 2, 59–60; control of, during 1930s, 174–79; by Europeans, 59–60; under Moulay Hassan, 59–60; legal

rights to, 179; royal control of, 59–60; water rights and, 174–77. *See also* Agriculture, state policies for
Nézière, J. de la, 110
Nogues, Charles, 182–84; trade unions as threat for, 183–84

OCIC. *See* Office Chérifien Interprofessionel Céréalière
October Protests, 207–10; butchers' role in, 208–9
Odinot, Paul, 141
Offal, 84–85
Office Chérifien Interprofessionel Céréalière (OCIC), 189
"Oriental despotism," 2
Ottoman Empire, 2–3; millet system in, 3; religious demographics in, 3
Ouali, Abdelwahed, 188, 216
Ouali, al-Arbi, 53, 138
al-Ouali, Si Mohamed Najib, 253n148
al-Ouazzani, Mohamed Hassan, 179, 205, 207
Oued Bou (river), 42–43. *See also* Water mills
Oued Fas (river), 42–43. *See also* Water mills

Peres, M., 126
Political instability, geoclimatic factors for, 4
The poor: in colonial Morocco, 101–2; enforced charity for, 33–34, 37–40; in 1930s Morocco, 179–85, 189
Portugal, commercial treaties with Morocco, 23
Potatoes, as alternative food source, 30
Potters, in colonial Morocco, 103
Pricing: for flour, 56–57; for meat, 74–75; royal control over, for water mills, 58–63; for wheat, 136–37; of wheat, during post WWI shortage, 128
Private property, under Islamic law, 25
Protégés, water mills and, investment in, 46–47
Public sanitation, butchers and, 86–87

al-Qabaj, al-M'feddel, 51–52
al-Qadmiri, Mohamed, 158
Qarawiyyin Mosque, 18–19, 33; religious endowments for, 36
Quwayshi (coarse flour), 57, 137

Rabani, Gilalli, 72
Rabani, Said, 72
Rabat, water mills in, 51
Rachid, Moulay, 29
Rahaba (designated market for cereals), 31
Al Raisuni, Moulay Ahmed, 147–48
René-LeClerc, Charles, 27, 32, 41–42, 59, 63–64, 72, 120
Ricard, Prosper, 102–3, 120, 156, 179, 188, 192
Rif War, 95, 116, 166; chevillards during, 169; Fez during, 139–40
Riots: during colonialism in Morocco, 94; during famines, 22; during The Great Sacrifice, 69–70; Tanners' Revolt, 27–28; from taxation, 27; violence against Jews during, 94; Water Riots, 205–7
Royal butchers, 79–80

Saadian dynasty, 29
Sabathier, Charles, 124
Sacrifices, 77–78; as assertion of masculinity, 77; by women, 77
al-Saghroushni, Sidi Abdelwahed al-Ghandour, 53
Saint, Lucien, 173
Saladin, Henri, 113
Sandillon, Antoine, 49
Sanhadji, Lahcen ben Ahmed, 138–39
Sarfaoui, Hamed, 113
Sattar, Mohamed, 113
Scott, James, 3
Sefrioui, Ahmed, 72
Semolina, 141
Sharqi, Hadj Mohamed, 216–17
Shias, 2
al-Shra'i, Mohamed ben Ahmed al-Mazglidi, 46
Shurafa' (scholars), 20, 164
Sidi Daqiq. *See* Abdallah, Abou
Sidi Mohamed ben Youssef (sultan), 6, 27, 47, 177
Singer, Amy, 3
Slaoui, Ahmed, 167
Slaoui, Ali, 105
Slaoui, Driss ben Mohamed, 204
Slaoui, El Hadi ben Mohamed, 139
Slaoui, M'hamed, 167
Slaoui, Mohamed, 156, 167–68

Slaughter, of animals, 71–75; in Fez, 73–74; gurnas, 73–74, 235n20; under Islamic law, 143–44, 217; legislation for limitation of, 165; in private homes, 78; as protection of culture, 143; religious rites before, 143–44

Slaughterhouses, 151–57; in Bayn al-Madun neighborhood, 151–54; in Casablanca, 157; construction of, 151–52; design structure of, 155–56, 193–94; increased bureaucracy for, 154; industrialization of, 193; location sites for, 151–52; municipal, 151–57; political importance of, 152; separation by religious faith in, 153; in Ville Nouvelle, 167. *See also* Butchers

Smith, Chales Euan, 70

Social responsibility. *See* Charity

Société Générale des Abattoirs Municipaux et Industriels, 157

Soldiers: food budgets for, 80; foreign, in colonial Morocco, 93–94; meat consumption by, 80

Soussi, Bireim, 24

Spain: in Battle of Tetouan, 27; in Spanish Moroccan War, 27

Spanish Moroccan War, 27

Spinsters, charity for, 37–38

Steeg, Jules-Joseph Théodore, 151, 178

Strikes: by butchers, 154–55; union, in Europe, 109

Sultans, in Morocco, 5–6; during colonization of Morocco, 95–96; conservative ideology of, 6; enforced social responsibility under, 34; during The Great Sacrifice, 67–68; guerjouma under, 85–88; as imam, 6; Jews tithing to, for protection, 35; line of succession for, 5–6; makhzan and, 6, 24; meat consumption determined by, 76–77; redistribution of wealth under, 37–40

Sunnis, 2

Suq (market), 19

Tahaniyyin (custom millers), 29

Tahar, M'hamed Youbi ould Hadj, 177

Tahiri, Hamza, 100, 179

Tahuna (mills), 231n38

Tangier, 41; water mills in, 50

Tanners, 181

Tanners' Revolt, 27–28

Tarrahiyyin (commercial millers), 29

Taxation, of food, 27, 30–31; during droughts, 160–61; for The Great Sacrifice, 201–2; guerjouma, 85–88, 160–61; for kosher meat, 158–59, 190; for meat, 157–63, 190–91; riots as result of, 27

Taya, Mouayya Ould Sid'Ahmed, 4

Tazi, Ahmed, 120, 177

al-Tazi, Hadj Abdelghani ben al-Said al-Taib, 36–37

Tazi, Mohamed, 72–73, 109, 175, 189

Tazi, Mohamed ben Larbi, 167–68, 170, 185, 194–95, 203

al-Tazi, Mohamed Ibn Idriss, 51–52

Tazi, Omar, 32, 61–62, 157

Tea, as import, 25

Tennessee Valley Authority, 4

Tourism, development of, 107, 115

Trade unions, 108–10, 243n127; in nationalist movements, 184–85; as political threat, 183–84; social unrest as result of, 108; workers' rights and, 111

Treaty of Fez, 119–20

Treaty of Versailles, 120, 127

Unions. *See* Trade unions

United States (U.S.): agricultural policies in, 3–4; Tennessee Valley Authority in, 4

Verde, Fava, 206–7

Veyre, Gabriel, 61–62

Ville Nouvelle, 111, 126; butchers in, 162; separation of slaughterhouses in, 167

La Villette slaughterhouse, 153

Water mills, 41–64; under Moulay Abdelaziz, 49–51, 61; anti-industrial actions toward, 54; attacks on, 232n64; in Casablanca, 48–49; dam construction v., 54; design structure for, 43–44; during droughts, 47–52; energy sources for, 59; European investments in, 49–51, 58–59, 123, 134–35; in Fez, 42–47; flour production by, 49, 52–55; during Great Famine, policy for, 44, 56; grinding capacity of, 43; under Moulay Hassan, 48, 50–51, 61; historical development of, 42, 230n8; hubus and, 43–44, 121; importation of equipment for, 126–27;

"indigenous," 122–23; industrialization and, 123–27; Maristan Fund and, 43–44; in Marrakech, 48, 51, 59, 61; mechanization of, 47–52, 60–61; owners' rights for, 44–45; political lobbying for, 52–55; private investment in, 42–45, 121–23; production capacity of, 43; protégé investment in, 46–47; in Rabat, 51; royal investment in, 45–46; royal price controls for, 58–63; subletting of, 45; in Tangier, 50; wartime investment in, 120–23. *See also* Moulin du Quartier

Water rights, 174–77, 211

Water Riots (1937), 205–7

Water shortages, 173

Westermarck, Edward, 70

*What Went Wrong?: The Clash Between Islam and Modernity in the Middle East* (Lewis), 1

Wheat: agricultural strategies for, 30; devaluation of, 128; distribution policy for, 132–36; global surplus of, 141–42; hoarding of, 129; importation of, into Morocco, 129–30, 136; majlis and, distribution under control of, 132–35; millers for, 29–31; muhtasib control over, 32–33; political importance of, 129–31; pricing for, 136–37; production levels for, 185–86; quota system for, 136, 141; in rahaba, 31; royal distribution of, 29–34; shortages of, after WWI, 127–32, 207; storage of, 32–33; tahaniyyin for, 29; tarrahiyyin for, 29; thefts of, 138–39. *See also* Flour

Wheat crisis, 127–32; political implications for, 129–31

Wittfogel, Karl, 2

Women, sacrifices by, 77

Workers' rights, 111

World War I: flour importation limits during, 120; investment in waters mills during, 120–23; wheat crisis after, 127–32

Worster, David, 2

Yashua, Mordechai ben, 22

Youssef, Moulay, 6, 95–96, 101, 121, 144–46, 149–50, 164, 200; The Great Sacrifice under, lack of public support for, 145–46; political rise of, 150

Zemrani, Driss, 165

Zrif (fine flour), 57, 137

Stacy E. Holden is associate professor of history at Purdue University.